D0858702

Beginning Web Development, Silverlight, and ASP.NET AJAX

From Novice to Professional

■ ■ ■

Laurence Moroney

apress®

Beginning Web Development, Silverlight, and ASP.NET AJAX: From Novice to Professional

Copyright © 2008 by Laurence Moroney

ISBN-13 (pbk): 978-1-59059-959-4

ISBN-10 (pbk): 1-59059-959-4

ISBN-13 (electronic): 978-1-4302-0582-1

ISBN-10 (electronic): 1-4302-0582-2

Printed and bound in the United States of America 9 8 7 6 5 4 3 2 1

Trademarked names may appear in this book. Rather than use a trademark symbol with every occurrence of a trademarked name, we use the names only in an editorial fashion and to the benefit of the trademark owner, with no intention of infringement of the trademark.

Lead Editor: Kevin Goff
Technical Reviewers: Fabio Claudio Ferracchiati, Bob Lair
Editorial Board: Clay Andres, Steve Anglin, Ewan Buckingham, Tony Campbell, Gary Cornell,
    Jonathan Gennick, Kevin Goff, Matthew Moodie, Joseph Ottinger, Jeffrey Pepper, Frank Pohlmann,
    Ben Renow-Clarke, Dominic Shakeshaft, Matt Wade, Tom Welsh
Project Manager: Richard Dal Porto
Copy Editor: Damon Larson
Associate Production Director: Kari Brooks-Copony
Production Editor: Ellie Fountain
Compositor: Dina Quan
Proofreader: April Eddy
Indexer: Brenda Miller
Artist: Kinetic Publishing Services, LLC
Cover Designer: Kurt Krames
Manufacturing Director: Tom Debolski

Distributed to the book trade worldwide by Springer-Verlag New York, Inc., 233 Spring Street, 6th Floor, New York, NY 10013. Phone 1-800-SPRINGER, fax 201-348-4505, e-mail orders-ny@springer-sbm.com, or visit http://www.springeronline.com.

For information on translations, please contact Apress directly at 2855 Telegraph Avenue, Suite 600, Berkeley, CA 94705. Phone 510-549-5930, fax 510-549-5939, e-mail info@apress.com, or visit http://www.apress.com.

Apress and friends of ED books may be purchased in bulk for academic, corporate, or promotional use. eBook versions and licenses are also available for most titles. For more information, reference our Special Bulk Sales–eBook Licensing web page at http://www.apress.com/info/bulksales.

The information in this book is distributed on an "as is" basis, without warranty. Although every precaution has been taken in the preparation of this work, neither the author(s) nor Apress shall have any liability to any person or entity with respect to any loss or damage caused or alleged to be caused directly or indirectly by the information contained in this work.

The source code for this book is available to readers at http://www.apress.com.

I'd like to dedicate this book to my family: my wife, Rebecca, and my wonderful children, Claudia and Christopher. I'd also like to dedicate it to the one who has made all this possible. John 3:16

Contents at a Glance

About the Author xv
About the Technical Reviewer xvii
Introduction xix

PART 1 ■ ■ ■ Building Web Applications

■CHAPTER 1   Introduction to Web Development 3
■CHAPTER 2   Basics of Web Development with ASP.NET 9
■CHAPTER 3   Web Forms with ASP.NET 37
■CHAPTER 4   Data Binding with ASP.NET 69
■CHAPTER 5   ASP.NET Web Services 105
■CHAPTER 6   Deploying Your Web Site 129

PART 2 ■ ■ ■ Next Generation Technologies for Web Development

■CHAPTER 7   .NET 3.0: Windows Communication Foundation 155
■CHAPTER 8   .NET 3.0: Windows Presentation Foundation 177
■CHAPTER 9   .NET 3.0: Windows Workflow Foundation 209
■CHAPTER 10   .NET 3.0: Programming with CardSpace 233
■CHAPTER 11   Ajax Applications and Empowering the
              Web User Experience 253
■CHAPTER 12   AJAX Extensions for ASP.NET 279
■CHAPTER 13   Ajax Scripts and Services 309
■CHAPTER 14   JavaScript Programming with ASP.NET AJAX 331
■CHAPTER 15   Enhancing the Web Experience with Silverlight 353
■CHAPTER 16   Programming Silverlight with XAML and JavaScript 375

■INDEX 415

Contents

About the Author. xv

About the Technical Reviewer. xvii

Introduction. xix

PART 1 ■■■ Building Web Applications

■CHAPTER 1   Introduction to Web Development 3

The Internet and the Birth of the Web 3

Going Beyond the Static Web 6

The Arrival of ASP.NET 7

Summary. 8

■CHAPTER 2   Basics of Web Development with ASP.NET. 9

Using Visual Studio 9

Creating the Application 9

Exploring the IDE 12

Visual Studio and Solutions 17

The Code and Design Windows. 28

Architecture of ASP.NET. 32

The ASP.NET Worker Process and State Management. 33

Using the Web Configuration File 34

Summary. 36

■CHAPTER 3   Web Forms with ASP.NET 37

Understanding Page Processing. 37

Looking at Web Forms 39

HTML Forms 39

An HTML Forms Example in ASP.NET 41

Using a Server Control to Provide Feedback. 46

Using ASP.NET Events and Automatic Postbacks 52

View State. 55

Processing Web Forms. 56

Page Framework Initialization 57

Application Code Initialization 57

Performing Validation 58

Performing Event Handling. 58

Performing Data Binding 59

Server Tidies Up Objects 59

Pages and Controls. 59

Accessing the Page Head. 62

Creating Controls at Runtime. 64

The Page Object. 66

The Request Object. 66

The Response Object 66

Summary. 67

▪CHAPTER 4   Data Binding with ASP.NET 69

What Is ADO.NET?. 69

Using ADO.NET. 70

SQL Server 2005 Express 71

Downloading and Installing SQL Server 2005 Express 72

Starting the Install 72

Using SQL Server Management Studio Express. 78

Installing the AdventureWorks Database. 79

Using ADO.NET to Build Data-Driven Applications. 82

The Connection Class and Connection Strings. 82

Using Commands 86

Data Binding with Server Controls 91

Using the SQLDataSource Control 92

Using the GridView Control. 96

Using the DataList Control 99

Summary 103

CHAPTER 5   ASP.NET Web Services 105

Web Services Architecture. 106

Building a Web Service in Visual Studio 108

The ASMX and Code-Behind Files 108

Running Your Web Service. 110

Creating the Address Service 112

Adding Data to a Web Service. 113

Using the DataSet in a Web Method. 117

Creating a Web Service Client. 120

Data Binding in a Web Service 122

Summary. 127

CHAPTER 6   Deploying Your Web Site 129

Internet Information Services 129

Creating Web Sites and Applications with IIS Manager 131

How IIS Handles URLs. 134

Side-by-Side Execution 138

Manually Deploying Your ASP.NET Applications 138

Configuring Your Data Connections 140

Deploying Your Service Tier. 146

Deploying Your Client Tier 148

Summary. 150

PART 2 ■ ■ ■ Next Generation Technologies for Web Development

CHAPTER 7   .NET 3.0: Windows Communication Foundation 155

WCF and Productivity 156

WCF and Interoperability 158

WS-Security 159

WS-ReliableMessaging. 159

WS-Transactions 160

WCF and Service Orientation 160
Programming WCF 161
    Creating an Address Service in WCF 168
    Creating the Address Service Client 172
Summary 176

■**CHAPTER 8** **.NET 3.0: Windows Presentation Foundation** 177

XAML 177
Using Expression Blend 182
    Creating UIs with Blend 184
    Using Layout 188
Using Expression Blend to Build a Data Application 196
    Adding a Simple Timeline Animation 203
    Using the Blend Artifacts in Visual Studio 206
Summary 207

■**CHAPTER 9** **.NET 3.0: Windows Workflow Foundation** 209

Using WF 211
Using Visual Studio to Build Workflows 211
    Adding Input Parameters to an Application 218
Out-of-the-Box Activities 223
Workflow and the Web 224
Summary 230

■**CHAPTER 10** **.NET 3.0: Programming with CardSpace** 233

Using CardSpace 234
    Adding a New Card to Your CardSpace Wallet 235
    Using Cards on the Web 237
Creating a Web Site That Uses CardSpace 240
    Preparing Your Development Environment for CardSpace 240
    Creating Your Own CardSpace-Secured Web 244
Summary 251

CHAPTER 11 **Ajax Applications and Empowering the Web User Experience** 253

A Brief History of Ajax 253
    Coding with Ajax 256
    Communicating with the Web Server 256
Simple Ajax and ASP.NET Example 257
    Improving the UI Using Ajax 259
Using Ajax for Forward Caching 265
    Building the Image Server 266
    Accessing the Image Server from HTML 270
    Writing the Forward-Caching Ajax Client 271
Summary 277

CHAPTER 12 **AJAX Extensions for ASP.NET** 279

ASP.NET AJAX Overview 279
Editions of ASP.NET AJAX 282
Getting Started with ASP.NET AJAX 282
Migrating ASP.NET to AJAX 289
Building a Simple Ajax Application with ASP.NET 292
Using Ajax with Web Services 300
Summary 308

CHAPTER 13 **Ajax Scripts and Services** 309

The ScriptManager Class 309
    Partial Page Rendering 309
    Managing Custom Scripts 311
    Using Web Services from Script 312
    Using Application Services from Script 314
    Using Profile Data 327
Summary 329

■CHAPTER 14   JavaScript Programming with ASP.NET AJAX 331

Object-Oriented Extensions to JavaScript. 331

Using Classes in JavaScript. 331

Using Namespaces in JavaScript 332

Creating and Using a Simple JavaScript Class. 333

Using Inheritance in JavaScript. 338

Using Interfaces in JavaScript. 341

Reflection in JavaScript 343

Array Type Extensions to JavaScript 344

Adding Items to an Array 344

Adding a Range of Items to an Array 345

Clearing an Array. 345

Cloning an Array. 345

Checking Array Contents 345

Dequeuing an Array. 346

Looping Through an Array 346

Finding a Specific Element in an Array 346

Inserting an Item into an Array 347

Removing an Item from an Array 347

Boolean Type Extensions 348

Date Type Extensions 348

Formatting a Date 348

Formatting a Date Using Locale 348

Parsing a Value into a Date 349

Error Type Extensions. 349

Number Type Extensions 350

Formatting a Number 350

Parsing a Number 350

String Extensions. 351

String Matching 351

String Trimming 351

Summary 351

CHAPTER 15   Enhancing the Web Experience with Silverlight 353

Introducing Silverlight. 354
Silverlight Feature Highlights. 355
Current and Future Versions of Silverlight. 355
The Anatomy of a Silverlight Application. 356
Using Silverlight.js 357
Using XAML. 357
Creating an Instance of the Silverlight Plug-In 358
Writing Application Logic 359
Putting It All Together in HTML 360
Programming with the Silverlight Control 362
The Silverlight Control Properties 362
The Silverlight Control Events 368
The Silverlight Control Methods 370
Using the Downloader Object 371
Summary. 373

CHAPTER 16   Programming Silverlight with XAML and JavaScript 375

Layout in XAML 375
Using Brushes in XAML 378
The SolidColorBrush 379
The LinearGradientBrush 379
The RadialGradientBrush 381
The ImageBrush. 383
The VideoBrush 385
Using Strokes with Brushes. 386
Using Visual Elements in XAML. 388
Dimension and Position Properties. 388
Opacity. 388
Cursor Behavior 388
Using Shapes in XAML 389
The Ellipse. 389
The Rectangle. 390
The Line. 390
The Path 390

XAML Controls 391

The Image Control 392

The Glyphs Control 392

The TextBlock Control 392

Transformations 393

Storyboards and Animation 394

Programming with JavaScript 394

Editing Properties 395

Using Common Methods 396

Using MediaElement Methods 398

Handling Events 399

MediaElement Events 401

Putting It All Together: Creating a Casual Game in Silverlight 401

Designing the Game XAML 402

Implementing the Code 408

Summary 414

■INDEX 415

About the Author

 **LAURENCE MORONEY** is a senior technology evangelist at Microsoft. He specializes in Silverlight and promoting how Silverlight can be used in real-world systems to enhance the user experience. Author of many computer books and hundreds of articles, he's usually found tapping at his keyboard. Outside of his computer passions, he's big into all kinds of sports, and has been involved with professional men's and women's soccer.

About the Technical Reviewer

■**FABIO CLAUDIO FERRACCHIATI** is a senior consultant and a senior analyst/developer using Microsoft technologies. He works for Brain Force (www.brainforce.com) at its Italian branch (www.brainforce.it). He is a Microsoft Certified Solution Developer for .NET, a Microsoft Certified Application Developer for .NET, a Microsoft Certified Professional, and a prolific author and technical reviewer. Over the past ten years, he's written articles for Italian and international magazines and coauthored more than ten books on a variety of computer topics. You can read his LINQ blog at www.ferracchiati.com.

Introduction

This book is aimed at equipping you, the developer, to understand the technologies that are available to allow you to rapidly build secure, quality web experiences. Note that I use the term *experiences* and not *applications* or *sites*. That is because the user experience is the heart of the future Web.

Before you can start looking at the future, it is good to understand the current suite of web development and deployment technologies that are available to you. In Part 1 of this book, you'll look at the Microsoft stack of technologies that allow you to build web services and applications, and how you'll deploy them. It will be scenario-driven, so instead of going into depth on the various APIs, you'll get your hands dirty in a step-by-step approach to building, testing, and deploying multitier web applications. You'll look at databases and how to connect your application to them, and you'll manage these connections through the deployment process. Ultimately, in the first six chapters, you'll get a whirlwind tour of the full life cycle of application development using the .NET Framework (which always looks good on a resume!).

If you are new to ASP.NET, these six chapters will condense everything you need to know to get up and running with the framework. By the end of them, you'll have learned the technology, the tools, and the servers, and gained the know-how to deploy a multiple-tier web service–based application to the enterprise server technology from Microsoft. Even if you are experienced with ASP.NET, this is a nice refresher!

Chapter 1 will give you a tour of the history of web development, from static HTML served up from the network, through activation of servers using CGI, to activation of pages using ASP, PHP, and other technologies. It ends with a survey of the managed APIs that are available for building web applications, including J2EE, PHP, and ultimately ASP.NET.

In Chapter 2, you will look into ASP.NET in a little more detail, going through the basics of web development with this API. You'll see its architecture and how it uses the concept of *controls* to generate markup from the server. You'll see how it hangs together with the standard web technologies of HTML, JavaScript, DHTML, and more. There is a great suite of tools available to the ASP.NET developer, including the free Web Developer Express, and you'll look at how to download, install, and use this to build, deploy, and debug ASP.NET server applications. Finally, you'll survey the lifetime of an ASP.NET application, learning how the framework can provide stateful communication in an inherently stateless environment.

Chapter 3 takes you further into building ASP.NET web applications through the use of web forms. You'll look into the page processing model, postbacks, and how events are handled in web applications. You'll also start to look into data in your web applications. You'll see how to download, configure, and manage a SQL Server Express instance, and how to access the data and functionality in it from code, from UI tools, and from data binding.

Chapter 4 brings you further down the data path, looking at data binding in ASP.NET and explaining the fundamentals of the ADO.NET API. You'll look into the architecture of this flexible data framework, including data providers, and the DataSet and DataAdapter components. You'll also see how some of the data-aware controls such as the GridView are used to provide great data experiences for your users.

Chapter 5 takes you in a different direction, looking at Web Services and how this vital technology is implemented using ASP.NET. You'll see how to build a web service that wraps a database and exposes its contents to users in a platform-agnostic, technology-agnostic way. With Web Services, the technology that implements the service should be abstract, and you'll see how this is achieved using XML and the WS-I basic profile. You'll see how you can build your services to be consumed by applications running on other technologies, such as Java. You'll expand on some of the examples from Chapter 4, seeing how a multitier application can be built using Web Services as the data tier, and binding controls such as the GridView to them.

Part 1 of the book wraps up in Chapter 6. Here you will look at how to get your applications deployed and running using Windows Server 2003, SQL Server, and IIS 6. You'll look at how IIS serves pages up, and go through the scenario of deploying the multiple-tier application that you built in Chapter 5, moving it in a phased manner, performing unit testing on each tier. You'll also look at how to use the tools to automatically set up the virtual web sites that your application will run in.

Once you've wrapped all that up, you'll be ready to move into Part 2, which delves into the next-generation web technologies, and take an in-depth look at AJAX extensions for .NET, Windows Communication Foundation, Windows Presentation Foundation, Silverlight, and more.

PART 1

Building Web Applications

■ ■ ■

Introduction to Web Development

To understand web development, you have to understand the Web, and to understand the Web, you have to understand the Internet that the Web is built on. This chapter will give you a brief history of the connected world, discussing first the origins of the Internet, then the origins of the Web, and finally the technologies used by developers to build applications on the Web. It will hopefully be a fun and informative ride!

The Internet and the Birth of the Web

The Internet dates back to the early development of general communication networks. At its heart, this concept of a computer network is an infrastructure that enables computers and their users to communicate with each other. There have been many types of computer networks over time, but one has grown to near ubiquity: the Internet.

Its history dates back to the 1960s and the development of networks to support the Department of Defense as well as various academic institutions. Interoperability of these different networks was a problem. In 1973, Robert E. Kahn of United States Defense Advanced Research Projects Agency (DARPA and ARPANET) and Vinton Cerf of Stanford University worked out a common "internetwork protocol" that they called the TCP/IP Internet Protocol Suite. This was both a set of standards that defined how computers would communicate as well as conventions for how the computers should be named and addressed, and thus how traffic would be routed between them.

At its core, TCP/IP follows most of the OSI (Open Systems Interconnection) model, which defines a network as an entity of seven layers:

Application layer: Provides the user interface (UI) to the network as well as the application services required by this interface, such as file access. In terms of the Internet, these application services are those typically provided by the browser, giving access to the file system to save favorites, print, and more.

Presentation layer: Translates the data from the network into something that the user can understand and vice versa, translating user input into the language used by the network to communicate. For example, when you use a browser to access a page, you type the address of that page. This address gets translated for you into an HTTP-GET command by the browser.

Session layer: Used to establish communication between applications running on different nodes of the network. For example, your request from the browser sets up a session that is used to communicate with the server that serves up the page. The lower levels are used to discover that server and facilitate the flow, but at this level you have a communication session storing all the data needed to manage the flow of data to the presentation tier for representation on the client.

Transport layer: Handles the task of managing message delivery and flow between nodes on the network. Networks are fundamentally unreliable because packets of data can be lost or received out of sync. Thus, a network protocol has to ensure delivery in a timely manner or trigger an action upon nondelivery. It also works to ensure that the messages are routed, assembled, and delivered correctly. For example, when using an Internet browsing session, your message is broken down into small packets as part of the TCP/IP protocol. The TCP/IP stack manages sending these packets to the server and assembling them correctly once they reach it.

Network layer: Used to standardize the way that addressing is accomplished between different linked networks. For data to flow from A to B, the locations and paths between A and B need to be known. This address awareness and routing is achieved by the network layer. There is almost never a direct connection between a client and a server. Instead, the traffic has to be routed across a number of networks through connections that involve changes of addresses between them. For example, a server might have the Internet protocol (IP) address 192.168.0.1 on its internal network, but that internal network faces the world using a different IP. A client calling the server calls the external IP, and has traffic on the web port routed to 192.168.0.1. This is all handled by the network layer.

Data link layer: Defines how the physical layer is accessed—that is, what protocols are used to talk to it, how the data is broken up into packets and frames, and how the addressing is managed on the physical layer. In the example just described, TCP/IP is the protocol. This is used on the network layer and above to manage communication between the client and the server. At this layer, the frames and routing information for TCP/IP packets are defined as to how they will run on the line as electrical signals. Network bridges operate at this layer.

Physical layer: Defines the type of medium, the transmission method, and the rates available for the network. Some networks have broadband communication, measured in megabits per second, whereas others have narrower communication in the kilobit range or less. Because of the wide variance in bandwidth, different behavior can be expected, and applications that implement network protocols have to be aware of this. Thus, the physical layer has to be able to provide this data to the next layer up, and respond to command instructions from it.

You can see this seven-layer model, and how typical TCP/IP applications such as the web browser fit into it, in Figure 1-1.

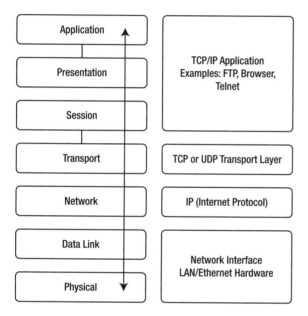

Figure 1-1. *OSI seven-layer model*

This model provided the foundation for what would become the Internet, and the Internet provided the foundation for what would become the World Wide Web.

By using TCP/IP, it became possible to build first a file transfer protocol (FTP) and ensuing application. From there, Tim Berners-Lee expanded the idea to having a "live" view of the file in an application called a "browser." Instead of just transferring a document from a distant machine to your own, the application would also render the file. To do this, the file would need to be marked up in a special way that could be understood by the browser. A natural progression to this is to allow documents to be linked to each other, so that when the user selects a link, they are taken to the document that the link refers to. This introduced the concept of *hypertext,* and thus HTML (Hypertext Markup Language) was invented.

An *HTML document* is a text document containing special markup that provides instructions to the browser for how to render the document. *Tags* such as <H1> and <H2> are used to provide styling information so that the document can be viewed as more than just text. Links to other documents are provided via another tag, <a> (for anchor), where a piece of text is defined as linking to another document, and the browser renders it differently (usually with a blue underline).

Once HTML was developed, the Web grew rapidly. Thanks to TCP/IP and the Internet, people could put documents on any server in the world and provide an address, called a *URL* (Universal Resource Locator), which could enable these documents to be found. These URLs could then be embedded as links in other documents and used to find those documents. Quickly, a huge network of interconnected, browsable documents was created: the World Wide Web.

Going Beyond the Static Web

This Web—a network of linked documents—was very useful, but in essence very static. Consider the scenario of a store wanting to provide links to potential customers of their current products. Their inventory changes rapidly, and static documents require people who understand the inventory and can constantly generate documents containing new details. Every time something is bought or sold by the store, these documents need to be updated. This, as you can imagine, is a time-consuming, difficult, and non-cost-effective task!

We needed some way to automatically generate documents instead of creating them manually. Also, these documents needed to be generated not in overnight batch runs, but rather upon request so that the information would always be up-to-date.

Thus, the "active" Web was born. New servers were written on the Common Gateway Interface (CGI) standard, which allowed developers to write code (usually in C) that executed in response to user requests. When a request came in for a document, this code could run, and in the case of our store scenario, that code could read a database or an inventory system for the current status and generate the results as an HTML document. This document would then be sent back to the browser. This system worked well, and was very powerful and widely used.

Maintenance of CGI applications became quite difficult, however, and CGI applications were also platform-specific, so if you had a cluster of servers, some of which were based on different technologies and/or versions of operating systems, you could end up with multiple versions of the same program to support! So, for example, if you wanted to run the same program on your cluster, but had different versions of an operating system, your code would have to be tailored for each machine.

But when there is a problem, there is also opportunity. And where there is opportunity, there is innovation. One of these opportunities was moving toward a *managed cross-platform code* approach in which a high-level language such as Java could be used to build an application that generates dynamic pages. Because Java is a cross-platform language, the platform on which the code ran no longer mattered, and server-side Java, called *servlets*, became an effective replacement for CGI.

But the problem of generating HTML still existed. In these applications, string management, or `printf` statements, were used to write HTML, leading to ugly and onerous code. In another approach, HTML defined the output, and special extension tags instructed the server to do something when it reached those tags and fill in the placeholders. The code would look like the pseudocode here:

```
<h3>We have <% nQuantity %> widgets in stock. </h3>
```

The `<% %>` contains code that will be executed by the server. In this case, it is a value calculated on the fly as part of the session. When it's evaluated, the result is injected into the HTML and returned to the browser.

This is the underpinning of technologies such as classic ASP, which runs on Internet Information Server (IIS) and uses a Microsoft Visual Basic–like language between the tags. A similar architecture is used by Personal Hypertext Processor (PHP), which runs on its own interpreter that can be an IIS or other web server extension, and uses its own C++-like language. There are many other examples as well, such as Java Server Pages (JSP), which uses an approach where the HTML is not written out using code, but instead contains tags that are interpreted and replaced at runtime with calculated values; or Ruby, an object-oriented scripting language that works well for generating web content.

The opportunity was there for a best-of-both-worlds approach. And here is where ASP.NET arrived to fill the gap.

The Arrival of ASP.NET

ASP.NET was the result of developers and architects sitting back and thinking about the direction in which web development had taken to date. In some ways, developers had been painted into a corner by rapid innovation and were now in a nonoptimal development environment.

ASP.NET was designed to get around a number of issues regarding how to develop web applications at the time. At the same time, it began spurring innovation of new types of applications that previously might not have been possible.

First, it was designed to be a code-friendly environment using sophisticated object-oriented methodology that allowed for rapid code development and reuse, as opposed to the scripting-like environment used previously.

Second, it was designed to be a multiple-language single runtime, allowing developers from different backgrounds to use it with minimal retraining. For the Visual Basic folk, Visual Basic .NET was available, and for those used to more traditional object-oriented languages such as C++ or Java, a new language—C#—was introduced.

Third, the concept of *web services* was identified as being vital for the future of the Web, because they are a device-agnostic, technology-agnostic means for sharing data across the multi-platform Internet. ASP.NET was designed to make the complicated process of creating, exposing, and consuming web services as simple as possible.

Finally, performance of the Web depends not only on the speed of the network, but also on the speed of the application serving you. Absolute performance, defined as the overall speed of the application, is difficult enough, but application performance under different user loads implemented concurrently across multiple servers is more of a trick. ASP.NET was designed with optimizations for this in mind, including a compiled code model, where all the source code is turned into native machine language ahead of time, instead of an interpreted one, where all the source code is turned into native machine language step by step as it executes. It also includes a scalable data access mode, a way to keep state between client and server, data caching, and much more.

Summary

This chapter has given you a very brief background on what the Internet is, how the Web fits into the Internet, and how web application development has evolved to this point. It has also introduced you to the ASP.NET technology.

In this book, you'll look at ASP.NET in the .NET Framework and how it is used to build the web applications and services of today and tomorrow. In Part 1, you'll learn about the framework for building traditional web applications. Then, in Part 2, you'll move on to looking at how innovations for technologies such as Ajax and Windows Presentation Foundation (WPF) allow you to start improving the overall user experience. You'll also look at the development frameworks of tomorrow to learn how you can take the Web into the next phase of its evolution—that is, toward the next-generation Web, where the user experience is at the heart of everything you do.

■■■

Basics of Web Development with ASP.NET

In Chapter 1, we looked at the history of web development technologies, culminating in smart server-oriented code that generates client-side markup as well as script that gets rendered by the browser for your users. The Microsoft technology that achieves this is ASP.NET, where *ASP* stands for Active Server Pages, and *.NET* is Microsoft's contemporary software runtime environment. In this chapter, you'll get an overview of what ASP.NET is and how it works. You'll first look at the tools that are available to build ASP.NET applications, from the free Microsoft Visual Studio Express tools to the various professional Visual Studio 2008–based packages. You'll see how to build an ASP.NET application with these tools before digging into the architecture of ASP.NET so that you can understand how it all fits together.

Using Visual Studio

Before we go into the architecture of ASP.NET, it's a good idea to create a simple ASP.NET application that can be used to demonstrate its architectural principles. This application is a multiple-tier application that consumes a back-end web service to expose a stock quote to the user. The examples in this chapter are built using Visual Web Developer Express (VWDE), downloadable for free from Microsoft at `http://msdn.microsoft.com/vstudio/express/vwd/`. (For those who are not familiar with Visual Studio, we will look into the different versions available in a little more detail later in this chapter.) This section assumes that you aren't familiar with building ASP.NET applications, so we will follow the process in small steps.

Creating the Application

VWDE enables you to create web site applications that run on either the Visual Studio 2005 Web Server (also known as Cassini), which comes with Visual Studio, or from Internet Information Services (IIS). The first example will use Cassini.

■**Note** When running Visual Studio in Windows Vista, if you want to debug your application you should run it as an administrator.

To begin creating the application, launch Visual Studio or VWDE, select the File menu, and then select New Web Site (see Figure 2-1).

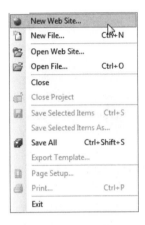

Figure 2-1. *Creating a new web site*

The New Web Site dialog box appears, in which you can select the type of web site application that you want to create. The available default options are as follows:

ASP.NET Web Site: This is a web site that uses ASP.NET to execute. It comes with a sample file called Default.aspx, which is an ASP.NET Web Forms application. (This is the type of web site application you'll create in this chapter; web forms are discussed in detail in Chapter 3.)

ASP.NET Web Service: A web service is a device- and platform-agnostic implementation of business logic. It does not have a UI, but instead is called using an XML vocabulary called Simple Object Access Protocol (SOAP). Web services are the underpinnings of the Service-Oriented Architecture (SOA) and methodologies of the Web. You'll be looking into this important technology in Chapter 5.

Personal Web Site Starter Kit: This kit includes a template for everything that you can use to create a simple personal-use web site that hosts pages, pictures, and more.

Empty Web Site: This option creates the stubs that you need to build a web site, including all the required ASP.NET configuration files, but no sample pages or web forms.

The Location drop-down list is important in this dialog box. As you can see in Figure 2-2, the options available are File System, HTTP, and FTP.

The *File System* option creates a directory on your hard drive for your web application and treats that directory like a web site. This option uses the embedded Visual Studio 2005 web server to run your application (that is to say, it uses Cassini as the web server rather than a full web server, easing administration and debugging).

The *HTTP* option is used to connect to an IIS instance. If you choose to create your web application on a remote server, that server will need to have IIS installed and running, as well as Front Page (Server) Extensions (FPE). You may also need to administer IIS in some cases to enable remote debugging (be sure to see an IIS administrator for help with this!). To run your new web application under IIS on your local machine, make sure IIS is installed and running (FPE will have been installed for you when you installed Visual Studio), and then specify http://localhost as the server. This will create a new directory under C:\Inetpub\wwwroot for your application, and IIS will serve it from there.

The *FTP* option enables you to use FTP to connect to a server. This server can be running IIS or another web server. However, to use ASP.NET applications as opposed to simple HTML pages, the server must be running IIS. If you use an alternative server, such as Apache, you can still create a blank web site and standard HTML pages by using VWDE and deploy those pages to Apache by using the FTP option.

In the following section, you'll learn about the integrated development environment (IDE) and use it to edit your web site application. But first, you need to create a new web site on your file system. To do this, select File System from the Location drop-down list (as shown in Figure 2-2) and select your preferred language. The examples in this book will be using C#, but if you prefer Visual Basic, converting between the two is fairly straightforward. Next, set a location for where you want the web site to be stored, as well as the desired name for your site. For example, Figure 2-2 shows the path as C:\WebNextBook\Chapter2Example1, so this will create a new web site called Chapter2-Example1 in the C:\WebNextBook directory. When you click OK, Visual Studio will create the web site and launch the IDE, which enables you to create and edit your application's various web form pages and support files.

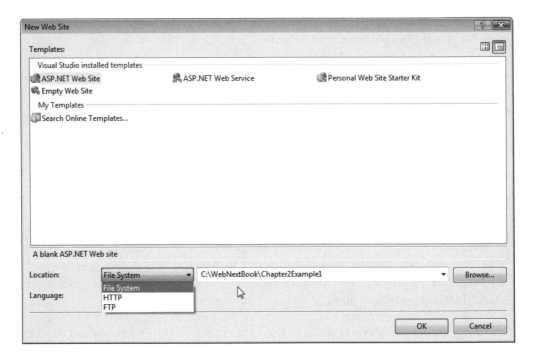

Figure 2-2. *New Web Site dialog box*

Exploring the IDE

Once you've created the web site, the IDE will launch and you will be able to edit your new web site, as shown in Figure 2-3.

VWDE provides you with a fully featured IDE that enables you to edit and maintain your web application. The IDE is divided into several distinct areas; we'll take a brief tour of them now.

The Toolbox

On the left side of the screen is the Toolbox, which enables you to drag and drop controls onto your web application. Controls can be either ASP.NET server controls, which wrap basic HTML controls but provide for a greatly enhanced programming interface; or standard controls, which represent basic HTML controls, such as buttons, input text controls, and lists, but without the enhanced programming interface (their programming interface mimics the basic control itself). Both types of controls are rendered into raw HTML when the page is compiled, which occurs either beforehand if you like, or when the page is first accessed on the server.

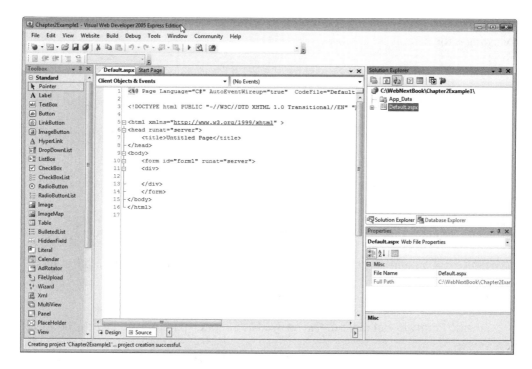

Figure 2-3. *The VWDE IDE*

Figure 2-4 shows the Toolbox with each group of controls hidden in collapsed tree control nodes commonly referred to as "tabs" (even though this isn't a Tab control!).

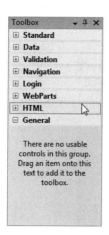

Figure 2-4. *The Toolbox*

The Toolbox gathers all your controls into logical groupings, accessed by tabs. Following is the default set of tabs:

Standard: Contains the standard suite of ASP.NET server controls

Data: Contains the suite of ASP.NET server controls that can be bound to data

Validation: Contains the suite of ASP.NET server controls that can be used to validate user input

Navigation: Contains the suite of ASP.NET server controls that can be used to build navigation on a web site

Login: Contains the ASP.NET server controls for login and user management

WebParts: Contains server controls used to build SharePoint WebParts applications

HTML: Contains standard, generic HTML controls

General: Empty by default, but can be used as a scratch pad for your favorite controls

You aren't limited to this group of tabs or the controls that they contain. You can right-click the Toolbox to add or remove tabs and to add or remove controls from a tab.

■Note Did you know that you can put code snippets in the Toolbox, too? Simply highlight them, and then drag and drop them onto the Toolbox!

It's pretty common for people to use a third-party or add-on control that isn't part of the default control suite. To add a new tab, right-click a blank area in the Toolbox and select Add Tab to create a new tab for your control (see Figure 2-5). A new tab with a text box placeholder appears. Type a name for the new tab (e.g., My Controls) and press Enter. You'll now have a new, empty tab on which you can place your controls.

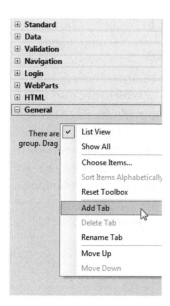

Figure 2-5. *Adding a new tab*

The next step is to add controls to the new tab. To do this, right-click in the blank area on the tab and select Choose Items from the context menu (see Figure 2-6).

Figure 2-6. *Adding a new control to your tab*

The Choose Toolbox Items dialog box will appear, as shown in Figure 2-7. This dialog box enables you to add either .NET Framework components, which are components written in managed code that will run anywhere you have the .NET Framework runtime, or Component Object Model (COM) components. COM components are binary components written in unmanaged code that may not necessarily run anywhere because all their binary dependencies are necessary. Remember this limitation when using COM components in a web application: You'll need to provide installers for the COM components so that your users can access them. Additionally, when COM components are used in .NET applications, the IDE will generate an interoperability (interop) layer that is used to communicate between the managed and the unmanaged worlds. If you are planning to use the COM components only on the server side, you'll still need to make sure that the deployment server has the full COM component and all its dependencies installed and versioned correctly, as well as the interop assemblies.

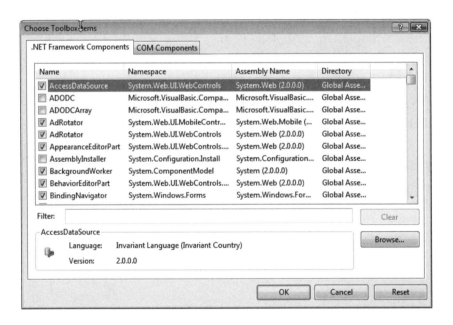

Figure 2-7. *The Choose Toolbox Items dialog box*

You can select any of the detected components from the Choose Toolbox Items dialog box, or use the Browse button to browse to the assembly that contains the component you want to add. To add the component to your Toolbox, simply select the check box beside it and click OK.

Now, to use controls in your Toolbox, simply drag them from the Toolbox to the design surface of your page. When we've finished the IDE tour, you'll build a simple application by doing just this.

The Solution Explorer

The Solution Explorer is a window in the IDE showing all the files, directories, and physical artifacts of your project. You can use it to manage your project, adding and deleting new content or moving existing content around. The Solution Explorer window is shown in Figure 2-8.

Figure 2-8. *The Solution Explorer window*

Visual Studio and Solutions

Visual Studio 2005 uses the concept of *solutions* for managing complex applications. Solutions are broken down into *projects*. If you have a single project present in your solution, as with the example so far, then the project and solution are one in the same. However, as soon as you add other projects, which may represent other web sites, related business logic code, web services, or whatever, then the solution will encompass all of those projects and compile them into a single web application.

Earlier in the chapter, you created an ASP.NET web site. If you look at your project in the Solution Explorer, you can see a couple of interesting things. The first of these is a folder named App_Data. This is a special directory used by ASP.NET to manage data and data connections within your project. You'll be examining this in more detail in Chapters 3 and 4.

The next item of interest Visual Studio created for you is a file called Default.aspx. ASP.NET uses the .aspx extension to denote a web form. This is a special type of web page on which server controls may be placed, and code associated with these forms may be executed by the server. The design and code implementation are separated by means of a *code-behind page*. The code-behind page is typically the name of the page with a .cs extension (or .vb if you are using Visual Basic). Therefore, if your page is called Default. aspx, its associated code-behind file is called Default.aspx.cs. You can see this in action in

Figure 2-8. You'll find out more about the page itself in the next section, but first, let's finish looking at the Solution Explorer.

The Solution Explorer is more than just a means to view the files in your project. You can right-click any item in the window to access a context menu of actions that you can take with your solution (see Figure 2-9). To get the solution options, it's best to select the project name at the top of the Solution Explorer and right-click that. Experiment with right-clicking each of the artifacts within the Solution Explorer to see what other actions are available.

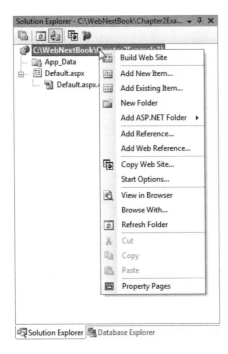

Figure 2-9. *Solution Explorer context options*

As you can see, the menu shown in Figure 2-9 is quite a long list. Let's look at each of these options.

Build Web Site

This option invokes the compiler to build each page and element on your web site. The compiler will check your pages for errors and flag them in the Errors window, which is typically in the middle of the IDE, beneath the code window.

Figure 2-10 shows an example of this. The error is described in the Errors window, along with metadata such as the file and its location. You can double-click the error description to jump to the error.

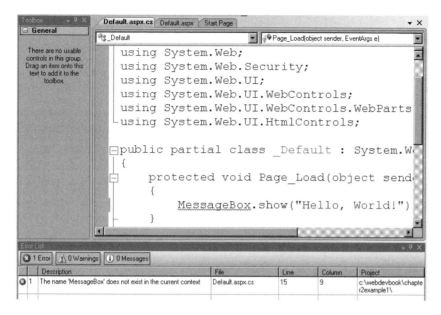

Figure 2-10. *Using the Errors window*

Add New Item

This option invokes the Add New Item dialog, enabling you to specify a new item name and type (see Figure 2-11).

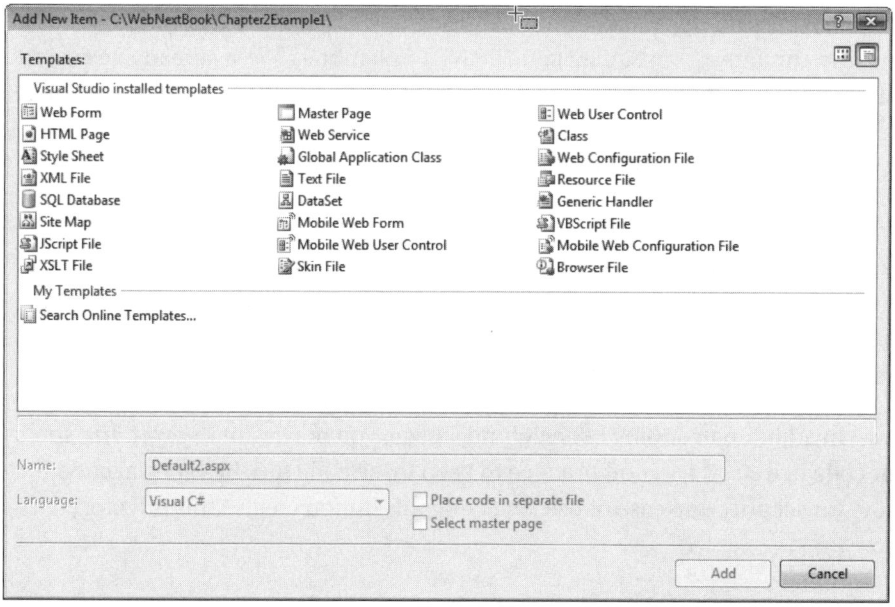

Figure 2-11. *Add New Item dialog box*

As you can see, there are a myriad of new items you can add to your project here. You'll be using many of these throughout this book.

Add Existing Item

This option enables you to browse your computer for an existing item to add to your web site. This can be anything from an HTML page to a cascading style sheet to a media item that you are going to reference from one of your pages. Note that the IDE will create a new copy of the item in the folder that contains your web site. That is, VWDE does not try to reference the item from its original location, since on the web server there are likely file system permission issues to deal with.

New Folder

This option creates a new folder within the directory that contains your web site. This new folder should be distinguished from an ASP.NET folder (discussed in the next section). Use the New Folder option to create directories that you will use to segregate your site or centralize content of a specific type, such as JavaScript (.js) files or media (images).

Add ASP.NET Folder

ASP.NET recognizes a handful of specially named web site directories as containing information required by the framework for specific purposes. For example, App_Code contains source files that will be compiled the first time the web site is accessed (or modified). The Bin subdirectory contains precompiled code in .NET assemblies. We've already discussed App_Data. If you want to use one of these directory types, you should use this menu instead of creating a new folder and giving it the associated name (such as Bin or App_Code).

The options available in the Add ASP.NET Folder submenu are as follows:

Bin: Adds a directory to your web site that contains referenced .NET assemblies ("binary" files). This directory is used to add the assemblies of components that you want to use on your web site, but aren't automatically referenced by ASP.NET. So, if you are referencing a third-party assembly, the dynamic-link library (DLL) file for that assembly will be placed in this directory.

App_Code: In addition to adding code behind a page, you may want to centralize some of your code in a class. It's good practice to keep these code files in a special code directory for security and ease of use. Selecting this option creates this directory for you.

App_GlobalResources: This is a directory that you use to store resources that are accessible to every page or project in a web application. It isn't really useful for web site projects because they have only one project, and local resources (see the next item in this list) would be more appropriate.

App_LocalResources: This is a directory that you can use to store resources that are accessible to every page in your project.

App_WebReferences: When you want to access a web service, you create a web reference to that service, and the IDE will create proxy code that can be used to communicate with the web service. This folder will contain the proxy code and other information necessary for this task. It is created automatically for you whenever you create a web reference.

App_Browsers: This directory is used to store files that can be used by ASP.NET in response to queries from different browsers. This is particularly useful if you create your own server controls because you can specify how the control behaves for different browsers by placing special XML files in this directory.

Theme: This creates a directory that can be used to store a *theme* for your web application. A theme is a "skin" file that contains definitions for how each control should be rendered.

When you use code in a .skin file and place the file in the Theme directory, you can then specify the theme to be used as part of the page declaration. It's a nice way of specifying look and feel without defining it on each control on your page. Building themes with ASP.NET is a powerful way of adding flexibility to your site. To learn a bit more about ASP.NET theme capabilities, see http://msdn2.microsoft.com/en-us/library/ykzx33wh.aspx.

Add Reference

If you are using an assembly containing .NET managed classes in your application, and that assembly is not delivered as a part of the core .NET Framework that ASP.NET pre-references, you can create a reference to the assembly with Add Reference. Doing so will add the classes within the assembly to the IDE for IntelliSense, as well as create a copy of the DLL for the assembly in the Bin folder. Selecting Add Reference will open the Add Reference dialog box (see Figure 2-12).

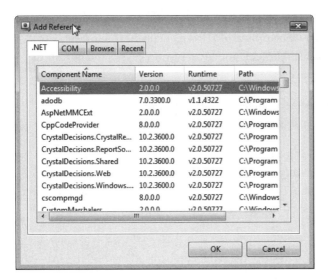

Figure 2-12. *Adding a reference*

One option is to add a .NET assembly from the .NET tab in the Add Reference dialog box, in which case the process is straightforward. Just make sure that you deploy the DLL containing the assembly with your site, and your application should work well. Another option is to add a COM component from the COM tab, which is a little more complex. As I mentioned previously, you'll have to make sure that the COM component is properly installed on the server as well as the COM interop assemblies that are generated by the IDE to enable your code to interact with the COM component from the .NET runtime environment.

If the component that you need isn't on the list, whether it's a .NET assembly or a COM component, you can look for it on the Browse tab, or the Recent tab, where, for your convenience, recently added components are listed.

So, for example, if you want to use the Microsoft AJAX Extensions for ASP.NET (formerly known as "Atlas" in its beta form), discussed in Chapters 11 through 14, you can use the Browse tab to go to their installation directory and pick them up from there (see Figure 2-13). (Note that you can select multiple files on this tab.) Once you locate the files using the Browse tab, you will be able to use the controls and functions from these DLLs in your web site.

ASP.NET AJAX: THE WHATS, WHYS, AND WHERES

Ajax is a technology that allows you to break through many of the typical restrictions of browser-based applications. While the acronym AJAX stands for Asynchronous JavaScript and XML, it has become synonymous with dynamic, flexible applications built on the asynchronous functionality that is provided with the `XMLHttpRequest` object and the styling innovations from CSS (Cascading Style Sheets).

ASP.NET AJAX is a technology that is designed to make Ajax applications much easier to develop, debug, and deploy. It's available at `http://asp.net/ajax/`, and will be covered in Chapters 11 through 14 of this book.

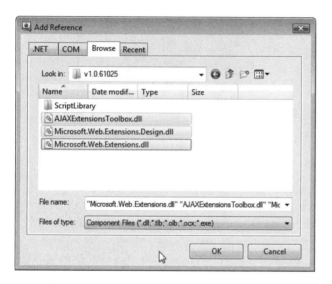

Figure 2-13. *Adding a reference to the AJAX assemblies*

Add Web Reference

A web service has an associated definition file called a WSDL (pronounced *WIZ-dull*). You can point the Visual Studio IDE at the WSDL for a web service, and the IDE will automatically create all the code necessary for talking to the web service by using the standard SOAP code that web services use.

So, for example, if you want to talk to a web service that is hosted at the following URL

```
http://www.swanandmokashi.com/HomePage/WebServices/StockQuotes.asmx?WSDL
```

you simply need to enter this into the URL field in the Add Web Reference dialog, as shown in Figure 2-14.

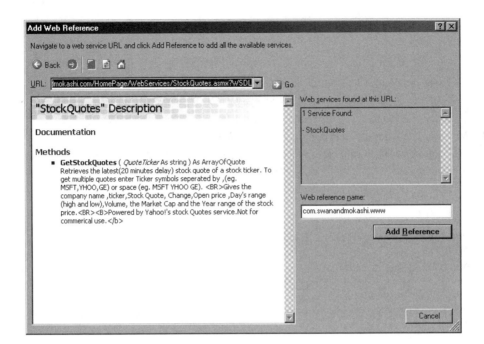

Figure 2-14. *Creating a web reference*

Visual Studio will then create a special type of class called a *proxy*. This is simply a local representation of the remote service, allowing you to call methods as if they were implemented on your local computer. However, under the covers, ASP.NET will forward all of the proxy method calls to the remote service for execution.

If Visual Studio interprets the file successfully, you will see a list of available methods (GetStockQuotes in the example in Figure 2-14). You can then create a name for the web reference and add the reference to your project. At this point in your project, you can create an instance of the web reference proxy class and call the method on it to get data back from the web service.

In fact, let's do that now so that we can call a remote web service to obtain stock quotes for our example. Right-click the project name and select Add Web Reference. When the Add Web Reference dialog box appears, type http://services.xmethods.net/ soap/urn:xmethods-delayed-quotes.wsdl into the URL field and click Go. We'll be using a service provided by XMethods (www.xmethods.com) that reports delayed stock quotes given a stock ticker symbol. You can see this in Figure 2-14. After clicking Go, Visual Studio contacts XMethods, downloads the WSDL, and displays the available methods it finds for you to review. Note the value in the Web reference name field (net.xmethods.services), which will ultimately form the namespace of the proxy class you'll be using. Change the value you find there to "QS" for "quote service," and then click Add Reference. At this point,

Visual Studio converts the WSDL into a C# class (the proxy) and stores it under the App_WebReferences folder, which Visual Studio also creates for you. Later in the chapter, we'll use this quote service to actually retrieve stock quote values.

Copy Web Site

This enables you to copy your web site to a new location. This can be another directory on your file system or a remote directory on an FTP or IIS server. Copy Web Site can also be used to back up or deploy your web site.

Start Options

This enables you to specify the action to take when you start the project. It's a shortcut to the Property Pages window, with the start options already selected (see Figure 2-15).

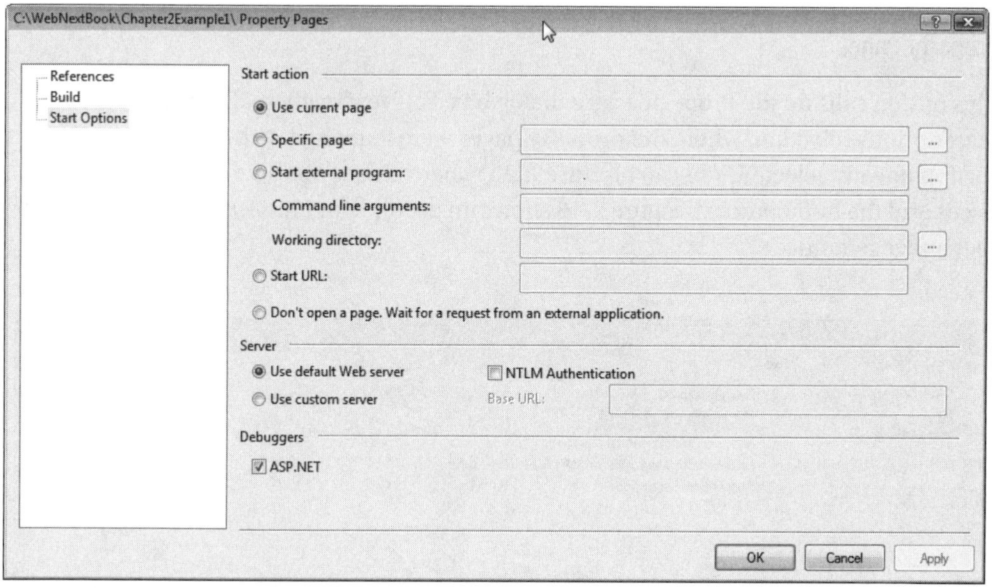

Figure 2-15. *Web Start options*

You can use this dialog box to specify how the application will start—for example, launching the current page (in the IDE) as the start page, specifying a particular page, or starting an external program first before launching the site. You can also specify the server to use and how to authenticate against that server.

View in Browser

The default browser on your system shows the currently selected page (or the default page as specified in Web Start options if nothing is selected).

Browse With

This option enables you to specify the browser that you will use to browse the site. By default, Microsoft Internet Explorer and the Visual Studio built-in browser are available, but you can easily use the dialog box to add other browsers such as Mozilla Firefox.

Refresh Folder

This option refreshes and redraws the contents of the Solution Explorer. If you've added new files or references and they haven't shown up yet, choose Refresh Folder to see them.

Property Pages

This option calls up the Property Pages dialog box. You've already seen this with the Web Start options selection, where the property pages were launched with the Start Options section already selected. You can also use the Property Pages option to manage references and the build process. Figure 2-16 shows an example of Property Pages being used to manage references.

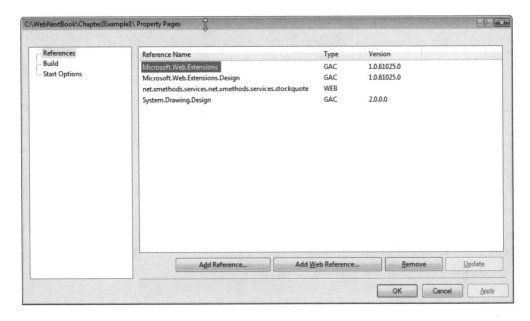

Figure 2-16. *Managing application references with Property Pages*

You can use Property Pages to view existing references, which will either be application references (type GAC) or web references (type WEB) on the references list. You can also add application or web references from this window, following the same workflow that you followed when you chose to add them directly from the context menu. If you want to remove unwanted references, select them and click Remove. Finally, web services may change over time, causing your proxy to break because it is out of sync with the originating service. If you want to make sure that your proxy is up-to-date and able to communicate with the service, select the web reference and click Update. Of course, when the update to your web reference indicates the originating service actually did change, you may need to change your own code that uses the web service.

Figure 2-17 shows the Build options.

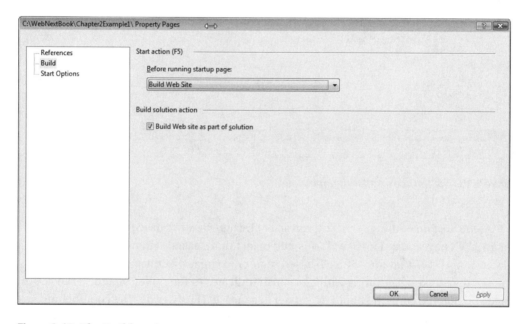

Figure 2-17. *The Build options*

In Visual Studio, pressing the F5 key starts your application. You can use the Property Pages dialog box to specify what should happen when the application starts. By default, the web site will be built every time, but there are other available options, including No Build (where the current build of the site will be run, ignoring changes since the last build) and Build Page (where only the current page will be built before executing). The latter option is useful, for example, in a larger site when you just want to unit test one page without rebuilding everything.

The Code and Design Windows

At the center of the IDE screen you'll see the Source and Design window. If you are view-ing an ASPX file and you select the Source tab at the bottom, the window will look like Figure 2-18.

Figure 2-18. *The Source and Design window*

At the bottom of the screen, you can select Design view or Source view. Source view for an ASPX page looks a lot like HTML, and in fact that's exactly what it is—specially marked-up HTML that the ASP.NET-based server recognizes. At the top of the document, you see the markup beginning with <%@, which indicates to the server that this is an active page and that the content should be parsed to generate HTML code. The code-behind file is specified as part of the Page tag at the top. In addition, as you place controls on the page, you'll see the server-side code specified using tags such as <asp:Button> for a server-side button. As the server parses the page, it recognizes tags like this and generates the appropriate HTML to render the desired content.

Design view shows the design surface for the page. In Design view, you can drag and drop controls from the Toolbox onto the page to create your web UI. See the example in Figure 2-19, where an ASP.NET Button, Label, and TextBox control have been added to the page.

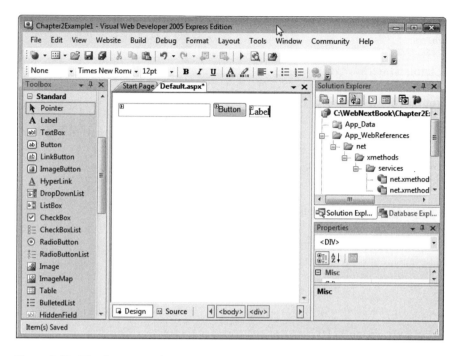

Figure 2-19. *The design surface*

You can use the Properties window to set the properties of the currently selected item. So, for example, you can change the label on the button from Button to Get by finding the Text entry in the Properties window and using it to set the button text to Get (see Figure 2-20). You can also change the name of a button using the ID property.

Figure 2-20. *Setting the label for a button by using the Properties window*

For the stock quote application you are creating, set the properties of the three controls as follows:

TextBox: Change the ID to `txtTicker`.

Button: Change the ID to `btnGet`, and change the text to `Get`.

Label: Change the ID to `lblQuote`, and change the text to `' '` (an empty string).

The page will now look something like what you see in Listing 2-1.

Listing 2-1. *The Stock Quote Application*

```
<%@ Page Language="C#" AutoEventWireup="true"
    CodeFile="Default.aspx.cs" Inherits="_Default" %>

<!DOCTYPE html
    PUBLIC "-//W3C//DTD XHTML 1.0 Transitional//EN"
    "http://www.w3.org/TR/xhtml1/DTD/xhtml1-transitional.dtd">

<html xmlns="http://www.w3.org/1999/xhtml" >
<head runat="server">
  <title>Untitled Page</title>
</head>
<body>
  <form id="form1" runat="server">
  <div>
    <asp:TextBox ID="txtTicker" runat="server"></asp:TextBox>
    <asp:Button ID="btnGet" runat="server" Text="Get" />
    <asp:Label ID="lblQuote" runat="server"></asp:Label></div>
  </form>
</body>
</html>
```

You can see the `<asp:>` labels for the three controls as well as their attributes, which define the properties that you just set. If you don't want to use the Property Editor to set the properties, you can instead use the source editor to enter these properties manually, and IntelliSense will even help you with this.

If you haven't done so already, make sure that you add a web reference to the XMethods quote service at `www.swanandmokashi.com/HomePage/WebServices/StockQuotes.asmx?WSDL`. Call the service reference `'QS'`.

Now, in the `Default.aspx` page's Design view, double-click the button, and a click event handler will be added to the code-behind file. This event handler will be called `btnGet_Click`. Edit the event handler so that it looks like this:

```
protected void btnGet_Click(object sender, EventArgs e)
{

    QS.StockQuotes myQuote = new QS.StockQuotes();
    QS.Quote[] res;
    res = myQuote.GetStockQuotes(txtTicker.Text);
    lblQuote.Text = res[0].StockQuote;

}
```

This code creates an instance of the web service proxy called `'MyQuote'`. It then calls the `getStockQuotes` method on this proxy (and by extension the web service), which returns a stock quote for the string ticker. As you can see from the code, the contents of the txtTicker text box are being passed to the quote retrieval web service. The service returns an array of `Quote` objects, and the label then has its text set to the value of the `StockQuote` property of the first element in this array, converted to a string. Do note, however, that this is just example code. In a real scenario, you would likely want to at least add some form of error handling to check for a timeout or other error in calling the web service. For production systems, you may also want to look into asynchronous web service calls.

Now if you run the application, type a stock ticker (e.g., MSFT, RTRSY, or BEAS) into the text box, and click Get, the web service will return a stock quote for that ticker. You can see this in action in Figure 2-21.

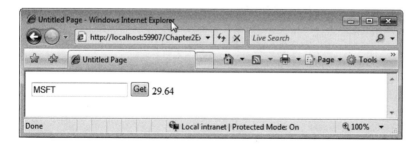

Figure 2-21. *The simple stock quote web site*

Architecture of ASP.NET

The simplicity of developing the stock quote application proves the power that ASP.NET affords you as a web developer. Some fairly complex stuff was going on behind the scenes, enabling you to focus on the business logic for your application, instead of all the underlying plumbing necessary to get it to work.

Figure 2-22 shows how the underlying ASP.NET components all work together in an ASP.NET application. At the bottom of the figure, you see the host operating system on which the web server runs. The web server for ASP.NET can be Cassini or IIS. The web server receives the incoming request from the browser and passes it to the ASP.NET runtime, which sits on top of the operating system.

This runtime can use a global application file, called Global.asax, to manage functions that are central to your web site. A number of modules are available to the runtime for handling sessions, authentication, and caching.

Finally, your application or web service sits on top of these modules and executes. Upon executing, it generates HTML markup that gets passed back to the process that initiated the request through the web server.

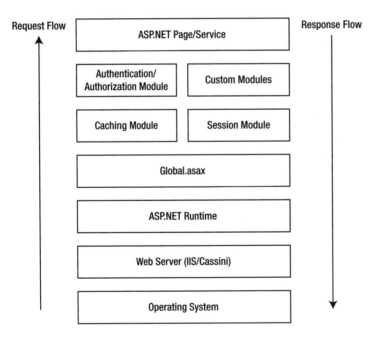

Figure 2-22. *ASP.NET architecture*

The ASP.NET Worker Process and State Management

In the stock quote application, when the web browser requested the page from the
server, the server recognized the `.aspx` page name extension as an ASP.NET page, and
passed the request to the ASP.NET runtime, which processed the ASP.NET code and
returned the output to the client. Take a look back at Listing 2-1, where the page was
defined using extended HTML. If you look at the code being rendered by the browser
(by selecting View Source from your browser when viewing the `Default.aspx` page), you'll
see something different. Take a look at Listing 2-2.

Listing 2-2. *The Stock Quote Application As Rendered by the Browser*

```
<!DOCTYPE html
    PUBLIC "-//W3C//DTD XHTML 1.0 Transitional//EN"
    "http://www.w3.org/TR/xhtml1/DTD/xhtml1-transitional.dtd">

<html xmlns="http://www.w3.org/1999/xhtml" >

<head>
<title>Untitled Page</title>
</head>

<body>
 <form name="form1" method="post" action="Default.aspx" id="form1">
 <div>
  <input type="hidden" name="__VIEWSTATE" id="__VIEWSTATE"
    value="/wEPDwUKMTU5MTA2ODYwOWRk1kQjjKUNXCMmyhw9mwUkqs1+CdU=" />
 </div>
 <div>
    <input name="txtTicker" type="text" id="txtTicker" />
    <input type="submit" name="btnGet" value="Get" id="btnGet" />
    <span id="lblQuote"></span>
 </div>
 <div>
    <input type="hidden" name="__EVENTVALIDATION" id="__EVENTVALIDATION"
    value="/wEWAwKQOuDFBALGsPqoBgKLk8m1COva3iCLI38aZ+8cKQVn2KcWFC3g" />
 </div>
 </form>
</body>
</html>
```

As you can see, the stock quote application as rendered by the browser is very different from the stock quote application you saw in Listing 2-1. The `<asp:>` controls have been replaced by pure HTML, the text box has been replaced by an input control of type `"text"`, the button has been replaced by a form input control of type `"submit"`, and the label has been replaced by an HTML span. There are also a couple of new, hidden input controls, called `__VIEWSTATE` and `__EVENTVALIDATION`, which contain a series of characters.

These fields simply contain a binary serialized representation of the page controls that are passed to the server and deserialized when the page inputs are submitted, or *posted back*, to the server. The server then uses this information to retrieve the contents of the controls (e.g., to reconstitute the text in the text box if the page is rerendered) and to change them when necessary (e.g., to set the value of the label). This is the concept of *page state management*, which is implemented for you by ASP.NET.

Using the Web Configuration File

When you first ran the stock quote application, the IDE should have noticed that debugging wasn't enabled, and would have asked if you wanted a default `Web.config` with debugging enabled. If you chose Yes, your project directory will include a new file, `Web.config`.

This file is used to define how the .NET Framework should handle your site. Information such as security, caching, debugging, and globalization settings are typically stored in `Web.config`.

Here's an example of the `Web.config` file:

```xml
<?xml version="1.0"?>
<configuration>
  <appSettings/>
  <connectionStrings/>
  <system.web>
    <!--
          Set compilation debug="true" to insert debugging
          symbols into the compiled page. Because this
          affects performance, set this value to true only
          during development.
      -->
    <compilation debug="true"/>
    <!--
          The <authentication> section enables configuration
          of the security authentication mode used by
          ASP.NET to identify an incoming user.
      -->
```

```
<authentication mode="Windows"/>
<!--

        The <customErrors> section enables configuration
        of what to do if/when an unhandled error occurs
        during the execution of a request. Specifically,
        it enables developers to configure html error pages
        to be displayed in place of an error stack trace.

    <customErrors mode="RemoteOnly" defaultRedirect="GenericErrorPage.htm">
        <error statusCode="403" redirect="NoAccess.htm" />
        <error statusCode="404" redirect="FileNotFound.htm" />
    </customErrors>
    -->
  </system.web>
</configuration>
```

Here, the configuration for the system.web namespace is being set up. As you can see, the compilation attribute is set to "true", enabling application debugging. Any references that were added will have their assemblies referenced here, and the authentication type that should be used to talk to the site is set. Web.config is a useful and powerful tool, and something you should become familiar with. As you step through the examples in this book, you'll be using it extensively to fine-tune and configure your site to work to the best of its abilities.

The recommended methodology for editing Web.config is to use the Web Site ➤ ASP.NET Configuration menu option within the IDE. This menu option launches an editor for Web.config, called the Web Site Administration Tool, which ensures that the settings are placed in the correct location in the file and that they are using the correct syntax. Invalid syntax or settings within Web.config will break your site, so be careful when editing it by hand! You can see the Web Site Administration Tool in Figure 2-23.

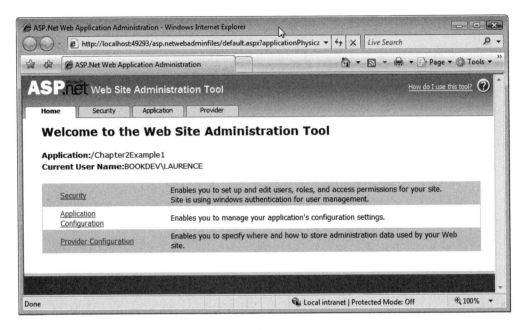

Figure 2-23. *The Web Site Administration Tool*

Summary

In this chapter, you took a brief look at ASP.NET and how you can use the VWDE tool to build a simple ASP.NET application. You were given a tour of the development environment and how it is used to build and manage web sites. After this tour, you should have an understanding of how development is done using a server-side paradigm—which was reinforced with a brief look at the architecture of ASP.NET.

Additionally, you looked at using configuration and web site administration to define how ASP.NET should behave when serving your site. Ultimately, you were able to build a site with some pretty sophisticated functionality using only four lines of code, demonstrating just how much the framework can do behind the scenes for you! One of the concepts that you were introduced to was the *web form*. Chapter 3 will go into this in more detail, looking at how pages are processed by ASP.NET and how the technology can be used to build scalable, performant web applications.

■■■

CHAPTER 3

Web Forms with ASP.NET

At the heart of web applications and web sites in ASP.NET are the elements that you use to build the pages that the user will see. These are called *web forms*, terminology that is a holdover from Windows development when windows were built using *forms*.

This methodology is unique and innovative in web development. It enables you to create your pages in a visual manner, using server-side controls (as you saw in Chapter 2) that are converted into HTML markup by the ASP.NET runtime at the time they are served to the client. This chapter will go into some detail about web forms and how they work in ASP.NET. You'll learn about the event model of a page, and how postbacks work.

This chapter will also show you the life cycle of a page, and it will go into the object model that the page supports, going through the control tree that ASP.NET exposes to you as a developer. Finally, you'll take an in-depth look at the Page class, and how it can be used to control the flow between the server and your users, enabling you to access the request and response streams, and parse and/or override them as necessary.

By the end of the chapter, you'll have a good understanding of how web forms work, and how you can use them to add great power to your web applications.

Understanding Page Processing

It is important to understand that there are a number of major differences between building web applications and building standard Windows client applications. If you are coming to web development from a Windows client development background, there are several aspects of web development that are significantly different from Windows client application development. Most Windows applications are designed to work with a single user, but web applications that don't scale to thousands of users are considered a failure. Also, the application from a user's perspective executes in a web browser, so local file system permissions and system access is very limited. And perhaps the hardest concept to grasp if you're used to virtually unlimited memory and computational horsepower is that web applications are by and large stateless, meaning that information isn't retained on the server between page invocations. (There are techniques to bypass this obstacle, but even those require some design thought.)

Web applications are multiuser: When building an application for the Web, you have to remember that your application should be designed to be scaled out to many users, which in some cases can number in the millions. This leads to two major challenges. The first is that when the application has to scale out to huge numbers of users, it will operate in a clustered environment, meaning that it is deployed to a number of servers, and the clustering hardware manages who speaks to which server. In an environment such as this, you have to make sure that the experience each user has when using your application is consistent. Thus, a level of commonality is necessary, and this is achieved using shared pools of resources such as data, styling, and connectivity to outside applications. You have to make sure that your application cooperates with other instances of itself in accessing shared application resources. Similarly, you have to make sure that the users accessing your application are doing so concurrently, leading to potential concurrency issues. This means that you have to be careful in how you write classes that are going to be shared by user sessions. The framework *helps* you in this regard, but it doesn't do everything for you. Your user classes will need to be carefully crafted and deployed.

Web applications are designed to execute on a server and be viewed in a browser: Your application is used within users' browsers on their machines, but the application actually executes (for the most part) on your server. So, if you think about the simple case where the user is filling out a form on the browser (like our stock quote application in Chapter 2), what is happening is that the user sets the state of some of the controls in the form and invokes an HTML form data submission process, which sends the data to the server. The server executes the application and then returns the results to the client. This process is called a *postback*. Newer application programming interfaces (APIs) and methodologies such as Ajax move some of the processing to the client, providing a richer client experience (they make more frequent asynchronous postbacks to the server to make the application appear more responsive), but your web applications still have a server element to them, and understanding how to handle this is vital as you write your web applications.

Typical web applications are stateless: To maintain a clean relationship between the client and the server, particularly to avoid confusion when in a clustered environment, no state of the condition of a client is stored on the server in a typical web application. This can be overridden to some degree, but the typical scenario has the server destroy all instances of web page objects residing in its memory for a particular page once the page has been sent to the client. This is great for scalability, but it can hurt the user and developer experience—for example, when information should be persisted throughout a number of sessions and a mechanism has to be grown to achieve this. ASP.NET assists you in building applications that maintain state through a process called *view state*, in which information about the form can be stored in hidden HTML form fields. You'll be looking at view state a little later in this chapter. Additionally, ASP.NET offers a session state mechanism that allows sessions to be persisted in a SQL server, allowing them to work in a clustered environment. This allows you to build a stateful web application, but the typical web application does not do this and is stateless.

Looking at Web Forms

In the next few sections, you'll look into different types of web forms and how they execute. First, you'll look at a typical HTML form and what goes on when the user submits it to the server.

HTML Forms

The World Wide Web Consortium (W3C) defines an HTML form as a section of an HTML document that contains normal content markup as well as special elements called *controls*. This is not to be confused with ASP.NET controls, which execute on the server. HTML controls are client-side controls that are part of the HTML specification and thus are handled and rendered by the browser. Examples of these HTML controls are text boxes, radio buttons, lists, and standard push buttons. When you use server controls to create a UI that has more sophisticated visual representations such as grids, ASP.NET generates HTML made up of these client controls to represent what you wanted. An HTML form is wrapped in a `<form>`, which contains a number of important attributes. The two most important that you'll use as a developer are the `action` and the `method` attributes. In the `action` attribute, you specify the Uniform Resource Indicator (URI) of the *agent* that handles the processing of the form. This agent can be a number of things, from a Personal HyperText Processor (PHP) script to an ASP page or a Common Gateway Interface (CGI). With the `method` attribute, you specify that the form will use either the `HTTP-POST` or the `HTTP-GET` *verb* to talk to the server. When using `HTTP-GET`, the URI of the agent is called with the parameters specified in the form as name/value pairs in the URI. As a result, the call will look something like this:

```
http://server/application?param=value &param=value
```

When using `HTTP-POST`, the values are embedded within the body of the HTTP request itself, following the HTTP header values:

```
POST /application HTTP/1.1
Accept-Language: en-us
Content-Type: application/x-www-form-urlencoded
User-Agent: Mozilla/4.0 (compatible; MSIE 7.0)
Host: server
```

```
Content-Length: nnnn
Connection: Keep-Alive
Cache-Control: no-cache

&param=value&param=value
```

The headers provide the server with client information for routing and processing. The name/value pairs follow the headers after a blank line. The HTTP-GET verb is generally used to request information from the server (pull model), such as when you want to see a web page or other resource, while HTTP-POST is used to send information to the server for processing (push model), such as when submitting data from a web form in response to a button click. In Chapter 2, the browser issued an HTTP-GET verb to request the Default.aspx page, and then an HTTP-POST verb in response to the button click, sending the stock ticker value recorded in the TextBox control to the server for processing by the web service.

Take a look at what happens when you create a new ASP.NET page. Create a new web application and take a look at the Default.aspx page that is created for you. You can see the HTML form by looking at the Source pane. Listing 3-1 shows an example.

Listing 3-1. *Standard Default ASP.NET Web Form*

```
<html xmlns="http://www.w3.org/1999/xhtml" >
<head runat="server">
    <title>Untitled Page</title>
</head>
<body>
    <form id="form1" runat="server">
    <div>

    </div>
    </form>
</body>
</html>
```

What is interesting is what is missing. There are no action or method attributes present in the <form> tag! What ASP.NET does for you is add a runat=server attribute. This isn't a tag that is defined by the W3C for handling forms, but that's OK, because this is something that is processed by the server and translated into action and method attributes at runtime, enabling the form to be rendered on any browser that supports the W3C standard. Run this application and use your browser's View Source functionality to look at the result. You'll see something like Listing 3-2.

Listing 3-2. *Viewing the Form in a Browser*

```
<form name="form1" method="post" action="Default.aspx" id="form1">
  <div>
    <input type="hidden" name="__VIEWSTATE" id="__VIEWSTATE"    value="..." />
  </div>

  <div>
  </div>
</form>
```

You can see that the ASP.NET runtime recognized that it encountered the `<form>` tag by saying `runat="server"`, and realized that the tag was a server control, not a raw HTML `<form>` tag. Therefore, it generated the required form, defaulting the `method` to `HTTP-POST` and specifying itself (`Default.aspx`) as the agent (via the `action` attribute) to handle the form feedback.

An HTML Forms Example in ASP.NET

The following example contains an ASP.NET form, which is a server-side control that generates a client-side form, as well as a number of client-side form elements. If this is confusing, don't worry—it will soon become second nature. I've deliberately chosen this complex scenario to demonstrate how ASP.NET makes it easy for you to mix and match server-side and client-side functionality to make your work as easy as possible.

First, use VWDE to create a new web site. Open the default page that is created for you for editing, and select Design view within the Visual Studio UI.

Now take a look at the Toolbox for the HTML controls. It should look something like Figure 3-1. Remember that you are going to use the ASP.NET HTML controls, which have a programming interface similar to the actual HTML controls they represent. (This is in contrast to the standard ASP.NET controls, which ultimately generate HTML but have a more robust programming interface.)

Figure 3-1. *The HTML controls tab in the Toolbox*

Drag three Input (Text) boxes, two Input (Radio) controls, and an Input (Submit) control to your design surface. Note that you will be using the HTML controls as shown in Figure 3-1, not the similar ASP.NET controls. Set their properties and arrange them so that they look like the layout in Figure 3-2. The label text can be added to the design surface by placing the cursor in the desired area and simply typing in the text.

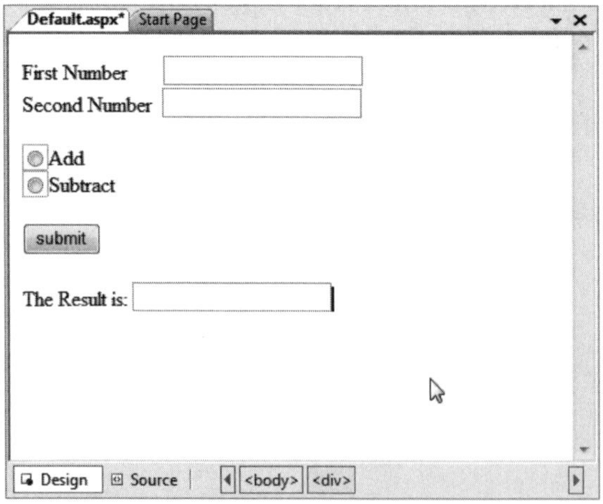

Figure 3-2. *The layout for your HTML form*

Next, be sure to use the Properties window to give your controls some friendly names. The names used in this example are shown in Table 3-1. You'll see what they look like in HTML in Listing 3-3.

Table 3-1. *Naming Your HTML Controls*

Control	Name
First Number TextBox	`txtFirst`
Second Number TextBox	`txtSecond`
First radio button (Add)	`optOption`
Second radio button (Subtract)	`optOption` (using the same name groups the radio buttons)
Submit button	`btnSubmit`
Result TextBox	`txtResult`

If you aren't familiar with HTML forms code, a few things may seem a little quirky, particularly when dealing with the radio buttons. To create a group of radio buttons where only one is selectable, use the `name` property and set each one to the same value. So, as you can see in Listing 3-3, each radio button is called `optOperation`. You distinguish them from each other using the `value` property. In this listing, you can see that they contain the values `Add` and `Subtract`, respectively.

Listing 3-3. *Your HTML Form*

```
<%@ Page Language="C#" AutoEventWireup="true"  CodeFile="Default.aspx.cs"
    Inherits="_Default" %>

<!DOCTYPE html PUBLIC "-//W3C//DTD XHTML 1.0 Transitional//EN"

    "http://www.w3.org/TR/xhtml1/DTD/xhtml1-transitional.dtd">

<html xmlns="http://www.w3.org/1999/xhtml" >
<head runat="server">
    <title>Untitled Page</title>
</head>
<body>
  <form id="form1" runat="server">
    <div>
      First Number      
      <input name="txtFirst" type="text" />
```

```
      <br />Second Number 
      <input name="txtSecond" type="text" /><br />

      <br />
      <input name="optOperation" value="Add"
            type="radio" checked="CHECKED"/>Add

      <br />
      <input name="optOperation" value="Subtract"
            type="radio" />Subtract
       <br />
       <br />
       <input name="btnSubmit" type="submit" value="submit" />
       <br />
       <br />
       The Result is:
       <input name="txtResult" type="text" /></div>
    </form>
</body>
</html>
```

Now if you load this page and click the submit button, the browser indicates some network activity because it is calling the agent (in other words, itself), resulting in a page refresh, or *postback*. However, since there is no server-side code to process the postback, very little actually happens!

Now let's add a little server-side code to the page so that the resulting button click on the server takes some tangible action. To do this, turn to the Solution Explorer and double-click the Default.aspx.cs file, which is the code-behind file for the page, and scan the C# code for the Page_Load method Visual Studio inserted for you when it created the page.

A nice tool that the ASP.NET Framework gives you is a class that can be used to examine and pull information from the HTTP request—HttpRequest. If there had been parameters encoded in the query string (the URL), as is the case with HTTP-GET, we could access those values through the HttpRequest.QueryString parameter. In this case, however, the form's method indicated we're to return parameters to the server using HTTP-POST, so the information is available in the HttpRequest.Form array, like this:

```
string strVal = Request.Form["ItemName"];
```

The HttpRequest is available to your ASP.NET page through the Page.Request property, which is available to all ASP.NET pages. You can use the Request.Form array to access and then process the form parameters, as shown in Listing 3-4.

Listing 3-4. *Handling the HTML Form in the ASP.NET Agent*

```
using System;
using System.Data;
using System.Configuration;
using System.Web;
using System.Web.Security;
using System.Web.UI;
using System.Web.UI.WebControls;
using System.Web.UI.WebControls.WebParts;
using System.Web.UI.HtmlControls;

public partial class _Default : System.Web.UI.Page
{
    protected void Page_Load(object sender, EventArgs e)
    {
        if (IsPostBack)
        {
            string sFirst = Request.Form["txtFirst"];
            string sSecond = Request.Form["txtSecond"];
            string sOperation = Request.Form["optOperation"];
            int nF = 0;
            int nS = 0;
            int.TryParse(sFirst, out nF);
            int.TryParse(sSecond, out nS);
            int nR = 0;              if (sOperation == "Add")
                nR = nF + nS;
            else
                nR = nF - nS;
        }
    }
}
```

In this listing, you see that the strings sFirst, sSecond, and sOperation contain the values entered into the txtFirst and txtSecond text boxes, and the value of the selection radio button, respectively. The values in the text boxes are converted to integers, and—depending on which operation is selected—are either added or subtracted.

Sending the results back to the user can be problematic, however. You may think that you could simply call into play the txtResult control using code like this:

```
txtResult.Value = nR.ToString();
```

But you can't, because the text box that you added earlier for `txtResult` was an ASP.NET HTML control. Based on the fact that web applications are stateless, the server doesn't recognize the control, and your code will not compile!

Why is this the case? The answer lies in the fact that ASP.NET was designed for efficiency. For ASP.NET to be able to change the value of a page control when the page posts back, ASP.NET needs to first be made aware that the control could potentially have its value changed, and then ASP.NET needs to keep track of the value. This is called control state. We'll see how to do this in the next section.

For completeness, I should mention that if you don't want to use the input text control to return the mathematical result to the user, you could use the `Page.Response` (`HttpResponse`) stream to write HTML directly to the response stream, overwriting the default HTML to be returned to the client (i.e., the HTML that makes up your form) with your own content. However, this isn't recommended in general, because you will completely overwrite your application within the browser.

Using a Server Control to Provide Feedback

Earlier, you added an ASP.NET HTML text box to your page markup with the expectation that it could be used to store the results of the mathematical operation. But simply assigning the mathematical result to the text box will yield a compilation error. Clearly ASP.NET needs to provide a mechanism for returning calculated page values to the user! The answer to providing feedback to a form operation is to introduce the control to ASP.NET's `view state` mechanism, which can be done in one of two ways.

If you want to continue to use the HTML input text box, simply add this attribute to its definition in your page markup:

```
runat="server"
```

Since the control has a `name` attribute but not an `id` attribute, which ASP.NET requires, you also need to add this:

```
id="txtResult"
```

By doing this, you make ASP.NET aware that this control, `txtResult`, should be accessible on the server (allowing you to change its content, or *state*).

But you may elect to forego the ASP.NET HTML controls and instead use the full-fledged ASP.NET server controls. In the following example, you'll modify the previous example to use a server-side Literal control, and this control will be populated with the results of the operation.

Go back to Design view for the `Default.aspx` page and amend it by removing the `txtResults` HTML control and replacing it with an ASP.NET Literal control. You can find this control on the Standard Visual Studio Toolbox tab. Once you've done so, your screen should look like Figure 3-3.

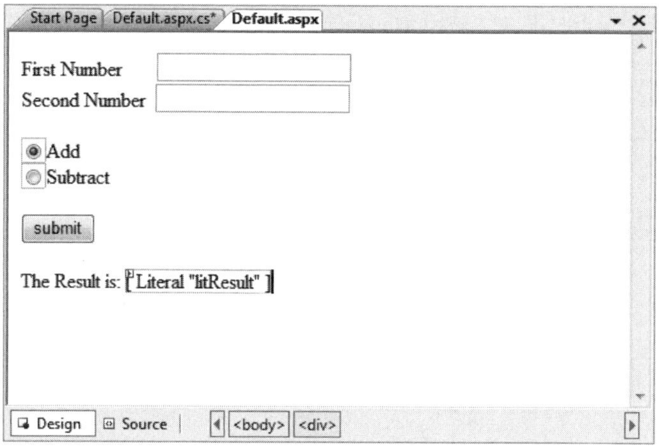

Figure 3-3. *Using the ASP.NET Literal control in your page*

The listing for this page will look like Listing 3-5.

Listing 3-5. *The Revised Form*

```
<%@ Page Language="C#" AutoEventWireup="true"  CodeFile="Default.aspx.cs"
    Inherits="_Default" %>

<!DOCTYPE html PUBLIC "-//W3C//DTD XHTML 1.0 Transitional//EN"
    "http://www.w3.org/TR/xhtml1/DTD/xhtml1-transitional.dtd">

<html xmlns="http://www.w3.org/1999/xhtml" >
<head runat="server">
    <title>Untitled Page</title>
</head>
<body>
    <form id="form1" runat="server">
    <div>
        First Number      
        <input name="txtFirst" type="text" />
        <br />
        Second Number 
        <input name="txtSecond" type="text" /><br />
        <br />
        <input name="optOperation" value="Add"
               type="radio" checked="CHECKED"  />Add<br />
        <input name="optOperation" value="Subtract"
```

```
                    type="radio" />Subtract<br />
        <br />
        <input name="btnSubmit" type="submit" value="submit" />
        <br />
        <br />
        The Result is:
        <asp:Literal ID="litResult" runat="server"></asp:Literal></div>
    </form>
</body>
</html>
```

You can see that the Literal control is prefixed with `<asp:>`, like this:

```
<asp:Literal ID="litResult" runat="server"></asp:Literal>
```

Now it is a simple matter to provide feedback of the operation to your users. Modify the Page_Load event handler to look like Listing 3-6.

Listing 3-6. *Modified Page_Load to Provide Feedback*

```
using System;
using System.Data;
using System.Configuration;
using System.Web;
using System.Web.Security;
using System.Web.UI;
using System.Web.UI.WebControls;
using System.Web.UI.WebControls.WebParts;
using System.Web.UI.HtmlControls;

public partial class _Default : System.Web.UI.Page
{
    protected void Page_Load(object sender, EventArgs e)
    {
        if (IsPostBack)
        {
            string sFirst = Request.Form["txtFirst"];
            string sSecond = Request.Form["txtSecond"];
            string sOperation = Request.Form["optOperation"];
            int nF = 0;
            int nS = 0;
            int.TryParse(sFirst, out nF);
            int.TryParse(sSecond, out nS);
```

```
            int nR = 0;
            if (sOperation == "Add")
                nR = nF + nS;
            else
                nR = nF - nS;
            litResult.Text = nR.ToString();
        }
    }
}
```

Now when you run your application, enter values into the text boxes, and click the submit button, you'll see that the value of the operation is loaded into the Literal control and displayed on the page. But the text boxes are then emptied! Why is this?

The same reasoning that applied to the ASP.NET HTML control for the mathematical results also applies to the text boxes containing the values to be added or subtracted. ASP.NET is unaware that your intention was to maintain the control's view state, and indeed, when the page posted back, ASP.NET very efficiently threw the values to be added or subtracted away once the page was refreshed.

As before, one solution is to add the `runat` and `id` attributes to these controls. And that works. But the best solution to this problem is to use the full-fledged ASP.NET TextBox controls and have ASP.NET manage their view state for you. Remember, ASP.NET converts the TextBox controls into HTML input text boxes for you, but the view state functionality ASP.NET employs can now be used to maintain their contents as the request flow passes back and forth. The next step is to replace the ASP.NET HTML text input controls with ASP.NET TextBox controls. You can find these on Visual Studio's Standard Toolbox tab alongside the Literal control.

Listing 3-7 shows the revised code for the `Default.aspx` page using `<asp:TextBox>` controls instead of HTML `<input>` controls for the text boxes.

Listing 3-7. *Modified Listing for ASP.NET Text Boxes*

```
<%@ Page Language="C#" AutoEventWireup="true"  CodeFile="Default.aspx.cs"
    Inherits="_Default" %>

<!DOCTYPE html PUBLIC "-//W3C//DTD XHTML 1.0 Transitional//EN"
    "http://www.w3.org/TR/xhtml1/DTD/xhtml1-transitional.dtd">

<html xmlns="http://www.w3.org/1999/xhtml" >
<head runat="server">
    <title>Untitled Page</title>
</head>
<body>
```

```
    <form id="form1" runat="server">
    <div>
        First Number          
        <asp:TextBox ID="txtFirst" runat="server"></asp:TextBox><br />
        Second Number   
        <asp:TextBox ID="txtSecond" runat="server"></asp:TextBox><br />
        <br />
        <input name="optOperation" value="Add"
                type="radio" checked="CHECKED" style="width: 20px" />Add<br />
        <input name="optOperation" value="Subtract" type="radio" />Subtract<br />
        <br />
        <input name="btnSubmit" type="submit" value="submit" />
        <br />
        <br />
        The Result is:
        <asp:Literal ID="litResult" runat="server"></asp:Literal></div>
    </form>
</body>
</html>
```

You will now need to modify the Page_Load method once again to handle the text boxes instead of the more general input fields. Because you'll be using ASP.NET controls that the server "sees" and can understand, you don't need to pull the values to add and subtract from the Request.Form array as you did previously. Instead, you simply access each TextBox control's Text property. You can see this in Listing 3-8.

Listing 3-8. *Page_Load Modified for ASP.NET Text Boxes*

```
using System;
using System.Data;
using System.Configuration;
using System.Web;
using System.Web.Security;
using System.Web.UI;
using System.Web.UI.WebControls;
using System.Web.UI.WebControls.WebParts;
using System.Web.UI.HtmlControls;

public partial class _Default : System.Web.UI.Page
{
    protected void Page_Load(object sender, EventArgs e)
    {
```

```
        if (IsPostBack)
        {
            string strOperation = Request.Form["optOperation"];
            int nF = 0;
            Int32.TryParse(txtFirst.Text, out nF);
            int nS = 0;
            Int32.TryParse(txtSecond.Text, out nS);
            int nR = 0;
            if (strOperation == "Add")
                nR = nF + nS;
            else
                nR = nF - nS;

            litResult.Text = nR.ToString();

        }
    }
}
```

Now when you type the values into the text boxes and click the submit button, the server will return the response *and*—thanks to view state—maintain the value of the text boxes.

Also, as ASP.NET generates client-side code, you will have <input> buttons rendered within the browser anyway! Take a look at the resulting HTML in your browser, and you'll see something like Listing 3-9.

Listing 3-9. *Viewing the Source Code of the Page in the Browser*

```
<!DOCTYPE html PUBLIC "-//W3C//DTD XHTML 1.0 Transitional//EN"
    "http://www.w3.org/TR/xhtml1/DTD/xhtml1-transitional.dtd">

<html xmlns="http://www.w3.org/1999/xhtml" >
<head id="Head1"><title>
    Untitled Page
</title></head>
<body>
  <form name="Form1" method="post" action="Default.aspx" id="Form1" nameid="form1">
<div>
<input type="hidden" name="__VIEWSTATE"
    id="__VIEWSTATE" value="/wEPDwUJNTAyODQ2MjExD2QWAgIDD2QWAgIFDxYC
        HgRUZXh0BQIxM2RkhaM9N8FFWr+8Gc
```

```
                  WSG7LHO3G2iHU=" />
</div>

    <div>
      First Number       
        <input name="txtFirst" type="text" value="6" id="txtFirst" />

      <br />Second Number 
          <input name="txtSecond" type="text" value="7" id="txtSecond" />
        <br />

      <br />
      <input name="optOperation" value="Add"
            type="radio" checked="CHECKED"/>Add

      <br />
      <input name="optOperation" value="Subtract"
            type="radio" />Subtract
       <br />
       <br />
       <input name="btnSubmit" type="submit" value="submit" />
       <br />
       <br />
       The Result is:
           13
        </div>

<div>

        <input type="hidden" name="__EVENTVALIDATION"
                   id="__EVENTVALIDATION"
                  value="/wEWAwLlz7E/AsLD9sIMAtyOu4cGtJL+4Fv
                          k4E5cn/wE9V57IheOlKE=" />
</div></form>
</body>
</html>
```

Using ASP.NET Events and Automatic Postbacks

Having access to the control view state means that your server-side code isn't limited to
getting and setting properties—it can also respond to events within the controls. Remember, as the code is running on the client, and since the client is constrained to the

workflow that HTML forms offer, something is necessary to bubble the events up to the server so that the server knows what event to respond to. The flow of processing follows this model:

- When the page first runs, ASP.NET parses through the declarations and generates HTML to be sent to the client. All objects that it uses are destroyed from server memory once the HTML has been generated and issued to the client.

- The user triggers a postback to the server, either by clicking an HTML submit button or performing an action that the server will interpret as an event, such as checking a CheckBox control.

- When the page is returned to the server, ASP.NET is able to interpret the view state information to restore the state of each of the controls.

- The view state information also contains the operation that triggered the postback. ASP.NET obtains this information and raises the appropriate event, and if you've written an event handler for this event, then your event handler's code will execute. Other events that didn't cause the postback will also fire, such as a list selection, and if you've provided an event handler for those events, you can process them as well.

- The modified page is rendered back into HTML and returned to the client, and all objects—including those invoked by the event handlers—are destroyed.

Not all client browser events fire a postback right away, and ASP.NET is designed to process each event at the most appropriate time. For example, if you come from a Windows development background, you may know that the Windows Forms TextBox fires a `TextChanged` event whenever the user types something into the text box. However, in a web context, you wouldn't want to do this, because you'd trigger a postback every time you press a key when the cursor is in a text box, severely hampering your application's performance and scalability. Instead, the web-based text box triggers a postback when you press Enter or Tab if so configured.

However, when you start getting into complex controls, you may not want to use a postback for every user interaction. Consider a scenario where you have a UI containing a list control. In some cases, you might want to have a postback when the user selects an item on the list (so that you can respond to it right away), and in other cases, you might not want one. You can set up the former situation using an *automatic postback* (using the control's `AutoPostback` property), where the control triggers the postback instead of the user. For the latter, just query the status of the list when the user selects a submit button or something similar to generate a postback for the page.

Listing 3-10 shows a simple web UI containing a three-item list. This list has an event handler defined for it that is designated to fire whenever the list selection changes.

Listing 3-10. *Web UI Containing a List Box*

```
<%@ Page Language="C#" AutoEventWireup="true"  CodeFile="Default.aspx.cs"
    Inherits="_Default" %>

<!DOCTYPE html PUBLIC "-//W3C//DTD XHTML 1.0 Transitional//EN"
    "http://www.w3.org/TR/xhtml1/DTD/xhtml1-transitional.dtd">

<html xmlns="http://www.w3.org/1999/xhtml" >
<head runat="server">
    <title>Untitled Page</title>
</head>
<body>
    <form id="form1" runat="server">
    <div>
      <asp:ListBox ID="ListBox1" runat="server"
        OnSelectedIndexChanged="ListBox1_SelectedIndexChanged">
        <asp:ListItem Value="Test1"></asp:ListItem>
        <asp:ListItem Value="Test2"></asp:ListItem>
        <asp:ListItem Value="Test3"></asp:ListItem>
      </asp:ListBox>
    </div>
    </form>
</body>
</html>
```

Visual Studio will create a code-behind page for this, which includes a Page_Load event handler. Add a handler for the ListBox1_SelectedIndexChanged event that looks like this:

```
protected void ListBox1_SelectedIndexChanged(object sender, EventArgs e)
{
    string strTest = ListBox1.SelectedItem.Text;
}
```

Put a breakpoint in this code (by selecting the line and pressing F9) and run the application. Select an item on the list. Nothing happens—the event doesn't fire because there is no postback typically associated with a list box. Only form submit buttons cause postbacks, at least when you're not using ASP.NET.

Now, there are a couple of things you can do here. First of all, you can put a button on the form, and when you press the button, a postback will be triggered. The postback contains information for *all* raised events, not just the action that caused the postback (the submit button). To see the postback and how it contains information for all events, add an ASP.NET button to the form, run it, select a list item, and then click the button.

You'll see that your breakpoint on the ListBox's `SelectedIndexChanged` handler still trips, even though your action was to click the form's submit button. (Note that if you provided a handler for the submit button, that handler code would also be executed.) This demonstrates that ASP.NET passed the event information for everything on the page when you triggered the postback. The information for the list selection changed got passed along, too, and when the server received the postback, it triggered the event.

Alternatively, you can use the automatic postback feature that the ASP.NET ListBox provides you with by setting the `ListBox.AutoPostBack` property to `true`. You can do this with the Property Editor or simply by adding the `AutoPostBack='True'` attribute to the `<asp:ListBox>` declaration.

Remove the button from the page and try running the application again with the `AutoPostBack='True'` attribute present in the list box's markup. Now whenever you select an item on the list box, the page triggers a postback, and the `SelectedIndexChanged` event fires. Right now, this just loads the text of the selection into a dummy string. In your application, you could use this to give feedback to the user, or you could determine its index to—for example—enter selection data into a database.

Thus, when using ASP.NET, you have a number of options for how and when events are handled by the framework, and you can design your UI accordingly.

View State

I've mentioned view state a couple of times in this chapter, but what is it? And what does it do for you? Typically, web applications are stateless. Normally when we think of a stateless web application, we're thinking of an application that doesn't correlate invocations of the various pages in the application. Conversely, if you visit an online store and place an item in your shopping cart, you expect that item to be available in your shopping cart for checkout. This is known as *session state*.

But there is another type of stateless behavior going on here—the server will lose the page's control information between postbacks unless we do something about it. From HTML's inception, servers (for performance reasons) throw control values away when pages are posted back. To do otherwise typically consumes resources on the server and dramatically affects the scalability of the application. And as we saw earlier, even in the simplest of applications—adding two numbers—statelessness drastically affects the usability of the application because of this.

A number of methods, such as *cookies*, could be used to maintain state on a page, but they can lead to security problems and privacy issues. Additionally, cookie use often requires a lot of development overhead, particularly for sophisticated applications.

ASP.NET has introduced the concept of view state to overcome these problems while minimizing the impact on the developer. When you define an ASP.NET page, you also establish the initial values of the controls on the page. For example, when you place a text box on a page, you set its initial text to a string (even if it's an empty string). Then, when you change its value from its default to another value in the Visual Studio editor, the new value is stored within the tag representing the text box. If the user edits the text box's value in their browser, ASP.NET detects the change in textual values but doesn't change the underlying HTML for the text box. Instead, when ASP.NET recognizes that the value has changed, it stores this change, as well as all other changes, into a name/value pair collection. This collection is then encrypted and serialized into a Base64 string, which will contain only letters and numbers (and perhaps the equal sign: =), and inserts this into a hidden field within the HTML page's form tag. As the page is transmitted between client and server, this information serves to maintain the state of each control on the page.

So, for example, if your text box is originally empty, it is rendered on the client as empty. If the user changes it and later triggers a postback, ASP.NET looks at the view state when it receives the response and sees that the text box value has changed. ASP.NET then processes the postback and fires all applicable events. When ASP.NET finishes this processing, it generates new HTML and then takes the current value of the text, which may have changed yet again by some server-side process, encrypts and serializes it into the view state hidden field once again, and then sends it back to the client. The client sees the changes in the text box, and the process starts all over again.

Thus, we get the best of both worlds. The server doesn't use precious resources keeping the state of the client, but yet the client state is still preserved. When the page is posted back to the server, the server can use the view state information to reinitialize the page controls to their correct state.

There is a downside, however, which is that the size of the page is increased by the view state information. This has additional costs: it takes longer for the page to download and initialize, and the volume of information posted back to the server is larger because it contains all the view state information. When using complex controls such as Grids, the additional overhead can be significant.

If an excessively large page is giving you a problem, you can override view state by setting the EnableViewState property to false. Thus, when designing your application, you can optimize it for page size by enabling view state only for the controls that you want to maintain state for.

Processing Web Forms

We've seen that ASP.NET processes the page, generating HTML as it goes, and this HTML is returned to the client. In this section, we'll look at this process in a little more detail and see the major steps performed as part of this action. These include page initialization, code initialization, validation, event handling, data binding, and cleanup. This happens for each page request. Figure 3-4 shows the order of these steps.

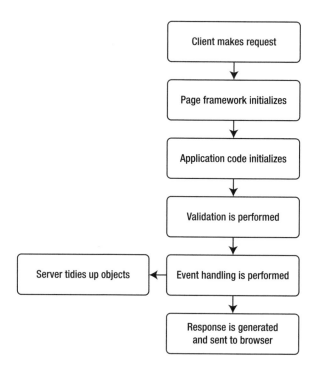

Figure 3-4. *ASP.NET page life cycle*

The following sections will look at each step in this cycle.

Page Framework Initialization

This is the stage at which ASP.NET initializes the page in memory on the server. It first parses through the definition of the ASPX, initializing each of the controls on the page as it was originally defined. Should this not be the first time the page has been requested, ASP.NET will then look through the view state and update the status of each control according to the name/value pairs that it deserializes out of view state.

At this point, it fires the Page.Init event. You can use this event to perform actions upon initializing the page, but UI actions are not permitted because the UI rendering has not yet occurred.

Application Code Initialization

Here is where the code behind your page is initialized so that validation and event handling (the next steps) can work. The important thing here is that the Page_Load event will fire at this point. Most applications will handle this event to perform their initialization. If you look back at the earlier add/subtract example, you'll see that Page_Load was used to handle the HTTP-POST from the form. Other initialization, such as configuring controls, retrieving database information, and so on, is usually done at this stage so that when the page is rendered, it is provided with all the information the user needs.

It's important to note that Page_Load always fires, whether this is the first time the page has loaded or it is a postback. With the latter, you might expect it not to load, because the page is already loaded, but it does. Due to the stateless nature of web applications, each postback is treated as a new request to the page, and view state is used to maintain state between calls, as discussed earlier.

As a developer, you may need to discern whether you are in a postback situation or an initial load situation, and ASP.NET provides this information for you via the IsPostBack property on the Page object.

Thus, Page.IsPostBack will be true upon a postback and false on the first load. If there are actions that you only want to perform on either case, you can gate them inside an if(Page.IsPostBack) clause.

Performing Validation

An important aspect of any web application is verifying that the data the user has input is valid. This ensures that your application is secure (e.g., so that no one is able to attempt Structured Query Language [SQL] injection attacks) and the user experience is optimized; only appropriate data is sent to the server and returned from the server. ASP.NET introduces a suite of self-sufficient validation controls that can be used to ensure that the content of your page meets validation rules. These are very useful controls, relieving you from writing reams of validation code to ensure that the correct data has been input.

Performing Event Handling

Earlier we saw how events are handled on a page. Some events provide an automatic postback that triggers an event handler. Others—such as a list box selection—aren't handled immediately, unless they have their AutoPostBack property set to true. At this stage of the life cycle, ASP.NET invokes the event handlers for each of the events that were tripped. So, if your page has a number of events before the postback occurs—for example, if a number of lists are used with no AutoPostBack, and the user selects items on them before pressing a button on the page—then *each* of these events will have their handler called at this stage.

In addition, a number of page-level events need to be performed. In the scenario in which two lists do not have AutoPostBack set to true, and there's no button that causes the postback, events will be fired in the following order:

1. Page_Init

2. Page_Load

3. `ListBox1_SelectIndexChanged`

4. `ListBox2_SelectIndexChanged`

5. `Button_Click`

6. `Page_PreRender`

7. `Page_Unload`

Note that the order in which the `SelectionIndexChanged` events occur might vary, depending on the order in which the user clicked them before pressing the button. They don't necessarily fire in chronological order, as this list indicates.

Performing Data Binding

Data binding is a vital part of making web applications easy to develop. In short, it enables us to automatically set properties on a control from the contents of a database or other data store. It involves little to no coding on the developer's part. It is a tool provided by the ASP.NET Framework. We'll be going into this very important functionality in more detail in Chapter 4.

One issue to note is the timing at which the data-binding functionality occurs. Any data binding that *updates* the data store via an insert, a delete, or an update will occur after all the control events are handled, but before the `Page_PreRender` occurs. Then, *after* the `PreRender` event, the functionality that queries the data store will fire. This ensures that data isn't stale, because any functionality on your page that updates the data store will happen before anything is read from the data store. Therefore, the data on your page is always up-to-date.

Server Tidies Up Objects

To maintain application scalability, the server sends the results of the page rendering to the client, and in its memory, cleans up everything for a particular session. The server now "forgets" about the page, and control is returned to the browser. Information that is necessary for the server to "remember" the page again at the next session is stored in view state, and the page is initialized with this information on the next postback.

Pages and Controls

Because ASP.NET is a true object-oriented development API, the page itself is an object that is accessible to the developer, as are the controls on the page (which are members of a collection within the page). Listing 3-11 shows the source code for a page containing several ASP.NET server controls.

Listing 3-11. *ASP.NET Page Containing Many Controls*

```
<%@ Page Language="C#" AutoEventWireup="true"
    CodeFile="Default.aspx.cs" Inherits="_Default" %>

<!DOCTYPE html PUBLIC "-//W3C//DTD XHTML 1.0 Transitional//EN"
    "http://www.w3.org/TR/xhtml1/DTD/xhtml1-transitional.dtd">

<html xmlns="http://www.w3.org/1999/xhtml" >
<head runat="server">
    <title>Untitled Page</title>
</head>
<body>
    <form id="form1" runat="server">
    <div>
        <asp:Label ID="Label1" runat="server" Text="Welcome to my Page!">
        </asp:Label>
        <asp:Panel ID="Panel1" runat="server" Height="168px" Width="286px">
            This is a Panel Containing some Controls<br />
            <br />
            <asp:CheckBoxList ID="CheckBoxList1" runat="server">
                <asp:ListItem>Item 1</asp:ListItem>
                <asp:ListItem>Item 2</asp:ListItem>
                <asp:ListItem>Item 3</asp:ListItem>
            </asp:CheckBoxList>
            <asp:Calendar ID="Calendar1" runat="server"></asp:Calendar>
        </asp:Panel>
        <asp:Panel ID="Panel2" runat="server" Height="50px" Width="435px">
            This is another Panel containing some controls<br />
            <asp:Button ID="Button1" runat="server" Text="Button" />
            <asp:ListBox ID="ListBox1" runat="server"></asp:ListBox>
            <asp:Button ID="Button2" runat="server" Text="Button" /><br />
        </asp:Panel>

    </div>
    </form>
</body>
</html>
```

You can see how this looks in Design view in Figure 3-5.

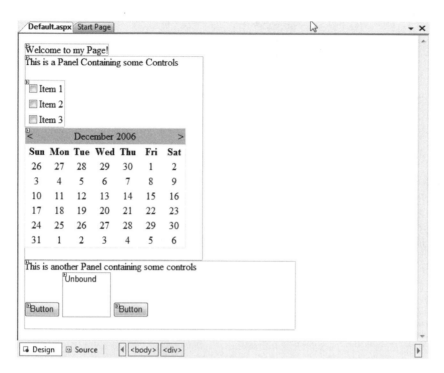

Figure 3-5. *Viewing the page in Design view*

You can see how these controls are held within the Page object by executing the following code:

```
protected void Page_Load(object sender, EventArgs e)
{
    foreach(Control ctrl in Page.Controls)
    {
        ListBox1.Items.Add(ctrl.GetType().ToString() + ":" + ctrl.ID);
    }
}
```

This code will access the Page.Controls collection and cycle through it, taking the type and ID of the control and adding them to the list. You can see the results of the code in Figure 3-6.

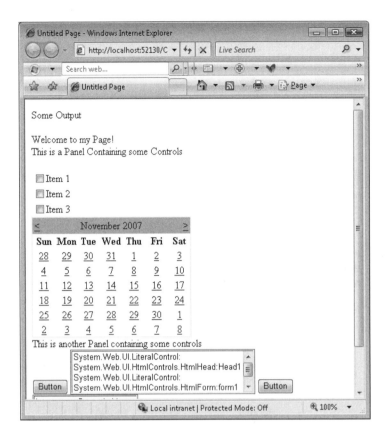

Figure 3-6. *Using the Page.Controls collection*

Accessing the Page Head

If you look closely at Figure 3-6, you'll see that the HTMLHead of the page is listed as one of the controls on this page. You can see the reason for this if you look back at Listing 3-11, where the <head> tag has a runat="server" attribute set.

This enables you to set HTML page attributes from the server dynamically so that you can, for example, set the attributes of the HTML header from within your code. For example, the page title can be set quite simply. (Note that this technique is identical to what you saw for accessing the ASP.NET HTML control properties with the add/subtract application.)

First, make sure that the <head> tag has an ID, like this:

```
<head runat="server" id="theHead">
    <title>Untitled Page</title>
</head>
```

Now you can access your HTML header in code. Here's a simple example of some code running in the `Page_Load` event that sets the title of the page:

```
theHead.Title = "Dynamically Created Title!";
```

You could, for example, interface this with a membership API to create a dynamic title that welcomes the user by name. Figure 3-7 shows the page with the new, dynamically created title.

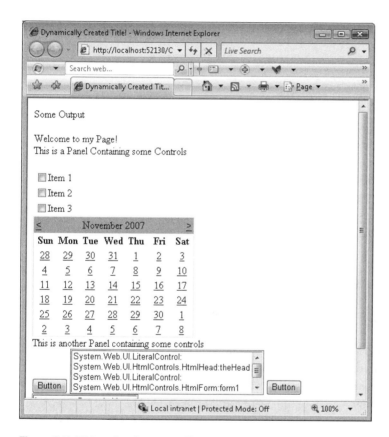

Figure 3-7. *Using the dynamically created title*

Also, if you look closely at the list containing the controls, you can see that the header ID has been set to `theHead` in Figure 3-7.

Creating Controls at Runtime

Because controls are objects, and because the page controls are a collection, you can also create controls at runtime. So, if you consider the previous example, you can add a new list box to the bottom of the form quite easily with this code:

```
protected void Page_Load(object sender, EventArgs e)
{
    foreach(Control ctrl in Page.Controls)
    {
        ListBox1.Items.Add(ctrl.GetType().ToString() + ":" + ctrl.ID);
    }
    theHead.Title = "Dynamically Created Title!";
    ListBox newListBox = new ListBox();
    newListBox.Items.Add(new ListItem("Item on my Dynamic List"));
    Page.Form.Controls.Add(newListBox);
}
```

Note that you have to add a control to a control container—you cannot add it directly to the page—so Page.Controls.Add will fail. If you want to add it to the top level of the page, use Page.Form.Controls.Add, as just shown. Additionally, you can add the control to an existing panel on the page. For example, you can add one to a named panel (Panel1) like this:

```
Panel1.Controls.Add(newListBox);
```

When you run the application, you can see the new list box on your page (see Figure 3-8).

Of course, you can also handle events on dynamically created controls. You do so by adding an event handler to the object, specifying the event that you want to handle. So, for example, if you want to handle a SelectedIndexChanged event on a dynamically created list, you would do this first by assigning the event handler like this:

```
newListBox.SelectedIndexChanged +=
    new EventHandler(newListBox_SelectedIndexChanged);
```

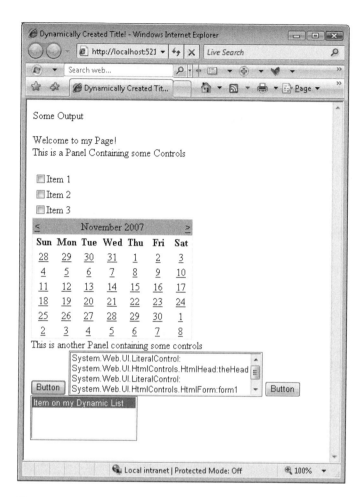

Figure 3-8. *Adding a list dynamically*

You would then create an event-handler function. This function takes a parameter, sender, which is a generic object that you can then cast to get the list box. Now that you have a list box, you have full IntelliSense in development so that you can handle it. Here's an example:

```
protected void newListBox_SelectedIndexChanged(object sender, EventArgs e)
{
    ListBox theBox = (ListBox)sender;
    String strTest = theBox.SelectedItem.Text;
}
```

The Page Object

When you are running an ASP.NET application, you have access to the Page object via the Page class. You can use this access to get valuable information such as the session, the cache, the HTTP request, and the HTTP response (which we looked at briefly earlier in the chapter), among others. Let's take a look at some of these.

The Request Object

The Request object contains the values associated with the HTTP request that the browser issued to the server to invoke your page. Its most common use is to interrogate the request parameters. You've seen many URLs that look like this:

```
http://server/page.aspx?param=value&param=value
```

When ASP.NET sees a call like this, it creates an array of name/value pairs that you can access from your code. So, for example, to test for a parameter called Test1 and pass it to a string in your code, you would have C# that looks like this:

```csharp
if (String.IsNullOrEmpty(Request.Params["test1"])){
    strTest1 = Request.Params["test1"];
}
else
{
    strTest = String.Empty;
}
```

You should always check to see if the parameter is present (non-null entry in the array) before you load it into an internal data store, such as strTest1 in the preceding case.

You should also sanitize all input parameters after loading them to avoid security holes through events such as SQL injections.

The Request object supports much more than managing the parameters, including cookies and certificates. See http://msdn2.microsoft.com/en-us/library/system.web. httprequest(vs.80).aspx for more information.

The Response Object

As you can imagine, if you can handle requests, you can also handle responses. This is done using the Response object, which can be used to write new output to the response buffer or to redirect the user to another page or site.

So, for example, to write new content to the output buffer, you'd simply call its `Write` method, like this:

```
Response.Write("New Content");
```

Or, to redirect the user to a new page, you can use this:

```
Response.Redirect(http://someserver/somepage.htm);
```

You can find more details here: `http://msdn2.microsoft.com/en-us/library/system.web.httpresponse(VS.80).aspx`.

Summary

In this chapter, you looked into ASP.NET and the page life cycle. You learned how ASP.NET processes pages and how page forms and server-side controls can be mixed to improve your developer productivity and your users' experience when accessing your application. You saw the differences between using ASP.NET HTML controls and ASP.NET server controls. You learned how maintaining page state can cause problems in scalability for applications, and how the ASP.NET view state functionality can give you a best-of-both-worlds approach—state maintenance in your application without consuming server resources.

You looked into how events can get stored and fired, and how they can be fired immediately using automatic postbacks. Finally, you reviewed the `Page` and `Controls` collections, looking into how you can use code to manage and manipulate controls on a page, or even dynamically add controls or dynamically change the status of your page at runtime. Our example was changing the page header in code.

In the next chapter, you'll look at more application-specific code using data binding so that you can build real-world applications that provide user access to secured data stores.

■■■

CHAPTER 4

Data Binding with ASP.NET

Most applications use some form of data store, with the application itself being a means to store, retrieve, manipulate, and view data. These applications might use a SQL Server 2005 database, a storage area network, or even a simple XML file. Web applications are no exception, and typically these applications are termed *data-driven applications*. When it comes to retrieving and representing data, a myriad of options are available; over time, the technology has evolved dramatically. The reason for this is that the code needed to access data and the engines that run the data itself tend to be resource heavy, and in situations such as on the Web where they may be used in clustered environments (i.e., the same application running on a number of machines) and serving millions of users, they can be expensive to maintain. As a result, the technology that developers use to create data-driven applications has evolved rapidly, driven by the needs of scaling to large audiences.

.NET provides a data programming technology for you to use in your applications. It is called ADO.NET. It consists of a number of managed classes that enable your applications to connect to data sources, execute commands, and manage disconnected data. In this chapter, you'll look at the architecture of ADO.NET and how it works to bring data to your application.

You'll look into the SQL Server 2005 Express edition, a free version of the industry-leading enterprise database software from Microsoft, as well as a sample database, AdventureWorks, that is used to demonstrate many of its features.

You'll wrap the chapter up with a tour through some of the server controls that can be used to provide data awareness to your web application through *data binding*.

What Is ADO.NET?

Scalability is typically achieved by breaking an application into functional tiers. As I mentioned in the previous chapter, keeping state between tiers has a high cost when it comes to scalability, performance, and security. Data-aware applications are no exception. ASP.NET offers view state as a great alternative to maintaining control state between the browser and server to provide both a nice programming interface and control state management with minimum resource consumption. When writing data applications, the cost of maintaining state between the tiers of your application can be much higher, as you may be passing large amounts of data (sometimes referred to as *data sets*) between them.

Thus, ADO.NET offers a *disconnected* model that enables you to access data from another tier, disconnect from that tier (thus breaking state), and access that data locally. To prevent data from being corrupted, ADO.NET provides the means for syncing back up with the data store when your transaction is complete, as well as locking mechanisms to prevent other processes from affecting the data while your application is holding it in a disconnected state.

At the heart of the disconnected model is XML. ADO.NET was designed with the XML classes of the .NET Framework in mind, and at the core of this is the DataSet object, which you'll undoubtedly encounter if you continue writing ADO.NET-based applications. (It's also used under the covers when controls are automatically bound to a database, although that's not obvious at a casual glance.)

Using ADO.NET

You use a .NET *data provider* to connect to the data store. A provider is one or more classes that give you programmatic access to a database, providing methods that enable you to read or update data stored in the supported data store. The main classes that you'll use when using a data provider to connect to databases are as follows:

Connection: As its name suggests, the Connection class is used to make and manage the connection with the database.

Command: You use Command to create and execute Structured Query Language (SQL) statements against your database, or to access stored procedures already on the database and execute them.

DataReader: When you want to access data in a read-only manner, moving forward through the data as you read, this class provides a lightweight, fast component that achieves this.

DataAdapter: The DataAdapter class is used to facilitate the communication between the disconnected DataSet and the data store. It fills the DataSet with data and provides the methods to apply changes to the data stored within the data store based on any modifications made within the (disconnected) DataSet.

DataSet: The DataSet is a disconnected representation of all or part of a database. It is much more sophisticated than something like a recordset or table because it can support a collection of tables, relationships, constraints, and more.

ADO.NET supplies you with a number of built-in providers, including a SQL Server provider that is optimized for SQL Server. This includes all of the preceding classes

(`Connection`, `Command`, etc.) that are written specifically for this database. In addition to this, there is also an Object Linking and Embedding for Databases (OLEDB) provider and an Open Database Connectivity (ODBC) provider, which are written to access any database that provides OLEDB or ODBC databases, respectively. Although these aren't optimized for a database such as SQL Server, they will still work. For older versions of SQL Server that do not support the ADO.NET provider (earlier than 7.0), they provide a viable option.

The built-in set of providers is rounded out with an Oracle provider, which is optimized for Oracle databases.

The recommendation if you are using Oracle or SQL Server is to use their dedicated providers, due to the optimization inherent in them. Should this not work, OLEDB is recommended, and then the ODBC provider as a final fallback option.

You are, of course, not limited to these providers, and a third-party ecosystem of providers around databases such as MySQL and PostGreSQL has evolved. Take note that these providers form dependencies that you'll need to account for when you deploy your application.

Despite the fact that you use different providers for different databases or versions of databases, the API has been carefully designed to avoid fragmentation. Each provider is built upon a standard set of interfaces that ensure that the method signatures for standard operations such as open and close are preserved. Because of this, your application data access code is buffered from change if you switch databases.

We'll go into ADO.NET programming a little later in this chapter, but first, it's a good idea to get a copy of SQL Server. If you don't have one already, the Express edition can be downloaded from MSDN at `http://msdn.microsoft.com/vstudio/express/sql`. We'll explore this in the next few sections before delving back into ADO.NET development to round out the chapter. Note that if you are using Windows Vista, you should find Service Pack 2 (SP2) for SQL Server Express and then download and install that. SP2 is available from the Visual Studio Express download site at `http://msdn.microsoft.com/vstudio/express/sql/register/default.aspx`.

SQL Server 2005 Express

If you've developed Windows applications before, you may have encountered a "mini" desktop database called Microsoft SQL Server Desktop Engine 2000 (MSDE). SQL Server 2005 Express edition is the next version of this and is free to download, redistribute, and embed in your applications. It's a great way to get familiar with SQL Server because it can be used with tools such as SQL Server Management Studio, which may be downloaded and installed from the same site as SQL Server Express. This tool is also used in the Enterprise editions. In this section, you'll look at downloading, installing, and configuring SQL Server Express for your applications.

Downloading and Installing SQL Server 2005 Express

There are a number of different options presented to you when you want to download SQL Server Express:

Core SQL Server Express: This provides the basic runtime engine for SQL Server. It can be embedded within Microsoft Visual Studio 2005 (but not the Express editions), is free to distribute, and can be seamlessly upgraded to Professional or Enterprise editions of SQL Server.

SQL Server Management Studio Express: This is the tool that you can use to manage instances of SQL Server or SQL Server Express. It is a recommended tool if you are using Express editions of Visual Studio, or if you want to learn about administration of the Professional versions of SQL Server. Please note that this is downloaded separately.

SQL Server Express with Advanced Services: This adds features to Core SQL Server Express, including Management Studio, reporting services, and full-text search.

SQL Server Express Edition Toolkit: This adds tools, including a report creator for reporting services, the business intelligence development studio for building stored procedures and other database-related functionality, and the SQL Server software development kit (SDK).

In this chapter, we'll be looking at SQL Server 2005 Express with Advanced Services, which provides a single download that gives you SQL Server and Management Studio.

Starting the Install

Once you've downloaded SQL Server 2005 Express with Advanced Services (available at www.microsoft.com/express/sql/default.aspx), launch it to get the installer. The first screen that you'll see is the End User License Agreement (EULA), which you will need to accept to continue (see Figure 4-1).

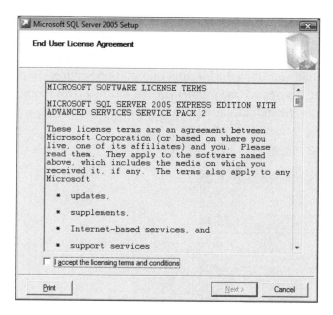

Figure 4-1. *SQL Server Express EULA*

Click Next to continue the installation, and the installer will install all the necessary setup files. Once this is complete, the installer will scan your system for prerequisites, and should you have them all installed, it will launch (see Figure 4-2). If there are any installation problems, a different dialog will show you what they are.

Figure 4-2. *Beginning the installation*

Clicking Next will take you to the System Configuration Check, at which point your system will be scanned for the required components. Should any of them be missing, you will receive a warning or an error message, and the Message column will instruct you what to do. Figure 4-3 shows an example in which the Internet Information Services (IIS) feature requirement hasn't been met; it isn't a critical problem, just a warning. This is one of the Windows Vista incompatibilities mentioned earlier—the current version of SQL Server Express doesn't recognize IIS 7.

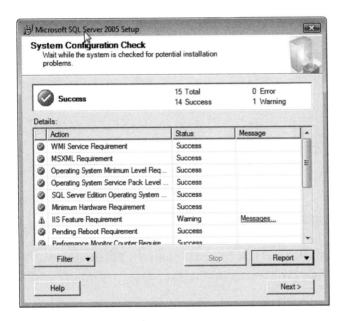

Figure 4-3. *System Configuration Check*

When you get to the Registration Information screen (see Figure 4-4), remember to uncheck the box that reads "Hide advanced configuration options."

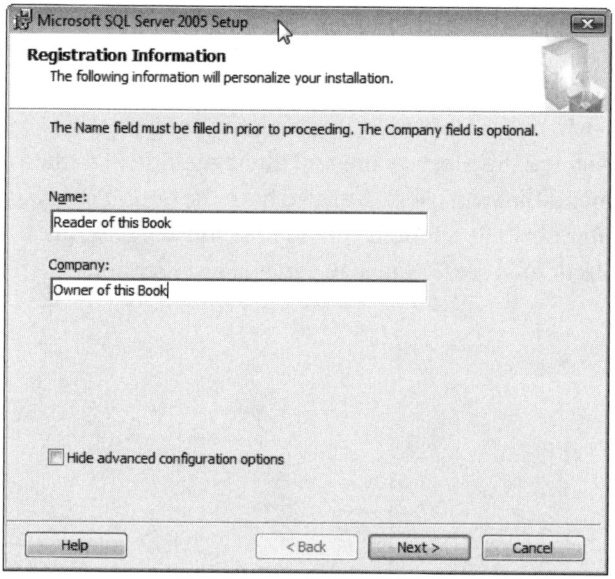

Figure 4-4. *Registration information*

The next screen is where you configure what you want to install. In this case, you should make sure that you install at least Database Services and Management Studio Express (see Figure 4-5).

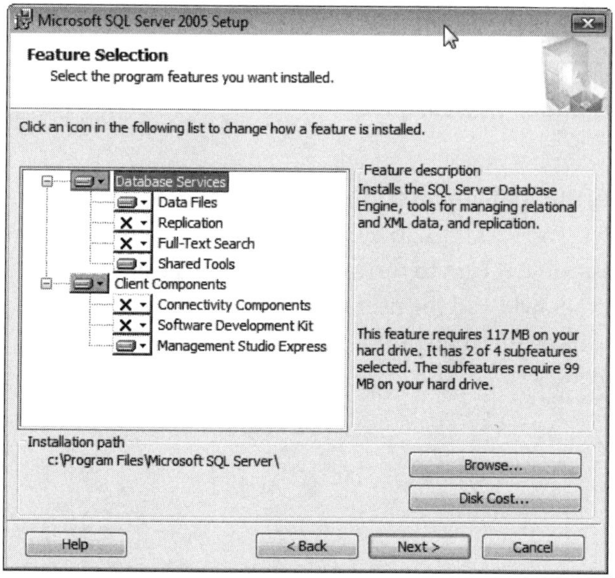

Figure 4-5. *Feature Selection screen*

Your next step is to set the authentication mode for SQL Server (see Figure 4-6). There are two ways you can log into the database. You can use Windows authentication only when your Windows sign-on credentials are used to access the database, and you can use Mixed Mode authentication when SQL Server has its own set of credentials.

Windows authentication is considered the most secure and direct method of authentication, and for this book, I recommend that you use it. You also have the option of using Mixed Mode authentication for greater flexibility. Should you do this, you will have to configure the sa login, which is the credential set for the SQL Server administrator.

Figure 4-6. *Configuring the SQL Server authentication mode*

The next screen allows you to set the configuration options (see Figure 4-7). There are two main options that you can set. The first is Enable User Instances, which if set will allow users that do not have administrative access to run separate instances of the SQL Server Express engine. The second, if set, will add the user that is installing the database as a SQL Server administrator. You can see this in Figure 4-7.

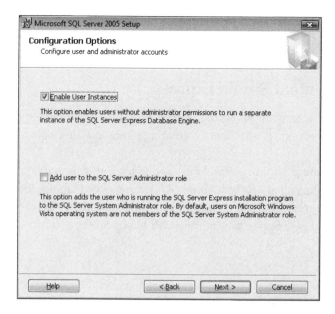

Figure 4-7. *Configuration options*

The final step is an option screen that allows you to configure feedback settings that, if set, will allow SQL Server to send errors back to Microsoft, allowing them to improve the product. This is shown in Figure 4-8.

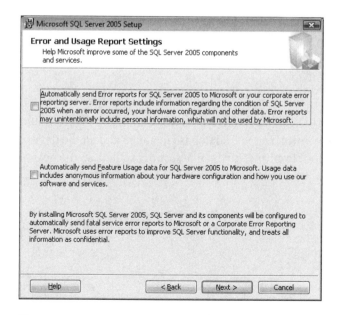

Figure 4-8. *Error and Usage Report Settings screen*

After this, SQL Server Express will install itself. When installation is complete, the specified services will run.

Using SQL Server Management Studio Express

Now you can launch the SQL Server Management Studio Express tool. This tool enables you to sign into a database and manipulate its artifacts for creating tables, queries, data, user accounts, and more.

When you first launch Management Studio, you will be asked to log into your database. By default, your database will be called *MachineName*\SQLExpress (see Figure 4-9). You can sign on with your Windows credentials, or if you specified Mixed Mode authentication and wish to, sign on with your SQL Server sa account. With Mixed Mode, you can sign on either way.

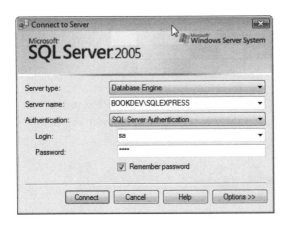

Figure 4-9. *Signing into SQL Server 2005*

Once you've successfully connected, Management Studio will launch (see Figure 4-10).

From here, you have complete control over your database instance and all the databases attached to it. At this point in our example, no databases are installed, so the next step is to download and install a sample database.

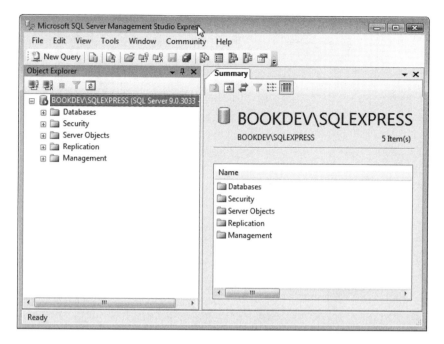

Figure 4-10. *SQL Server Management Studio*

Installing the AdventureWorks Database

You can download the AdventureWorks database from `http://msdn.microsoft.com/ vstudio/express/sql/register/default.aspx`. This will take you to the SQL Server 2005 downloads page, where a number of different downloads are available. Select the SQL Server 2005 Samples option to download the AdventureWorks sample database. Note that several versions are available for different hardware, so be sure to select the one that is appropriate for your setup. The preceding link takes you first to a registration page, but registration isn't necessary to get the AdventureWorks sample. Simply choose the "No, I do not wish to register" option if you just want to directly access this sample.

Run through the setup process, and the database will be installed on your machine. However, you won't be able to do anything with it until you attach it to your current SQL Express instance. You can do so by using Management Studio. Launch Management Studio and select the Databases node. Right-click it and select Attach. The Attach Databases dialog box will appear (see Figure 4-11).

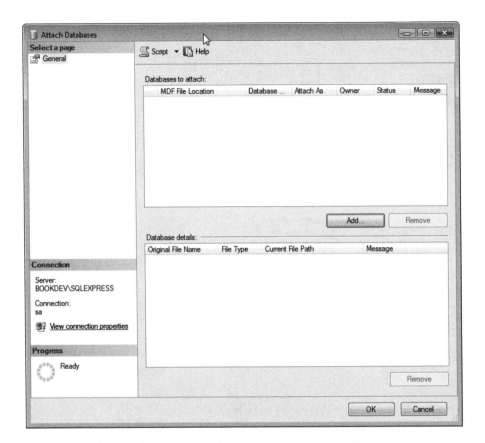

Figure 4-11. *Attach Databases dialog box*

You use this dialog box to attach database files (files with the `.mdf` extension) to your instance of SQL Server. Click Add, and a file browser will open on the default location for MDF files on your system. This will likely be: `C:\Program Files\Microsoft SQL Server\ MSSQL.1\MSSQL\Data`, but its exact location depends upon the location you selected when you installed SQL Server 2005 Express.

Find the `AdventureWorks_data.mdf` file and click OK. You can see this dialog box in Figure 4-12.

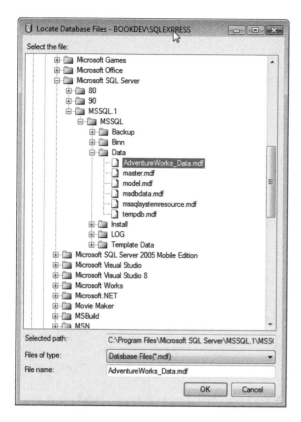

Figure 4-12. *Finding a database to attach*

Once you've done this, the database and its log file will be attached to your SQL Server instance, and you will be able to write applications that access it from within Visual Studio.

Note that if you are using Windows Vista, the operating system will prevent you from writing to the Data directory for security reasons, and this operation will fail. You will need to navigate to the MDF and LDF files for AdventureWorks from within Windows Explorer and use the security settings in the Properties dialog box. Add permissions for the SQL Server processes to have full control over these files.

Once you've connected the database, you can view its contents within Management Studio. See Figure 4-13 for an example of the data that this table contains, namely the addresses of the (fictional) people who are part of the AdventureWorks customer database.

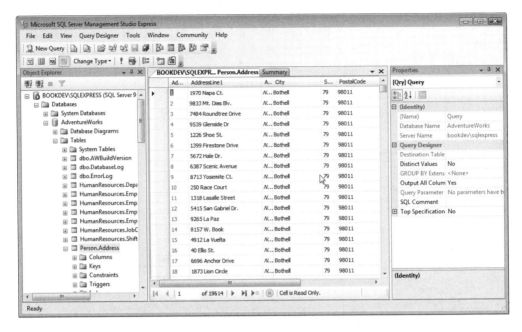

Figure 4-13. *Browsing data with Management Studio*

Using ADO.NET to Build Data-Driven Applications

Now that you've installed and configured a SQL Server database, the next step is to learn more about ADO.NET and start building some applications designed to work with databases and data. You'll do this in two steps. First, you'll learn how to use the coding environment to create connections to the data and to retrieve data sets that you'll manipulate, and then you'll start looking at the graphical user interface (GUI) tools that provide this for you, as well as the server controls that you can use to provide sophisticated data-binding functionality in your application.

The Connection Class and Connection Strings

ADO.NET provides a connection class that you use to connect to your database. A specially formatted string, called a *connection string,* contains the specifications for how you will connect to it. An example of a connection string is shown here:

```
Data Source=BOOKDEV\SQLEXPRESS;
    Initial Catalog=AdventureWorks;
    Integrated Security=True
```

It contains a semicolon-separated list of name/value pairs. You need at least three pairs in any connection string: the name of the database server (Data Source), the database on that server to connect to (Initial Catalog), and the sign-on credentials. If you set Integrated Security to True, SQL Server will use the Windows account of the current process to sign into SQL Server. Or, you can specify a user ID and password to sign in using SQL Server credentials in Mixed Mode.

You can easily hard-code a connection string into your application like this:

```
string strConn = "Data Source=BOOKDEV\SQLEXPRESS;" +
    "Initial Catalog=AdventureWorks;Integrated Security=True";
```

However, it makes much more sense to store the connection string in your Web.config file, because you may want to change it over time and prefer not to recompile your code just to reconfigure the connection to your database. You do this by using the <connectionStrings> section within Web.config. Here's an example:

```
<configuration>
  <connectionStrings>
    <add name="AW" connectionString="Data Source=BOOKDEV\SQLEXPRESS;
          Initial Catalog=AdventureWorks;Integrated Security=True" />
  </connectionStrings>
</configuration>
```

Now, from your code, you can use WebConfigurationManager (found in System.Web. Configuration) to access the connection string like this:

```
string connectionString =
    WebConfigurationManager.ConnectionStrings["AW"].ConnectionString;
```

Visually Designing Your Connection String

Visual Studio gives you a nice tool to help you build your connection strings. This tool also works with the Express editions.

From the tools menu in Visual Studio, select Connect to Database. The Add Connection dialog box will appear. From here, fill out the details for your database, including the server instance name, the database to connect to, and the sign-on credentials. You can see an example of this in Figure 4-14.

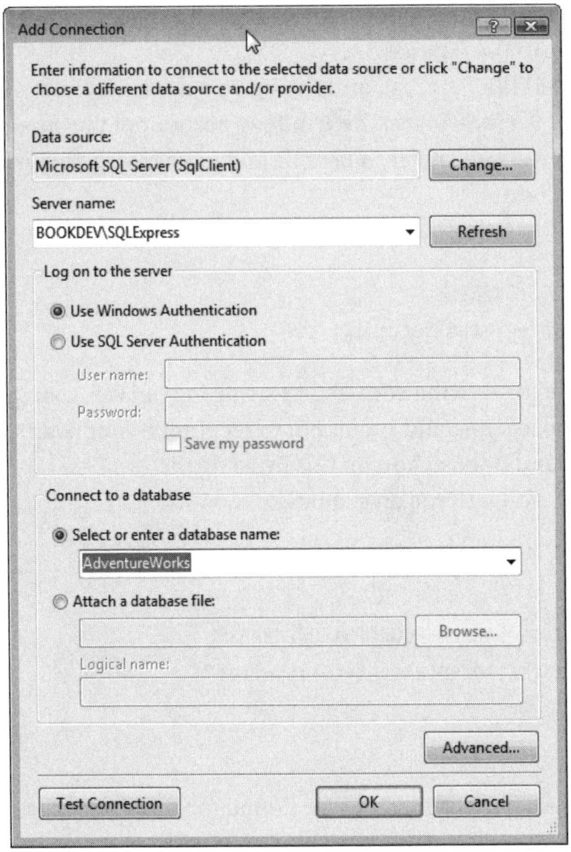

Figure 4-14. *Connecting to a database*

You can also test the connection from this dialog box to work out any bugs in your connection string. When you are done (i.e., you are connecting successfully), click OK.

An entry for this connection will be added to the Database Explorer in Visual Studio (see Figure 4-15).

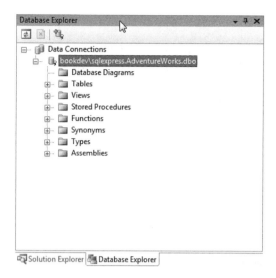

Figure 4-15. *The Database Explorer*

At this point, you can see that the connection string is displayed for you in the Properties window (see Figure 4-16).

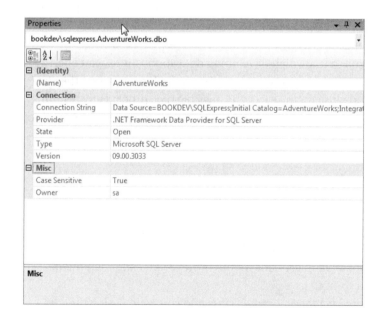

Figure 4-16. *Using the Properties window to view the connection string*

Accessing a Connection

You use the SqlConnection class, which is derived from the generic ADO.NET Connection class, to access your SQL Server database. This is part of the SQL Server–specific ADO.NET Providers suite found in System.Data.SqlClient.

Here's a simple piece of code that opens a connection, queries the server, and then closes the connection:

```
string connectionString =
    WebConfigurationManager.ConnectionStrings["AW"].ConnectionString;
using (SqlConnection sqlCon = new SqlConnection(connectionString))
{
    sqlCon.Open();
    lblVersion.Text = sqlCon.ServerVersion;
}
```

Note that connections are expensive resources on a server, and you should take every precaution to prevent connection leaks, which are orphaned connections. Every time you open a connection, you must close that connection. Therefore, it's best to wrap your data access code in a try...catch block and place the SqlConnection.Close method invocation in a finally block, or create the SqlConnection in a using statement. The using statement will call the connection's Dispose method when it goes out of scope, thereby closing the database connection for you. This way, the connection is assured to be closed, even if your code sustains an error while accessing the data.

It is also highly recommended that when developing data applications, you open them as late as possible (i.e., perform all required initialization before you open the connections to your database) and close them as early as possible (i.e., process any resulting DataSet after you close the connection), unless you have to keep the connection open for some compelling reason. The goal here is to minimize the time connections are held open, which serves to increase scalability.

Using Commands

A *command* represents any kind of SQL statement made against your database. This gives you powerful application control over your database structure and contents, enabling you to create and delete databases, insert and retrieve data, and manipulate table structures, among other things.

A command is implemented via the SqlCommand class and controlled using the SqlCommand.CommandType and SqlCommand.CommandText properties, which are often used in tandem. If you set the CommandType to CommandType.Text, the CommandText property (a string) should contain the SQL statement that you want to execute. If the type is CommandType.StoredProcedure, the CommandText should contain the name of the stored procedure to execute. Finally, if the type is CommandType.Table, the command text should contain the name of a table in your database. Executing this type of command will return all records stored in that table.

So, for example, if you want to create a query that returns the street address for customers in the AdventureWorks address database who live at postal code 98011, you would use code like this:

```
string connectionString =
  WebConfigurationManager.ConnectionStrings["AW"].ConnectionString;

SqlConnection sqlCon = new SqlConnection(connectionString);
SqlCommand sqlComm = new SqlCommand();
sqlComm.Connection = sqlCon;
sqlComm.CommandType = CommandType.Text;
sqlComm.CommandText =
    "SELECT AddressLine1 FROM Person.Address " +
    "WHERE (PostalCode = N'98011')";
```

Executing the Command

Now that you have your command, you are going to want to execute it to do anything meaningful. There are four different methods for executing an ADO.NET command:

ExecuteNonQuery: This is used to execute a query for which you do not want to return a result set. For example, if you are inserting, updating, or deleting records, you can use the command's ExecuteNonQuery method. It will return an integer containing the number of records that were affected.

ExecuteScalar: This executes the query and returns the first column of the first row of the result set. This is very useful for queries that use SQL COUNT or SUM, or other queries that return a desirable value.

ExecuteReader: This executes a SELECT query and returns a DataReader object that can be used to provide forward-only read access to your data.

ExecuteXmlReader: This is similar to ExecuteReader except that it gives you an XmlReader to access the data.

So, executing a command to generate the required feedback is very straightforward. Here's an example of executing the previous query, with the results available via a SqlDataReader:

```
SqlDataReader sRead = sqlComm.ExecuteReader();
```

In the next section, you'll see how to use this reader to step through the results of the query and access the first line of the returned addresses.

Reading the Data

When you execute the previous command, ADO.NET returns a `SqlDataReader`. This reader is a forward-based read-only cursor that moves forward by one record every time you call its `Read` method. The `Read` method returns `True` if it reads a record and `False` otherwise. Upon a successful read, it will then load an array of values with the index of the array representing the column name—so `reader["ColumnName"]` will contain this record's value for `ColumnName`.

Thus, we can iterate through the returned result set using a `while` loop, and upon a successful read, retrieve the result set's data by simply accessing the reader as if it were an array.

Listing 4-1 contains the complete code to access the addresses for postal code 98011 in the AdventureWorks database.

Listing 4-1. *Using Connection, Command, and Reader to Access Data*

```
using System;
using System.Data;
using System.Configuration;
using System.Web;
using System.Web.Security;
using System.Web.UI;
using System.Web.UI.WebControls;
using System.Web.UI.WebControls.WebParts;
using System.Web.UI.HtmlControls;
using System.Web.Configuration;
using System.Data.SqlClient;
using System.Text;

public partial class _Default : System.Web.UI.Page
{
  protected void Page_Load(object sender, EventArgs e)
  {
    string connectionString =
      WebConfigurationManager.ConnectionStrings["AW"].ConnectionString;
    StringBuilder strReturn = new StringBuilder();
    using (SqlConnection sqlCon = new SqlConnection(connectionString))
    {
      SqlCommand sqlComm = new SqlCommand();
```

```
    sqlComm.Connection = sqlCon;
    sqlComm.CommandType = CommandType.Text;
    sqlComm.CommandText =
      "SELECT AddressLine1 FROM Person.Address " +
      "WHERE (PostalCode = N'98011')";
    sqlCon.Open();
    SqlDataReader sRead = sqlComm.ExecuteReader();
    while (sRead.Read())
    {
        strReturn.Append("<li>");
        strReturn.Append(sRead["AddressLine1"]);
        strReturn.Append("</li>");
    }
  }
  litResults.Text = strReturn.ToString();
 }
}
```

You can see the results of running this in Figure 4-17.

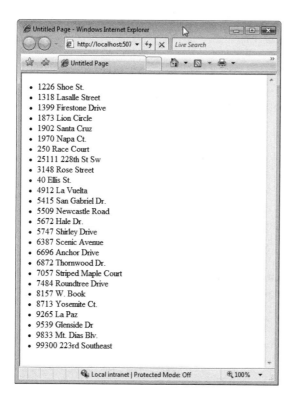

Figure 4-17. *Viewing the results of the postal code query*

Using Parameters in Commands

Now, this is all very well for a fixed SQL statement like the one we had hard-coded to query for postal code 98011. But what happens if you want the user to specify the postal code that they are searching for? You achieve this using parameters. Thus, you can provide an application where the user specifies (using text input, request parameters, or other input mechanisms) what they want, and your application responds accordingly.

Be careful when using parameters in SQL statements that are derived from user input, as this is a common source of SQL injection attacks. This type of hacker attack involves a cleverly crafted parameter value on the user's part and an insecure application that doesn't validate user input. This attack can allow a malicious user to access private data or even destroy your database.

To use a parameter in SQL, you specify a placeholder for the parameter by prefixing it with the @ character. So, for example, our hard-coded query from earlier could be changed to this:

```
sqlComm.CommandText =
  "SELECT AddressLine1 FROM Person.Address WHERE (PostalCode = @strZIP)";
```

Then, before executing, you add the value of the parameter to the command, like this:

```
sqlComm.Parameters.Add("@strZIP", strParamZIP);
```

The value you'll assign to the parameterized postal code is contained in the variable strParamZIP. The value can be the result of text input, or, if you prefer, taken directly off the query string. The code to access it from the query string will look like this:

```
string strParamZIP = "98011";
if (Request.Params["ZIP"] != null)
  strParamZIP = Request.Params["ZIP"];
```

But if you use code like this, don't forget to sanitize strParamZIP before passing it to the database to avoid injection attacks. By *sanitize*, I mean that you should evaluate the value contained within strParamZIP and make sure it's a valid postal code, not some other (invalid) text.

Now if you run your application, your query string can contain a postal code, and the query results for that postal code will be displayed. Figure 4-18 shows an example of this where I used a postal code of 14111.

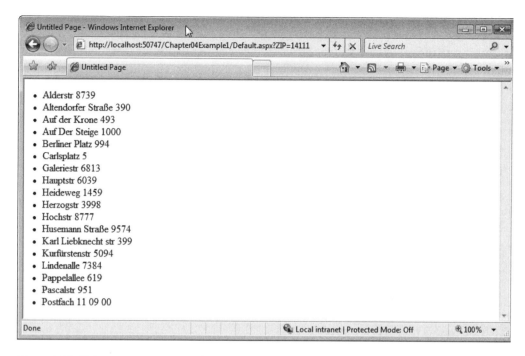

Figure 4-18. *Using a parameterized query*

Data Binding with Server Controls

You've seen in the previous sections how ASP.NET and ADO.NET can be used to connect to databases and manipulate the data therein through connections, commands, and readers. However, most modern applications require flexible, graphical access to the same data. As a developer, you aren't going to want to develop all of this complex data access and binding code from the ground up.

ASP.NET provides controls that give you visual- and designer-based access to data through data binding, but all of them use a DataSource control to provide access to the underlying database. Because we are using SQL Server data in this example, the SQL Server–specific DataSource control will be used. You aren't limited to using this control, because .NET provides several others, such as ObjectDataSource and XMLDataSource, but these go beyond the scope of this chapter. Still, the principles that you learn from the SqlDataSource control will apply across all data sources when data binding is taken into context.

Using the SQLDataSource Control

When you are using Visual Studio or Visual Web Developer Express, open the Designer to edit any ASP.NET page. You will see a Data tab on the Toolbox. This tab contains the SqlDataSource control. Drag and drop it onto the design surface, and its Tasks pane will open (see Figure 4-19).

Figure 4-19. *The SqlDataSource control*

This pane contains a Configure Data Source link. Selecting this link will launch the SQL Server Connection wizard (see Figure 4-20). The first step in this wizard is to select a database connection, if one already exists.

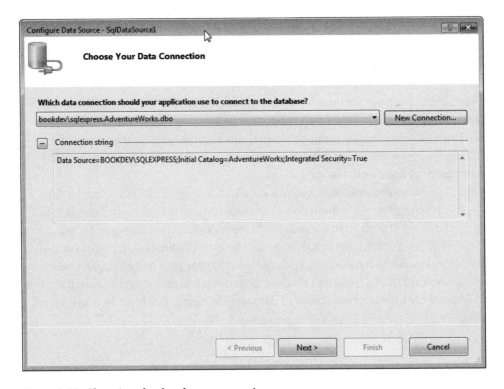

Figure 4-20. *Choosing the database connection*

Earlier in this chapter, you saw how to create a connection to a database. If you've already created a connection, you can select it in the SQL Server Connection wizard. Alternatively, you can click the New Connection button to create a connection now. You can also view the connection string for this connection in this dialog box. When you're happy with the connection, click Next to go to the application configuration selection step, where you can specify what to call the connection string in your Web.config file (see Figure 4-21).

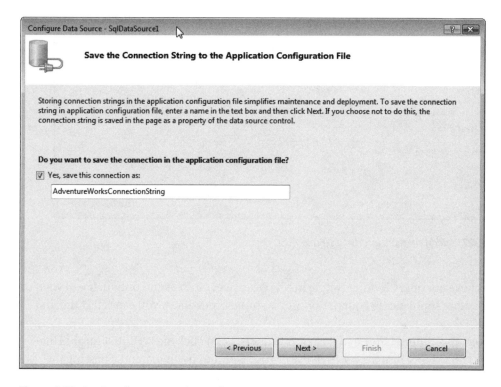

Figure 4-21. *Saving the connection string*

The next step in the wizard is very powerful, enabling you to specify a custom SQL statement or stored procedure, filter an existing table, or drill down to a viewable set of records. You can see this page in Figure 4-22.

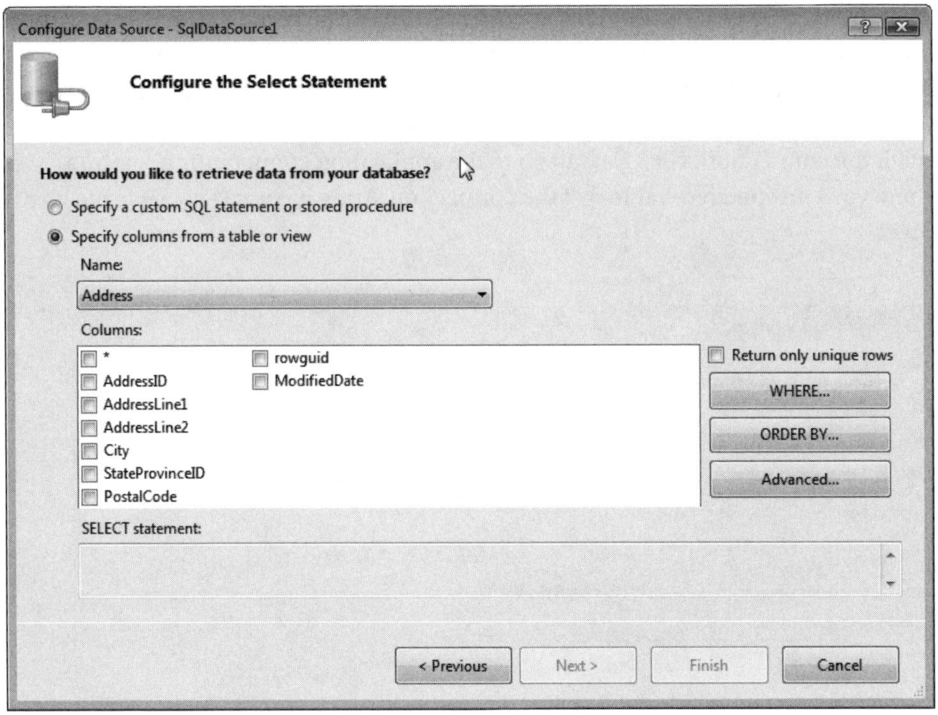

Figure 4-22. *Specifying which data to use*

Because our query is quite simple in this case, select the second option. If you want to build more sophisticated queries or access stored procedures, you can select the first option.

Select the AddressLine1 and PostalCode fields. Then click the WHERE button. This enables you to configure the WHERE clause of your SQL and use it to handle passing the parameter for the ZIP postal code value from the query string. This launches the Add WHERE Clause dialog box (see Figure 4-23).

You can use this dialog box to specify the column operation and source for the WHERE clause. So, for example, if you want to specify that the returned data should be all records that match a postal code passed in on a query string, you would set Column to PostalCode, Operator to " =", and Source to =" QueryString".

You then fill out the properties for the parameter, giving it a name and a default value. You can see the sample version in Figure 4-23, which uses a parameter called ZIP taking a default value of 98011. Clicking Add will add this WHERE filter to the SQL expression.

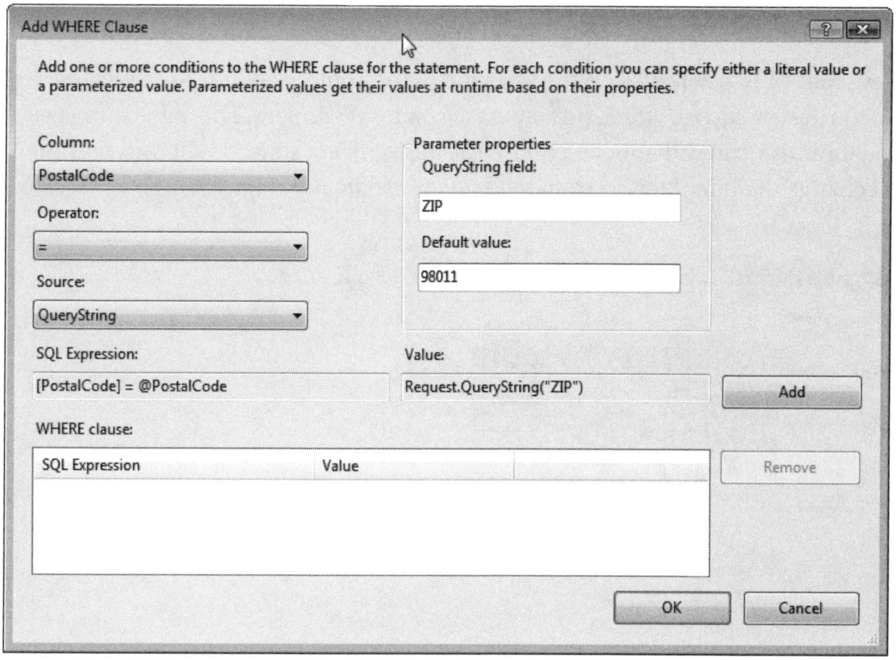

Figure 4-23. *Adding a new WHERE clause*

If you now finish the wizard, SqlDataSource will be set up to access the set of records that are defined by this query. This can be seen in the declaration for the SqlDataSource in the Source view of your page:

```
<asp:SqlDataSource ID="SqlDataSource1" runat="server"
  ConnectionString="<%$ConnectionStrings:AdventureWorksConnectionString2 %>"
  SelectCommand="SELECT AddressLine1, PostalCode FROM Person.Address WHERE
             (PostalCode = @PostalCode)">
  <SelectParameters>
    <asp:QueryStringParameter DefaultValue="98011" Name="PostalCode"
                          QueryStringField="ZIP" />
  </SelectParameters>
</asp:SqlDataSource>
```

You now have the root functionality that will enable you to bind your page's UI to your data source.

Using the GridView Control

The GridView control is also found on the Data tab of the Toolbox. When you drag and drop it onto the design surface, the GridView Tasks pane will appear. This pane enables you to format how the grid will appear, choose the desired data source, edit the columns to view, and change the templates used to represent the data (see Figure 4-24).

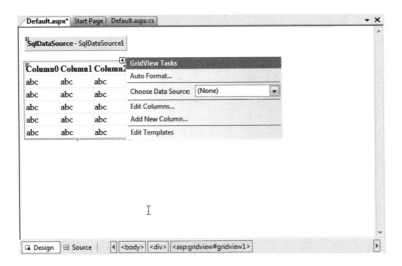

Figure 4-24. *The GridView Tasks pane*

You can hook the GridView control up to the data source by using the Choose Data Source drop-down list. Choose the SqlDataSource control that you created in the previous step and run the application. You'll now have the same functionality as you had in earlier examples (that being the ability to view the addresses of people in the Adventure-Works database, filtered by a ZIP code passed in the query string), and you didn't have to write a single line of code to achieve this!

With the GridView control, you can go a lot further. The Auto Format dialog box enables you to choose from a large set of preset styles to determine how your grid will appear. You can see the Auto Format dialog box, including a live preview of how your grid will appear, in Figure 4-25.

The set of columns that you want to display can be edited from within the Tasks pane. If you select Edit Columns, the Fields dialog box will display, enabling you to add or remove columns from the set of selected fields. The query on the SqlDataSource in this example returns two columns—AddressLine1 and PostalCode—which have been automatically added to the GridView. If you only want to show the AddressLine1 column values, you can easily do this by selecting the PostalCode column and deleting it from this dialog box (see Figure 4-26). Alternatively, you may want to be able to access the column from code, but not show it to the user. In this case, you can set the column's Visible property to False.

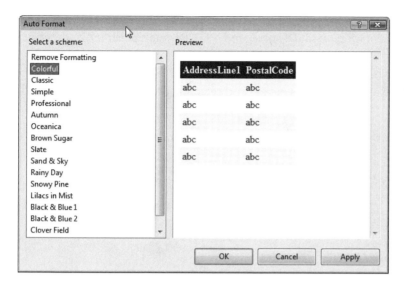

Figure 4-25. *Auto-formatting your GridView*

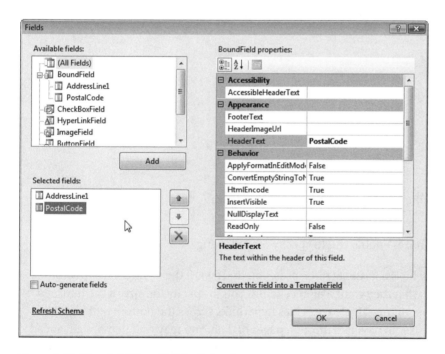

Figure 4-26. *The GridView Fields dialog box*

In addition to having columns that are bound to your data source (called BoundField types; see Figure 4-26), you can also add a number of different column types to your grid. These include check boxes, hyperlinks, buttons, and so on. The GridView control has a huge amount of functionality, going well beyond the scope of this book, so it is worth checking out the documentation on MSDN or a good ASP.NET reference book if you want to go into more detail.

You may notice that once you've configured your data source, the Tasks pane will change, giving you more options, such as paging and selecting the data (see Figure 4-27).

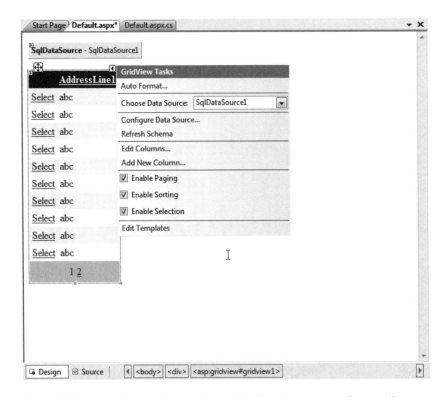

Figure 4-27. *Accessing paging, sorting, and selection on your data grid*

These check boxes enable you to specify the following:

Paging: If you have a large set of records, you don't want the user to have to scroll down to find what they want. Paging enables you to specify the size of the returned grid in number of rows. It also provides hyperlinks across the bottom of the grid, enabling the user to navigate through pages of data. You may find in more advanced applications that the developer chooses to perform the paging in the database tier within their stored procedures. This is very effective in that it doesn't persist a large amount of data on the presentation tier, and it reduces the amount of traffic on the wire. ASP.NET gives you the facility to page on the client, should you choose to, and SQL Server gives you the facility to page on the database tier, should you choose to. It's all about flexibility!

Sorting: This makes the columns clickable, enabling the data to be sorted based on clicking the column.

Selection: This adds a Select hyperlink, enabling an event to be fired when the user selects a row of data.

You can see an example of the postal code filter application using a GridView control in Figure 4-28.

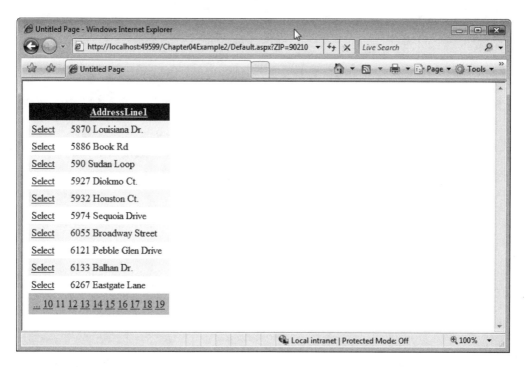

Figure 4-28. *Your application including paging, sorting, and selection*

You have all this functionality, and you still haven't written a line of code, thanks to the GridView control and ADO.NET data binding!

Using the DataList Control

The GridView is a large control with a wealth of functionality, and in the previous section, you barely scratched the surface of what you can do with it. If you just want to return a list of data and codelessly control how that list appears, you can achieve this with the DataList control. This control is a server control, found on the Data tab of your Toolbox.

Make sure you have a fully configured SqlDataSource control on your web form, and then drop a DataList control onto the same web form. The Tasks pane will appear, and your environment will look something like that in Figure 4-29.

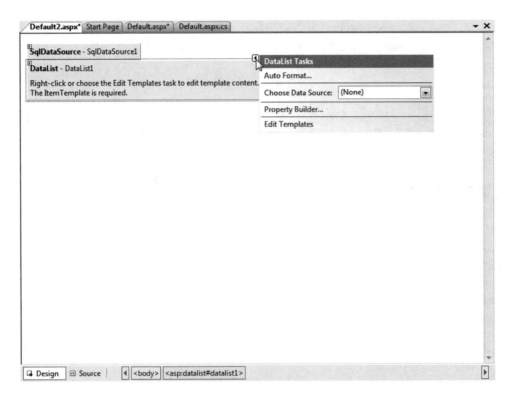

Figure 4-29. *Using the DataList control*

Now, you can choose your data source and run your application. You'll see that you get the list of data returned, as shown in Figure 4-30.

You can see that the page the DataList control builds for you isn't the prettiest of displays, but fear not, you can use the same Auto Format feature as with the GridView control, and you can define the template that dictates how the data should appear by using a visual editor. To do this, select Edit Templates in the Tasks pane (see Figure 4-31).

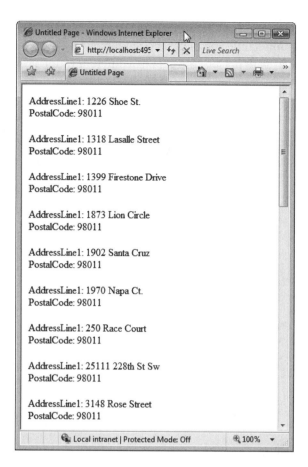

Figure 4-30. *Output of the DataList control*

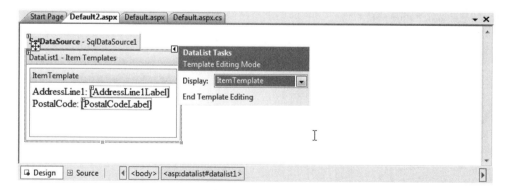

Figure 4-31. *Editing your DataList control's template*

The DataList template is automatically configured for the data fields that you've selected. It has a label containing the column name, and a placeholder for where the data should appear. You can change this easily to present the data in a different way. For example, if you don't want a postal code label, and just have a comma between the address line and the postal code, you can visually edit this. Figure 4-32 shows one example of how the editor can be used to make the appearance of the data more visually pleasing.

Figure 4-32. *Editing the template for the DataList control*

View this page in your browser now to see the visual improvements (see Figure 4-33).

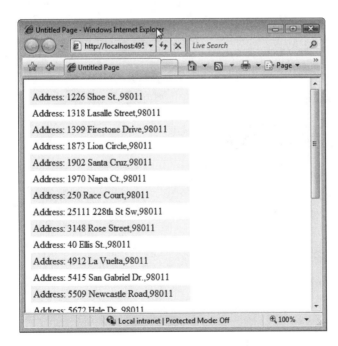

Figure 4-33. *Running the application with the revised DataList control*

Summary

This chapter gave you a whirlwind tour of data in ASP.NET and showed how your web applications can be used to access data. You looked at ADO.NET and how it works, as well as how to download and install SQL Server 2005 Express. Next, you started writing ADO.NET code to access and read from the database. Then, you wrapped up with a tutorial on how to use the Visual Studio designers and tools to create connections to the database, and bind the GridView and DataList controls to present your data, which resulted in a pretty decent web-based data display application, complete with styling, selection, and pagination without writing a single line of code.

You've barely touched the surface of what is possible with ADO.NET in the .NET Framework, but working through this chapter hopefully has given you a taste of what is possible with this powerful and flexible framework!

In the next chapter, you'll take a look at how ASP.NET can be used to deliver web services. These are units of business logic that can be accessed over the network or Internet using standard XML-based messages, and are the foundation of the principles of Software as a Service (SAAS).

CHAPTER 5

■ ■ ■

ASP.NET Web Services

In Chapter 4, you looked at an application that queried data from a database and presented the results as HTML to the browser. This is considered a *tightly coupled* application, where the logic for the UI and the logic for the database are part of the same application module. Consider a case in which a third party would like to use your information and integrate it in their application with their branding and styling—delivering HTML wouldn't be sufficient. With requirements like this in mind, XML (Extensible Markup Language) has grown in popularity. It is a way of representing data in a machine-readable format.

Here's an example of a simple XML document:

```
<recordset>
  <record id="1">
    <address>Street Address</address>
    <zip>11801</zip>
  </record>
  <record id="2">
    <address>Street Address</address>
    <zip>11811</zip>
  </record>
</recordset>
```

XML has an associated technology called XSLT, which enables you to transform one form of XML into some other form, including XML, simple text, and (of most benefit to web developers) HTML. For a best-of-both-worlds approach, you could provide a layer that generates XML from your database and a presentation layer that renders it, thus enabling you to render and resell your own data. This is called a *loosely coupled* approach.

The notion of loose coupling is a powerful one, and the desire to create a mechanism for sending XML between applications to facilitate loosely coupled architectures sparked a technology called *Web Services*. A web service is a device-agnostic implementation of business logic. You generally invoke a web service by using an HTTP-POST verb to send an XML document containing your request details, and the service returns another XML document containing its response to you (this style of web service is more formally called an *XML web service*).

Another interesting facet of modern XML web services is that the service describes itself also using XML. Based on this description, you can craft your requests and understand the responses you receive. Nowhere in this picture are you bound to a particular web presentation technology; therefore, when using web services, you can (in theory at least) present your data to clients that use a different technology base (such as Java 2 Platform Enterprise Edition [J2EE]), or conversely, consume data that is available on a different technology base.

In this chapter, you'll look at web services with ASP.NET. You'll look into how to create and consume them, and you'll explore interoperability technologies that will ensure that your applications can be consumed by others.

Web Services Architecture

XML web services are defined by the W3C as a software system designed to support interoperable machine-to-machine interaction over a network. The XML Web Services specification serves as the basis for communicating information that is well defined and generally available for any technology that implements the specification. The concept of computer-to-computer data communication isn't new; technologies such as DCOM (Distributed Component Object Model) and CORBA (Common Object Request Broker Architecture) have had this functionality for some time. Where XML web services differ is in how they achieve this goal. Instead of using a proprietary data representation, often called a "wire protocol," they use XML, which has become a leading standard for communicating data across the network.

Web services come from the application of several different technologies. These are as follows:

Hypertext Transmission Protocol (HTTP): This is the well-known means of client-server communication that the Internet is built on.

XML: This enables data to be encoded in a machine-readable, richly attributed format.

Simple Object Access Protocol (SOAP): This is a variant of XML and is used to encode requests to a service and response data from the service.

Web Services Description Language (WSDL): This is a variant of XML and is used to describe a web service. This description can be interpreted by a client machine to decipher how the SOAP document structure will be set up to talk to a specific server's web service.

If you haven't used XML web services before, this may sound like an odd mix of technologies, but in practice they work together very well. (From here through the rest of the book, I'll simply refer to the XML web service as a "web service.") If you build a web service, your intention is generally for someone to be able to invoke it. If you have millions of clients, you don't want each of them calling you asking you how to access your service; rather, you want to publish the methodology for talking to your service and understanding its responses. This is the purpose of the WSDL document your service should generate. Fortunately, if you build your web service by using ASP.NET, the WSDL document is automatically generated for you, as you'll see later in this chapter.

Next, you need a way to communicate with the service, and this is where SOAP and HTTP come in. The simplest method is to post a document to a service and have the response returned to you by the service. This is exactly what the SOAP architects intended. You can see the bigger picture in Figure 5-1.

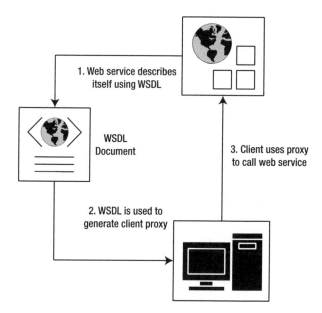

Figure 5-1. *Web service architecture*

Exposing your functionality in this manner and allowing it to be generally used by outside organizations leads to the concept of *Service-Oriented Architecture (SOA)*. Instead of designing monolithic applications that deal with everything from data to presentation in a single tier, you can design small, nimble services that implement functionality. These services can then be combined and orchestrated into an application. In addition to this, you can interface with services from business partners in a manner that may have been difficult, if not impossible, before this technology became commonplace.

Building a Web Service in Visual Studio

Microsoft Visual Studio and Visual Web Developer Express make it easy to build web services. In this section, you'll look at adapting the postal code address browser from Chapter 4 to become a web service.

First, launch Visual Studio or Visual Web Developer Express and select File ➤ New Web Site. In the New Web Site dialog box, select ASP.NET Web Service (see Figure 5-2). This will create a new web site containing the service, called Service.asmx, and the code-behind file for the service (Service.cs) will be placed in the App_Code folder.

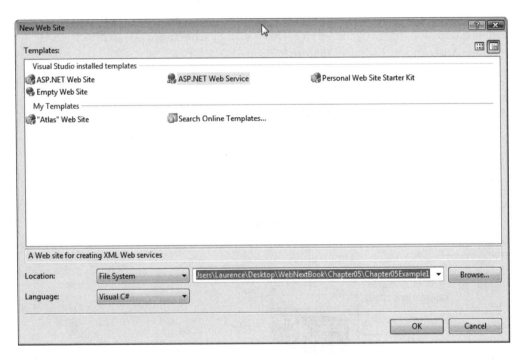

Figure 5-2. *Creating a new web service*

The ASMX and Code-Behind Files

When you browse to a file (HTTP-GET) with the .asmx extension, the ASP.NET-based server recognizes it as a web service request and delivers the service's description page, which often includes test capabilities and a link to the service's WSDL. (You download the WSDL by adding ?WSDL to the URL.) That ASP.NET does this for you saves you from building these for yourself, providing a huge productivity boost. Moreover, the WSDL files that describe your service are generated automatically for you based on your web service code. This ensures that your WSDL description is always up-to-date with your latest code.

This isn't always the case when you use technologies other than ASP.NET, where you may end up with differences between your service code and its description.

You can see what the default ASMX file markup looks like here:

```
<%@ WebService Language="C#"
  CodeBehind="~/App_Code/Service.cs"
  Class="Service" %>
```

It's pretty straightforward and might seem like little more than a file that describes the language of the code-behind file, the location of the code-behind file, and the main class that implements your service. However, note the <%@ and trailing %>. These denote an ASP.NET directive and tell ASP.NET to get ready to work its magic. The WebService is the directive itself, and in this case you're telling ASP.NET to fire up its web service–processing infrastructure (if you look back to Listing 3-3, you'll see another ASP.NET directive, Page, which tells ASP.NET to generate a web page).

The code-behind file is where the action happens in your web service. You can see the default example in Listing 5-1.

Listing 5-1. *Default Web Service*

```
using System;
using System.Web;
using System.Web.Services;
using System.Web.Services.Protocols;

[WebService(Namespace = "http://tempuri.org/")]
[WebServiceBinding(ConformsTo = WsiProfiles.BasicProfile1_1)]
public class Service : System.Web.Services.WebService
{
  public Service () {

    //Uncomment the following line if using designed components
    //InitializeComponent();
  }

  [WebMethod]
  public string HelloWorld() {
    return "Hello World";
  }

}
```

The code in Listing 5-1 defines a class called Service. As you recall, the WebService directive specified this class when it defined Service as the implementing class of the web service logic.

The class is decorated with a couple of attributes. The first one ([WebService (Namespace = "http://tempuri.org/")]) sets the namespace for your web service. You should use a namespace when publishing your web service to distinguish it from other services on the Web that may have the same name and to help reinforce your branding.

The second attribute ensures that your web service conforms to the WS-I basic profile. The WS-I is a group of technology vendors, including Microsoft, who have developed a set of rules called *profiles* to define how a web service should work. Profiles ensure that different technologies won't prevent web service clients and servers from communicating with each other. The most common profile is called the Basic Profile. In its simplest sense, the Basic Profile ensures that only data that is common to all technology platforms can be exposed via a web service. Thus, to conform to the Basic Profile, a Java web service cannot expose a Java-specific data type such as Vector. Conversely, a .NET-based service cannot expose a .NET-specific data type such as DataSet. The WebServiceBinding attribute ([WebServiceBinding(ConformsTo = WsiProfiles.BasicProfile1_1)]) forces your web service to conform to the Basic Profile version 1.1, thus ensuring interoperability.

Your final responsibility when developing a web service in ASP.NET is to define which methods your class will export by using the WebMethod attribute. Only the methods that have been attributed with WebMethod will be exposed to the outside world.

Running Your Web Service

When you view the running web service in the browser, you'll see the ASP.NET web service description page. From here, if you select methods from the bulleted list, you can inspect and test the web methods that have been exposed using the WebMethod attribute. Should those methods require input parameters, the test page for that method will provide text boxes for you to enter the parameter values. You can see the test page for the default Hello World web service in Figure 5-3.

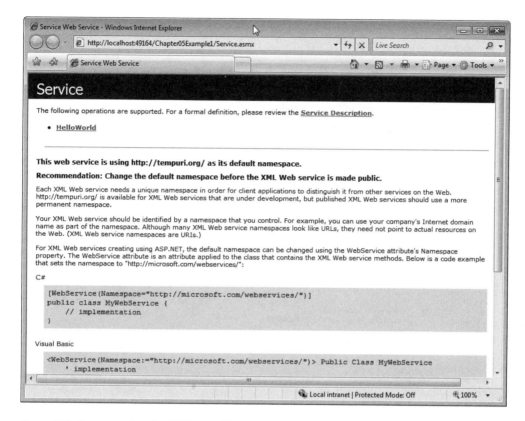

Figure 5-3. *Test page for the Hello World web service*

If you like, you can view the service description by clicking the Service Description link on the test page or by postfixing the URL of the service with ?WSDL, like this:

```
http://localhost:49164/Chapter05Example1/Service.asmx?WSDL
```

Note that the URL you use may vary, but the addition of ?WSDL still applies. This will render the WSDL XML document within the browser. If you want others to access your web service, you just need to provide them with this URL, and they will be able to use it to generate the code necessary to communicate with it.

Figure 5-4 shows your WSDL being rendered in the browser.

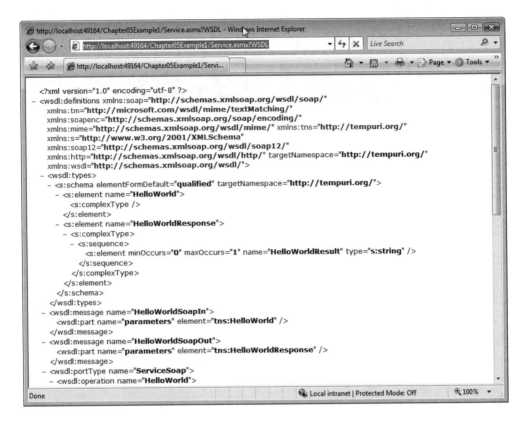

Figure 5-4. *WSDL in the browser*

Creating the Address Service

Now it's time to go beyond Hello World and provide a web service that exposes the address table from the AdventureWorks database. The web service will take a single parameter in the call: the postal code that will be used to filter the desired records.

Because the service requires access to data, you will need to create a data connection. To do this, you will use a strongly typed DataSet object in your solution. Creating this object is very straightforward. You'll look at how to use the DataSet wizard to do this in the next section.

Adding Data to a Web Service

To add a (strongly) typed DataSet to your web service, you use the Solution Explorer. Right-click your project and select Add New Item. The Add New Item dialog box displays (see Figure 5-5).

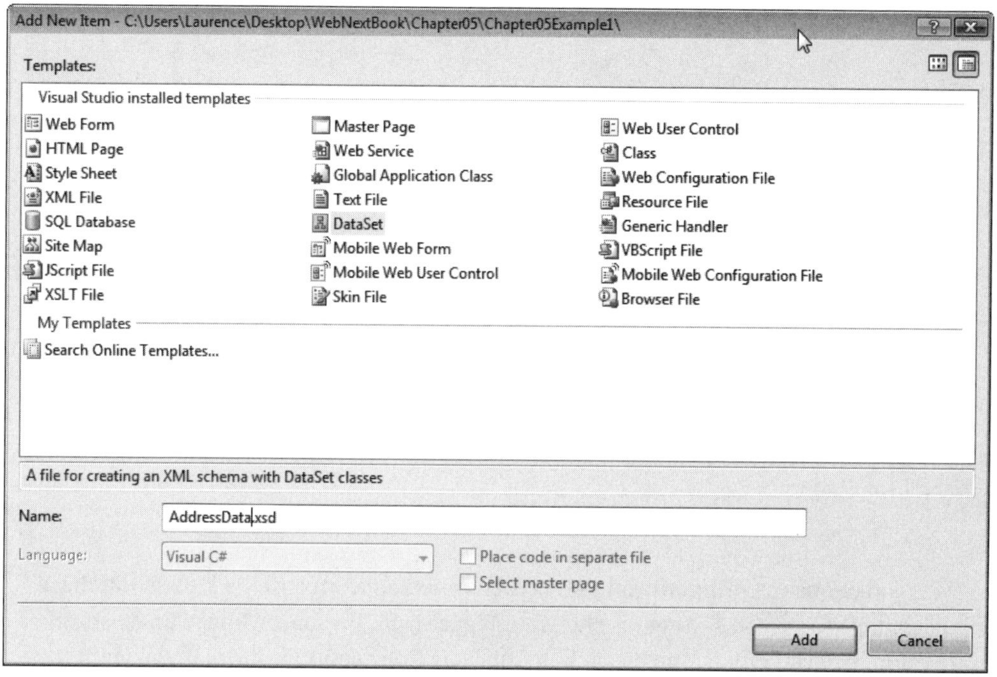

Figure 5-5. *Adding a typed DataSet to your project*

Select the DataSet and give it a friendly name. To use the code later in this section, for the purposes of this example, you should call it AddressData. The IDE will warn you that the code should be placed in the App_Code folder. Click Yes, and the TableAdapter Configuration wizard will launch. The first page of the wizard configures the desired database connection (see Figure 5-6).

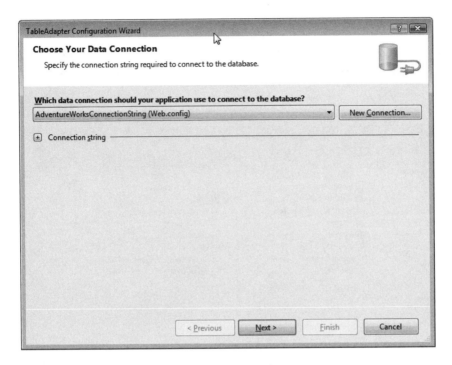

Figure 5-6. *Configuring your database connection*

You can choose a configuration that is preconnected from either a known database or an existing Web.config setting (as shown in Figure 5-5). If you don't have an existing connection, you can create one by clicking the New Connection button. If you want to look at the steps involved in doing this, refer to Chapters 3 and 4.

Once you have selected your connection, click Next. This will take you to the command type configuration page (see Figure 5-7).

You can choose from three options on this page. The first is to use SQL statements embedded in your code (dynamic SQL), which can be used to select, insert, update, or delete data from the database. The second option enables you to create a stored procedure, which is precompiled code that resides on the database and therefore provides performance, security, and code maintenance benefits. Finally, if you have existing stored procedures in your database, you can use them by selecting the third option.

For this example, pick the first option—because we will be using a parameterized SQL query and there is no existing stored procedure—and then click Next.

The next page enables you to type or build the SQL that you'll use to access the database. You can see this in Figure 5-8.

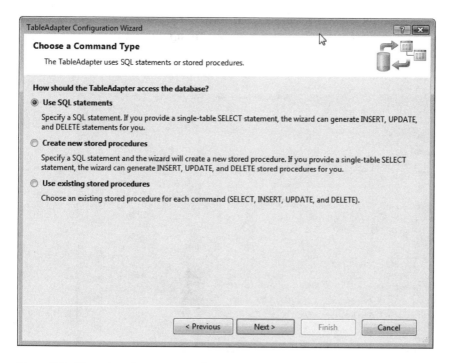

Figure 5-7. *Choosing the command type*

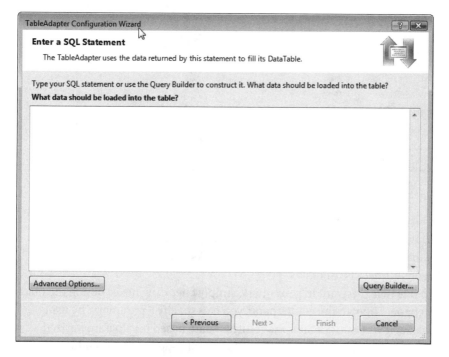

Figure 5-8. *Building your dynamic SQL statement*

You can manually type your SQL on this page (or cut and paste an existing known query), or you can use the Query Builder. Click the Query Builder button, and this builder will launch (see Figure 5-9).

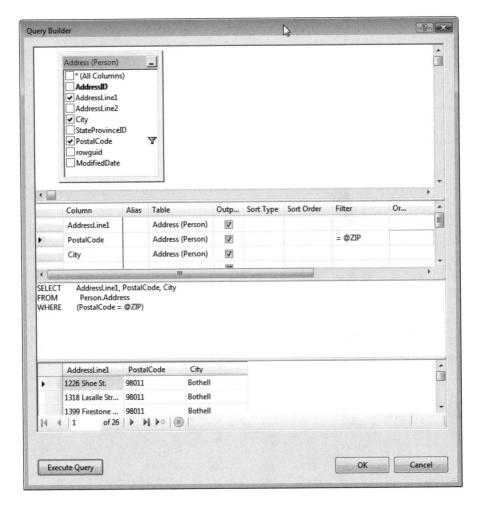

Figure 5-9. *The Query Builder*

The Query Builder dialog box enables you to visually create your query. First, select the tables that you want to add to your query and the links that join them. In this case, a single table, Person.Address, is used.

To pick the fields that you want in your query, simply check the boxes beside the field names in the top pane. Then, in the center pane, you can specify a parameter by using the Filter column. So, if you want to filter the returned data based on a parameterized postal code, you can place a filter called @ZIP on the PostalCode field. This embeds a parameter called ZIP in the SQL statement. Later, when you write your code for the query, you'll see how to use this parameter.

Your SQL can be viewed and tested at the bottom of the screen. You're now ready to hook this query up to your code and use it to expose the data from the database through the web service.

Click OK on the Query Builder and click Finish to exit the wizard. You now have a typed DataSet in your project, tied to the Person.Address table, that can be seen in the Designer (see Figure 5-10).

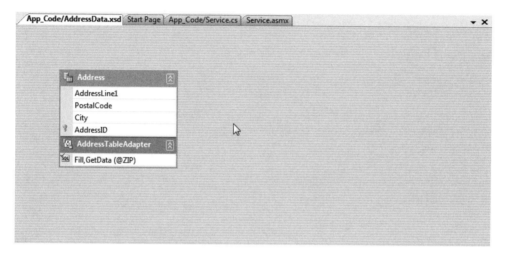

Figure 5-10. *Viewing the DataSet in the Designer*

The Designer shows you the fields that are available once you run the query, as well as the methods (Fill and GetData) that are available to the programmer to write to and read from the database, respectively.

Using the DataSet in a Web Method

To retrieve the data in a strongly typed DataSet, you use the corresponding *data adapter*. So, by creating a strongly typed DataSet, such as AddressData, you'll have a reference to the AddressDataTableAdapters collection. From this collection, you create an instance of an AddressTableAdapter, like this:

```
AddressDataTableAdapters.AddressTableAdapter da =
    new AddressDataTableAdapters.AddressTableAdapter();
```

This table adapter implements the Fill and GetData methods that enable you to write and read data from the table, respectively. Because we specified a parameter (@ZIP), the postal code value is passed as a parameter to the GetData method named strZIP.

This returns an `AddressDataTable` object, so you can instantiate a new object like this:

```
AddressData.AddressDataTable dt = da.GetData(strZIP);
```

You now have a data table containing the returned results from your query. However, you may not want to return this from your web method, because you may have clients written on J2EE, PHP, or other web technologies that will not be able to parse the `AddressDataTable` object (it is bound to ADO.NET and therefore .NET).

A better approach is to use well-formed XML to return your data. In this case, you are returning addresses to the client, so you can set up a class to store a specific address, and another to contain a list of addresses. Here's the code:

```
public class Address
{
    public string AddressLine1 = String.Empty;
    public string City = String.Empty;
    public string PostalCode = String.Empty;
    public int AddressID = -1;
}


public class Addresses : List<Address>
{
}
```

Now your web method can build this list of addresses with the data that was returned from the database query. You can see the code that implements this here:

```
[WebMethod]
public Addresses GetAddress(string strZIP)
{
    AddressDataSetTableAdapters.AddressTableAdapter da =
        new AddressDataSetTableAdapters.AddressTableAdapter();
    AddressDataSet.AddressDataTable dt = da.GetData(strZIP);

    Addresses addrs = new Addresses();
    foreach (AddressDataSet.AddressRow row in dt.Rows)
    {
        // Create a new Address object
        Address addr = new Address();

        // Assign the new address information
        addr.AddressID = row.AddressID;
        addr.AddressLine1 = row.AddressLine1;
```

```
        addr.City = row.City;
        addr.PostalCode = row.PostalCode;

        // Add to the list
        addrs.Add(addr);
    } // foreach

    return addrs;
}
```

This cycles through each row in the data table and creates an instance of the Address class with the data from that row. It then adds this instance to the list of addresses. Once the loop is complete (i.e., when you've iterated through each row), the list is returned to the caller.

Figure 5-11 shows the results of running this web method in its test page.

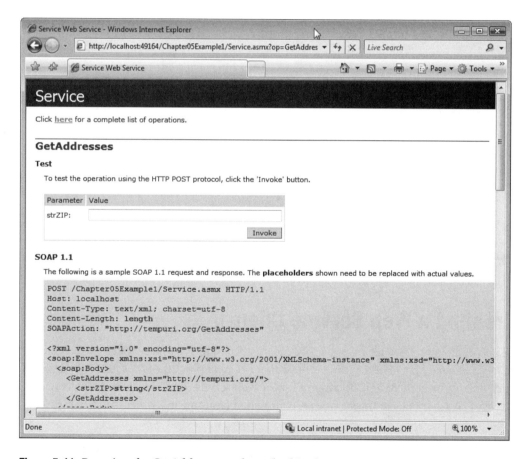

Figure 5-11. *Running the GetAddresses web method in the test page*

You can type a postal code into the field on this form and click Invoke. You'll get the results of the query, formatted as XML, returned to you (see Figure 5-12). Web service clients can now consume this XML and render it as they please.

Figure 5-12. *The XML returned from the web service*

Creating a Web Service Client

Visual Studio offers you a convenient way to create clients for web services via a facility called *web references*. When adding a web reference, you point the IDE's Add Web Reference dialog box at the WSDL document for the web service, and Visual Studio will create a proxy class that talks to the service on your behalf (you saw this process in Chapter 2).

In order to add a web reference, and therefore use the underlying web service, the first thing you'll need is the WSDL for your web service. You can get this by appending ?WSDL to the URL of your service if it is an ASP.NET web service (the mechanism for other services varies and is beyond the scope of this chapter to describe). For example, if your service's endpoint is located at http://url/Service.asmx, you can get the WSDL by using the URL http://url/Service.asmx?WSDL.

Knowing this, you can create a client web site, a Windows application, or another web service to easily consume this service. From your project, right-click the project name in the Solution Explorer and select Add Web Reference. You'll see the Add Web Reference dialog box, as in Figure 5-13. Use the URL field to enter the URL of the WSDL file, and then click Go.

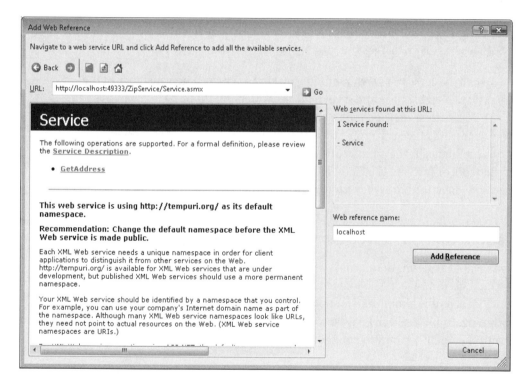

Figure 5-13. *Adding a web reference*

Once the IDE parses the WSDL, the list of methods will be displayed, and the web reference name will be given a default value. It's a good idea to change this name to something more meaningful before you click Add Reference.

Clicking the Add Reference button will then generate the proxy classes that communicate to the web service and get the results on your behalf. Communication with an XML web service is via SOAP, so your request is serialized into a SOAP message, which is then posted to the web service. The web service cracks open this message, parses out the method request and parameters, executes the method, and serializes the results back into a SOAP document for return. This document is then returned to the caller. When you use a proxy, the hard work of encoding the request and decoding the response is done for you by the proxy and its underlying infrastructure (provided by the .NET Framework). All you see is a (local) method signature for the web method. Having this capability provided for you by the .NET Framework saves you a lot of code and potential bugs!

To call this web service (assuming the web reference name was changed to Address-Data), you can simply reference the proxy like this:

```
AddressData.Service myAdr = new AddressData.Service();
AddressData.Address[] theAdrs = myAdr.GetAddress("90210");
```

To call the GetAddress web method, you simply create a new instance of the AddressData.Service class and invoke the GetAddress method.

The GetAddress method took a string containing the postal code and returned an array of Address objects, so you can simply assign a new array of addresses to the return of this method call. The complexities of handling SOAP to call the distant service over the network or Internet is all handled for you, allowing your code to look just like it was accessing data from your local computer.

Data Binding in a Web Service

If you want to use this data in data binding to a GUI control such as a GridView control, you do it via the ObjectDataSource control. You can find this control on the Data tab of your Visual Studio Toolbox. Before placing it on the design surface, add a TextBox and a Button control. These will be used to pass parameters to the ObjectDataSource control at runtime. You'll see how to configure these using the ObjectDataSource wizard a little later.

When you first place the ObjectDataSource control on the design surface, you'll see the control adorner, which gives you the option to configure the data source (see Figure 5-14).

Figure 5-14. *Placing an ObjectDataSource*

If you select the Configure Data Source link, you will be taken into the wizard that allows you to configure the data source for the ObjectDataSource control. As this project is using a table adapter for the address database, you'll see this as an option in your business objects. However, you won't see the web service unless you uncheck the "Show only data components" check box. Once you've done this, you can select your web service (i.e., AddressData.Service). See Figure 5-15.

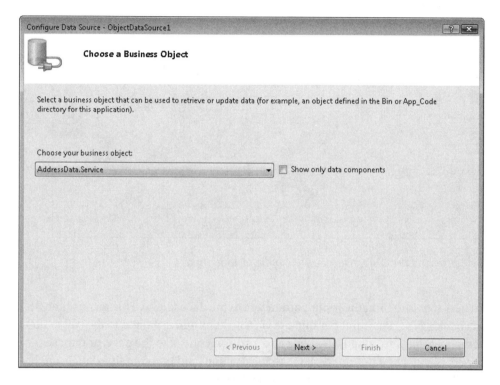

Figure 5-15. *Configuring the business object for your ObjectDataSource control*

The next step is to select the data method that this ObjectDataSource control is going to use. You can select, update, insert, or delete using this control, but in your case you're reading the response from a web service, so you use the Select tab and choose the GetAddress web method that was created earlier. You can see this in Figure 5-16.

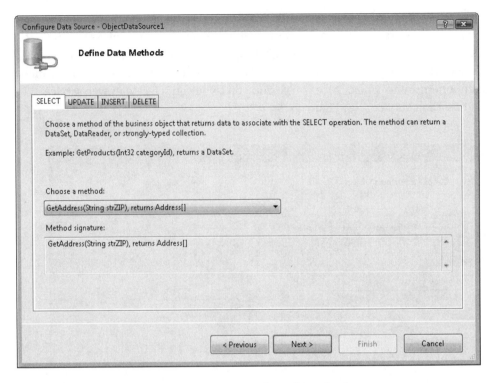

Figure 5-16. *Binding the ObjectDataSource to the web method*

The next step is to bind the input parameters to the data source. This means that you can codelessly accept input parameters via a text box and use them in the call to the web method. Earlier you added a text box and a button control to the page, and these will be used. Clicking the button triggers the form action, and this contains data from the text box. As a result, you should specify Form as the parameter source, and the text box as the form field that contains the parameter data. The default text box name is TextBox1, so if you didn't change the name of the text box, you would use this name, as shown in Figure 5-17.

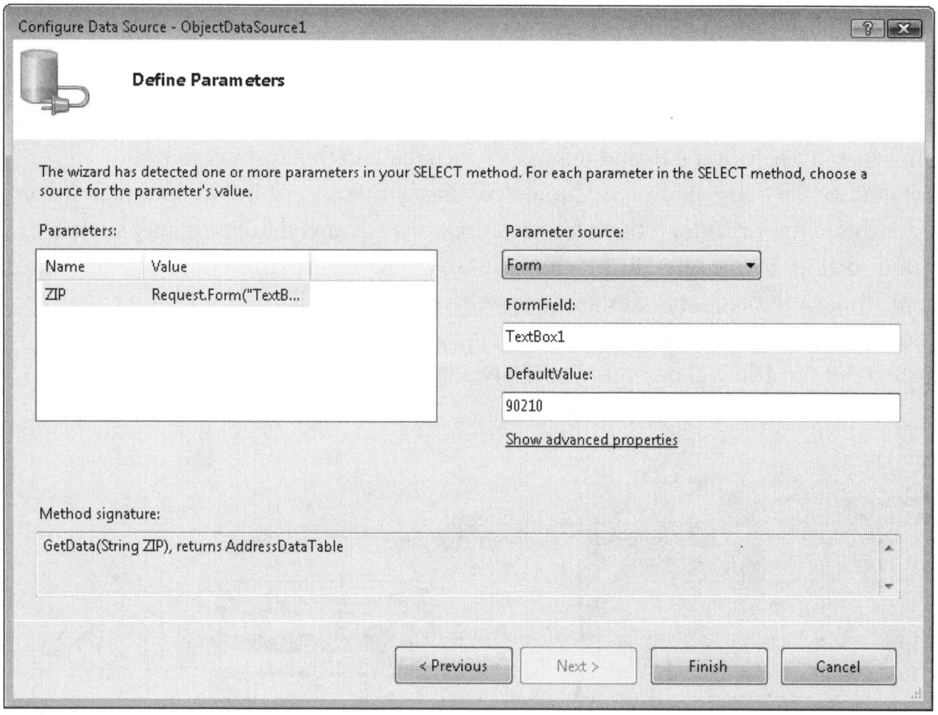

Figure 5-17. *Binding the input parameters*

Next, finish the wizard, and the ASP.NET code for the ObjectDataSource and form
bindings will be generated for you. It should look something like this:

```
<form id="form1" runat="server">
<div>
  <asp:TextBox ID="TextBox1" runat="server"></asp:TextBox>
  <asp:Button ID="Button1" runat="server" Text="Button" />
  <asp:ObjectDataSource ID="ObjectDataSource1" runat="server"
      SelectMethod="GetAddress"
      TypeName="AddressData.Service">
      <selectparameters>
          <asp:formparameter DefaultValue="90210"
              FormField="TextBox1" Name="ZIP"
              Type="String" />
      </selectparameters>
  </asp:ObjectDataSource>
</div>
</form>
```

You can see here how the `<asp:ObjectDataSource>` uses the `TypeName` parameter to set up the web service binding and the `SelectMethod` to configure the method that it will call on this service. As we are running a Select (i.e., a read-only query) from this web service, the `<selectparameters>` child is present. This contains an `<asp:formparameter>` node, which configures the name, form field, and default value to call on this web service.

Now that we have the binding set up, we can easily place a control to bind to. A great control for this is the GridView control, which provides advanced functionality such as paging and sorting. To use one, simply drag the GridView control from the Data tab on the Visual Studio Toolbox to the design surface. The adorner will open, and you can use this to configure the data source. Select the ObjectDataSource control that you configured earlier and the grid will be bound to it (see Figure 5-18).

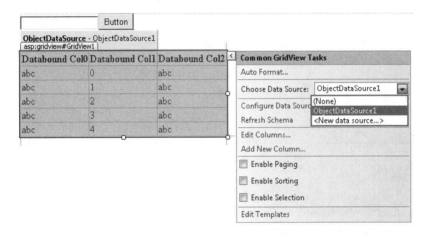

Figure 5-18. *Data binding a grid to a web service via an ObjectDataSource*

If you now execute the application, the grid will bind to the web service and render the data for the default parameter. You can also type new parameters into the text box and click the button, and they will be fetched and rendered for you. And this was all achieved without writing a single line of code on the client!

Summary

This chapter introduced you to web services and their architecture. You looked at the theory of web services and how the group of technologies—HTTP, SOAP, XML, and WSDL—are used in the Web Services ecosystem. You then looked into how to create a web service using Visual Studio and Visual Web Developer Express. You looked into how to tie a web service to databases using DataSets, and finally you built a web service client by using the IDE to access the WSDL document for your web service to generate a proxy class. This client then consumed the data and used it in a data-binding scenario with a GridView control.

CHAPTER 6

■■■

Deploying Your Web Site

In this chapter, you will look at an important step in your application life cycle—deploying it to a web server and ensuring that it works post-deployment. You will look at Microsoft Windows Server 2003 and how to use it to run IIS to serve your application. Deployment involves a lot more than just copying your application to the target server. You'll need to configure the server, configure security scenarios, add dependencies, configure data connections, fine-tune your server performance, and a whole lot more besides!

In IIS, you use the concept of a *virtual directory* to run your application. A virtual directory maps a URL (Universal Resource Locator, or in other words, the Internet address for the page you're about to display) to a physical directory handled by IIS. For example, if you have a directory C:\MyApp on your server, you can configure IIS to treat this as a web application by configuring it as a virtual directory. The virtual directory will then be accessed from the browser through http://url/<virtual_directory_name.

You'll look at how this and many of the other features of IIS work, and how you can configure them. You'll also look into how you can deploy your ASP.NET applications.

Internet Information Services

At the heart of running web applications and sites on the Windows technology stack is IIS. This is a Windows service that is responsible for managing the servicing of requests on a number of IP ports, typically including 80 (HTTP), 443 (HTTPS), and 21 (FTP). When this service is running, requests on the configured ports are handled by this service.

The service allows for multiple web sites to be configured on the same server, with traffic being directed based on settings in the IIS Manager tool. By default, one web site is configured, serviced from port 80.

You can see IIS Manager in Figure 6-1. This tool is accessible from the Administrative Tools folder.

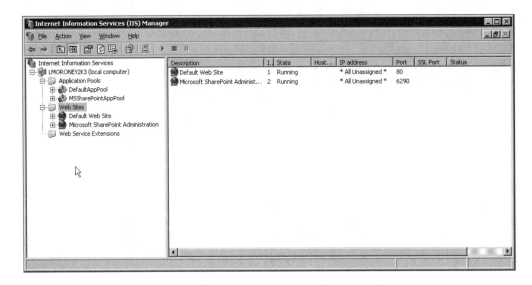

Figure 6-1. *IIS Manager*

Within IIS Manager, you will see the default web site, as in Figure 6-1. This web site is the entire site that manages a number of web applications. You can create and manage sites from here.

IIS 7.0

While this chapter covers IIS 6.x, Windows Server 2008 will have a new version of IIS, version 7.0, which has the following enhanced features:

- Fully customizable install that allows you to reduce your attack surface, footprint, and patching

- Automatic sandboxing of new sites

- XCopy deployment and a new simplified configuration system

- Easy sharing of configuration information across servers in a web farm

- Updated diagnostics and troubleshooting tools

More details can be found at the Windows Sever 2008 site at www.microsoft.com/windowsserver2008/default.mspx.

Creating Web Sites and Applications with IIS Manager

If you right-click the Default Web Site node, you will get a context menu with a selection of available actions. From these, you can create a new web site, which is a whole new site to be managed by IIS. This has to operate on a unique Transmission Control protocol/Internet protocol (TCP/IP) port. So, for example, if your default web site is running on port 80, and you want to run a new site, you'll have to put it to a different unused port. Doing so will also enable you to create a new virtual directory, which is an application that will run on your existing site. Finally, you can create (FrontPage) Server Extensions Web and Administration sites, which provide browser-based configuration of your server, as well as external access and control. You can see this in Figure 6-2.

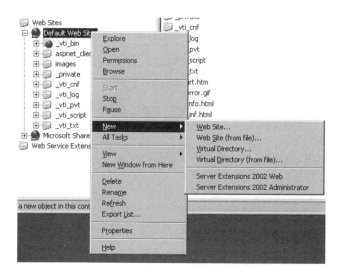

Figure 6-2. *Web site actions*

To create a new application on your existing site, select Virtual Directory from the context menu. This will launch the Virtual Directory wizard. The first step (see Figure 6-3) is to give your virtual directory a name. This is the name of the context root (URL) that the browser will use when accessing your application. So, for example, if you use the name Chapter6Test as the virtual directory, your users will access the application using http://servername/Chapter6Test.

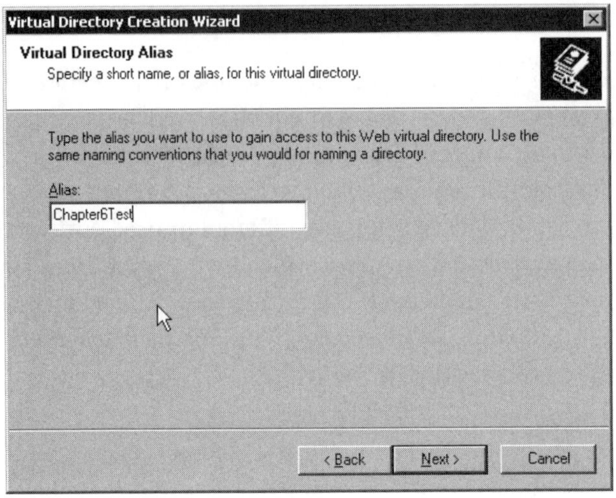

Figure 6-3. *Configuring the virtual directory name*

The next step is to configure the *physical* path on your hard drive to where the files for this web application will be stored. This can have the same name as the virtual directory, but this is not necessary. The location can be anywhere on your drive, but the typical location for web content is under C:\InetPub\wwwroot. You can see this step in Figure 6-4.

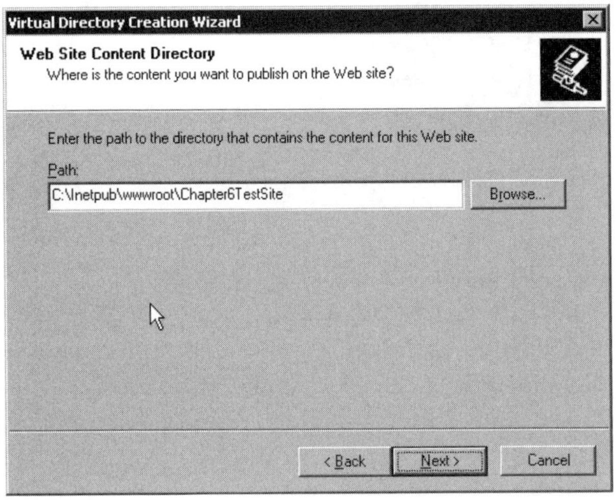

Figure 6-4. *Configuring the physical directory*

The next step is to set the access permissions for users accessing your site (see Figure 6-5). By default, only the Read setting is checked, which means that users can read supported files hosted by your site. Supported files include HTML pages, text files, and other files as configured using IIS Manager—including files with an `.aspx` extension, perhaps!

If you are planning on using scripts such as ASP, ASP.NET, or PHP on your site, the "Run scripts" check box should be selected, too.

Some older technologies for active web content, such as Internet Server Application Programming Interface (ISAPI) and CGI, can also be supported by IIS. These involve compiled, executable files, and should you need to use these, you can configure the server to allow for their execution by selecting the Execute check box.

If you want to allow the user to upload files to this directory, select the Write check box. By default, this is disabled for security reasons. You'll want to be careful when using this setting for obvious reasons.

Finally, if you want to allow users to browse your site and retrieve a listing of the pages in the site and its subdirectories when they do not specify a page, then you should select the Browse check box. You should also use the Browse option for creating sites where no default page exists.

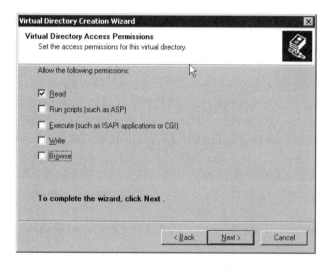

Figure 6-5. *Virtual directory access permissions*

The wizard will complete, and your virtual directory will be ready, but empty.

Add a new text file to the directory by using IIS Manager or Windows Explorer. Call it `test.htm` and give it the following contents:

```
<html>
  <body>
   <h1>My HTML Page</h1>
  </body>
</html>
```

Now, from a browser, you can call `http://serverIP/Chapter6Test/test.htm` or `http://serverurl/Chapter6Test/test.htm`, and the browser will render a page according to the instructions in the preceding HTML code. You can see this in Figure 6-6 where the IP address of the server is used.

Figure 6-6. *Viewing your page*

How IIS Handles URLs

As you can see from the preceding example, the user types a URL into the browser, and IIS serves the HTML page in response to their request. The HTML code is then rendered by the browser as shown in Figure 6-6.

When IIS received this request, the first thing it did was to examine this URL and establish the location of the content. First, it recognized that no port was specified on the URL, so it used port 80, which is the standard (default) HTTP port. If this server had been running on port 81, for example, then the URL of the server should be postfixed with `:81`, like this: `http://servername:81/`.

It then decodes the virtual directory and/or subdirectories that determine where the content is located. In the preceding example, the URL dictated that the content should be found in Chapter6Test, which is a virtual directory that maps to `C:\InetPub\wwwroot\Chapter6TestSite` for this example.

Finally, at the end of the URL is the content itself, which in this case is `test.htm`. If this content is present in the specified location, it will be rendered and the resulting content returned to the requesting user. Note that if you want to deliver nonstandard web content, you will have to specify its Multipurpose Internet Mail Extensions (MIME) type by using IIS Manager. Later in this book, you'll use Extensible Application Markup Language (XAML), which is a variant of XML that is used to deliver graphical information. This is an example of a MIME type that you'll to need add for the server to recognize it as a valid content request. If you don't, IIS and its default security lockdowns will prevent you from serving resources with nonstandard content.

To manage the served MIME types, select Properties for the site, and then select the HTTP Headers tab (see Figure 6-7).

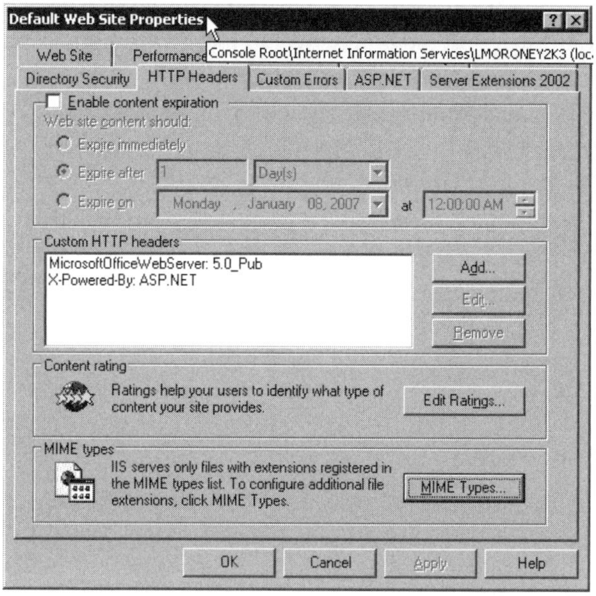

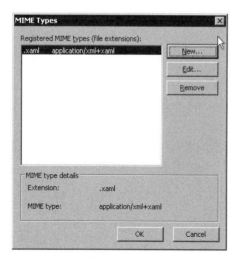

Figure 6-7. *HTTP headers configuration for the site*

On this dialog box, you can click the MIME Types button to invoke the MIME Types dialog box, which can be used to add, remove, or edit registered MIME types (see Figure 6-8).

Figure 6-8. *Configuring the MIME types*

The MIME type for XAML is application/xml+xaml, which you can see configured in Figure 6-8.

In addition to automatically serving configured MIME types, IIS sometimes uses ISAPI filters to process specific file types. In the previous example, you were serving an HTML file, which is a static file that is simply rendered and delivered to the browser. However, if you are instead serving an ASPX page, as in earlier chapters, to return this type of resource the server runs an ISAPI extension that is assigned to requests for content with the .aspx extension. It then receives the response from the ISAPI extension as HTML and dispatches it back to the client.

Here's an example of a simple ASPX web page. Save it in a file called Test.aspx in the same folder you used earlier (i.e., C:\InetPub\wwwroot\Chapter6TestSite).

```
<%@ Page Language="C#" %>

<!DOCTYPE html PUBLIC "-//W3C//DTD XHTML 1.0 Transitional//EN"

  "http://www.w3.org/TR/xhtml1/DTD/xhtml1-transitional.dtd">

<script runat="server">

</script>

<html xmlns="http://www.w3.org/1999/xhtml" >
<head runat="server">
  <title>Untitled Page</title>
</head>
<body>
  <form id="form1" runat="server">
  <div>
  <% Response.Write(System.DateTime.Now.ToString()); %>
  </div>
  </form>
</body>
</html>
```

When you use the browser to navigate to this file, the C# code will execute and ASP.NET will generate HTML containing the current time and date. You can see this in Figure 6-9.

Figure 6-9. *Viewing the ASPX page*

Note that you will need execute permissions on the virtual web to be able to run the script code. You can set up these permissions by right-clicking the virtual web in IIS Manager, selecting Properties, and then viewing the Virtual Directory tab in the Properties dialog box. At the bottom of the screen, you'll see the "Execute permissions" drop-down list, which should read "Scripts only" or "Scripts and executables" (see Figure 6-10).

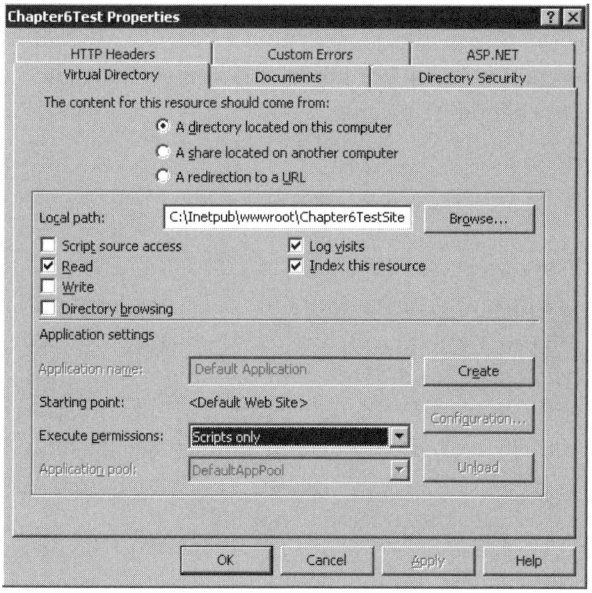

Figure 6-10. *Setting the execute permissions for ASP.NET files*

You can see the registered handlers for various file extensions in IIS Manager. To view the configured handlers, select your web site (e.g., "Default Web Site") in IIS Manager, right-click it, and select Properties. In the Properties dialog box, select the Home Directory tab and then select Configuration. The Application Configuration dialog box will appear (see Figure 6-11).

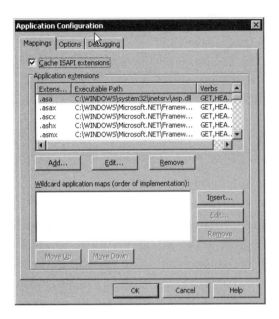

Figure 6-11. *Managing your application extensions*

You can browse through the settings in this dialog box to see the handlers for each file type. For example, the ASPX file type is handled by `aspnet_isapi.dll`.

Side-by-Side Execution

There are several versions of the .NET Framework available: 1.0, 1.1, 2.0, 3.0, and 3.5. These are installed in separate directories in your primary Windows folder (the location of which varies by operating system). You may have noticed that the Application Configuration dialog box is a property of the *virtual directory* and not of the machine itself. Thus, you can specify different versions of `aspnet_isapi.dll` to handle each site. Therefore, you can configure a site in one virtual directory to use ASP.NET 2.0 and another site in a different virtual directory to use ASP.NET 3.0.

Thus, a single web server isn't bound to a specific version of ASP.NET.

Manually Deploying Your ASP.NET Applications

Because ASP.NET 2.0 has a runtime compilation model, deployment is a lot easier than in previous versions of ASP.NET—for simple applications, you just deploy your ASPX and code-behind files, and the web server handles the rest.

However, many applications may have more artifacts than just these files. For example, you may be using a database and need to configure the connection for the server; in your code, you may be using a third-party assembly for which you don't have the source code; or you may need to set custom permissions on the server.

Each application has different requirements, but in general, if you follow these steps, your application will work on your server.

The first step is to configure your database and database connections to the server-side deployment database.

Next, add your application code to the server. If it is a multitier application, you should do this tier by tier, starting with the tiers that are closest to the database. Deploy the first tier, update the references from the tier below it, unit test, and continue.

As part of this process, you may encounter a situation in which you are using third-party components that you don't have the source code for. You'll have to make sure that these components are installed, configured, and referenced correctly in your runtime code. Each component has its own nuances, so it's best to work with its documentation at this stage. For example, if you are using a charting component that uses a SQL Server database for caching, you'll have to install it on your server, configure it for database access, and then reference it in your application. This type of process is usually well documented in the third-party component's deployment instructions.

Finally, you configure IIS if necessary. You may need to look into advanced IIS topics that are beyond the scope of this book, such as application pooling, which helps you to isolate ASP.NET applications from each other and increase their overall reliability.

Configuring the server and deploying an application to it is best illustrated by example, so as you proceed through this chapter, you'll take a look at what is involved in deploying the multitier application that provided the addresses from the Adventure-Works database to the browser that you built in Chapter 5. You didn't make any changes to the database structure or contents, so you don't need to deploy any new database information. But if you had, you would of course have to make sure that the database on the server matches the one in your development environment.

APPLICATION POOLING

One really nice feature of IIS is the facility to provide and use application pools. An application pool can contain a number of applications, and it allows you to configure levels of isolation between different web applications. For example, if you want to isolate each ASP.NET application on your web server from every other one, you could create a separate application pool for each one, and then place your applications in them. As each application pool runs in its own worker process, an error in one application will not affect others.

Configuring Your Data Connections

Remember, your web service is connected to your database, so the first step is to change the web service connection from pointing to your local database to pointing to the server-based one. You do this by changing the connection string.

Earlier, you had a connection string that looked like this:

```
Data Source=localhost\SQLExpress;Initial Catalog=AdventureWorks;
Integrated Security=True
```

You should change it to look like this:

```
Data Source=servername\SQLExpress;Initial Catalog=AdventureWorks;
Integrated Security=True
```

You may face some issues when trying to connect to this remote database. The most common ones will be that SQL Server isn't configured for remote access and that the server firewall isn't permitting the SQL Server traffic to pass.

You'll see how to resolve these issues in the next sections.

Configuring SQL Server for Remote TCP/IP Access

SQL Server is configured using SQL Server Configuration Manager. From here, you can control the services, the native client, and the network configuration.

On the network configuration screen (see Figure 6-12), you should make sure that the TCP service is enabled *and* running.

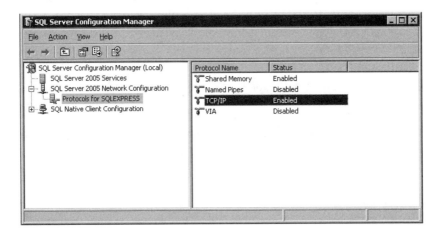

Figure 6-12. *SQL Server Configuration Manager*

It's a common trap to think that the TCP service is enabled and actively running based on the fact that it shows up as enabled on this screen. However, you should double-click it to get the TCP/IP Properties dialog box (see Figure 6-13), and make sure that both the Active and Enabled properties are set to Yes.

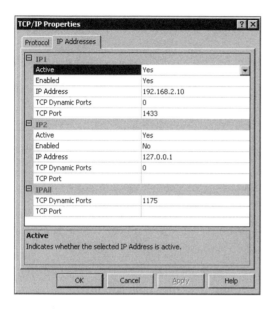

Figure 6-13. *TCP/IP properties for SQL Server*

You'll also have to make sure that port 1433 is open on the firewall of both your web and database servers to be able to communicate.

Configuring SQL Server Security

Now, recall your connection string that you've been using to connect to the database. When it came to logging in, the connection string specified something known as *integrated security*. Integrated security means you'll log into the database as a Windows user, which ultimately means the username and password necessary to access the database do not require encoding in the connection string. This is more secure since Windows is handling the authentication credentials for you.

Most likely, however, logging in remotely will not work in this situation. Quite often, the database server and the web server aren't on the same computer. ASP.NET will execute using the Windows user account ASPNET, which probably doesn't exist on the database server. Unless the ASP.NET worker process (ASPNET) is configured as a user on the database server, or unless you've configured a Windows domain account that's shared by both computers, you'll probably be relegated to using SQL Sign-In to access the database.

This, in turn, means you'll need to place a valid database username and password in your connection string.

You can configure existing Windows users or add new database users to SQL Server directly from within the management console (see Figure 6-14).

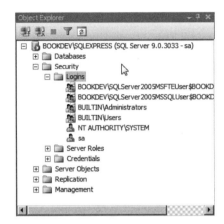

Figure 6-14. *Database user administration*

From Object Explorer, open the Security node and then the Logins node to see the presently configured users. You can add a new user by right-clicking the Logins folder and selecting New Login from the context menu. This takes you to a sophisticated user login dialog box. You can use this to create a new user—for example, you can set up the user WebServiceUser by entering this as their login name and then configuring a password (see Figure 6-15). For the sake of example, use WebServiceUser as the password, too.

You have the option of setting up either a Windows authentication or a SQL Server authentication login. For the former, pick an existing Windows user on the system and then establish their database access. The ASP.NET worker process is a Windows user, so you can configure its access to the database in this manner.

The second option is to use a SQL Server login. In this case, you specify the user's name and password as well as their password policy. Because this isn't going to be a manual login (your application will be logging in), make sure you deselect the "User must change password at next login" check box.

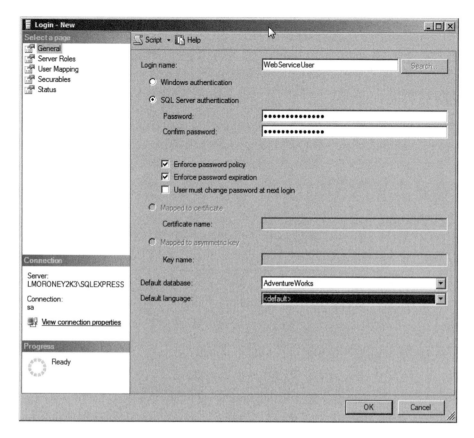

Figure 6-15. *Creating a new database login*

This process simply creates the database login. SQL Server will also require the user you just created to be associated with a specific database. To enable the user to access the AdventureWorks database, you have to authorize this new user to access that database. You don't want every user to be able to access every database, particularly in a large, multi-application environment, so you assign specific users to specific databases using SQL Server Configuration Manager.

To do this, find the database in Object Explorer and expand it until you see the Users node (see Figure 6-16).

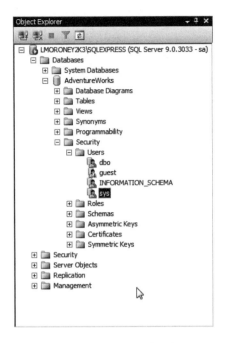

Figure 6-16. *Configuring database users*

At this point, Object Explorer shows the list of approved database users and their associated login accounts that are configured to have access to the database. Windows usernames will be prefixed by either the machine name or the domain name. So, users on the domain MyDomain will appear as MYDOMAIN\username. Similarly, a user from a machine called DBServer will be prefixed DBServer\username.

To add your new WebServiceUser login to the database, right-click the Users folder and select New User. The Database Users – New dialog box will then appear (see Figure 6-17).

In this dialog box, you can (for this database only) change the user's name by assigning a different name to the user's login account. This is known as *aliasing*. To avoid confusion, I recommend keeping the database user access name the same as the user's SQL Server login name. For example, if you created a SQL Server user called WebService-User, then you should also use WebServiceUser as the username for accessing the database in the Database Users – New dialog box (as I've shown in Figure 6-17).

You'll also need to assign the user a role or roles when you authorize them to access a given database. For security reasons, I recommended you give them the minimum amount of control that they need to get their job done. In this case, we know the web service is just reading data, so the db_datareader role is selected.

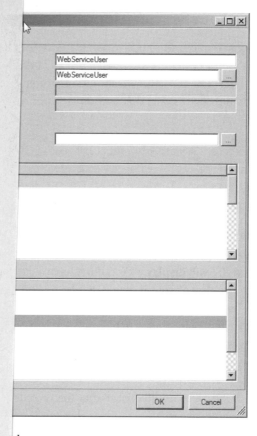

Figure 6-17. Adding a user to your database

By this point, you should be able to sign into the database that resides on your database server from the web service that resides on your web development system by changing the connection string to use the user you just created:

```
Data Source=SERVERNAME\SQLExpress;Initial Catalog=AdventureWorks;
user id=WebServiceUser;password=WebServiceUser
```

Do note here that storing your password in clear text in Web.config like this is a bad idea and a major security risk. In any real environment, you should encrypt the password. This is beyond the scope of this tutorial, but a great reference for how to handle encryption of sections of Web.config can be found here: http://msdn2.microsoft.com/en-us/library/dtkwfdky.aspx.

Deploying Your Service Tier

The best way to deploy your application is to use the IDE to deploy it directly to the server. Visual Studio will perform most if not all of the IIS administration for you if you do.

Before deploying, though, you should once again edit your Web.config file. You'll see that in the default Web.config, this section is commented out. You should remove the comments:

```
<customErrors mode="RemoteOnly" defaultRedirect="GenericErrorPage.htm">
   <error statusCode="403" redirect="NoAccess.htm" />
   <error statusCode="404" redirect="FileNotFound.htm" />
</customErrors>
```

These lines configure how your ASP.NET application will deal with specific errors. In this case, if the user attempts to access something on your web site they shouldn't, ASP.NET (and IIS) will display a "You don't have access to that resource" error page. If the resource simply isn't found, it will display a "File not found" error page. These pages come as part of ASP.NET, but feel free to provide your own. Just replace the page file names you see here with the page file names of the pages you create, and ASP.NET will use your pages. You can add other error pages as well, following the same model. Just add the HTTP error code in the statusCode attribute and the page file name in the redirect attribute, as shown here.

Note also that you should ensure that the <compilation> setting in Web.config is set to turn off debugging, like this:

```
<compilation debug="false">
</compilation>
```

Once the Web.config file is ready, you then use the Copy Web Site tool on the Web Sites menu to access the deployment tool (see Figure 6-18).

At the top of the screen, you'll see a Connect button. Click this to specify the server that you want to connect to. One helpful feature is that if you specify an IIS server and a URL containing a subdirectory, IIS will automatically create the virtual web directory for you. So for example, if you want to deploy the web service to a virtual web directory called ServiceTier, you simply add it to the URL of the server you want to open and then click New Web Site (see Figure 6-19).

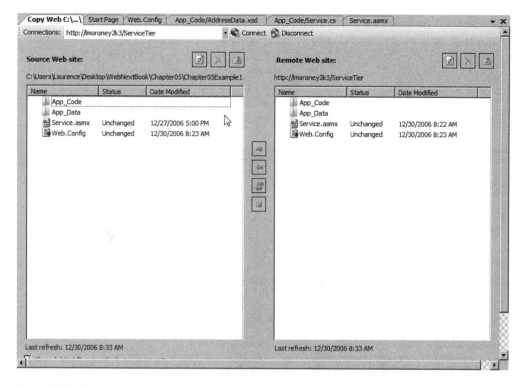

Figure 6-18. *Copy Web Site tool*

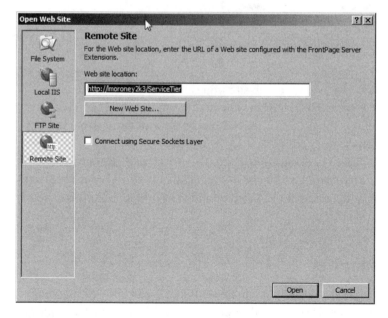

Figure 6-19. *Creating a remote web site*

Finally, the most common problem when deploying an application like this involves mismatched ASP.NET versions. If your server is configured for ASP.NET 1.1 (as Windows Server 2003 will be by default) but your application was written to use ASP.NET 2.0, your application will fail once deployed. Check IIS Manager on the server and ensure that ASP.NET 2.x is configured. You can see this in Figure 6-20, where ASP.NET Version 2.0 is selected.

Figure 6-20. *Setting the ASP.NET version on the server*

Once you copy your files to the remote web site, you can launch your site to test your pages. You'll notice with a web service that when you view it remotely, you cannot access its test page. Don't worry, this is intentional. ASP.NET blocks the automatic generation of this page for security reasons.

For similar reasons, if you're browsing remotely and your web page sustains an exception, you will not see any exception details. To debug this situation, open a browser on the server machine rather than a remote computer and view the site from there—you'll get a more meaningful error page.

Deploying Your Client Tier

Before you deploy your client tier, you should remember that it is currently configured with a service reference to the service on your development machine. When you deploy it to the server, it will then refer back to the development machine, which isn't what you want it to do! So, the first thing you should do is update your client references to your newly deployed service tier on your server.

When you originally built the client tier, you added a web reference to the server running on the Visual Studio development web server, Cassini. The important thing to remember to prevent breaking your code is the name that you gave the reference. Looking back through Chapter 5, you'll note we named the web reference AddressData. This is because once you remove the reference, the proxy class will be destroyed, your code will no longer recognize it, and your code will thus not compile. When you create the new web reference to the deployed service, should you give it the same name, then a new proxy class with that name will be created, and your code will compile again.

To destroy the reference, right-click AddressData in the Solution Explorer and then select Delete (see Figure 6-21).

Figure 6-21. *Removing the web reference*

Now you just need to find the WSDL of your deployed service, which will look something like this:

```
http://server/servicetier/service.asmx?WSDL
```

(If you created the virtual web service tier on the server when deploying the service in the last step, you'll have this URL. Otherwise, use the virtual web that you created.) Remember to use AddressData as the name of the new service reference, and your client should be ready to deploy.

Now, deployment is simply a matter of using the Copy Web Site tool as you did in the previous section (Figure 6-18) to add your site to the server. At this point, your server should have a ServiceClient web site that contains your client. This references a web service on the ServiceTier web site, which wraps the database access. You can now call your service client by using your browser and pointing it to the new web site. Here's an example:

```
http://server/serviceclient/default.aspx?ZIP=90210
```

You can see the results in Figure 6-22—note that in this case the server name is lmoroney2k3.

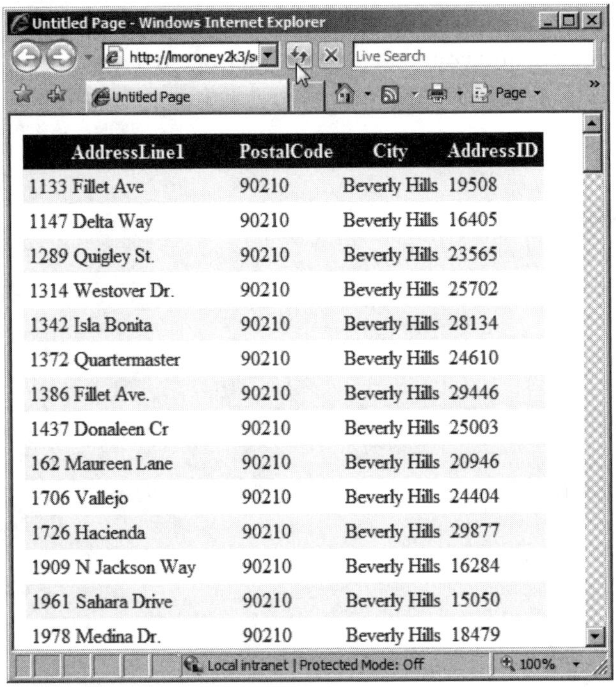

Figure 6-22. *Running the deployed application*

Summary

An integral part of any application development life cycle is deploying the application and ensuring that it works once deployed. The Microsoft suite of development tools is designed for maximum consistency between the development environment and the deployment environment, but you will always encounter minor differences between these environments. For example, in development, you'll likely use the Cassini web server, which provides dynamic port assignment. Alternatively, in production, you'll want to use IIS, which has a fixed port (usually port 80) for your web applications. You'll also face different database configuration issues (e.g., using SQL Server Enterprise as opposed to Express), but all of these tools have been carefully designed to minimize the impact on deployment.

In this chapter, you looked at the deployment environment, using IIS and SQL Server on Windows 2003, and what it takes to move a multitier application from the development environment to the deployment one. The scenario we explored in this chapter took a hands-on approach, covering most of what you'll likely encounter in a real-world deployment.

You followed a data-down deployment process, first configuring the database on the server (i.e., installing AdventureWorks), and then adding the required credentials for your application to sign into the database. If this isn't deployed on your server already, go back to Chapter 4 and follow the steps there. You then had your development-based service sign into this database to ensure that it worked. Once this was achieved, you deployed your service to the server. Once that was ready, you changed your client to point to this service. Finally, you deployed your client web application to the server and made it available to all users who can access the web server.

This chapter showed the power and flexibility of IIS and Windows as a web server environment and how easy it is to build your applications and make them ready for public consumption. Going beyond what you've learned in this chapter, you can look into advanced server configuration, creating application pools and health monitoring, tweaking the compilation models, using FTP and security, and much more. Many excellent resources are available on these topics, both in book form (an excellent example being *Internet Information Services 6.0 Resource Kit*, from Microsoft Press) and as Internet resources, including, for example, MSDN (`http://msdn2.microsoft.com`) and TechNet (`http://technet.microsoft.com`).

PART 2

■ ■ ■

Next Generation Technologies for Web Development

CHAPTER 7

■■■

.NET 3.0: Windows Communication Foundation

Windows Communication Foundation (WCF), formerly known as Indigo, is the next-generation unified framework for building applications that are secure and reliable, supporting transactions and providing standards-based interoperability.

WCF as a technology is primarily intended for *connected* applications, be they connected across the Internet, inside the corporate firewall, or even on your machine. At the heart of this imperative is interoperability and integration. When systems work as decoupled, connected systems, the interfaces and interaction between them needs to be secure—bytes flying across the wire can be sniffed and compromised by malicious users. They need to be reliable—communications breakdowns shouldn't cause the application to break, but instead should be handled gracefully. They also need to be transacted, with batches of communications being managed by the framework so that each node in the communication network has the best, freshest data available to it. When these three goals are met, then the desirable goal of dynamic, decoupled, connected applications becomes possible.

Prior to .NET 3.0 and WCF, there were many technologies that would help the developer to achieve these goals. Messaging systems could provide reliable message delivery, database systems could provide support for transactions and standards for security, and security products could secure your messaging and your web services. But a plethora of APIs and skills were needed to achieve these goals, and in many cases, expensive third parties would have to be involved, making the overall cost-benefit ratio suffer. With WCF, the development APIs for services, Remoting, messaging, and more have been taken under one hood—and the runtime environment for them is the freely available .NET Framework 3.0. Thus, the possibilities of meeting the goals and being productive are greater than ever before.

WCF and Productivity

As mentioned earlier, there are many technologies available for building distributed applications. From Microsoft alone, you can use COM+, .NET Enterprise Services, MSMQ, .NET Remoting, Web Services, and Web Services Enhancements (WSE), to name just a few. Each of these requires different domain knowledge and different programming skills.

WCF incorporates all of these into a single programming model, reducing this overall complexity and making it easier for the developer to focus on the business logic that you are paid to produce. Additionally, this allows you to combine each of these technologies into an application in ways that may not be possible today. As you work through this chapter, you'll see how, through configuration changes in .config files, you will be able to finely control different services that may have required reams of code before WCF!

Figure 7-1 shows the pre-WCF stack of technologies that can be used to build connected applications.

These technologies are described in the following list:

ASMX Web Services: You've used this throughout this book. It is a technology that makes web services easy to implement and deploy. It includes the basic Web Services technology and interoperability stack, allowing for stateless connected applications that use SOAP to communicate with clients and servers on Microsoft or other technology stacks.

WSE: As web services have evolved, so have the standards that implement them. New requirements have brought about new standards in security, addressing, and more. Microsoft continually updates WSE to bring these standards to ASMX services.

Messaging: The System.Messaging namespace in the .NET Framework allows programmatic access to Microsoft Message Queuing (MSMQ). This allows developers to build messaging-oriented middleware applications where reliable delivery of messages between systems is paramount.

Remoting: The System.Remoting namespace in the .NET Framework allows object sharing across the network, giving remote users access to application classes, objects, and more. This also provides location transparency, easing distributed application development.

Enterprise Services: The System.EnterpriseServices namespace in the .NET Framework allows programmatic access to a set of classes that allow you to build enterprise-grade applications that use COM+ to support critical systems functionality such as transactions.

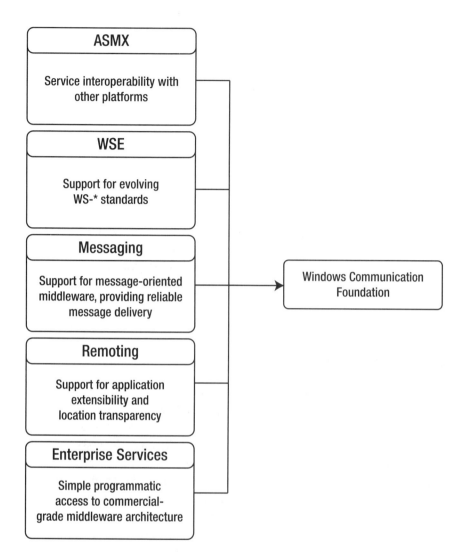

Figure 7-1. *Connectivity technologies and WCF*

These provide a terrific range of functionality, providing great power to you to develop connected applications, but the fact remains that they are in silos—each having its own development design, requiring the developer to train in each one to understand it well. For example, you may have expertise in Remoting, but this expertise would not transfer easily to Enterprise Services without extensive training. Consider a scenario where you want to expose a messaging system via Remoting—two completely separate and independent APIs are necessary. Or consider another scenario where you want to expose functionality as an ASMX web service, but also want to ensure reliable message delivery.

While these scenarios are possible, they are difficult, often involving thousands of lines of code to achieve them.

WCF incorporates all of this functionality into a single .NET development namespace: System.ServiceModel. This allows for *composability*, in which different functionality types can be "layered" into an application. For example, a web service can be implemented that provides reliable messaging by using both aspects of WCF in a composed service.

It's important to note that WCF is part of the .NET Framework, and as such is composed of a number of runtime class libraries, packaged as assemblies, with a companion SDK that allows you to build applications that run on those assemblies. Thus, any platform that has the .NET 3.0 runtime installed can run WCF applications. You do not have to have dedicated servers or software for messaging, transactions, or any of the other enterprise-class facets of WCF—you simply need .NET 3.0 on the runtime.

Similarly, as WCF is part of the .NET Framework, developers can continue using their familiar .NET development tools such as Visual Studio and the Visual Studio Express line to build WCF applications!

WCF and Interoperability

When you build connectable applications, you'll often be faced with the need to make your application talk to others that aren't built on the same APIs or technology. Consider the plumbing necessary to get a .NET Remoting application to talk to PHP, for example! Standards-based interoperability is a core design tenet of WCF. Using WCF allows you to quickly build services that use the advanced Web Services protocols (WS-*)—this way, developers of applications that use other platforms can use the frameworks that implement the same standards on their platforms to talk to yours. It also allows you to easily upgrade your existing services and applications to use these standards, so you have a smooth glide path to upgrade your existing assets to standards-based interoperability. Finally, as new standards emerge, updates to the framework will become available, allowing you to use the standards with the peace of mind that Microsoft is supporting you.

Any strategy for interoperability has two facets. The first is *cross-platform interoperability*, which is defined as support for communication between WCF and services built on non-Microsoft platforms. The strategy for this is to support the Web Services specifications extensively. The second is *integration*, which is defined as how WCF services will communicate with existing applications built on the Microsoft stack, including, for example, ASMX or Enterprise Services.

At the heart of cross-platform interoperability is the support for the suite of Web Services standards, typically called WS-*. Three of the most important of these are WS-Security, WS-ReliableMessaging, and WS-Transactions, which provide for the secure, reliable, transactable services that are at the heart of WCF. You can see how these work in the abstract architecture diagram in Figure 7-2.

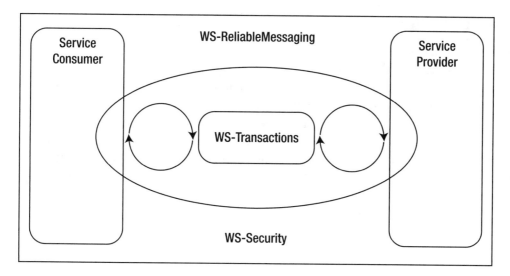

Figure 7-2. *WS-* support*

WS-Security

WS-Security is a set of enhancements to SOAP that allow you to specify how a message can be secured when being passed to and from a service. It can ensure that the message isn't tampered with, and that sensitive information, such as a password, is encrypted. The message is protected through authentication, confidentiality, and assurance of integrity. The original specification for WS-Security was drawn up by OASIS (Organization for the Advancement of Structured Information Standards), and is available at www.oasis-open.org.

WS-ReliableMessaging

WS-ReliableMessaging builds on WS-Reliability, which is a set of enhancements to SOAP designed to guarantee message reliability to and from a web service. It has guaranteed delivery and duplication elimination, as well as the facility to ensure that the ordering of messages is maintained.

WS-ReliableMessaging expands on this to provide reliable message delivery between applications, and is not limited to SOAP and Web Services, making it ideal for integration with existing systems. WS-ReliableMessaging is an important next step in ensuring the reliability of message interchange between distributed applications in that it is designed to also maintain reliability characteristics in the presence of component, system, or network failures. It is transport-independent, allowing it to be implemented on network technologies and protocols other than SOAP, but a SOAP binding is also defined within its specification.

WS-Transactions

The WS-Transactions specifications define the mechanism for how applications running across Web Services domains can interoperate in a transactable manner. It is also designed to provide a means of composing transactional quality-of-service attributes into Web Services applications. The transaction standards are built on a number of other standards, including WS-Coordination for an extensible coordination framework, and specific types for different types of transactions, such as short-term atomic ones (WS-AtomicTransaction) and longer-running business transactions (WS-BusinessActivity). WCF aims to allow these diverse specifications to be programmable using a single attribute-driven API. Later in this chapter, you'll build some simple WCF applications that implement security, reliability, and transactability under the hood so you won't have to worry about the complexity of dealing with their messaging structure manually.

WCF and Service Orientation

Software as a Service (SAAS) is a major initiative for the future of the Web. This is an evolution of Service-Oriented Architecture (SOA), where a paradigm shift in how software is developed is taking place. Instead of thinking of traditional application development, developers are encouraged to think about small, nimble, reusable components, and to build these as services that can be exposed reliably and securely across the network. These components can then be assembled into distributed applications. Using next-generation presentation technology, these applications can provide a great user experience.

At the heart of it all is the question of how we reuse the code that we write. We want long-term returns on our investments in building software assets—but how do we achieve this?

In the 1980s, object orientation was the craze. It was based on the idea of building reusable abstract definitions of functionality (called classes), which provided the template for objects, and for more complex inherited objects. So, for example, a class that defines a type of object called a "car" could be defined, and a more sophisticated object called a "sports car" could derive from this, inheriting (and thus reusing) the attributes of the original "car" class. In a world where code was written procedurally, and most reuse was in cutting and pasting code from one routine to another, this was revolutionary. It brought about new benefits such as *polymorphism*, where dynamic binding to methods and events could happen at runtime, and *encapsulation*, the facility to hide and expose certain parts of your code to the outside world. However, the drawback was that once an application was built, it was built, and it was static. There was no easy way to put new functionality into an application other than to recode, rebuild, and redeploy it.

Later, the concept of components evolved from object orientation. It was designed to make the developer think about the external interface of their application and how other people could use it. Now an application could load and bind to new functionality at runtime—and the application became a "pluggable" organism, where new modules could be easily plugged in at runtime. To achieve this, rich metadata and type information had to be available, leading to the concept of self-describing systems.

Extending the concept of self-describing systems to the network gave rise to service orientation. And because the application is now distributed across the network, the design of the application has moved away from monolithic event and method "messaging" on a single machine toward a true message-oriented system where requests, responses, and streams are message-oriented across the network. Thus, the self-description of the application had to extend to the format of messages that it made and accepted, and service orientation was born. The typical application was built from a number of service components, each component having a well-defined interface and messaging structure, and each providing a unique, discoverable service that can be found and invoked dynamically.

There are four main rules or tenets regarding what makes true service orientation. Following these tenets enables you to create a loosely coupled system of nimble services that can be orchestrated and integrated into an application.

Explicit boundaries: Based on the concept of encapsulation, service orientation dictates that services are agnostic of their underlying implementation, and that they have well-defined "public" interfaces. WCF allows for this through an opt-in code attribute–based model.

Autonomy: It is recognized that the service will evolve over time, be it through bug-fixing internally in the service, the location of the service changing, or the "footprint" of the service changing with the addition or removal of public methods. The system must be designed to support this, and loose coupling of services helps achieve this end.

Sharing based on contract and schema: You should not have to know about the internal workings of a service in order to exchange data with it—you simply use the defined contract according to the explicitly defined boundary.

Policy-based compatibility: A service defines its communication policy based on its configuration, class attributes, and method footprint. This policy can then be retrieved by the client in order to configure itself to communicate with the service.

Programming WCF

Programming WCF is all about remembering the ABC of *Address, Binding, and Contract*. You'll step through some scenarios of building a WCF service that returns the address data from earlier, and add onto it with security, transactability, and reliability. This is a huge topic deserving of several books in its own right, but hopefully you'll glean enough from these sections to understand the big picture and get confident enough for a deep dive into the technology, should that be what you desire.

To get started building WCF, you'll first build a new WCF service. Visual Studio 2008 supports these; if you are using Visual Studio 2005 or VWDE 2005, however, note that you'll need the .NET Framework 3.0 runtime components and the .NET 3.0 extensions for Visual Studio (code-named Orcas) before you continue.

Launch your IDE and select File ➤ New Web Site. The New Web Site dialog will appear (see Figure 7-3). If you are using Visual Studio 2008, remember that you need to use the .NET Framework 3.0 or .NET Framework 3.5 filter to be able to see WCF Service as an option.

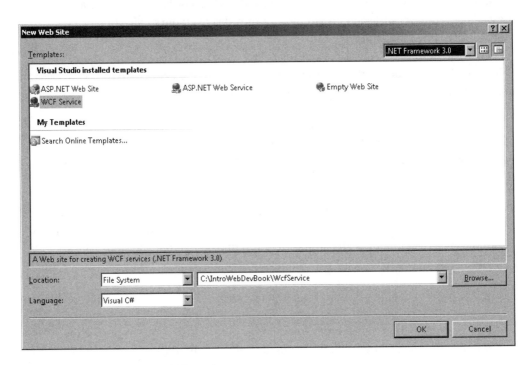

Figure 7-3. *Creating a new WCF service*

Once you've selected your service and placed it on either the file system or your local IIS, Visual Studio will create the project files and open the editor. You'll notice a new file type, with the .svc extension. As you can probably guess, this is a service. The SVC file structure is a lot like the base ASMX file that we saw earlier. It simply defines the language, the debug mode, the service class, and the location of the code-behind. Here's an example:

```
<% @ServiceHost Language=C# Debug="true"
    Service="MyService" CodeBehind="~/App_Code/Service.cs" %>
```

The code-behind is a standard C# class, but there are some new attributes on the code that WCF uses to determine contracts and binding. The basic service created by the IDE will look like this:

```
using System;
using System.ServiceModel;
using System.Runtime.Serialization;


// A WCF service consists of a contract
// (defined below as IMyService, DataContract1),
// a class that implements that interface (see MyService),
// and configuration entries that specify behaviors associated with
// that implementation (see <system.serviceModel> in web.config)

[ServiceContract()]
public interface IMyService
{
    [OperationContract]
    string MyOperation1(string myValue1);
    [OperationContract]
    string MyOperation2(DataContract1 dataContractValue);
}

public class MyService : IMyService
{
    public string MyOperation1(string myValue1)
    {
        return "Hello: " + myValue1;
    }
    public string MyOperation2(DataContract1 dataContractValue)
    {
        return "Hello: " + dataContractValue.FirstName;
    }
}

[DataContract]
public class DataContract1
{
    string firstName;
    string lastName;
```

```
    [DataMember]
    public string FirstName
    {
        get { return firstName;}
        set { firstName = value;}
    }
    [DataMember]
    public string LastName
    {
        get { return lastName;}
        set { lastName = value;}
    }
}
```

This probably looks a little different than what you are used to—but don't worry, it will become second nature in due course! There are three classes implemented in this module. The first is the interface that is used to template and declare the web methods and the contracts that will be understood around them, also known as operation contracts. As it is an interface, if your service class implements it, then it will get those methods; and as the methods have already been attributed as a contract, you don't need to worry about configuring them again.

Note that this example bundles the interface and implementation into the same code module. In a real-world application, it would be a good idea to separate these, and reference the interface class from the implementation class for good architectural separation. For simplicity, I've put them together in the same class in this example.

The interface defines the overall service contract, and to inform the compiler that this is your desire, you attribute it with [ServiceContract()].

The methods mentioned earlier will become service operations, and as we want the service to display its contract openly and freely, they too get attributed, but this time as [OperationContract()] attributes, as that is their task.

Finally, for interoperability's sake, when passing complex data structures around, you should define a contract for how they behave. Thus, a client consuming your service will know how to build and parse the data structure. This (largely) avoids type mismatch issues when crossing application platforms. For example, a complex data type that is made up of two strings with getters and setters for each is given to you by the wizard.

Let's take a look at it again:

```
[DataContract]
public class DataContract1
{
    string firstName;
    string lastName;
```

```
[DataMember]
public string FirstName
{
    get { return firstName;}
    set { firstName = value;}
}
[DataMember]
public string LastName
{
    get { return lastName;}
    set { lastName = value;}
}
}
```

Here you have a complex data type made up of two strings, each with a getter and a setter. You attribute the data class with the [DataContract] attribute, and each of its members with the [DataMember] attribute. You could of course have a larger class, with some data elements that you would want to keep private—in this case, you simply do not attribute them as DataMembers.

When you execute your application and browse to the Service.svc file, you'll see the service harness, as in Figure 7-4.

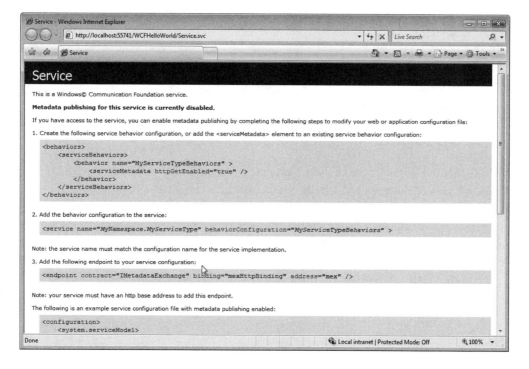

Figure 7-4. *Service harness*

As you can see in the screenshot, metadata publishing for the service is disabled. As a result, you cannot browse and understand the endpoints of the service using the harness without making a change to the Web.config file.

The first change you'll need to make is in the behaviors section. Here is an example of a Web.config that has been modified for this Hello World service:

```
<system.serviceModel>
  <services>
    <!-- Before deployment, you should remove
         the returnFaults behavior configuration to avoid
         disclosing information in exception messages -->
    <!--<service name="MyService" behaviorConfiguration="returnFaults">
      <endpoint contract="IMyService" binding="wsHttpBinding"/>
    </service> -->
    <service name="MyService"
             behaviorConfiguration="MyServiceTypeBehaviors">
      <endpoint contract="IMyService" binding="wsHttpBinding" />
    </service>
  </services>
  <behaviors>
    <serviceBehaviors>
      <!--<behavior name="returnFaults" >
        <serviceDebug includeExceptionDetailInFaults="true" />
      </behavior> -->
      <behavior name="MyServiceTypeBehaviors" >
        <serviceMetadata httpGetEnabled="true"></serviceMetadata>
      </behavior>
    </serviceBehaviors>
  </behaviors>
</system.serviceModel>
```

Note that the original service definition that returned fault details in exception messages has been commented out (as has its associated behavior definition in serviceBehaviors), and replaced by a new service definition tag that defines the behavior configuration as being available in the MyServiceTypeBehaviors section. In this section, ServiceMetadata has its httpGetEnabled property set to true, enabling the metadata for the service to be displayed in the service harness.

If you change it as specified, then you'll get the full service harness, as in Figure 7-5.

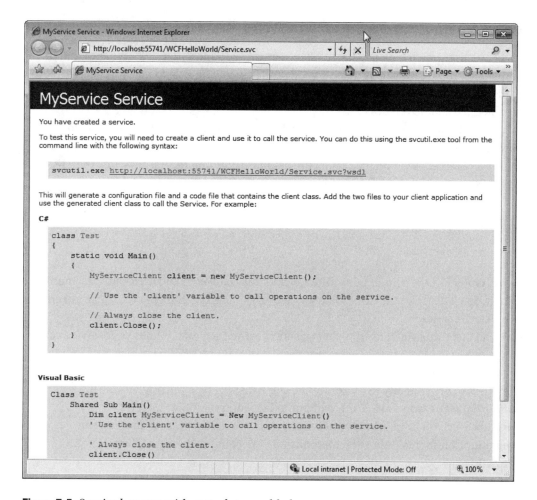

Figure 7-5. *Service harness with metadata enabled*

If you've built ASMX web services, you'll probably be familiar with the ability to test them with a simple form that is generated for you by the application. Unfortunately, your WCF service doesn't offer the same functionality, so you have to use the svcutil.exe tool to generate a client.

This screen demonstrates how you can do this. The svcutil.exe tool creates a proxy class that can be used to talk to the service, as well as the desired configuration information that enables the WCF pipelines to communicate with it. So, if you had for example enabled security or transactability on your service, the client will be configured to use the same features automatically.

This is best demonstrated by example, so in the next section, you'll look at how to use these attributes to build a "real-life" service. This will extend the examples in the previous chapters using the address data from the AdventureWorks database.

Creating an Address Service in WCF

In this section, you'll look at what it takes to create an address service similar to that in earlier chapters. However, as this is a WCF service, you'll be able to take it to the next level with some simple configuration changes—for example, adding reliability, security, and transactable characteristics to it.

First, create the service using the WCF Service template in the File – New dialog. Next, add a new DataSet to it. The DataSet should be based on the following SQL, which makes a parameterized query against the database, filtering the addresses by the ZIP code associated with it. Here's the SQL:

```
SELECT     AddressLine1, City, PostalCode
FROM       Person.Address
WHERE      (PostalCode = @ZIP)
```

Chapter 5 shows the steps required to add this DataSet, if you aren't already familiar with it. You'll be using the same DataSet here as you used in that chapter when you created a web service.

The first thing you'll need to do is create the interface that defines your service contract. In the Chapter 5 web service, you passed an XmlDocument type, which is a complex object requiring some pretty sophisticated data contracts to be set up in order to use it. For the sake of simplicity in this example, you'll instead pass a string. As a string is a simple data type, you don't need to define a data contract for it.

However, you'll still need the ServiceContract to define the interface, and an OperationContract to define the methods that are consumable by a client. Here's the code:

```
[ServiceContract()]
public interface IAddressService
{
    [OperationContract]
    string GetAddresses(string strZIP);

}
```

Next, you build your class that implements this interface. This class will also implement the specified operation (GetAddresses).

First, here's the class description:

```
public class AddressService : IAddressService
{
}
```

As you can see, this is just a straightforward class implementation. The idea is that your "custom" code to define a WCF service exists outside of your implementation code, and is configured via a `Web.config` file. This means that the business logic developers concentrate on the business logic and don't wrap it up in the plumbing. It's a very neat aspect of the WCF design that will make the implementation of enterprise-grade services easy.

Next, you build the operation itself. Here's the code:

```
public string GetAddresses(string strZIP)
    {

        string strReturn = "";
        AddressDataTableAdapters.AddressTableAdapter da =
            new AddressDataTableAdapters.AddressTableAdapter();
        AddressData.AddressDataTable dt = da.GetData(strZIP);
        strReturn = FormatDTasXML(dt);

        return strReturn;
    }
```

This takes in a string, the ZIP code, and uses it as a parameter in pulling the address data (as a DataTable) from the AddressTableAdapter, which is implemented by the DataSet. Then it sends this data to a helper function to format it as XML and serialize it into a string. This string will then be returned by the service.

Here's the listing for this helper function:

```
private string FormatDTasXML(AddressData.AddressDataTable dt)
    {
        MemoryStream memStream = null;
        XmlTextWriter xmlWriter = null;
        try
        {
            memStream = new MemoryStream();
            xmlWriter = new XmlTextWriter(memStream, Encoding.Unicode);
            dt.WriteXml(xmlWriter);
            int count = (int)memStream.Length;
            byte[] arr = new byte[count];
            memStream.Seek(0, SeekOrigin.Begin);
            memStream.Read(arr, 0, count);
            UnicodeEncoding utf = new UnicodeEncoding();
            return utf.GetString(arr).Trim();
```

```
        }
        catch
        {
            return String.Empty;
        }
        finally
        {
            if (xmlWriter != null)
                xmlWriter.Close();
        }


    }
```

The DataTable has the facility to write XML to an XMLWriter. This XMLWriter can then write to a memory stream that can be read out as a string. Thus, the XML is loaded into a string that can be returned. And as the string is a simple data type, it can be passed across the wire without a DataContract.

Now, to control how this service behaves, you'll use the Web.config file. Here's a sample Web.config file that will work with this service. You'll build on this later to provide attributes such as security to your service.

```xml
<?xml version="1.0"?>

<configuration xmlns="http://schemas.microsoft.com/.NetConfiguration/v2.0">
  <connectionStrings>
    <add name="AdventureWorksConnectionString"
      connectionString="Data Source=BOOKDEV\SQLEXPRESS;
          Initial Catalog=AdventureWorks;Integrated Security=True"
      providerName="System.Data.SqlClient" />
  </connectionStrings>
  <system.serviceModel>
    <services>
      <service name="AddressService"
              behaviorConfiguration="AddressServiceTypeBehaviors">
        <endpoint contract="IAddressService" binding="wsHttpBinding"/>
      </service>
    </services>
    <behaviors>
```

```
    <serviceBehaviors>
      <behavior name="AddressServiceTypeBehaviors" >
        <serviceMetadata httpGetEnabled="true" />
      </behavior>

    </serviceBehaviors>
  </behaviors>
  <bindings>
  </bindings>

</system.serviceModel>

<system.web>
  <compilation debug="true"/>
</system.web>

</configuration>
```

The important thing to remember here is the `<service>` node and how it is used to set up the service. Look at this node:

```
<service name="AddressService"
         behaviorConfiguration="AddressServiceTypeBehaviors">
  <endpoint contract="IAddressService" binding="wsHttpBinding"/>
</service>
```

Here you can see that the service called AddressService is being configured. Its behaviors are defined in a later part of Web.config called AddressServiceTypeBehaviors. But for now, what is most important is the endpoint. Here you define the contract (the name of the interface that defines the service that we saw earlier) and the binding type. In this case, it's an HTTP service, but WCF isn't limited to HTTP. MSMQ, Remoting, and other communications types are supported. Not only are multiple communication types supported, but multiple endpoints and bindings can be specified for a single service, offering you great flexibility. While this is all beyond the scope of this book, there are a number of good references that will help you understand these, including *Pro WCF: Practical Microsoft SOA Implementation* (Apress, 2007).

Now if you run the service, you'll see a result like that in Figure 7-6.

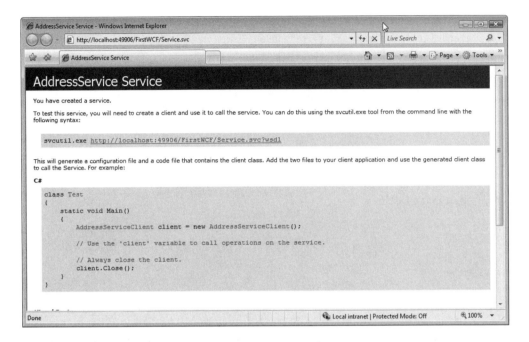

Figure 7-6. *Viewing the AddressService harness*

The next thing to do is to create a client that allows you to access this service. You'll see how to do this in the next section.

Creating the Address Service Client

To create a service client, you use the svcutil.exe tool that comes with the Windows SDK or as part of the Orcas add-ons to Visual Studio. You'll find it in the Program Files\ Microsoft Visual Studio 8\Common7\IDE folder.

In the service harness of your service, you can see the WSDL file that defines the service interface. In the simplest case, you just pass this as a parameter to svcutil.exe, and two files will be created for you. These are a proxy class and a configuration file.

So, from a command prompt, type the following:

```
Svcutil http://localhost:49906/FirstWCF/Service.svc?wsdl
```

■**Note** Remember to replace the URL with that of the WSDL in your service.

CASSINI VS. IIS

When you are developing with Visual Studio, if you create your web site or service using the file system, Visual Studio will launch the Cassini web server to allow you to test and debug your application. This will use a random port other than port 80, such as port 49906, as in the example in the "Creating the Address Service Client" section. When following along with the code in this section of this book (as well as any other book where Visual Studio and Cassini are being used), understand that you are likely to have a different port, so your URL will be `http://localhost:xxxxx`, where *xxxxx* is the port that was randomly assigned.

When you deploy your application to a production web server running IIS, you'll be using port 80. Remember to update proxies or any references to the correct port.

The tool will respond with output like the following:

```
Microsoft (R) Service Model Metadata Tool
[Microsoft (R) Windows (R) Communication Foundation, Version 3.0.4506.30]
Copyright (c) Microsoft Corporation.  All rights reserved.

Attempting to download metadata from
'http://localhost:49906/FirstWCF/Service.svc?wsdl'
using WS-Metadata Exchange or DISCO.
Generating files...
C:\Program Files\Microsoft Visual Studio 8\VC\AddressService.cs
C:\Program Files\Microsoft Visual Studio 8\VC\output.config
```

As you can see, the files are generated in the current directory. You will add them to your new client next.

You can use any type of application as a service client as long as you use this configuration information. If you're building a Windows app, you add the information to your App.config; otherwise you add it to your Web.config. For this example, you'll build a web client that takes the information back from the WCF service and renders it on a DataGrid.

First, create the web application that implements the client using the File – New dialog. You'll have a basic web application set up containing a Default.aspx page. You'll need to add a Web.config file to the project. The easiest way to do this is to just run the application in debug mode, and Visual Studio will automatically generate a Web.config file for you.

Next, you should copy the two files AddressService.cs and output.config to the directory that the new web site is implemented in, and add them to your project.

The next step is to add the settings from output.config to your Web.config file. Once you are done, Web.config will look something like this:

```
<system.serviceModel>
  <bindings>
    <wsHttpBinding>
      <binding name="WSHttpBinding_IAddressService" closeTimeout="00:01:00"
          openTimeout="00:01:00" receiveTimeout="00:10:00" sendTimeout="00:01:00"
          bypassProxyOnLocal="false" transactionFlow="false"
          hostNameComparisonMode="StrongWildcard"
          maxBufferPoolSize="524288" maxReceivedMessageSize="65536"
          messageEncoding="Text" textEncoding="utf-8" useDefaultWebProxy="true"
          allowCookies="false">
        <readerQuotas maxDepth="32" maxStringContentLength="65536"
            maxArrayLength="16384"
            maxBytesPerRead="4096"
            maxNameTableCharCount="16384" />
        <reliableSession ordered="true" inactivityTimeout="00:10:00"
            enabled="false" />
        <security mode="Message">
          <transport clientCredentialType="Windows" proxyCredentialType="None"
              realm="" />
          <message clientCredentialType="Windows"
              negotiateServiceCredential="true"
              algorithmSuite="Default" establishSecurityContext="true" />
        </security>
      </binding>
    </wsHttpBinding>
  </bindings>
  <client>
    <endpoint address="http://localhost:49906/FirstWCF/Service.svc"
        binding="wsHttpBinding"
        bindingConfiguration="WSHttpBinding_IAddressService"
        contract="IAddressService" name="WSHttpBinding_IAddressService">
      <identity>
        <userPrincipalName value="BookDev\Laurence" />
      </identity>
    </endpoint>
  </client>
</system.serviceModel>
```

This configures the service model on the client to talk to the server using the contract specified by the server via the generated proxy (AddressServiceIIS).

Add a DataGrid control to your ASPX page and use the Auto Format feature to style it in the Colorful style. You'll end up with markup that looks like this:

```
<%@ Page Language="C#" AutoEventWireup="true"
    CodeFile="Default.aspx.cs" Inherits="_Default" %>
<!DOCTYPE html PUBLIC "-//W3C//DTD XHTML 1.0 Transitional//EN"
    "http://www.w3.org/TR/xhtml1/DTD/xhtml1-transitional.dtd">
<html xmlns="http://www.w3.org/1999/xhtml" >
<head runat="server">
    <title>Untitled Page</title>
</head>
<body>
    <form id="form1" runat="server">
    <div>
        <asp:GridView ID="GridView1" runat="server" CellPadding="4"
            ForeColor="#333333" GridLines="None">
            <FooterStyle BackColor="#990000" Font-Bold="True" ForeColor="White" />
            <RowStyle BackColor="#FFFBD6" ForeColor="#333333" />
            <SelectedRowStyle BackColor="#FFCC66"
                Font-Bold="True" ForeColor="Navy" />
            <PagerStyle BackColor="#FFCC66"
                ForeColor="#333333" HorizontalAlign="Center" />
            <HeaderStyle BackColor="#990000" Font-Bold="True" ForeColor="White" />
            <AlternatingRowStyle BackColor="White" />
        </asp:GridView>
    </div>
    </form>
</body>
</html>
```

Next, you'll add code into the Page_Load event handler to call the WCF service and fill in the grid with the results of the call. This is done with code like this:

```
public partial class _Default : System.Web.UI.Page
{
    protected void Page_Load(object sender, EventArgs e)
    {
        AddressServiceClient myAddressService = new AddressServiceClient();
        string strData = myAddressService.GetAddresses("6105");
        XmlDocument xmlDoc = new XmlDocument();
        xmlDoc.LoadXml(strData);
        XmlNodeReader nRead = new XmlNodeReader(xmlDoc);
        DataSet d = new DataSet();
```

```
        d.ReadXml(nRead);
        nRead.Close();
        GridView1.DataSource = d;
        GridView1.DataBind();
    }

}
```

This code first creates an instance of the address service client (called myAddress-Service) and then uses it to get addresses for the ZIP code 6105. The rest of the code then reads the results into an XML document, creates a DataSet from it, and binds the grid to this DataSet. As you can see, from a coding point of view, you don't do anything special to communicate with the service—everything is handled by the autogenerated proxies, which were built based on the defined contracts.

Now that you have a simple service that runs with WCF, you can start playing with how to make it transactable, or add certificate-based security, or use WS-Reliability, among other things.

A great resource for getting started on this is the Windows SDK. It contains a file (WCFSamples.zip) that contains step-by-step instructions and code on how to achieve the most common tasks. Check out the extensibility samples in particular.

Summary

This chapter has given you an introduction to WCF and how it can be used to navigate the murky seas of different connectivity technologies and standards without needing to write thousands of lines of code. WCF is a critical component of .NET 3.0, and is something that you will find invaluable as you build the next Web. Your need to build applications that use standards around security, reliability, transactions, and more is only going to grow over time, and this framework is your best friend in empowering this.

You've barely scratched the surface of what is possible in this chapter, but hopefully you've gleaned enough to understand how it all works and hangs together. For further resources, take a look through the SDK and more in-depth books like *Pro WCF: Practical Microsoft SOA Implementation* (Apress, 2007).

In the next chapter, you'll look at another of the new pillars of .NET 3.0—Windows Presentation Foundation, a technology that can be used to bring your user experience to the next level. It's also the big brother of a technology that you'll be seeing a lot of in the future of the Web: Silverlight.

CHAPTER 8

.NET 3.0: Windows Presentation Foundation

Windows Presentation Foundation (WPF) is the unified presentation subsystem for Windows. It is made up of a display engine and a suite of managed classes that you can use to build applications that use it. It introduces XAML—an XML format that is used to define the UI, animations, interactions, and bindings, which are the "glue" of an application. Its ultimate aim is to provide a user experience beyond the traditional gray form-like interfaces of client applications. It introduces a new graphics driver model that is designed to use the power of the graphics processing unit (GPU) that is available to most modern desktop computers.

In this chapter, you'll take a look at the managed classes that provide the underpinnings of a WPF application, the XAML language that defines a WPF application, and the tools that can be used to build WPF applications, including Expression Blend, Expression Design, and Visual Studio 2008 (or alternatively, Visual Studio 2005 with the .NET 3.x extensions). You'll wrap up the chapter by building a WPF-based UI on top of the AdventureWorks address data service that you've been using in earlier chapters.

XAML

WPF constructs its UIs using Extensible Application Markup Language (XAML), an XML-based markup language that is used to compose, define, and interrelate WPF elements. It supports a number of built-in control definitions, such as `<Button>` to define a button. Here is how you would define a simple XAML document that contains a single button:

```
<Window x:Class="WPFIntro.Window1"
    xmlns="http://schemas.microsoft.com/winfx/2006/xaml/presentation"
    xmlns:x="http://schemas.microsoft.com/winfx/2006/xaml"
    Title="WPFIntro" Height="300" Width="300">
    <Grid>
```

```
        <Button>Hello, Web.Next Readers!</Button>
    </Grid>
</Window>
```

WPF parses this document and uses the elements that are defined within it to implement and render the UI. You can see the results of this in Figure 8-1.

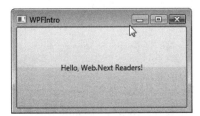

Figure 8-1. *Rendering the XAML button*

As WPF provides a vector-based rendering system, the application can be resized, and the button will be resized along with it without losing fidelity. Figure 8-2 shows the same application window where the user has resized it to make it much larger.

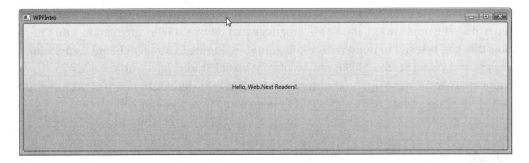

Figure 8-2. *Resizing the button window*

As you can see, the button resized and fit itself according to the dimensions of the window. This approach provides a number of distinct advantages over the previous form/control methodologies for defining and running UIs:

It allows for the separation of UI definition and application logic. Designers can use tools such as Expression Blend (which you will see later in this chapter) to define the UI look and feel, as well as how interactions take place within the UI. Design output is expressed in XAML, which is then taken up by developers to implement the application logic. Prior to XAML, there was a huge impedance mismatch between professional designers, who would implement their designs and express them as storyboards, Flash movies, or other such outputs; and developers, who would then reimplement them using Visual Basic, C#, COM, .NET, or others. This led to a huge gap between the intended design and the experience of the end product.

XAML is often more expressive than code for defining UIs. As such, it typically makes UI design simpler. It also opens the door for multiple tools to be used in designing a UI, and doesn't restrict usage to developer tools such as Visual Studio.

XAML works by a set of rules that map its elements, attributes, and namespaces onto classes or structures in the .NET 3.0 Framework. It typically follows the format where an element in XAML maps to a .NET type, and the attributes of that element map to members of that type. So, for example, take a look at the XAML used earlier:

```
<Button>Hello, Web.Next Readers!</Button>
```

The `<Button>` tag maps to the WPF Button control. As the contents of the tag were `Hello, Web.Next Readers!`, the default property of the Button was set to this value. In the case of a button, the default property is its `Content` property, so you could have achieved the same result by setting the `Content` attribute in XAML, which in turn sets the `Content` property on the Button. In that case, your XAML would look like this:

```
<Window x:Class="WPFIntro.Window1"
    xmlns="http://schemas.microsoft.com/winfx/2006/xaml/presentation"
    xmlns:x="http://schemas.microsoft.com/winfx/2006/xaml"
    Title="WPFIntro" Height="300" Width="300">
    <Grid>
      <Button Content="Hello, Web.Next Readers!" />
    </Grid>
</Window>
```

You can of course use multiple attributes to set multiple properties on the control. If you want to, for example, override the default background color, foreground color, and font type, you merely have to set the appropriate attributes on the `<Button>` element. Here's an example:

```
<Window x:Class="WPFIntro.Window1"
    xmlns="http://schemas.microsoft.com/winfx/2006/xaml/presentation"
    xmlns:x="http://schemas.microsoft.com/winfx/2006/xaml"
    Title="WPFIntro" Height="300" Width="300">
    <Grid>
      <Button Background="Black" Foreground="White"
FontFamily="Verdana" FontSize="20"
```

```
Content="Hello, Readers!" />
    </Grid>
</Window>
```

Figure 8-3 shows how this will render.

Figure 8-3. *Overriding the default background, foreground, and font properties*

When programming in WPF and defining elements in XAML, you'll encounter many complex properties that cannot be expressed in a simple string. For these, XAML provides a sub-element syntax, called *property element syntax*, that allows you to define them. This works by using dot syntax to define a property element. This example shows how the dot syntax may be used for complex properties and the attribute syntax may be used for simple ones:

```
<Window x:Class="WPFIntro.Window1"
    xmlns="http://schemas.microsoft.com/winfx/2006/xaml/presentation"
    xmlns:x="http://schemas.microsoft.com/winfx/2006/xaml"
    Title="WPFIntro" Height="300" Width="300">
    <Grid>
      <Button FontFamily="Verdana">
        <Button.Background>
          <SolidColorBrush Opacity="0.5">
            <SolidColorBrush.Color>Blue</SolidColorBrush.Color>
          </SolidColorBrush>
        </Button.Background>
        Hello, Web.Next Readers!
      </Button>

    </Grid>
</Window>
```

Here, a SolidColorBrush type is used to define the button's background. This has properties of its own, such as its color and opacity. These are not properties of the button, but of the SolidColorBrush that is created to implement the background color of the button. So, you cannot use attributes of the button to define the properties of this brush. Instead, you define the <Button.Background> and define a <SolidColorBrush> underneath it. This also shows that you can mix your property declarations between using attributes (see the Opacity declaration) or dot syntax (see the Color declaration). When you use tools such as Expression Blend to define your UI, you'll have a Property Editor dialog, and this will generate this code for you.

You can also define the properties of an element using *markup extension syntax*, where you refer to the properties of another element on the page. This can be used, for example, to set a common style on the page for a number of controls, and then have each control set itself according to the properties of that style. Markup extension uses curly braces ({}) to define the reference point. Here's an example:

```
<Window x:Class="WPFIntro.Window1"
    xmlns="http://schemas.microsoft.com/winfx/2006/xaml/presentation"
    xmlns:x="http://schemas.microsoft.com/winfx/2006/xaml"
    Title="WPFIntro" Height="300" Width="300">
  <Window.Resources>
    <Style TargetType="Button" x:Key="ButtonStyle">
      <Setter Property="Background" Value="Black"></Setter>
    </Style>
  </Window.Resources>
    <Grid>
      <Button FontFamily="Verdana" Style="{StaticResource ButtonStyle}">
        Hello, Readers!
      </Button>

    </Grid>
</Window>
```

In this case, a style has been defined and given the name ButtonStyle. Now all buttons can have their style property set to this style using markup extension syntax. Style is a static resource on the page, and as such you load the style for a button by pointing it at the named static resource using this syntax: {StaticResource ButtonStyle}.

This wraps up a very brief introduction to XAML and how you use it to define a UI. In most cases, you'll be using tools to create your XAML visually, going back into the XML to do some fine-tweaking. As such, the next sections introduce you to the new Expression Blend product, which allows you to define UIs in XAML; Expression Design, which complements Blend and allows you to define graphical assets, expressed as XAML; and Visual Studio 2005's Cider designer, which is part of the Orcas extensions for the IDE.

Using Expression Blend

Not only is Expression Blend a nice application to show how you can quickly define rich XAML interfaces, but it is also a demonstration of one of those interfaces itself, as Blend has been written using WPF. It's a great example of how you can create dynamic, rich, vector-based UIs using WPF.

You can download the beta version of Expression Blend from `www.microsoft.com/products/expression/en/Expression-Blend/default.mspx`.

Once you've downloaded and installed Blend, launch it to view the Blend IDE (see Figure 8-4).

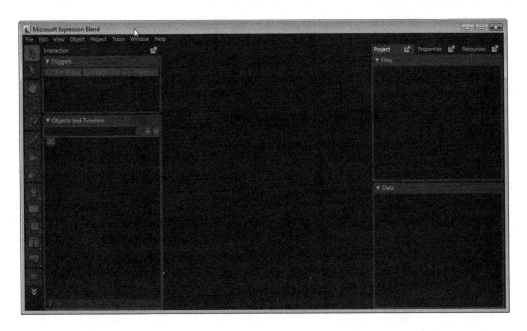

Figure 8-4. *The initial Blend screen*

If you are used to using Visual Studio, then the process of getting started will be very familiar. Select New Project from the File menu, and you'll be given the choice of a standard application (`.exe`) or a control library, and a programming language of Visual Basic or C# (see Figure 8-5).

Once you create a standard application, the IDE will create a new workspace containing the project, its core references, an assemblyinfo file, and two XAML files: `App.xaml` and `Window1.xaml`. This is shown in Figure 8-6, after which we'll look at each of these files in turn.

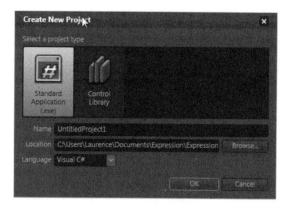

Figure 8-5. *Creating a new Blend project*

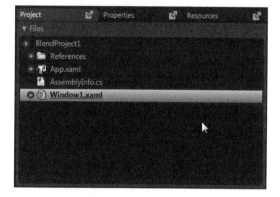

Figure 8-6. *The default Blend project*

The References folder contains references to each of the assemblies that your project uses. When you first set up a project, it will reference PresentationCore.dll, PresentationFramework.dll, and WindowsBase.dll from WPF, as well as System.dll and System.Xml.dll from the .NET Framework.

App.xaml is an application file that is used to contain settings and resources that are global to your application. For example, you can specify the markup to configure the behavior upon application startup, or define resources to be shared across all windows. By default, App.xaml looks like the following—you can see where it is setting up Window1.xaml as the initial page to view when the application launches.

```
<Application
  xmlns="http://schemas.microsoft.com/winfx/2006/xaml/presentation"
  xmlns:x="http://schemas.microsoft.com/winfx/2006/xaml"
  x:Class="BlendProject1.App"
  StartupUri="Window1.xaml">
```

```
<Application.Resources>
  <!-- Resources scoped at the Application level should be defined here. -->
</Application.Resources>
</Application>
```

Finally, `Window1.xaml` is the default window that the template provides. It is a basic XAML page defining a window, and a grid is placed on it. The Grid is a basic layout control, in which controls placed within it can appear using a "grid layout" methodology— meaning that they appear at the coordinates specified using their x and y properties. There are several layout controls available in WPF, allowing you to place controls in a stacked or flow manner (you'll be looking at these a little later on in this chapter). Here's the code for `Window1.xaml`:

```
<Window
  xmlns="http://schemas.microsoft.com/winfx/2006/xaml/presentation"
  xmlns:x="http://schemas.microsoft.com/winfx/2006/xaml"
  xml:lang="en-US"
  x:Class="BlendProject1.Window1"
  x:Name="Window"
  Title="Window"
  Width="640" Height="480">  <Grid x:Name="LayoutRoot"/>
</Window>
```

The basic layout of the Blend IDE when you are editing a project is shown in Figure 8-7. At the very left is the toolbar. To the right of this are the interaction tools, where timelines, triggers, and animations are designed. In the center is the Designer/XAML Editor. F11 puts you into Visual Design mode, where you can drag and drop XAML controls onto the page, and use a code editor that allows you to tweak your current XAML code. The right side of the screen is the management area, where you control your project, your connections to outside data sources, and the properties of the components you are currently editing.

Creating UIs with Blend

The left-hand side of the screen contains the control bar. When you hold the mouse down on any of the control icons (they have a triangle on their bottom-right-hand corner), the controls within that family will pop up. For example, if you hold the mouse on the Button icon, the list of selectable controls (such as CheckBox and RadioButton) will appear (see Figure 8-8).

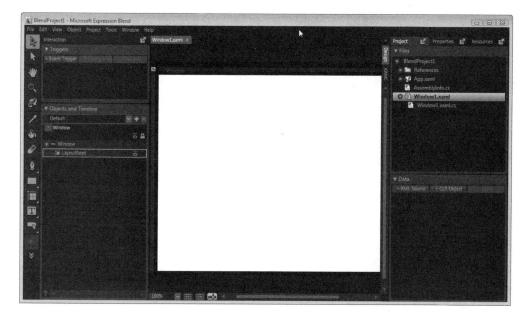

Figure 8-7. *Default Blend IDE layout*

Figure 8-8. *Accessing controls*

You then simply select any control and drag the mouse onto the design surface to place and size it, or alternatively double-click it to get a default position and size on the design surface. As the current layout for the Window1.xaml is using the grid layout methodology, you can place the control anywhere you like.

Once a control is on the design surface, you can edit its properties using the Property Editor on the right-hand side of the screen (see Figure 8-9).

Figure 8-9. *The Property Editor*

The sheer number of properties that WPF makes available for even the simplest of controls (such as a Button) can be overwhelming. Figure 8-9 shows that the properties have been broken down into families such as Brushes, Appearance, and Layout. Fortunately, Blend gives you the facility to search for a property. For example, if you type *f* into the search box, the Properties window will try to keep up by closing all property panes that do not contain a property beginning with *f*. Then if you type another letter—for example, *o*—it will redraw again. You can see the results in Figure 8-10.

As you can see in Figure 8-10, the results are showing FocusVisualStyle and Force-Cursor. If you then type an *n* into the search box (so that it reads *fon*), it collapses to just show the Text pane. This shows how smart the search engine is—nowhere in this dialog is the word *font* shown—but because you have typed *fon*, the likelihood that you are looking for font settings is pretty high, so you are shown the text settings properties (see Figure 8-11).

Figure 8-10. *Searching the Property Editor*

Figure 8-11. *Searching for a property*

Most properties have visual setters, and the interface is quite intuitive, helping you to get very fine-grained control over how you want your UI to look. You can, of course, also override the settings that the Properties windows give you by hand-editing the XAML.

Using Layout

WPF has a number of layout controls that act as containers for other controls. These give you control over how and where those controls appear on the screen. In addition, they dictate the behavior of the controls when the window is resized, allowing you to design your application for multiple-user flexibility. The following list describes the layout controls that are available to you:

Canvas: This is a simple layout control that allows you to freely place your controls anywhere you like, but you lose flexibility when the screen is resized.

Grid: This control gives you flexibility to place the controls anywhere you like on the screen. The Grid allows you to divide its area up into rows and columns and place child controls within each of the resulting cells. Thus, when the screen is laid out, the controls will appear within their grid cell.

StackPanel: This control lays out its children in a horizontal or vertical stack. It is very useful for implementing UI elements such as toolbars or vertical button bars.

DockPanel: This allocates an entire edge of the screen to its children. The toolbar interaction windows and management areas of the Blend IDE are great examples of DockPanels. If you consider any area like this (such as the dockable controls in Visual Studio or Office), you'll get the idea of how a DockPanel works.

WrapPanel: This lays its children out from left to right in sequence. When it hits the edge of its bounds, the controls wrap to the line below.

Using the Grid Layout Control

The default window created by Blend when you create a new project already has a Grid control placed on it. This is a single-cell grid, so it behaves just like a Canvas, allowing you to freely place controls anywhere on the screen. However, to get the most out of your Grid, you should create columns and rows. This can be done from within the Property Editor. This Grid, by default, is called LayoutRoot, so be sure that this is selected in the Objects and Timeline pane, on the left side of the screen (see Figure 8-12).

Figure 8-12. *Selecting an item in the Objects and Timeline pane*

When it is selected, it will be highlighted in yellow. Next, you should create some rows and columns using the Property Editor. These are found in the extended layout section of the Properties window. To find them, expand Layout and then click the extend button at the bottom of the Layout pane, or simply search for "Row" or "Column" as described earlier.

ColumnDefinitions and RowDefinitions are collections, so you'll see an ellipsis (. . .) button beside them in the Property Editor. Click this, and the Collection Editor (Figure 8-13) will appear.

Figure 8-13. *The Collection Editor*

Click the "Add another item" button to create a new definition in the collection. Figure 8-13 shows the ColumnDefinition Collection Editor; pressing this button adds new column definitions. When a definition is selected, you can edit its properties using the Properties window at the right of this dialog.

After adding three columns and three rows, your XAML in the main window will look like this:

```
<Window
  xmlns="http://schemas.microsoft.com/winfx/2006/xaml/presentation"
  xmlns:x="http://schemas.microsoft.com/winfx/2006/xaml"
  xml:lang="en-US"
  x:Class="BlendProject1.Window1"
  x:Name="Window"
  Title="Window"
  Width="640" Height="480">

  <Grid x:Name="LayoutRoot" HorizontalAlignment="Left">

    <Grid.ColumnDefinitions>
      <ColumnDefinition/>
      <ColumnDefinition/>
      <ColumnDefinition/>
    </Grid.ColumnDefinitions>
    <Grid.RowDefinitions>
      <RowDefinition/>
      <RowDefinition/>
      <RowDefinition/>
    </Grid.RowDefinitions>

  </Grid>
</Window>
```

You can see this grid (center-aligned) on the screen, as shown in Figure 8-14.

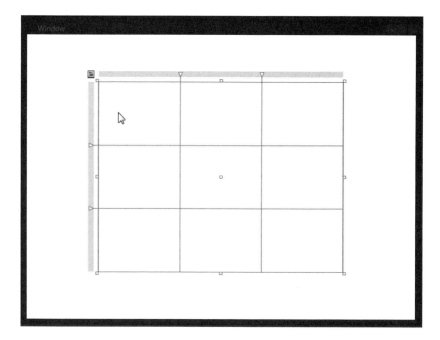

Figure 8-14. *A three-by-three grid layout*

Now you can add and lay controls out on your window. Note that the window itself can only contain *one* child control, and in this case that is the Grid. If you want more than one control within the window, you can use a container and place the controls within it. So, if you had selected the window in Objects and Timeline view (see Figure 8-12) and double-clicked the Button tool, then the grid would be replaced by a new button. So, be sure to select the grid in the Objects and Timeline selector and double-click the Button tool to add a button to the grid. Repeat this several times to add a few buttons. You'll notice that all the buttons are added to the top-left-hand corner of the grid. To see why this is the case, check out the XAML again. It looks like this:

```
<Grid x:Name="LayoutRoot" HorizontalAlignment="Center"
Width="391.247" Height="296">
    <Grid.ColumnDefinitions>
      <ColumnDefinition/>
      <ColumnDefinition/>
      <ColumnDefinition/>
    </Grid.ColumnDefinitions>
    <Grid.RowDefinitions>
      <RowDefinition/>
      <RowDefinition/>
      <RowDefinition/>
    </Grid.RowDefinitions>
```

```
    <Button HorizontalAlignment="Left"
VerticalAlignment="Top" Content="Button"/>
    <Button HorizontalAlignment="Left"
VerticalAlignment="Top" Content="Button"/>
    <Button HorizontalAlignment="Left"
VerticalAlignment="Top" Content="Button"/>
    <Button HorizontalAlignment="Left"
VerticalAlignment="Top" Content="Button"/>
    <Button HorizontalAlignment="Left"
VerticalAlignment="Top" Content="Button"/>

</Grid>
```

As you can see, the buttons aren't placed on the grid, so WPF draws them in the default position, which is the top left of their container. Select any button in the Designer and look at its layout properties. You'll see cells where you can enter a row and a column, and these are used to place the button in its containing grid (see Figure 8-15). Grid cells are zero-based, so setting Row to 1 and Column to 1 in a three-by-three grid sets the button to the center of the grid.

Figure 8-15. *Setting where the button resides in the grid*

After setting the Row and Column properties for a few buttons, your XAML will now look something like this:

```
<Grid x:Name="LayoutRoot" HorizontalAlignment="Center"
 Width="391.247" Height="296">

  <Grid.ColumnDefinitions>
    <ColumnDefinition/>
    <ColumnDefinition/>
```

```
    <ColumnDefinition/>
  </Grid.ColumnDefinitions>
  <Grid.RowDefinitions>
    <RowDefinition/>
    <RowDefinition/>
    <RowDefinition/>
  </Grid.RowDefinitions>
  <Button HorizontalAlignment="Left" VerticalAlignment="Top"
Content="Button" Grid.Row="1"/>
  <Button HorizontalAlignment="Left" VerticalAlignment="Top"
Content="Button" Grid.Column="2"/>
  <Button HorizontalAlignment="Left" VerticalAlignment="Top"
Content="Button" Grid.Column="1"/>
<Button HorizontalAlignment="Left" VerticalAlignment="Top"
Content="Button"/>
  <Button HorizontalAlignment="Left" VerticalAlignment="Top"
Content="Button" Grid.Column="1" Grid.Row="1"/>
</Grid>
```

This will look like Figure 8-16 when it is in the Designer.

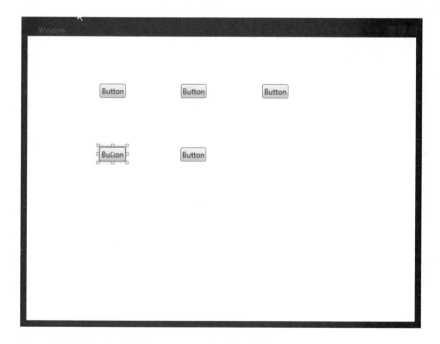

Figure 8-16. *Laying the buttons out in the grid*

Using the Other Layout Controls

Once you understand one layout control, you pretty much understand them all. The important thing to remember is that layout controls can be stacked (i.e., a layout control can contain another layout control), and with this in mind you can get great control over your window's behavior.

Here's an example of an application that uses multiple DockPanel and StackPanel controls to create a typical MDI-style application with a toolbar, a status bar, docks on the left and right, and a client area:

```
<Window
  xmlns="http://schemas.microsoft.com/winfx/2006/xaml/presentation"
  xmlns:x="http://schemas.microsoft.com/winfx/2006/xaml"
  xml:lang="en-US"
  x:Class="BlendProject1.Window1"
  x:Name="Window"
  Title="Window"
  Width="640" Height="480">

  <DockPanel LastChildFill="True" x:Name="MainWindow">
    <StackPanel x:Name="DockTop" Width="Auto" Height="33"
    Background="{DynamicResource {x:Static SystemColors.MenuBrushKey}}"
    DockPanel.Dock="Top" Orientation="Horizontal">
      <Button Content="Button"/>
      <Button Content="Button"/>
      <Button Content="Button"/>
      <Button Content="Button"/>
      <RadioButton Content="RadioButton"/>
      <RadioButton Content="RadioButton"/>
      <Button Content="Button"/>
    </StackPanel>
    <StackPanel x:Name="DockBottom" Width="Auto" Height="41"
    Background="{DynamicResource {x:Static SystemColors.MenuBarBrushKey}}"
    DockPanel.Dock="Bottom" Orientation="Horizontal">
      <Label Content="Label"/>
      <Label Content="Label"/>
    </StackPanel>
    <StackPanel x:Name="DockLeft" Width="70" Height="Auto"
    Background="{DynamicResource {x:Static SystemColors.MenuBarBrushKey}}">
      <Button Content="Button"/>
      <Button Content="Button"/>
      <Button Content="Button"/>
      <Button Content="Button"/>
```

```
    </StackPanel>
    <StackPanel x:Name="DockRight" Width="196" Height="Auto"
    Background="{DynamicResource {x:Static SystemColors.MenuBarBrushKey}}"
    DockPanel.Dock="Right">
      <Label Content="Label"/>
      <Label Content="Label"/>
      <Button Content="Button"/>
      <Button Content="Button"/>
      <Button Content="Button"/>
    </StackPanel>

    <RichTextBox x:Name="txtEdit">
      <FlowDocument>
        <Paragraph><Run>RichTextBox</Run></Paragraph>
      </FlowDocument>
    </RichTextBox>

  </DockPanel>
</Window>
```

When you run this application, you'll see something like that in Figure 8-17. When you resize the window, the layout controls manage the UI for you, with the dock panels filling the top, bottom, left, and right of the screen, and the text area automatically stretching (or shrinking) to fit its bounds.

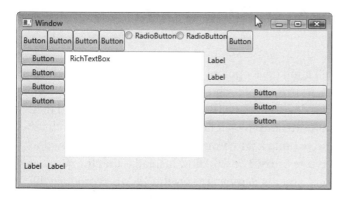

Figure 8-17. *Running the application*

You can see in Figure 8-18 how the application behaves upon resizing.

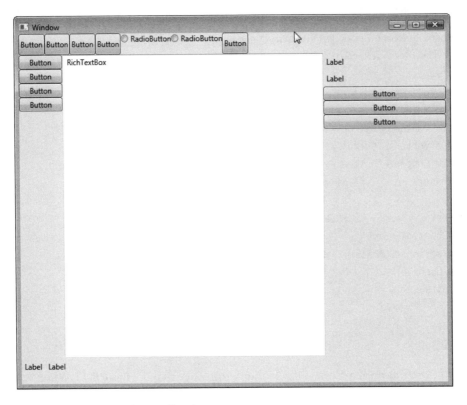

Figure 8-18. *Resizing the application*

Using Expression Blend to Build a Data Application

While Blend is a fully featured application development IDE, including the ability to data bind to XML or object data sources, it isn't suited for building a full n-tier web application from end to end. It is more suited for developing the UI and interaction layers, and then having a developer take the output XAML and "plug it in" to the full application architecture. For example, if you want Blend to build a WPF front end for a web service, you don't have the facility to create a web services proxy. The workflow instead is that the *designer* uses Blend to design the interactions, and the *developer* takes this XAML to produce the finished application in Visual Studio. In the case of a Web Services consumer, the developer can provide the designer with an XML document that is an example of what would be returned from the service, allow the designer to do their thing, and then take the resulting XAML and plug it into a "real" web service using some C# code.

Here's a snippet of XML as returned from the web service that you used in Chapter 5—fronting the AdventureWorks database with a query for address data.

```
<DocumentElement>
  <Address>
    <AddressLine1>1226 Shoe St.</AddressLine1>
    <PostalCode>98011</PostalCode>
    <City>Bothell</City>
    <AddressID>5</AddressID>
  </Address>
  <Address>
    <AddressLine1>1318 Lasalle Street</AddressLine1>
    <PostalCode>98011</PostalCode>
    <City>Bothell</City>
    <AddressID>11</AddressID>
  </Address>
  <Address>
    <AddressLine1>1399 Firestone Drive</AddressLine1>
    <PostalCode>98011</PostalCode>
    <City>Bothell</City>
    <AddressID>6</AddressID>
  </Address>
  <Address>
    <AddressLine1>1873 Lion Circle</AddressLine1>
    <PostalCode>98011</PostalCode>
    <City>Bothell</City>
    <AddressID>18</AddressID>
  </Address>
  <Address>
    <AddressLine1>1902 Santa Cruz</AddressLine1>
    <PostalCode>98011</PostalCode>
    <City>Bothell</City>
    <AddressID>40</AddressID>
  </Address>
</DocumentElement>
```

The designer can take this as a static XML file and bind to it when creating their interactions.

So, for example, if this XML snippet is saved out as a file called addressexample.xml, the designer can build a simple XAML UI that binds to it with Blend using the following steps:

1. Add a new window to your Blend application by right-clicking the project in the project explorer and selecting Add New Item. In the ensuing dialog, select Window, and give the window a friendly name such as GetAddresses.xaml.

2. Open the App.xaml file in XAML view and change the StartupURI attribute to the name of the window that you just created (i.e., GetAddresses.xaml). This instructs the application to load that window at startup.

3. The window will have a grid on it called LayoutRoot. Select this and find the property called DataContext. Click the small square to the right of the New button in the DataContext editor to open the advanced properties drop-down (see Figure 8-19).

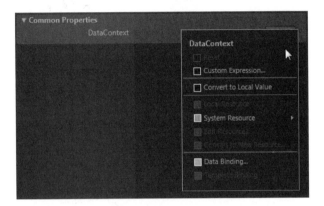

Figure 8-19. *Setting the advanced properties for the Grid's DataContext*

4. On this list, select Data Binding.

5. In the dialog that pops up, select + XML Data to add an XML data source.

6. This gives another dialog (Figure 8-20 shows both dialogs), where you can name the XML data and point it to the XML file that you created earlier.

7. When you click OK, the data source will be created and added to the "Data sources" list on the Create Data Binding dialog. Its fields will be listed on the right. As the data source has a collection of Address nodes, these will be indicated as an array in the Fields list (see Figure 8-21).

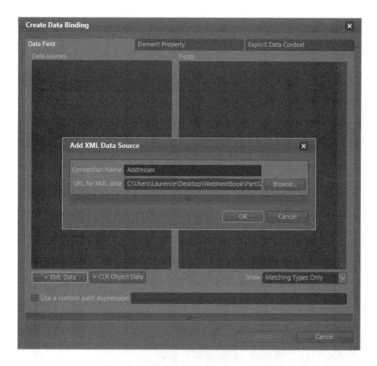

Figure 8-20. *Adding an XML data source*

Figure 8-21. *Binding to a data source*

8. Select Address (Array) and click Finish. This sets the DataContext for the Grid (and thus all its child controls) to the set of addresses that are found in the XML file.

9. Next, add a TextBox, a Button, and a ListBox to the window. You are going to set up the data binding for the ListBox. Select it and look at its common properties. You will see that its DataContext property has already been initialized because the control is on the Grid that had its DataContext set, and the ListBox inherited this. You can of course override it and point to a different data source to get the context for this control, but for now, this is perfectly OK.

10. To bind the ListBox to the data source, you use the ItemsSource property. Click it and select Data Binding in the ensuing dialog.

11. The Create Data Binding dialog will appear. This time, you want to bind to the context that is already present, so select the Explicit Data Context tab and pick your data source from there. If you don't see all the fields, change the Show dropdown to All Properties (see Figure 8-22).

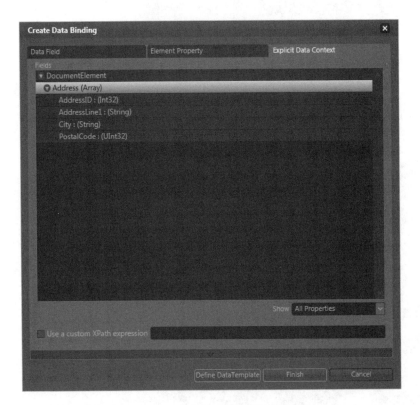

Figure 8-22. *Binding to the current DataContext*

12. Select Address (Array) and click Define Data Template. This allows you to define which fields you want to appear in the list. If you only want one field, you don't have to go this route—just select it in the Create Data Binding dialog—however, data templates allow you more flexibility.

13. The Create Data Template dialog appears and gives you three options for how you want your data to appear: Default ListBox Styling, which gives you all the fields stuck together into a single text line, with each entry having one line; Current or Predefined Data Template, which allows you to pick an existing data template and apply it to this ListBox; and New Data Template and Display Fields, which allows you to design a simple data template based on the fields that are currently available (see Figure 8-23).

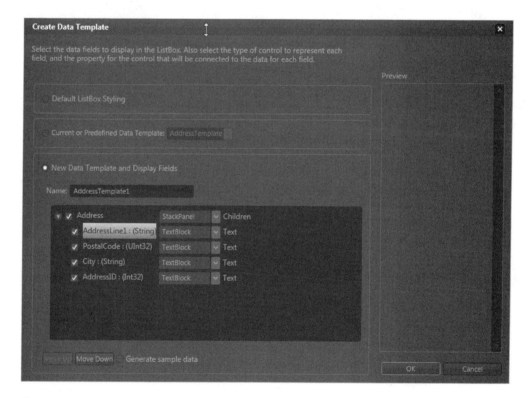

Figure 8-23. *Creating a new data template*

14. Select the fields that you want in the data template, and click OK. The dialog will close, and you'll be taken back to the Designer, where the list box will be populated with the data as expected (see Figure 8-24).

Figure 8-24. *Binding the ListBox to data with a template*

15. Because the definition of the ListBox and its binding is in XAML, you can easily edit it to customize the template. Open the XAML view of this window, and you can add a new node to separate the list items from each other.

    For example, here is a data template that was designed to just render the Address1 and ZIP code fields:

```
<Window.Resources>
  <XmlDataProvider d:IsDataSource="True"
      Source="C:\...\addressexample.xml"
      x:Key="Addresses"/>
  <DataTemplate x:Key="AddressTemplate1">
    <StackPanel>
      <TextBlock Text="{Binding Mode=OneWay, XPath=AddressLine1}"/>
      <TextBlock Text="{Binding Mode=OneWay, XPath=PostalCode}"/>
    </StackPanel>
  </DataTemplate>
</Window.Resources>
```

16. You see that it uses two TextBlock controls: one is bound to the AddressLine1 field, and the other to the PostalCode field. You can add a new XAML node underneath, for example, for an empty label that will create spacing between the elements. Here's an example:

```
<Window.Resources>
  <XmlDataProvider d:IsDataSource="True"
    Source="C:\...\addressexample.xml"
    x:Key="Addresses"/>
  <DataTemplate x:Key="AddressTemplate1">
    <StackPanel>
      <TextBlock Text="{Binding Mode=OneWay, XPath=AddressLine1}"/>
      <TextBlock Text="{Binding Mode=OneWay, XPath=PostalCode}"/>
      <Label Content=" " Height="8" />
    </StackPanel>
  </DataTemplate>
</Window.Resources>
```

17. Running the application will now give you the data neatly separated within the list (see Figure 8-25).

Figure 8-25. *Binding the data with an enhanced template*

Adding a Simple Timeline Animation

Now, the designer is likely to want to have some kind of UI glitz happening. For this example, we will make the list box fade in from invisible as it slides in from the left-hand side. This is achieved using animation timelines.

First you will want to create the trigger that fires when the button is clicked. You do this by selecting the button in the Objects and Timeline pane, and then the + Event Trigger button in the Triggers pane. The IDE will create the default trigger, which is Window.Loaded. Don't worry!

Underneath the Window.Loaded entry in the Triggers window, you will see the trigger definition section—it reads "When Window Loaded is raised," with "Window" and "Loaded" as drop-downs (see Figure 8-26).

Figure 8-26. *Creating the button click trigger*

Select the drop-down to the right of When (which should read "Window" right now) and change its setting to read "Button." Change the dialog that reads "Loaded" to "Click." The Triggers pane should now read "When button Click is raised" (see Figure 8-27).

Figure 8-27. *Setting the button click trigger*

A pop-up box will appear, pointing out that no timeline for this event trigger is present, and asking if you want a new one. Click OK to create it (see Figure 8-28).

Figure 8-28. *Creating a new timeline*

The timeline will be created, and a new timeline will start recording. This is a neat feature that allows you to define your animations and how they will run by setting the various properties that you want to animate visually. We want the list box to fly in from the left as it fades in from invisible to visible, so you should drag it off the left-hand side of the screen now and set its opacity to 0.

On the timeline, you will see that a key marker is set on the list box at time 0 (see Figure 8-29).

Figure 8-29. *Setting the first key frame on the timeline*

Drag the yellow line that indicates the time position to the 3 second mark. Go back to the Designer and drag the list from its position off the left-hand side of the screen to the final position that you want it to appear, and set its opacity to 100%. You'll see a few things happen: a new key marker will appear at the 3 second mark, the area between the two markers will be filled in, and a guide line showing the path of the animation will appear on the Designer (see Figure 8-30).

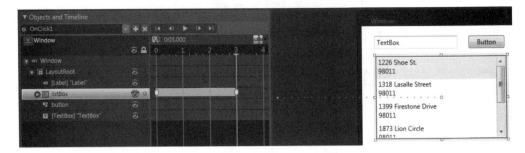

Figure 8-30. *Finishing off the timeline animation*

Now when you run your application, clicking the button will cause the list to fly in from the left as it slowly fades in.

This is a very simple example of an animation and an interaction that have been designed with Blend. No designer in his right mind would do something like this, but it shows the technology and how it works. With a little experimentation, you can build on this to produce the perfect interface for your needs. In the next section, you'll see how a programmer can take this work and add "real" data to the interaction using Visual Studio.

Using the Blend Artifacts in Visual Studio

Blend uses the same project file system as Visual Studio, so you can take your Blend projects and use them in Visual Studio to make them the front end in a multitier application.

In this case, the procedure is very simple. You first want to add a web reference to the address data service that you created in Chapter 5. Call it AddressService. This gives you a proxy out to the web service. Remember that you used the results of the web service call earlier when you templated the application, so it should be relatively easy to change the application to accept the live results.

You'll need to add a handler to the click event on the Button. You do this by adding a Click= attribute to the Button. Then you fill the attribute content with the name of the function you want to call upon the button being clicked.

Your XAML for the Button will look like this:

```
<Button Click="Handle_Click" HorizontalAlignment="Left"
  Margin="200,18,0,0" VerticalAlignment="Top"
  Width="67" Height="23" Content="Button"
  x:Name="button"/>
```

Now, all you need to do to implement this in your code-behind page is to write a function with the following syntax:

```
public void Handle_Click(Object obj, RoutedEventArgs e)
{
}
```

This is the typical function layout for a WPF event handler, where it accepts an object and an argument (usually RoutedEventArgs). When you click the button, the WPF runtime knows to invoke the code in this function. So let's fill it in. What you need to do is pretty simple.

Pull the ZIP code out of the text box, which is called tZIP:

```
string strZIP = tZIP.Text;
```

Create an instance of the proxy and call it with this ZIP code:

```
AddressService.Service d = new AddressService.Service();
XmlNode xNode = d.GetAddresses(strZIP);
```

Use the returned XML as the new DataContext for the layout root:

```
LayoutRoot.DataContext = xNode.InnerXml;
```

Your finished function will look like this:

```
public void Handle_Click(Object obj, RoutedEventArgs e)
        {
            string strZIP = tZIP.Text;
            AddressService.Service d = new AddressService.Service();
            XmlNode xNode = d.GetAddresses(strZIP);
            LayoutRoot.DataContext = xNode.InnerXml;


        }
```

Now when you run your application, you can enter text in the text box, click the button, and presto—you'll have live data in the interaction that the designer handed off to you.

Summary

In this chapter, you took a first look at WPF and how it all hangs together. You spent a lot of time with the new Expression Blend tool for designing WPF applications. However, you've barely scratched the surface of what is possible with WPF—there's a whole world of possibilities with dozens of controls, sophisticated timeline- and key frame–based animations, 3D, graphics APIs, multimedia, and more. If you want to look more into WPF, it's a good idea to check out *Foundations of WPF: An Introduction to Windows Presentation Foundation* (Apress, 2006), which takes you through a primer in this development API, and *Applications = Code + Markup* (Microsoft Press, 2006), which gives a very detailed look at the XAML API, going into depth on each of the tags, from controls to timelines and from layouts to multimedia.

CHAPTER 9

■ ■ ■

.NET 3.0: Windows Workflow Foundation

Workflow is what happens when an item is moved through various stages or people through a fixed business process. This process contains a number of steps or activities that can be acted on by machines, people, or a combination of both, and can involve various rules. For example, when you first join a new company, a set of business processes gets invoked. You need to be added to payroll, you need an office to be assigned, equipment and furniture need to be set up, and so on. Behind the scenes, a business process kicks in for the new hire. Or, when a company sells something, it typically begins with receipt of a purchase order. The purchase order has to be entered into the business system. This sets up a requisition for the product from stock. If not enough of the product is available, more needs to be ordered. When enough of the product is available, it is moved to shipping. Shipping boxes them up and sends them to the customer. Billing then generates an invoice to send to the customer. Billing also tracks payment, and if the customer pays, the order is flagged as such. If they don't pay by the time of the terms of the invoice, a new process for collections is kicked in.

Throughout this entire scenario, an "item," the purchase requisition, flows throughout the system. The item morphs and changes throughout, but as you can see from this example, it changes into what makes sense for the current stage in the process. The entire scenario is termed a *workflow*, and each of the actionable elements in it (entering the purchase order, building the order, etc.) is termed an *activity*.

A workflow isn't always linear. In fact, it is *rarely* linear. In the preceding scenario, the workflow could have gone in different directions based on different scenarios. For example, if the company has enough stock of whatever was ordered, the next step is to go to shipping and billing. If it doesn't, the next step is to order new product and wait for the order to be fulfilled before it can go to shipping and billing. In this case, it is likely that a customer service workflow, informing the customer of the delay, would also kick in. This is what is called *branching* in workflow terminology.

There are a number of different types of possible workflows. The preceding example is what is known as a *sequential* workflow, where the item flows from a known beginning point (receipt of the order) to a known endpoint (shipping, billing, and collecting).

Another type of workflow is called a *state* workflow, where the item moves between different states when certain criteria are met. An example of this is when an item is constructed in response to a purchase request (as opposed to just being sold from stock). Many computer manufacturers create a computer to order nowadays, and this process can be seen as a stateful workflow.

When the order is first received, the computer hasn't been created yet, and this is its initial state. Its next state could be Ready to Assemble, but before it can transition to this state, all of the components need to be available and assignable to this order. Once those criteria are met and the components assigned, the computer transitions to the Ready to Assemble state. In this state, it still isn't a computer, just a bunch of parts. It could remain in this state for some time, until the assembler has time to complete it. When the assembler has put together the computer, he may find that some of the components are broken, and he cannot complete assembly, so he returns it to the previous state; or if assembly has been completed, he could transition it to the new Assembled: Ready to Test state.

At this point, the test process kicks in, and should it pass, the computer will be transitioned to a Working state. Now we have a working computer, but the order likely includes a mouse, software add-ons such as manuals and discs, a monitor, and so forth. When these components are available and assigned to the order, the state then transitions into a Ready to Ship state. Once it reaches this state, the product is sent to shipping, and once it goes out the door it transitions to the Shipped state. Finally, when the order is received and acknowledged, the state machine transitions to the Completed state and is effectively destroyed.

Now consider the difficulties involved in developing business process scenarios using a programming language. The sheer complexity of even simple systems like those just described can make for some real spaghetti code, and because multiple departments and individuals are concerned, each with their own priorities and requirements, the overall scenario becomes a very complex one.

It is with this in mind that Microsoft has added Windows Workflow Foundation (WF) to .NET 3.0, providing a runtime environment for sequential and state-based workflows that are (mostly) visually designed, and compiled into code that will execute on the WF host that is present in the framework, and soon to be available to other applications such as Office.

This chapter gives you an introduction to this framework, and takes you through some of the tools that are available to you. It will focus on the web-oriented aspects of building WF applications, namely how they can be exposed as web services (you can compile your sequential or state-based workflow into a web service that the rest of your application can use); and also how they can compose web services—where your existing web services can be integrated into a workflow, giving you the ability to tie departments together into a coherent, centralized workflow.

Using WF

WF is at its heart a programming model along with the runtime engine and the tools to create workflow applications. The programming APIs are encapsulated in the .NET 3.0 namespace System.Workflow. The best place to get started is with the tools themselves. They are available already with Visual Studio 2008, or as an add-on to Visual Studio 2005. Please note that if you have downloaded and installed the Orcas add-ons for Visual Studio 2005, WF is *not* included. It is a separate download that can be obtained from the Windows Vista downloads section of MSDN, at http://msdn2.microsoft.com/en-us/ windowsvista. You'll look at the workflow templates in Visual Studio in the next section. Just as a real business process is composed of a number of activities connected by rules and flow, a WF process application also uses activities, of which the template provides many out-of-the-box activities dealing with branching, input/output, managing external services and activities, and so on. You can also compile your own activities into an activity library that can be reused by other workflow applications. In addition, a workflow can of course contain another workflow as an activity within it.

The next component in the WF architecture is the WF runtime engine. This executes the workflow, handling scheduling, rules, and everything necessary to make the workflow run as intended and designed. When long-running stateful transactions are needed, the workflow will often need to be persisted to save on resources when it isn't being used.

Finally comes the host process. The WF runtime engine is not an executable environment. You have to host it within an application, be it a console, Windows, or web application, in order for it to work. Thus, you can, for example, "embed" a workflow application in your web site that gets executed upon filling in a form on a web page, or you can host it to an external web service that gets called from your web applications, but the WF activity runs on the ASP.NET server that manages the web service. Any application can host a WF process as long as it is capable of invoking the .NET 3.0 runtime.

Using Visual Studio to Build Workflows

To build a workflow application using Visual Studio, select File ➤ New Project. In the New Project dialog, select Workflow as the project type (available to C# and Visual Basic), and you'll see the available project templates (see Figure 9-1).

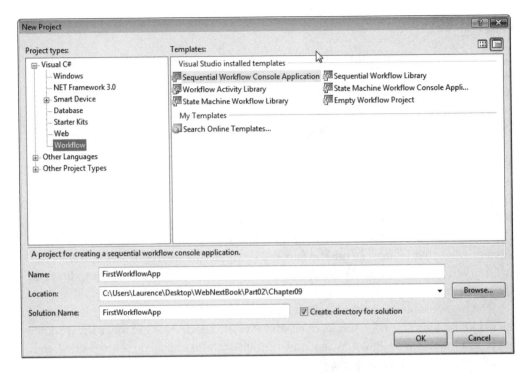

Figure 9-1. *Creating a new WF application*

The available templates are as follows:

Sequential Workflow Console Application: This contains a simple sequential workflow and the code for a Windows console application that can host it.

Sequential Workflow Library: This contains a simple sequential workflow that can be published as an activity or a web service.

Workflow Activity Library: This allows you to create a new activity for the WF Toolbox.

State Machine Workflow Console Application: This contains a state machine workflow and the code for a Windows console application that can host it.

State Machine Workflow Library: This contains a simple state machine workflow that can be published as an activity or a web service.

Empty Workflow Project: This provides a simple workspace that allows you to add your own workflow application types.

You can experiment with these to find the template that best suits you. For this example, you will step through building a simple sequential workflow console

application called FirstWorkFlowApp (see Figure 9-1). And, yes, if you were wondering—
this will be a Hello World application!

When you create this application using the template, you'll be taken to the Visual
Studio IDE with the Workflow Designer open, and the set of available activities open in
the Toolbox (see Figure 9-2).

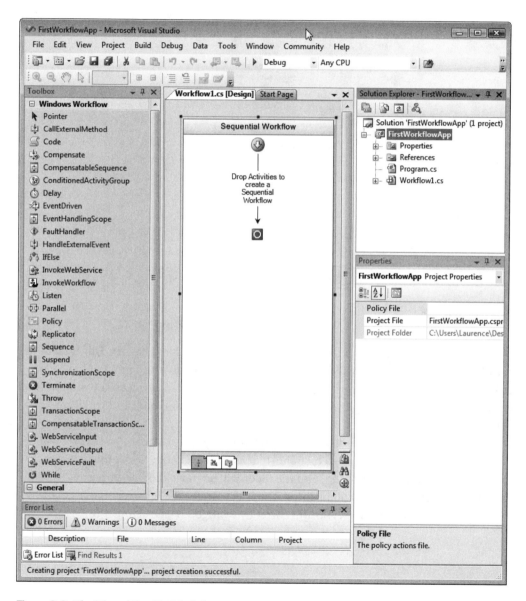

Figure 9-2. *The Visual Studio Workflow Designer*

The available activities can be seen on the left side of the screen. In the next section, you'll be taken on a tour of the major ones, but for now you'll use the Code activity. Drag it from the Toolbox to the Workflow Designer onto the sequential line where it indicates that it should be dropped. Alternatively, you can double-click the activity in the Toolbox. You should see something like Figure 9-3 when you complete this.

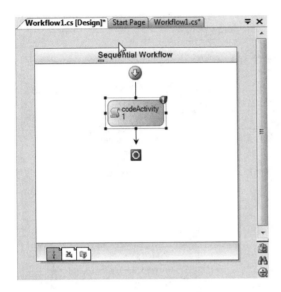

Figure 9-3. *Adding a Code activity*

Note that the activity has a red alert icon in its top-right-hand corner. This is feedback from the Designer notifying you that the activity isn't fully configured or has an error of some sort. It's useful feedback allowing you to visually inspect your workflow for errors before you try to compile or run it. Click the exclamation mark and you'll get details of the error (see Figure 9-4).

As you can see, the Code activity needs the property ExecuteCode to be set or it will not work. The tool also gives you a nice shortcut as it is selectable. Select the message (Property 'ExecuteCode' is not set), and the focus will be moved to the Properties window with the ExecuteCode property highlighted. You'll also notice the red exclamation mark informing you that the activity is not yet correctly configured (see Figure 9-5).

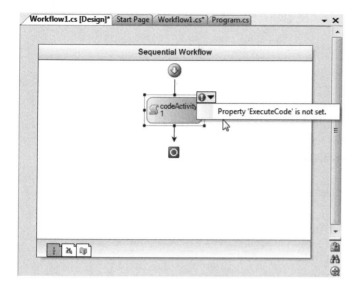

Figure 9-4. *Using the error tooltips on an activity*

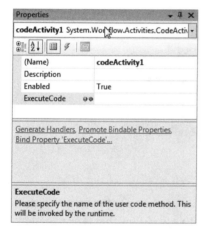

Figure 9-5. *Using the Properties window in WF*

The ExecuteCode property defines a code procedure that gets executed when the CodeActivity node is encountered in the workflow. You can code up a procedure yourself and add its name to this property, or you can have the IDE generate one for you. To do this, make sure that the ExecuteCode property is highlighted (as in Figure 9-5) and select the Generate Handlers link (which can also be seen in Figure 9-5). Pick a name for the function and place the name of this function in the ExecuteCode property. The IDE will then generate the code for you. If you select the name codeActivity1_ExecuteCode as the event handler, the code will look like this:

```
private void codeActivity1_ExecuteCode(object sender, EventArgs e)
        {

        }
```

This is now the code that will execute when this code block is reached. To turn this application into a Hello World application, you just need to add a couple of lines of code to it to get it to write out the message, and read in a new line before exiting. When you're done, the ExecuteCode function will look like this:

```
private void codeActivity1_ExecuteCode(object sender, EventArgs e)
        {
            Console.WriteLine("Hello, World!");
            Console.ReadLine();
        }
```

You can now execute the application to get the wonderfully sophisticated Hello World application running as a workflow hosted in a Windows console application (see Figure 9-6).

Figure 9-6. *Running the Hello World application*

The simplicity of the application belies the complexity of what is going on under the hood, where the sequential design has been compiled into a workflow that is executed by the WF runtime hosted in the console application.

You can see the code for the console application here (it is in Program.cs in your workspace):

```
namespace FirstWorkflowApp
{
    class Program
    {
        static void Main(string[] args)
        {
            using(WorkflowRuntime workflowRuntime = new WorkflowRuntime())
            {
```

```
AutoResetEvent waitHandle = new AutoResetEvent(false);
workflowRuntime.WorkflowCompleted +=
    delegate(object sender, WorkflowCompletedEventArgs e)
    {waitHandle.Set();};
workflowRuntime.WorkflowTerminated +=
    delegate(object sender, WorkflowTerminatedEventArgs e)
{
    Console.WriteLine(e.Exception.Message);
    waitHandle.Set();
};

WorkflowInstance instance =
    workflowRuntime.CreateWorkflow(typeof
        (FirstWorkflowApp.Workflow1));
instance.Start();

waitHandle.WaitOne();
            }
        }
    }
}
```

This code creates the new instance of the WorkflowRuntime called workflowRuntime. With this, it creates a waitHandle that exits the workflow when set. It adds a couple of event handlers to execute when the workflow completes or is terminated. When the workflow completes, you simply set the waitHandle. When it terminates, you dump out the error message and then set the waitHandle.

Next, it uses the workflowRuntime to create a WorkflowInstance. This instance is initialized with the workflow that you want to run, which in this case is called Workflow1 and is in the FirstWorkflowApp namespace.

It will then start the instance, calling the waitOne method on the waitHandle. This locks activity until the waitHandle is set.

Thus, when your application is run, the line instance.Start() kicks off the workflow sequence. This hits the CodeActivity node, which causes its ExecuteCode function to run. This function writes the text out to the console window and waits for a key to be pressed. When the key is pressed, the sequence moves to the next node, which is the end of the workflow. This causes the WorkflowCompleted event to fire, which sets the waitHandle, which in turn completes the waitOne method on the instance. At this point, the flow passes to the next line, which is the end of the application, so the application terminates.

Adding Input Parameters to an Application

In most cases, a workflow will require some form of input stimulus, like the details of a purchase order in our earlier scenarios. In this example, we'll expand on the Hello World application to allow the user to enter their age as a parameter to it. Then, depending on their age, different things may happen!

Create a new sequential workflow console application, but this time go directly to Program.cs before you design the workflow.

When you create an instance of the workflow, an overload exists that allows you to specify the parameters. You define the parameters as a dictionary with code like this (you'll see where they go in the next listing):

```
Dictionary<string,object> parameters= new Dictionary<string,object>();
parameters["age"] = 125; // Could replace with args[0] if you like :)
```

Now, when you instantiate the workflow instance, you pass this parameters dictionary to it. The call looks like this:

```
WorkflowInstance instance = workflowRuntime.CreateWorkflow(
    typeof(SecondWorkflowApp.Workflow1),parameters);
```

And here is the entire Main procedure from Program.cs:

```
static void Main(string[] args)
{
  using(WorkflowRuntime workflowRuntime = new WorkflowRuntime())
  {
    AutoResetEvent waitHandle = new AutoResetEvent(false);
    workflowRuntime.WorkflowCompleted +=
      delegate(object sender, WorkflowCompletedEventArgs e) {waitHandle.Set();};

    workflowRuntime.WorkflowTerminated +=
      delegate(object sender, WorkflowTerminatedEventArgs e)
      {
        Console.WriteLine(e.Exception.Message);
        waitHandle.Set();
      };
    Dictionary<string,object> parameters= new Dictionary<string,object>();
    parameters["age"] = 125; // Could replace with args[0] if you like :)
```

```
WorkflowInstance instance =
  workflowRuntime.CreateWorkflow(typeof(SecondWorkflowApp.Workflow1),parameters);

instance.Start();
waitHandle.WaitOne();
  }
}
```

Now that you're passing parameters to the workflow, the workflow has to know how to accept them—and it does this using the .NET property model. If you look at the preceding listing, you'll see that a parameter called age is used. Thus, you'll need to have a settable age property in your workflow. You can do this by adding some simple code to Workflow1.designer.cs:

```
partial class Workflow1
{
        private int ageVal=0;
        public int age
        {
            set { ageVal = value; }
        }
        private CodeActivity codeActivity2;
        private IfElseBranchActivity ifElseBranchActivity2;
        private IfElseBranchActivity ifElseBranchActivity1;
        private IfElseActivity ifElseActivity1;
        private CodeActivity codeActivity1;
}
```

This code has a private variable that is used to store the age, and a public settable one that maps whatever comes into the private variable.

The next step is to add the workflow activities. For this application, you are going to implement an IfElse activity driven off a simple rule. If the entered age is over 100, you will go down one activity route; otherwise you will go down another.

Drag an IfElse activity onto the design surface. The Designer should look like Figure 9-7.

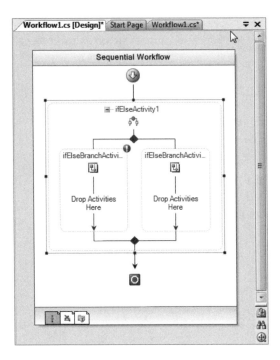

Figure 9-7. *Adding an IfElse activity*

You will see that the left branch of the IfElse activity is flagging an error. This is because the conditions of the IfElse have not yet been set up. Selecting it will take you to the Properties dialog. It will show you that the condition hasn't been set, and give you the option of adding a code condition or a rule condition (see Figure 9-8).

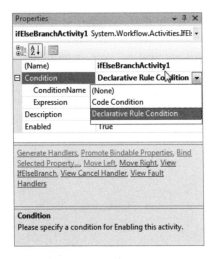

Figure 9-8. *Setting a new condition*

Adding a code condition allows you to specify a function that will fire off to evaluate the condition, and a declarative rule allows you to specify a simple rule. In our case, we're just using a very simple rule, so choose this option. Next, notice that the ConditionName is given a red alert because it isn't yet set. Change this field to a good name for the rule, such as ageOver100.

Once you've done this, notice that the alert moves to the ConditionExpression field, as you haven't yet defined it. Click the ellipsis button (. . .) and the Rule Condition Editor will open (see Figure 9-9).

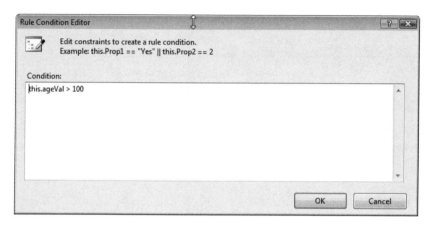

Figure 9-9. *Adding the rule condition with the editor*

Enter the rule this.ageVal > 100, as shown in Figure 9-9. You'll notice that you have full IntelliSense, which is a nice touch.

Click OK and the Rule Condition Editor will close, entering the rule into the `Expression` property. You'll also notice that the IfElse node on the Designer now has no alerts, so it is configured correctly.

Drag a Code activity to the left branch of the IfElse. This is the path that the sequence will follow if the rule is met (i.e., if the age is over 100). Use the procedures you followed earlier to add an `ExecuteCode` function to it, and put this code in that function:

```
private void codeActivity1_ExecuteCode(object sender, EventArgs e)
{
    Console.WriteLine("You say you are " + this.ageVal
                    + " years old? I don't believe you!");
    Console.ReadLine();
}
```

Repeat this process for the right-hand branch of the IfElse activity. When you get to the Properties dialog, wire up the `ExecuteCode` function as before and then add the following code to it:

```
private void codeActivity2_ExecuteCode(object sender, EventArgs e)
{
    Console.WriteLine("Hello World to you who is " + this.ageVal + " years old!");
    Console.ReadLine();
}
```

When you are done, the Designer should look like Figure 9-10. No errors, no red alerts.

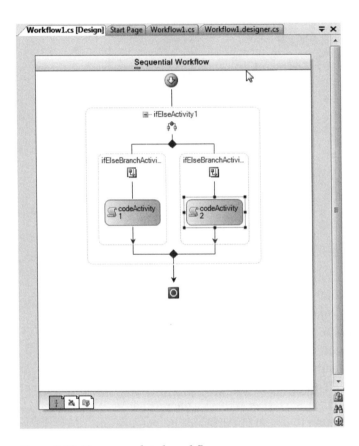

Figure 9-10. *Your completed workflow*

Now when you run the application, take a look at what happens. Remember you hard-coded the age to be 125 in Program.cs? The output that is rendered as a result is shown in Figure 9-11. Change the age parameter to a value less that 100, and you'll see the output in Figure 9-12.

Figure 9-11. *Running the parameterized workflow with age greater than 100*

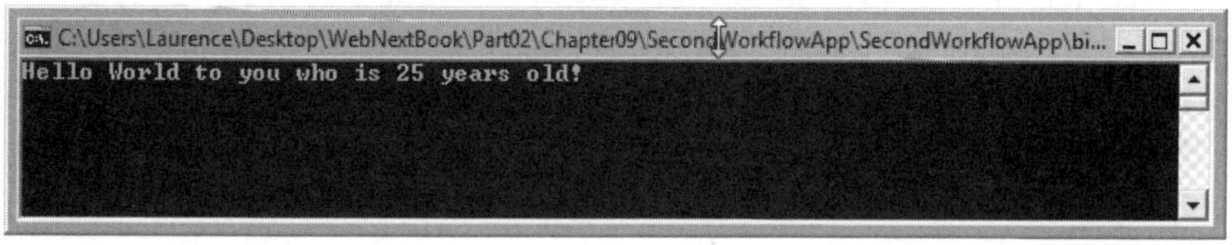

Figure 9-12. *Running the parameterized workflow with age less than 100*

Out-of-the-Box Activities

If you followed along in the previous examples, you will have noticed that a variety of out-of-the-box activities were available to you. You used two of them—the Code activity and the IfElse activity. In addition to these, WF offers a few more:

Compensate: This is an activity that you can use in case of an error, and is used with the FaultHandler activity. You use the Compensate activity to undo actions that have already been performed, in a similar manner to a rollback in database transactions.

ConditionedActivityGroup (CAG): You use a CAG to specify a group of activities where each one has its own criteria. When a condition for the group as a whole is met, execution passes out of the group.

Delay: This activity allows you to put pauses of a specified duration into your workflow.

EventDriven: This contains other activities to execute in response to an event firing.

FaultHandler: This allows you to handle errors. When an error occurs, you can direct to a fault handler (like a Catch statement in code) and specify the actions to follow.

InvokeWebService: This is used to communicate with a web service via its proxy class. A proxy class can be generated by the IDE when you make a reference to a web service.

Parallel: This allows you to specify multiple parallel routes of execution, and will not complete until all routes are complete.

Replicator: This is a conditional looping activity that creates a number of instances of a single activity. When they are all complete, the activity will be complete.

Sequence: This is used to link activities together in sequence. Once all have been completed, it will complete.

Terminate: This activity ends the current workflow.

Throw: This is used to raise an exception from within a workflow or other activity.

While: This works like a While loop in programming parlance, executing an activity repeatedly until a condition is met.

Workflow and the Web

These simple examples of workflow applications were hosted within a console application. When it comes to the Web, you may want to consider using workflow for your middleware and back-end transactions. As such, you will either want to host it in an ASP.NET web page or web service, or ideally, publish it as a web service that your other applications can use. Fortunately, WF supports the latter—you can publish your workflows as web services and reuse them, calling them with SOAP standards from other applications or web sites.

The best way to learn how to do this is by example, so let's create a new project, but this time make it a sequential workflow library and call it CToFService.

Once it is done, you'll get the design surface for the workflow. The first thing you'll need to do is to expand the Workflow1.cs node in the Solution Explorer, select Workflow1.designer.cs, and add the following interface declaration to it:

```
public interface CToF
    {
        double doCToF(double nC);
    }
```

This sets up the interface to describe the web service method(s) that the activities will recognize and invoke.

Next, you should drag a WebServiceInput activity to the design surface. You'll see an alert on it as it isn't an activating input. The first WebServiceInput in a sequence must be an activating input (see Figure 9-13).

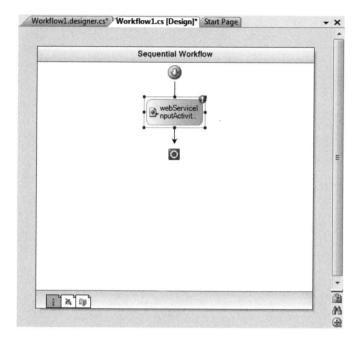

Figure 9-13. *Adding a WebServiceInput to your workflow*

You'll need to go configure a few properties to make sure that your WebServiceInput activity is properly configured:

1. First, as the error tag indicates, you'll need to make this WebServiceInput activity an activating input. You do this by setting the IsActivating property to true.

2. The error alert will move to the InterfaceType property, indicating that you need to specify the type of interface for this service. Click the ellipsis button (. . .) and you'll get the Browse and Select a .NET Type dialog. Select Current Project and you'll see the interface that you defined earlier as an option (see Figure 9-14).

3. Once you've selected the CToF interface and clicked OK, you'll see that the error alert moves to MethodName. The method that you specified on the interface was called doCToF, so select that here.

4. You'll now see that a property exists for nC, which is the value (of type double) that the interface declared as being passed into the web service. It has the alert beside it. You need to bind it to a member of your workflow, so click the ellipsis button (. . .), and the binding dialog will appear (Figure 9-15).

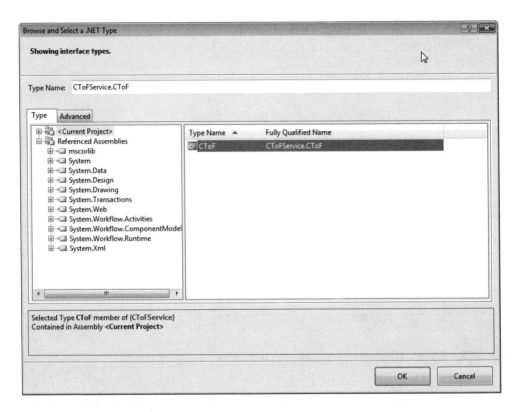

Figure 9-14. *Specifying the interface type*

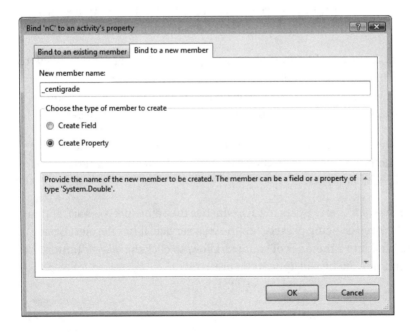

Figure 9-15. *Binding activity values to properties*

5. Give the new member the name _centigrade, and choose Create Property. Click OK.

6. The properties will now all be properly bound with no errors, but the WebServiceInput activity still shows an error—this is because it also requires a WebServiceOutput, which isn't yet present. So, rectify that by dragging a WebServiceOutput activity onto the design surface underneath the input (see Figure 9-16).

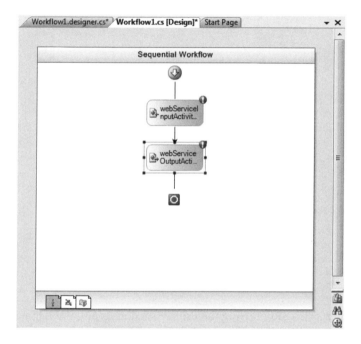

Figure 9-16. *Adding a WebServiceOutput activity*

7. You'll see that it still has an error flag, because it hasn't been assigned to a Web-ServiceInput. Fix that by going to the InputActivityName property and assigning it to the WebServiceInput activity (which will probably be called webServiceInput-Activity1).

8. You'll see that the return value is flagging an error because it isn't set. Select it and click the ellipsis button to bind the return value to a member. This member doesn't exist yet, so select the "Bind to a new member" tab and create a new property called _fahrenheit—the same as you did for the input parameter back in Figure 9-15.

9. You'll see that the WebServiceInput and WebServiceOutput activities are no longer showing any errors. However, you still need to perform one more step—the conversion of centigrade to Fahrenheit, which you do by adding a new Code activity between the existing activities (see Figure 9-17).

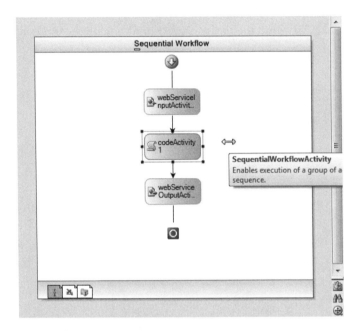

Figure 9-17. *Adding a Code activity between the input and the output*

10. Generate an `ExecuteCode` handler using the Properties dialog, and the IDE will generate the code handler, wire it up to the workflow, and then open the code window. Edit the handler so that it reads like this:

```
private void codeActivity1_ExecuteCode(object sender, EventArgs e)
      {
          _fahrenheit = 32 + ((9 * _centigrade) / 5);
      }
```

The environment is taking the burden of mapping the input from the web service caller to `_centigrade`, and mapping `_fahrenheit` to the output that is sent back to the caller. This function derives one from the other using the standard centigrade-to-Fahrenheit formula.

11. The next step is to publish this library as a web service. You do this by selecting the project in the Solution Explorer, right-clicking, and selecting Publish as Web Service from the context menu (see Figure 9-18).

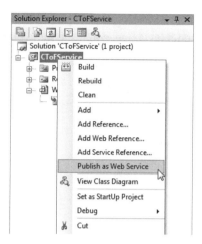

Figure 9-18. *Publishing a workflow as a web service*

12. Should all go according to plan, you'll have a new web site created within your solution. This site will contain the compiled workflow (CToFService.dll) and a web service that invokes it called CTOFService.Workflow1_WebService.asmx. Right-click this service and click View in Browser. The browser will launch and show the standard Web Services test harness (see Figure 9-19).

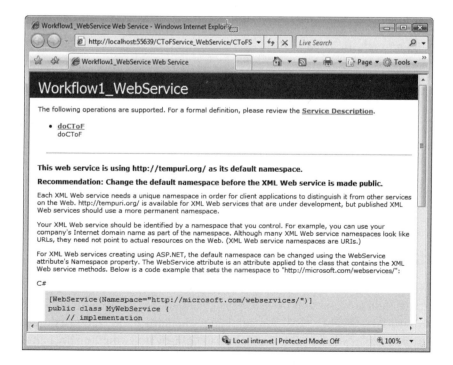

Figure 9-19. *Running the workflow as a web service*

Notice that the exposed web method is called doCToF, as this is what you defined on the interface. Also, when you select doCToF to call up its test page, you'll see that you can enter the value for nC (see Figure 9-20).

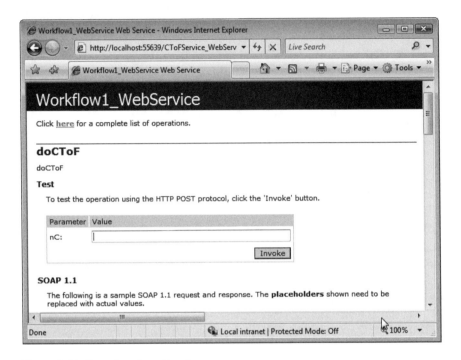

Figure 9-20. *Entering the nC value*

Clicking Invoke will now call the workflow and convert the input value from centigrade to Fahrenheit, returning the answer in an XML-encoded double.

This example shows how straightforward it is to use WF to create a workflow and expose it as a web service. It's worth playing and experimenting with, as, particularly for large complex transactions, you can drastically reduce the amount of code that you have to write and encapsulate business processes in easy-to-manage redistributable libraries that can be published as web services or hosted within web applications.

Summary

WF is a powerful and flexible design and runtime environment that allows you to encapsulate your business processes into a visual design and then compile and implement that design into a working program. This can come in particularly handy for web development, where you can neatly bundle up some very sophisticated functionality behind redistributable libraries or hosted, sharable web services. As you design your web application infrastructure, it's a good idea to start thinking about it in terms of workflow—and if complex systems and interactions can be designed as a workflow, you may save yourself and your company a lot of time and money by implementing it in WF. As such, WF, as one of the foundations of .NET 3.0, has a well-deserved place in the architecture of the future Web, and is a resource well worth learning and understanding. The simple applications that you learned in this chapter are but a taste of what is possible with WF. If you want to learn more about WF, a terrific resource to begin with is *Microsoft Windows Workflow Foundation Step by Step*, by Kenn Scribner (Microsoft Press, 2007).

CHAPTER 10

■■■

.NET 3.0: Programming with CardSpace

Windows CardSpace (formerly known as InfoCard) is a client application that allows your users to provide their digital identity and credentials to your application and other online services in a simple way while maintaining the essential qualities of security and trustworthiness. The interface it provides is typically known as an *identity selector*. Instead of logging into a web site with a username and password that can easily be forgotten, lost, or faked, the CardSpace application provides a UI with a set of "cards" that the user can choose from. These can either be cards that you generate yourself as a replacement for usernames and passwords, or *managed cards*, which are provided by an identity provider that is trusted—such as your employer or bank.

When you choose a card in response to a challenge from an online service, the application makes a request to the identity provider, signing and encrypting the communication, and the requested data is returned, also signed and encrypted. Should the user then want to relay the data to the online service, they can then do so, again in a secure encrypted and signed manner. The user is in charge of the communication at all times—the identity provider never sends the information directly to the requestor.

The ecosystem and architecture upon which CardSpace is built makes up what is usually termed the *Identity Metasystem*. This ecosystem is not limited to Microsoft and its technologies, but is a shared vision that is ultimately based on the WS-* standards. In this chapter, you'll take a look at getting started with using CardSpace on your site, seeing how you can accept information that comes from a card.

For the sake of simplicity, you'll be using user-issued cards only—which for all intents and purposes appear to be the same to you as the receiver of the information. You'll look at how to set up your system to try out CardSpace on your local IIS, and delve into some programming examples around accepting and parsing information out of cards that the user sends to you. First, however, you'll take a look at the client UI for CardSpace.

Using CardSpace

In Windows XP, you can launch CardSpace by using the Windows CardSpace entry in the Control Panel. This will launch the Information Cards window (see Figure 10-1).

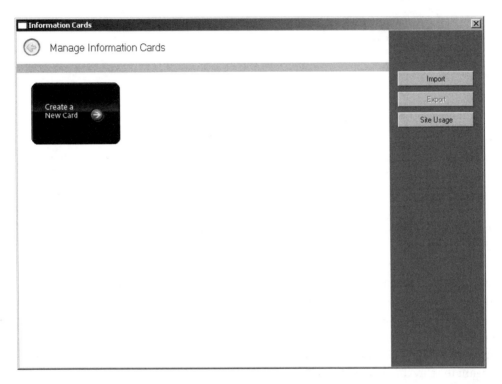

Figure 10-1. *Using CardSpace information cards in Windows XP*

This application has the same functionality, but a slightly different UI from the Windows Vista version that will be shown throughout the rest of this chapter. Using this application, you can create a new self-issued card containing your credentials, or import cards that have been provided by managed identity providers as CRD or CRDS files.

The Vista interface is shown in Figure 10-2. You can access Windows CardSpace from the Control Panel in the User Accounts and Family Safety section.

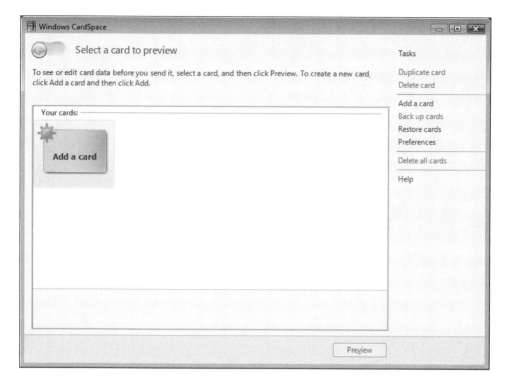

Figure 10-2. *Using CardSpace in Vista*

The first time you use CardSpace, you'll likely see a setup like that in Figure 10-2. You have no cards in your wallet, but you have the facility to add a new self-issued card or import one from a managed provider.

Adding a New Card to Your CardSpace Wallet

To add a new card to your CardSpace wallet, click the "Add a card" icon ("Create a new card," if you are using XP). You'll be taken to the next step of the wizard, where you can either create a personal card or install a managed card (see Figure 10-3).

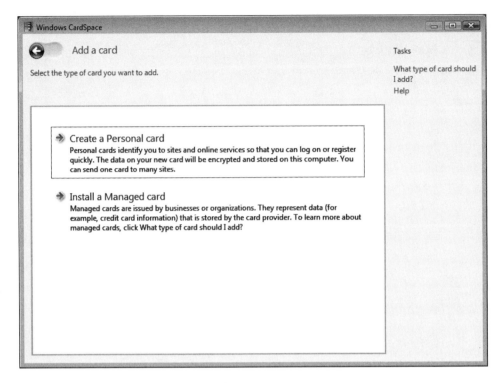

Figure 10-3. *Adding a new card to CardSpace*

Select the first option, "Create a Personal card," and you will be taken to the "Edit a new card" screen, where you can enter your personal details. Use as many or as few items as you like. Different sites may require different sets of information, but what you choose to provide is up to you. You can see the "Edit a new card" screen in Figure 10-4.

Once you've completed the card and entered your details, you can save it, and the wizard will return you to the CardSpace screen, where your new card will be visible. Now whenever you go to a web site that requests your card, you can select it from here and send it. You'll see an example of this in the next section.

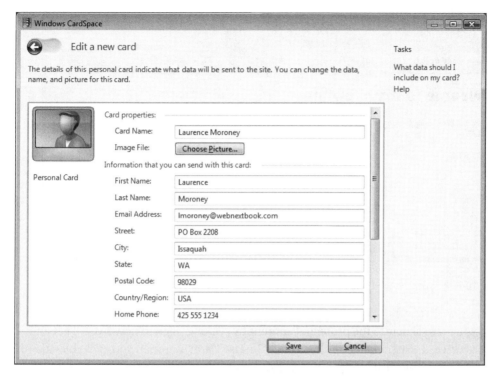

Figure 10-4. *The "Edit a new card" screen*

Using Cards on the Web

When you visit a web site that requires you to pass credentials using a card, the Card-Space application will automatically launch and ask you for the card to use. Different sites have different requirements, and the more sensitive the information, the more secure the card will need to be. As you can imagine, banking and brokerage sites will have different security needs from simple social networking sites, and they will likely require managed cards issued by a trusted authority. In this simple example, a personal card like the one you created in the previous section is enough.

Figure 10-5 shows a simple web site that requests you to sign in using a CardSpace card.

Figure 10-5. *A Simple CardSpace-secured site*

If you try to sign into the protected content by clicking "Sign in now!" you'll get an error, as no card is associated until you click the Use Card! button. If you click this, the page will invoke the CardSpace manager, requesting you to select a card (see Figure 10-6).

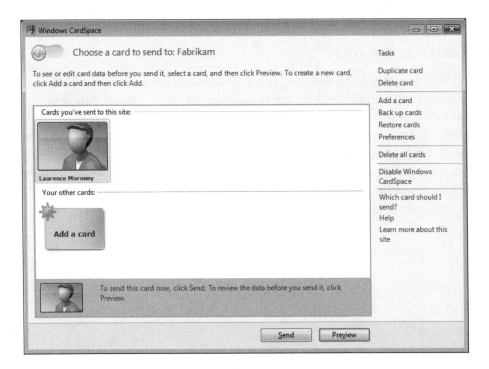

Figure 10-6. *Choosing a card to sign into the site*

You'll notice that it lists any cards that you've used on this site before at the top of the screen for your convenience. The Tasks pane on the right also provides useful tools and help, including which cards you should send.

When you select the card and click Preview, you can see the details for this card, including what the site is requesting from the card (see Figure 10-7).

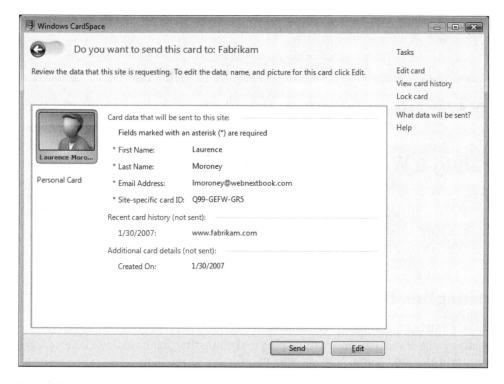

Figure 10-7. *Previewing the card*

As you can see in Figure 10-7, the first name, last name, e-mail address, and card ID are required. If these fields aren't filled in, CardSpace will not allow you to send the card to the server (the Send button will be disabled).

Clicking the Send button will then issue the card to the site. You can now click the "Sign in now!" button to send the credentials to the signed-in page. You can see this page in Figure 10-8. Note that this is just passing your identity credentials to the site. In most cases, the site will map these credentials to its account store, and based on a match there it will recognize you (or not).

Figure 10-8. *The CardSpace card has signed you into the site.*

Creating a Web Site That Uses CardSpace

The previous example demonstrated how a web site can use CardSpace on the client site to request and receive client credentials. In this section, you'll step through what it takes to build this application and run it on IIS. While CardSpace works on IIS 5, 6, and 7, this tutorial demonstrates installing certificates on IIS 7.

Preparing Your Development Environment for CardSpace

Your development environment will need some configuration before you can use CardSpace effectively. Before you do anything else, make sure that you have the Windows SDK installed. Within the Windows SDK, find the file WCFSamples.zip in the samples directory. In here, you'll find the technology samples folder containing CardSpace samples.

Look at the UsingCardSpacewithIE7 sample (note that CardSpace is not supported on earlier versions of Internet Explorer) and open the setup.bat file, using Notepad to inspect it.

Each CardSpace sample uses a similar setup, and they all follow the same four steps. Execute the setup.bat file to install the sample. The next sections will describe how it sets up CardSpace on your server.

Step 1: Registering CAPICOM.dll

The batch file should register CAPICOM.dll for you. On some systems this fails, so if you are having trouble installing the CardSpace samples, register it manually. You do this by changing to the Bin folder in the Windows SDK directory and issuing the following command from a DOS prompt:

```
Regsvr32 /s capicom.dll
```

This registers the DLL for you. Using /s does a silent installation, where you don't get the various status updates.

CAPICOM.dll is the implementation of the CAPICOM security layer, which allows for easy integration of security, digital signing, and encryption onto web pages. It is part of the Windows SDK, and can be found in the Bin directory. It provides a COM interface to the Microsoft CryptoAPI and exposes a set of its functions allowing for easy incorporation of digital signing and encryption into your programs. It provides support for smart cards, software keys, verification of digitally signed data, certificates, and more. It's well worth a look at its functions, but a deep dive goes beyond the scope of this book. However, the SDK documentation is a great place to start if you are serious about security in your web applications.

Step 2: Installing Certificates

The next function that the batch file performs is installing the certificates that are necessary to allow the site to be authenticated and trusted with HTTPS in the browser. This is performed by the install-certificates.vbs script.

The SDK ships with four sample certificates, used by the following URLs:

https://www.contoso.com

https://www.fabrikam.com

https://www.woodgrovebank.com

https://www.adatum.com

When you browse to a site, the certificate has to match the site—so if you visit http://localhost and it is certified by a certificate from https://www.contoso.com, you will get an error in the browser. This offers you two levels of security. The first is that Internet Explorer will present you with a blocking page letting you know that there is a problem with the certificate (see Figure 10-9).

This security measure is in place to prevent a "bad" site from delivering the certificate from a "good" site and betraying the user's trust. However, Internet Explorer still gives you the choice to proceed to the site, but lets you know that it isn't recommended. Should you decide to do this, you'll see another visual indicator that there is a problem with the site—the address bar is colored red and a certificate error is highlighted (see Figure 10-10).

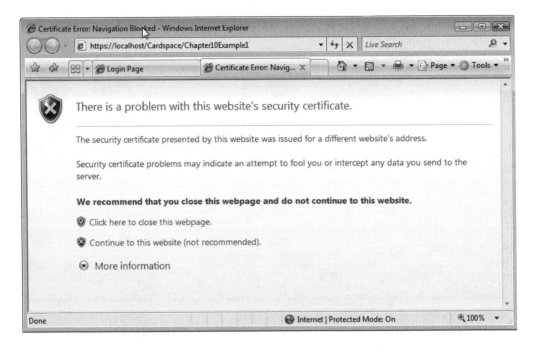

Figure 10-9. *Internet Explorer presents a blocking page when the certificate is issued for the wrong address.*

Figure 10-10. *Second level of certificate security*

To avoid these problems on your machine, see step 3.

Step 3: Editing the hosts File

The next step in the setup script is to edit your hosts file. Internet Explorer matches the domain name in the browser address bar to that in your certificate. If they don't match, you get the errors in Figures 10-9 and 10-10. When you are setting up a development environment, you will of course be hosting the applications on localhost, which doesn't match the certificates—but Windows provides a methodology to allow you to map IP addresses to domain names (taking a bypass around the DNS): the hosts file.

This file, found in Windows\System32\drivers\etc, is just called hosts (no extension). You can open it in Notepad to inspect it. Its structure is very simple: an IP address, followed by at least one space, followed by the domain name, and an optional comment denoted by a #.

The default hosts settings will likely look like this:

```
127.0.0.1        localhost
::1              localhost
```

The samples installer adds the adatum.com, contoso.com, fabrikam.com, and woodgrovebank.com sites to hosts, mapping them to 127.0.0.1 (your machine) also. When the script is done, your hosts file will likely look like this:

```
127.0.0.1        localhost
::1              localhost
127.0.0.1        www.adatum.com
127.0.0.1        adatum.com
127.0.0.1        www.contoso.com
127.0.0.1        contoso.com
127.0.0.1        www.fabrikam.com
127.0.0.1        fabrikam.com
127.0.0.1        www.woodgrovebank.com
127.0.0.1        woodgrovebank.com
```

Now, whenever the browser is instructed to go to www.fabrikam.com, it will bypass the DNS and consider 127.0.0.1 to be the server for this domain. Now the browser will match the domain name on the URL with that on the certificate, and you'll be able to access the site securely.

As the hosts file can be used to bypass the DNS and potentially fool users into thinking they are on one site when they are on another, it is protected by Windows and requires administrative access for it to be edited. However, you should check your hosts file regularly to make sure that it hasn't been hijacked.

Now that everything is in place, the final step is to install the samples themselves.

Step 4: Installing the Webs

The final step is very straightforward, and depending on which sample set you are installing, it creates the virtual web mapping IIS to the directory containing the web content so you can access it via `http://localhost/samplename`.

Creating Your Own CardSpace-Secured Web

Now that the SDK setup scripts have configured your environment by installing the certificates, registering the `CAPICOM.dll`, and editing your `hosts` file, you are ready to create your own CardSpace-secured web.

Note that CardSpace-secured webs run on HTTPS, so you will create this application as an HTTP web application on IIS, not a file system site as you have been doing in earlier chapters in this book.

Run Visual Studio (with administrative permissions on Vista) and select File ➤ New Web Site. You'll get the New Web Site dialog (see Figure 10-11).

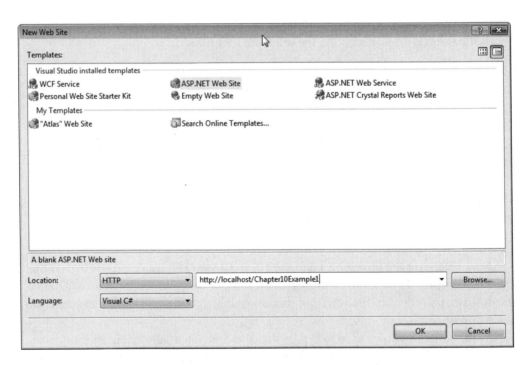

Figure 10-11. *Creating a new HTTP site*

Call the site Chapter10Example1, as shown in Figure 10-11.

The site will have a page, `Default.aspx`, that is used as the welcome page, and will redirect to `SignedIn.aspx` when the user passes credentials and attempts to sign in. In addition, it uses a set of helper classes in the `Microsoft.IdentityModel.TokenProcesser` namespace, which is implemented in the `TokenProcessor.cs` file that is part of the Windows SDK. We'll take a closer look at it a little later in the chapter.

Edit your `Default.aspx` page so that it looks like Listing 10-1.

Listing 10-1. *Default.aspx*

```
<%@ Page Language="C#" AutoEventWireup="true"
    CodeFile="Default.aspx.cs" Inherits="_Default" %>

<!DOCTYPE html PUBLIC "-//W3C//DTD XHTML 1.0 Transitional//EN"

"http://www.w3.org/TR/xhtml1/DTD/xhtml1-transitional.dtd">
<html xmlns="http://www.w3.org/1999/xhtml" >
<head>
    <title>CardSpace Secured Site</title>
        <object type="application/x-informationcard" name="_xmlToken">
            <param name="tokenType" value="urn:oasis:names:tc:SAML:1.0:assertion" />
            <param name="requiredClaims"
value="http://schemas.xmlsoap.org/ws/2005/05/identity/claims/givenname
http://schemas.xmlsoap.org/ws/2005/05/identity/claims/surname
http://schemas.xmlsoap.org/ws/2005/05/identity/claims/emailaddress
http://schemas.xmlsoap.org/ws/2005/05/identity/claims/privatepersonalidentifier"
/>
        </object>
    <script language="javascript">
            function GoGetIt()
            {
                var xmltkn=document.getElementById("_xmltoken");
                var thetextarea = document.getElementById("xmltoken");
                thetextarea.value = xmltkn.value ;
            }
    </script>
</head>
<body>
    <form id="form1" method="post" action="SignedIn.aspx">
    <div>
        <h1>
            Welcome to my Web Site</h1>
        This site is secured using Windows CardSpace.
        Please press the 'Use Card' button
        to retrieve your card and then click 'Sign In'
```

```
        <br />
        <br />
        <button name="go" id="go" onclick="javascript:GoGetIt();">
            Use Card!</button><br />
        <br />
        <br />
        <button type="submit">
            Sign in now!</button><br />
        <br />

        <input id="xmltoken" name="xmlToken" type="hidden" />
    </div>
    </form>


</body>
</html>
```

Running this page will give you the simple site that you saw earlier in this chapter. It is shown again in Figure 10-12.

Figure 10-12. *The CardSpace site*

You'll see that there are two buttons on here: Use Card!, which interfaces with Card-Space to get a card from the user; and "Sign in now!", which passes the token from the user's card to the SignIn.aspx page. Let's take a look back at the code and see how this hangs together.

The Use Card! button is defined with this markup:

```
<button name="go" id="go" onclick="javascript:GoGetIt();">
        Use Card!</button>
```

Upon clicking the button, the JavaScript function GoGetIt is invoked. Here's the function:

```
function GoGetIt()
{
    var xmltkn=document.getElementById("_xmltoken");
    var thetextarea = document.getElementById("xmltoken");
    thetextarea.value = xmltkn.value ;
}
```

This script uses the element _xmltoken to get its value and load that into a var that will fill a text box on the page. The _xmltoken field is a CardSpace object, whose definition looks like this:

```
<object type="application/x-informationcard" name="_xmlToken">
  <param name="tokenType" value="urn:oasis:names:tc:SAML:1.0:assertion" />
  <param name="requiredClaims"
value="http://schemas.xmlsoap.org/ws/2005/05/identity/claims/givenname
http://schemas.xmlsoap.org/ws/2005/05/identity/claims/surname
http://schemas.xmlsoap.org/ws/2005/05/identity/claims/emailaddress
http://schemas.xmlsoap.org/ws/2005/05/identity/claims/privatepersonalidentifier"
/>
</object>
```

This is how you use CardSpace on a page—by declaring an object of type application/x-informationcard and naming it. There are a number of properties supported by this object, including the facility to specify the data that's required by the site. Remember the earlier example in which the last name, first name, and so on were required data from the site—it is the requiredClaims property that dictates this. As you can see, it contains a list of the schemas of the required values.

When you query its value property, the object invokes the CardSpace client and allows you to specify a card. Should you specify and send a card, the value will become the token associated with that card; otherwise it will be null. The JavaScript code then loads the value of the token into the hidden text field xmltoken.

Next, when the user clicks "Sign in now!" they are in fact invoking a standard HTML form whose action is the SignedIn.aspx page, and one of whose elements is the hidden text field. This causes the token to be submitted to SignedIn.aspx from where it can be parsed.

If you don't have this page already, add a new web form to your project and call it
SignedIn.aspx.

Listing 10-2 shows the code for this page.

Listing 10-2. *SignedIn.aspx*

```
<%@ Page Language="C#"  Debug="true" ValidateRequest="false" %>
<%@ Import Namespace="System.IdentityModel.Claims" %>
<%@ Import Namespace="Microsoft.IdentityModel.TokenProcessor" %>

<!DOCTYPE html PUBLIC "-//W3C//DTD XHTML 1.0 Transitional//EN"
 "http://www.w3.org/TR/xhtml1/DTD/xhtml1-transitional.dtd">

<script runat="server">

    protected void ShowError(string text)
    {
        fields.Visible = false;
        errors.Visible = true;
        errtext.Text = text;
    }
    protected void Page_Load(object sender, EventArgs e)
    {
        string xmlToken;
        xmlToken = Request.Params["xmlToken"];
        if (xmlToken == null || xmlToken.Equals(""))
        {
            ShowError("Token presented was null");
        }
        else
        {
            Token token= new Token(xmlToken);
            givenname.Text = token.Claims[ClaimTypes.GivenName];
            surname.Text = token.Claims[ClaimTypes.Surname];
            email.Text = token.Claims[ClaimTypes.Email];
        }

    }
</script>
```

```
<html xmlns="http://www.w3.org/1999/xhtml" >
<head id="Head1" runat="server">
    <title>Login Page</title>
</head>
<body>
    <form id="form1" runat="server">
    <div runat="server" id="fields">
        <h1>
            Welcome to my Site!</h1>
        Thank you for signing in:  
        <asp:Label ID="givenname" runat="server"
            Text="" ForeColor="Red"></asp:Label>
        <asp:Label ID="surname" runat="server"
            Text="" ForeColor="Red"></asp:Label><br />
        <br />
        <br/>
        Email Address:
      <asp:Label ID="email" runat="server"
        Text="" ForeColor="Blue"></asp:Label><br/>
    </div>
    <div runat="server" id="errors" visible="false">
        Error:<asp:Label ID="errtext" runat="server" Text=""></asp:Label><br/>
    </div>

    </form>
</body>
</html>
```

When this page loads, it takes the xmlToken value off the request parameters. This value was passed in as a hidden form field by the Default.aspx page, and if a card was assigned by the user, it will contain the token associated with that card.

It creates an instance of the Token class from this value. This class is implemented in the SDK TokenProcessor.cs class, so make sure you have included it in your solution within the App_Code folder. It provides a collection of the metadata associated with the token (such as name or e-mail address) as a text collection. The page then pulls the values of the First Name, Last Name, and Email Address claims and assigns them to the Text property of the associated ASP.NET label controls.

Then, when the page renders, the labels get filled with the values from the card, received via the token and exposed via the claims. You can see the result in Figure 10-13.

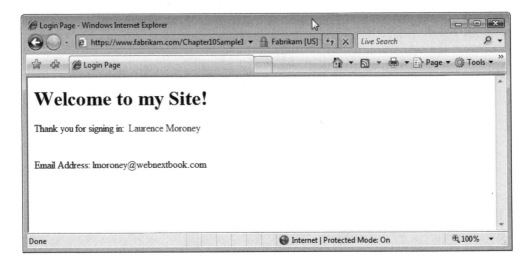

Figure 10-13. *Rendering the data from the card on the site*

As you can see, this example demonstrated that CardSpace is very easy to use once your site is set up to use HTTPS. At the heart of accessing and decrypting the information is the `Token` class, which is part of the `Microsoft.IdentityModel.TokenProcessor` namespace, which is supplied by the SDK (not a default part of .NET 3.0).

Exploring the TokenProcessor API

The TokenProcessor API provides a single class, `Token`, that is used to parse token information received from a card. It provides the following properties:

`IdentityClaims`: This returns a `System.IdentityModel.Claims.ClaimSet` collection, which contains all the claim objects in the token.

`Claims`: This returns a `ClaimTextCollection`, which is a read-only string collection of the claims in the token.

`IssuerIdentityClaim`: This returns a `System.IdentityModel.Claims.Claim` object with the issuer's identity claim (which is typically the private key of the issuer of a card).

`AuthorizationContext`: This is the `System.IdentityModel.Policy.AuthorizationContext` value that is returned when all the policies are evaluated by the `System.ServiceModel.ServiceAuthorizationManager`. This is used when handling tokens with WCF.

`UniqueID`: This gets the `UniqueID` (`IdentityClaim`) of this token.

The earlier example used the Claims property to pull the desired claims from the token and set the value of some label controls to their values like this:

```
Token token= new Token(xmlToken);
givenname.Text = token.Claims[ClaimTypes.GivenName];
surname.Text = token.Claims[ClaimTypes.Surname];
email.Text = token.Claims[ClaimTypes.Email];
```

Summary

As security is becoming more and more of a necessity as opposed to a luxury when dealing with the Web, it is essential to make users' experiences with security as friendly as possible, while still protecting them from malicious web sites.

CardSpace fills this void by providing an easy-to-use and attractive way of storing your personal information securely and digitally, and an easy means to send it to a web site that requests it. It is designed to be a long-term replacement for passwords, and can effectively form a client-based single sign-on for all of your favorite sites.

In this chapter, you explored CardSpace and how it looks from the user's point of view. You then went into putting together a development environment where you can host your own sites that accept CardSpace credentials. As part of this exercise, you looked briefly at site certificates and how they prevent domain spoofing. You then went into the process of building your own CardSpace-enabled site, looking at how to embed the CardSpace object on your pages and process it, taking user credentials and using them to customize the site for the end user.

Finally, you took a tour of a helper class that is provided by the SDK and that implements the token in an easily manageable way.

I hope this was a good taste of what you can do with CardSpace to make your users' lives a lot easier. There's a lot more information that you can drill into—and a great resource for this is the Windows SDK documentation.

In the next chapter, we'll get back onto the traditional web development route—looking at the technology that effectively gave birth to Web 2.0—Asynchronous JavaScript and XML, also known as Ajax.

■ ■ ■

CHAPTER 11

Ajax Applications and Empowering the Web User Experience

Ajax (Asynchronous JavaScript and XML) has become a major value proposition in the Web development industry. Indeed, 2006 was often called the "year of Ajax" because no matter where you turned, it seemed every software vendor was pushing their Ajax toolkit, Ajax sessions at conferences were filled to the rafters, and everybody wanted to use it on their web site. But Ajax has been around a lot longer than this—it's just that it seemed to hit critical mass in that year.

In this chapter, you'll look at what Ajax is at its core—no toolkits, no value-adds or complexities, just a good look at the technology underpinning the whole Ajax phenomenon. You'll start with a history of where it came from, an analysis of why it evolved, a good look at its architecture, and some hands-on experience in building some simple Ajax interactions using good old-fashioned JavaScript and HTML.

After that, the next few chapters will look at the AJAX extensions for ASP.NET and how these can empower your Ajax development experience by bringing the productivity of the server-side paradigm of ASP.NET and a suite of new JavaScript libraries to bear.

A Brief History of Ajax

The term *Ajax* was coined by Jesse James Garrett, and made its first public appearance in early 2005. At its heart is the ability to make web applications more responsive and more competitive with desktop applications. One part of this is to remove the need for the typical full page refresh that occurs when the user wants to see some new content on a page. For example, consider a page like MSN MoneyCentral (shown in Figure 11-1).

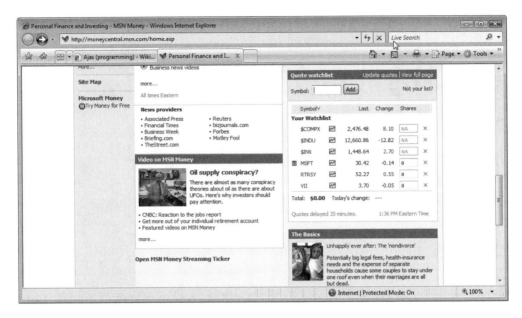

Figure 11-1. *MSN MoneyCentral*

This web site is a pretty typical one, presenting a portal of information to customers. There are many information panes on this portal, three of which can be seen in the screenshot (Video on MSN Money, Quote watchlist, and The Basics). Some of these information panes provide user interaction—for example, the Quote watchlist allows you to enter the stocks that you are interested in monitoring. It uses a simple HTML form where you enter the ticker of the stock you are interested in and click Add.

The typical web site will refresh the entire page once you click the Add button, causing a lag for the user, and the expense of traffic for the web site administrator. If you were to use a technique that allows for a *partial* refresh, then only the information pane that you want to change (i.e., the Quote watchlist) would be changed.

It was with use cases like this in mind that browser developers started adding new features long before the term *Ajax* was coined. The first attempt at allowing something like this was the IFrame, introduced in Internet Explorer 3 in 1996. This allowed you to use something similar to a frameset, but to have a frame showing a different set of content to be embedded within a page. Thus, in an application such as MoneyCentral, you would have one master page, and one complete subpage for each of the information panes. These pages would then be rendered on the master page using an IFrame. This technology still works and is useful today, but it makes for more complex management of a portal such as MoneyCentral, as many independent pages need to be maintained. The IFrame, and other new elements such as <div> and <span>, when grouped together with JavaScript, evolved into the generic term *DHTML* (Dynamic HTML), with the intent being that developers could produce pages that rewrite their own HTML in response to user actions, providing a dynamic environment that reduces postbacks and page refreshes.

Another increment to this came with Microsoft's Remote Scripting technology, which took this to the next level, providing a browser plug-in that could communicate with a server over sockets and expose the data that it received to JavaScript. This plug-in was a Java applet and was released with Internet Explorer 4.

After this, an ActiveX control that provided a dependency-free plug-in was produced by Microsoft. This object, called XMLHttpRequest, came with Internet Explorer 5. The first major application to use this functionality was the web-based version of Microsoft's popular Outlook e-mail program, Outlook Web Access. The e-mail scenario is perfect for asynchronous web page updates—when a new e-mail comes in, you would like it to appear in your inbox without a complete page refresh, just like it does in your desktop application.

This XMLHttpRequest ActiveX control is the heart of Ajax. Oddly enough, although it was released to the wild in 2000, it didn't really pick up until nearly five years later. There are a number of possible reasons for this, including browser support—initially, XMLHttpRequest was Internet Explorer–only. Another reason was likely the availability of broadband. Increasing broadband penetration over that five-year period lead to a greater demand for richer web applications and more incentive for web sites to provide richer experiences.

The first Ajax application that I used was Google Maps—with mapping being the perfect sweet spot for consumer-oriented rich applications. Consider your workflow when using a mapping application—you enter an address and receive a map showing the area around your address. You then likely want to inspect the area around that address, for example, to plot routes to that address. Before Ajax was used, you would pan around the map using North, South, East, and West buttons. The Ajax implementation used XMLHttpRequest to download the surrounding areas of the map in the background while you were inspecting the map. You would then drag the mouse around the map, and they would appear. Of course, if you dragged quickly, the tiles may not have been in place yet, and you would get a blank map while they downloaded—but the experience was still vastly superior to full page refreshes.

The improvement in the user experience and the reduced amount of bandwidth that needed to be served to provide it created an irresistible new design pattern for web sites and experiences, and it wasn't long before use of XMLHttpRequest became commonplace.

At the same time, the concept of Web 2.0 was emerging. This concept, invented by Tim O'Reilly, described the next phase of the Web, built around services that allowed users, not just web developers, to be contributors of information. Effective collaboration from novice users requires an enhanced experience, and Ajax was there to provide it. As such, in developer terms, Ajax is pretty synonymous with Web 2.0. In the next section, we'll take a look at getting started with Ajax programming and some of the neat things that you can do with it!

Coding with Ajax

As mentioned earlier, the heart of Ajax is the XMLHttpRequest object. For the rest of this chapter, you'll look at this object, building applications that use it to communicate with a back-end system.

XMLHttpRequest is as useful as it is simple—but as with anything that is powerful and simple, you should exercise caution in using it, and use it only when appropriate. It isn't, for example, appropriate to write a JavaScript function that uses XMLHttpRequest to script navigation between complete HTML pages, thus turning it into a browser within a browser!

While XMLHttpRequest is supported in all major modern browsers, there are differences that need to be coped with in your scripts. Internet Explorer 7, Firefox, Safari, and Opera support it as a native JavaScript object, whereas Internet Explorer 6 and earlier implement it as an ActiveX object—your code to implement the object needs to cater for all these browsers.

Listing 11-1 shows simple JavaScript code that loads an instance of XMLHttpRequest into a standard var.

Listing 11-1. *Creating an Ajax Instance*

```
var ajaxRequest
try
{
    ajaxRequest = new XMLHttpRequest();
}
catch(error)
{
    ajaxRequest = new ActiveXObject("Microsoft.XMLHTTP");
}
```

This code simply tries to create an instance of the native XMLHttpRequest object, which will succeed in Mozilla, Safari, Opera, and Internet Explorer 7. This instantiation will fail in Internet Explorer 6, but will be caught by the catch clause, and will then instantiate a Microsoft.XMLHTTP ActiveX object instead. The script will fail in older browsers that do not support Ajax, such as Internet Explorer 4.

Communicating with the Web Server

The XMLHttpRequest object supports two methods that allow communication with back-end servers. They are the open method, which you use to specify the request, and the send method, which you use to send it. The responses are returned asynchronously to call back JavaScript functions that you specify using the onreadystatechange property.

When building an Ajax application, you'll typically go through the same workflow to develop an asynchronous area on your page.

The first step is to use the open method, which supports up to four parameters:

- The first parameter, which is mandatory, is an HTTP command verb such as GET, POST, HEAD, PUT, or DELETE. You'll typically use GET to retrieve data when using Ajax.

- The second parameter is the URL of the resource that you are accessing. This is also a mandatory parameter.

- The third (optional) parameter predates Ajax, and is a Boolean determining whether an asynchronous request will be used. It defaults to true; setting it to false will disable asynchronicity, thus rendering the application non-Ajax. When this is false, the script processing will pause until the service returns.

- The fourth (optional) parameter is used to send a username to the service.

- The fifth (optional) parameter is used to send a password to the service.

The typical Ajax application will just use the first two parameters, as it will always be asynchronous, and it is very bad practice to put a username and password into a client script where they can easily be inspected with a View ➤ Source command in the browser.

The second step is to use onreadystatechange to set the name of the function to be used to handle callbacks. This function should be used to handle the different states of the transaction (available from the readyState property) to respond to these states. The states are uninitialized, open, sent, receiving, and loaded. You'll see how this is used in the examples later in this chapter.

The third step is to call the send method to send your request. This accepts a text parameter, which you'll use in the case of a POST transaction to contain the variables that you want to post to the server. When doing an HTTP-GET (which is typical for Ajax), you don't use this parameter—simply call send with no parameters.

That's it, your application is now using Ajax. Your callback function will typically wait until the readyState is loaded, meaning that all the data has been returned from the service, and you can update your page with the results.

In the next section, you'll look at a simple example—multiplying two numbers. You'll see how it will work in a typical ASP.NET page that uses postbacks, and then you'll see how it works with Ajax, and how just using Ajax can make the user experience better.

Simple Ajax and ASP.NET Example

Create a new ASP.NET web form called MultiplyNumbers using Visual Studio (or Visual Web Developer Express). Drag a couple of text boxes, a button, and three labels to it. Arrange them so that your screen looks something like that in Figure 11-2.

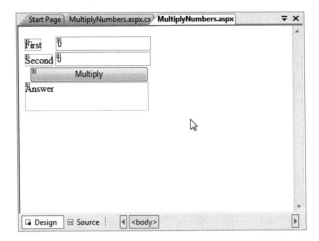

Figure 11-2. *Creating an ASP.NET number multiplier*

The associated markup for this page is shown in Listing 11-2.

Listing 11-2. *Markup for ASP.NET Multiplier*

```
<%@ Page Language="C#" AutoEventWireup="true" CodeFile="MultiplyNumbers.aspx.cs"
Inherits="MultiplyNumbers" %>

<!DOCTYPE html PUBLIC "-//W3C//DTD XHTML 1.0 Transitional//EN"
   "http://www.w3.org/TR/xhtml1/DTD/xhtml1-transitional.dtd">

<html xmlns="http://www.w3.org/1999/xhtml" >
<head runat="server">
    <title>Untitled Page</title>
</head>
<body>
    <form id="form1" runat="server">
    <div>
        <asp:Label ID="Label2" runat="server" Text="First"></asp:Label>
            
        <asp:TextBox ID="TextBox1" runat="server">0</asp:TextBox><br />
        <asp:Label ID="Label1" runat="server" Text="Second"></asp:Label>
        <asp:TextBox ID="TextBox2" runat="server">0</asp:TextBox> <br />
         
        <asp:Button ID="btnMult" runat="server" OnClick="btnMult_Click"
            Text="Multiply" Width="193px" /><br />
        <asp:Label ID="lblAnswer" runat="server" Height="45px"
```

```
                Text="Answer" Width="201px"></asp:Label></div>
    </form>
</body>
</html>
```

Finally, add a click event handler to the button, and add this code to it:

```
protected void btnMult_Click(object sender, EventArgs e)
{
    int nX = Convert.ToInt16(TextBox1.Text);
    int nY = Convert.ToInt16(TextBox2.Text);
    int nAns = nX * nY;
    lblAnswer.Text = nAns.ToString();
}
```

The ideal user experience for a program like this would be a dynamic one, whereby when you type the numbers, the answer displays while you are typing. For example, if the second field has 5 in it and you type 4 in the first, the answer would immediately show 20. If you then type a 0 in the first field so that it displays 40, the answer should update to 200.

The problem with this approach is that TextChanged events on ASP.NET controls do not fire until a postback, so this isn't possible in a web application. Of course, for a simple calculation like multiplication, you could always use JavaScript to do it on the client side—but consider a more complex mathematical scenario, such as calculating a moving average or Bollinger band on a time series of data for a stock, and you'll see that this rapidly becomes infeasible.

So, for a server-side calculation, you have to perform a postback, and then you cannot do it on the changed text, so the desired user experience hits a technical constraint. In this case, you add the button and get it to trigger the postback, and you can then perform the calculation on the button's click event.

Now when you run the application, you can type numbers in the two text boxes and click the button. You'll get a page refresh, and then you'll see the answer to your calculation.

Improving the UI Using Ajax

Now consider the same scenario using Ajax. Thanks to the asynchronous updates that don't use a postback, you can give more dynamic feedback to your users—as they type numbers in the text boxes, they'll get immediate feedback of the results of the calculation.

The first thing you'll do is split the application into two pages: the page that runs on the server and provides the calculation, and the page that provides the UI and calls the first page.

To add the server page, add a new ASP.NET Web Forms page to your project, and call it MultiplyAJAXServer.aspx.

In Source view, remove all the markup on the page *except* for the ASP.NET markup on the top line, which looks like this:

```
<%@ Page Language="C#" AutoEventWireup="true"
    CodeFile="MultiplyAJAXServer.aspx.cs"
    Inherits="MultiplyAJAXServer" %>
```

Now, in the Page_Load event handler, add this code:

```
protected void Page_Load(object sender, EventArgs e)
    {
        int nX = 0;
        int nY = 0;
        try
        {
            nX = Convert.ToInt16(Request.Params["nx"]);
            nY = Convert.ToInt16(Request.Params["ny"]);
        }
        catch (Exception ex)
        {
            nX = 0;
            nY = 0;
        }
        int nAns = nX * nY;
        Response.Write(nAns);
    }
```

This takes two HTTP parameters, nX and nY, and multiplies them out, writing the response back to the output buffer. You'll take these results and load them into the answer field when you write the Ajax UI layer. This is why you removed all the markup from the page earlier, as you do not want to write out unnecessary HTML tags from this service (such as <head> and <body>).

To create the Ajax UI, add a new HTML page to the solution and call it MultiplyAJAXClient.htm. Make a similar layout to the earlier example, but use HTML controls. When you are ready, the HTML should look like this:

```
<!DOCTYPE html PUBLIC "-//W3C//DTD XHTML 1.0 Transitional//EN"
  "http://www.w3.org/TR/xhtml1/DTD/xhtml1-transitional.dtd">
<html xmlns="http://www.w3.org/1999/xhtml" >
<head>
    <title>AJAX Multiplier Client</title>
</head>
<body>
    <div>First      <input id="Text1" type="text"  /><br /></div>
    <div>Second
        <input id="Text2" type="text" /><br /><br /></div>
    <div id="ans">Answer</div>
</body>
</html>
```

Figure 11-3 shows how this will look on the screen.

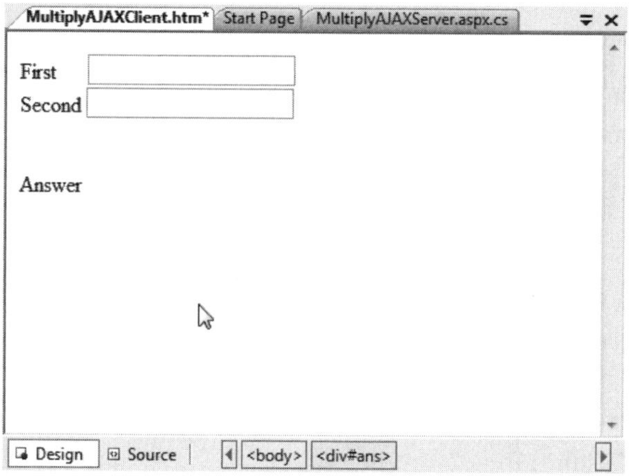

Figure 11-3. *MultiplyAJAXClient in the Designer*

The next step will be to make sure that the page instantiates the Ajax components. The logical place and time to do this is when the page loads and renders. To do this, add a `<script>` block to the page and add an initAJAX function to it. It should look like this:

```
<script type="text/javascript">
var ajaxRequest
function initAJAX()
{
    try
    {
        ajaxRequest = new XMLHttpRequest();
```

```
    }
    catch(error)
    {
        ajaxRequest = new ActiveXObject("Microsoft.XMLHTTP");
    }

  }
</script>
```

Now change your <body> tag to call this function when it loads using the onload parameter.

```
<body onload="initAJAX();">
```

Now that you're set up for Ajax, the next thing is to configure the text boxes to do something when a key has been pressed on them. You'll write the event-handler function in the next step. You do this by specifying the event handler for the onkeyup event on the text boxes, like this:

```
<input id="Text1" type="text" onkeyup="handleInput();" />
<input id="Text2" type="text" onkeyup="handleInput();"/>
```

The handleInput function then gets the value of the text boxes and uses Ajax to make a call to the server that you created earlier, passing in the parameters. It also sets up the callback handler using the onreadystatechange property. Here's the code:

```
function handleInput()
{
  var T1 = document.getElementById("Text1");
  var T2 = document.getElementById("Text2");
  var theURL = "MultiplyAJAXServer.aspx?nx=" + T1.value + "&ny=" + T2.value;

  ajaxRequest.open("GET", theURL);
  ajaxRequest.onreadystatechange = handleUpdate;
  ajaxRequest.send();
}
```

As you can see, this function gets a reference to each of the text boxes, and then uses their values to construct a URL to the server page. It then uses the open method on the ajaxRequest to set up an HTTP-GET to that URL, specifies the callback function (handleUpdate, which you'll see next), and starts the communication by calling send.

The final piece of the puzzle is the callback. When you specify a callback function, the XMLHttpRequest object will call it four times, setting the readyState property to the values 1, 2, 3, and 4, respectively. These correspond to the following states:

1: Communication open

2: Message sent to server

3: Payload downloading from server

4: Payload download complete

The responseText property contains the returned values from the server.

So, if you are only interested in updating the page when the server has completed its operation and sent its payload, then check the readyState for the value 4. You can see this in action here:

```
function handleUpdate()
{
    var ansDiv = document.getElementById("ans");
    if(ajaxRequest.readyState == 4)
    {
        ansDiv.innerHTML = ajaxRequest.responseText;
    }
}
```

This checks the readyState of the ajaxRequest, and when it is 4, it takes the responseText and loads it into the <div> element that is assigned to contain the answer.

If you run this application, you can see the effect. As you type in the text boxes, the Ajax code will execute, calling the server and processing the return, loading it into the answer <div>, and giving a much more fluid user experience.

Again, as this is a simple case (multiplying two numbers), you could argue that you don't need a server, and thus don't need Ajax—but it indicates the methodology that you would use in a scenario where the mathematical functions may be too complex to do in JavaScript, or may involve proprietary algorithms, as is the case with many financial analytics calculations.

You can see it in action in Figure 11-4.

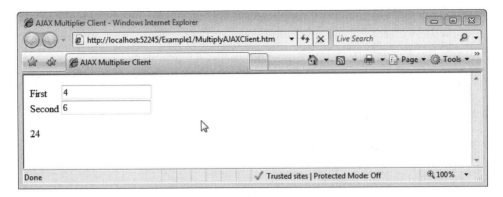

Figure 11-4. *Running the Ajax Multiplier*

The full listing for the client page is shown in Listing 11-3.

Listing 11-3. *The Full Ajax Client*

```
<!DOCTYPE html PUBLIC "-//W3C//DTD XHTML 1.0 Transitional//EN"
  "http://www.w3.org/TR/xhtml1/DTD/xhtml1-transitional.dtd">
<html xmlns="http://www.w3.org/1999/xhtml" >
<head>
    <title>AJAX Multiplier Client</title>
    <script type="text/javascript">
    var ajaxRequest
    function initAJAX()
    {

        try
        {
            ajaxRequest = new XMLHttpRequest();
        }
        catch(error)
        {
            ajaxRequest = new ActiveXObject("Microsoft.XMLHTTP");
        }
    }
    function handleInput()
        {
            var T1 = document.getElementById("Text1");
            var T2 = document.getElementById("Text2");
            var theURL = "MultiplyAJAXServer.aspx?nx=" +
                T1.value + "&ny=" + T2.value;
```

```
            ajaxRequest.open("GET", theURL);
            ajaxRequest.onreadystatechange = handleUpdate;
            ajaxRequest.send();
        }

    function handleUpdate()
    {
        alert(ajaxRequest.readyState);
        var ansDiv = document.getElementById("ans");
        if(ajaxRequest.readyState == 4)
        {
            ansDiv.innerHTML = ajaxRequest.responseText;
        }
    }


    </script>
</head>
<body onload="initAJAX();">
    <div>First      <input id="Text1"
        type="text" onkeyup="handleInput();" /><br /></div>
    <div>Second
        <input id="Text2" type="text" onkeyup="handleInput();"/><br /><br /></div>
    <div id="ans">Answer</div>
</body>
</html>
```

Using Ajax for Forward Caching

One popular methodology for Ajax is to use Ajax to do intelligent forward caching of data, improving the overall speed and usability of the application. This is commonly used in mapping applications.

Consider, for example, the mapping scenario shown in Figure 11-5. At this moment, the user is looking at a part of the Microsoft campus in Redmond, Washington.

The current zoom level is pretty close to the buildings, so the entire campus cannot be seen. If the user drags the mouse around, then they instantly receive new content. This is achieved using *forward caching*. In this scenario, a map is made up of a number of tiles. While the user is looking at a portion of the map, the Ajax application is downloading and caching the surrounding areas of the map. Thus, when the user drags the mouse around, the new tiles are already in the cache and are loaded from there, instead of waiting for a download from the server.

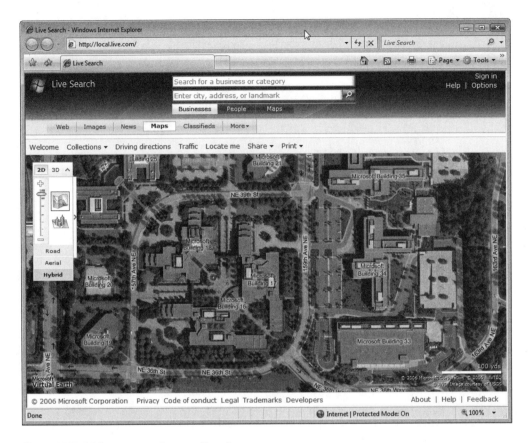

Figure 11-5. *Using a mapping application*

Implementing forward caching using Ajax is pretty straightforward. This example will step you through how to do it by building a browser for the product photos in the AdventureWorks database. It will show one picture, and give you browse buttons that allow you to look at the next and previous pictures in the set.

You'll build a server page that pulls a picture based on a parameter from the AdventureWorks database, and tie the Ajax front end up to it.

Building the Image Server

The image server fronts the AdventureWorks database. If you don't have it already installed on your machine, look back to Chapter 4 for a walk-through.

The image server will be a simple web form application that takes in a parameter, queries the database for the image with the corresponding ID, and writes the image back to the response when it finds one.

Unfortunately, AdventureWorks doesn't have a contiguous set of images, so you'll get a lot of broken links in your application. For example, there is an image corresponding to product ID 100, but none for product ID 101. To get around this, you would have to download a set of existing product IDs to the client and navigate through them—but for the sake of simplicity, this application just allows you to add and subtract 1 on the current ID, so you will end up with broken links in the final version.

The first step is to add a new ASPX web form to your project. Call it GetPicture.aspx. In the Source view for the page, delete all the HTML markup, leaving only the top line, which contains the ASP.NET directives. When you are done, the source for your page should consist of just one line, and look like this:

```
<%@ Page Language="C#" AutoEventWireup="true"
  CodeFile="GetPicture.aspx.cs" Inherits="GetPicture" %>
```

The next step is to add some code to the Page_Load event handler for this page. Make sure that the set of using includes everything that you'll need for this operation. This includes the IO stuff to handle the streams, the Sql.DataClient to handle the database connection, and the imaging APIs to handle the graphics.

Here's the complete set:

```
using System;
using System.Data;
using System.Configuration;
using System.Collections;
using System.Web.Configuration;
using System.Web;
using System.Web.Security;
using System.Web.UI;
using System.Web.UI.WebControls;
using System.Web.UI.WebControls.WebParts;
using System.Web.UI.HtmlControls;
using System.IO;
using System.Drawing;
using System.Drawing.Imaging;
using System.Data.SqlClient;
```

Now that you are ready to start coding, the first step will be to handle the input parameter. This page will be called using a URI like this: GetPicture.aspx?PicID= <something>, and the parameterized ID will be used to call the database for a specific picture. This is achieved with the following code:

```
int picID;
if (Request.Params["PicID"] != null)
    picID = Convert.ToInt16(Request.Params["PicID"]);
else
    picID = 100;
```

This simply checks to see if the parameter is present. If it is, it loads its value into the integer picID; otherwise it defaults it to 100.

Next, you set up your data connection and initialize a SQL query to use this parameter:

```
string connectionString =
WebConfigurationManager.ConnectionStrings["AdventureWorksConnectionString"]
.ConnectionString;

SqlConnection con = new SqlConnection(connectionString);
string sql = "Select * from Production.ProductPhoto where ProductPhotoID=@ID";
SqlCommand cmd = new SqlCommand(sql, con);
cmd.Parameters.Add("@ID", picID);
```

This code pulls the connection string from the Web.Config file for the web application. If you don't have one already, refer back to Chapter 4 for instructions on installing and configuring the database on your web site.

It then creates a new instance of a SqlConnection object, initializing it with this connection string.

The SQL is simply a string, and in SQL strings you can specify parameters using the @ directive, so it knows that when you say ProductPhotoID=@ID, it will be expecting a parameter.

Next, a new SqlCommand is created using this SQL code on the configured connection. Finally, the parameter is added to the command. SQLCommand objects have a collection of parameters that is empty by default. When you add parameters to this collection, you specify the parameter name (@ID in this case) and the parameter value (picID in this case). When the command is executed, the SQL is assembled with the parameter values filling in the placeholders.

The next step is to open the database and execute the SQL. When you execute a command, a SqlDataReader object is returned, allowing you to read the results line by line. This query will at most return one line (as there is only one picture per ProductPhotoId).

```
con.Open();
SqlDataReader sqlRead = cmd.ExecuteReader();
```

To access the contents of the SqlDataReader, the Read function is called. This reads a single record at a time. As we have at most one record, we call this once. Calling this function loads the next record, and returns true if it succeeds (i.e., if there is a next record), and false if it doesn't.

Thus, in this case, we can gate the sqlRead.Read, and in the true clause handle the loading and writing of the image to the response. In the false clause, we can provide an error message. Here's the code:

```
if (sqlRead.Read())
    {
        MemoryStream mems = new MemoryStream();
        BinaryWriter binw = new BinaryWriter(mems);
        byte[] bits = (byte[])sqlRead["LargePhoto"];
        binw.Write(bits);
        Bitmap b = new Bitmap(mems);
        sqlRead.Close();
        con.Close();
        Response.ContentType = "image/jpeg";
        //Response.Write(b);
        b.Save(Response.OutputStream, ImageFormat.Jpeg);
    }
    else
    {
        Response.Write("No image found");
    }
```

Once the record is read, some interesting stuff goes on. The image needs to be read from the database into a `Bitmap` type. You do this by reading the contents of the database into a byte array (called `bits` in the preceding code). This byte array then has to be written to an output stream using a binary writer. In this case, we are using a memory stream, as we don't need to write the data out to another process. The bitmap is initialized from this stream.

To write it out to the response buffer, you need to set the MIME type so that the browser will understand the content you are sending—in this case, it is an `image/jpeg` type, indicating that you are writing out an image.

You then call the `Save` method of the bitmap to write its contents out. This method allows you to specify a stream to save to and a format to save in. If you write it to `Response.OutputStream`, it will be returned to the caller of this URL. The format to be used is `ImageFormat.Jpeg`, as this matches the MIME type that was set earlier.

In this case, if no image is found, a simple "No image found" message is written out. For a more user-friendly application, you could perhaps have a default image that gets written out instead.

Now, if you run the application, you can pass it an ID, and if there is a photo for that ID, it will be rendered in the browser.

You can see it in action in Figure 11-6. Try doing a View ➤ Source command on this page—you won't see anything. Why do you think that is?

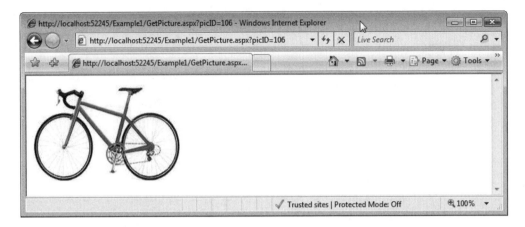

Figure 11-6. *The image server in action*

Accessing the Image Server from HTML

The reason why you do not see any source on this page is because there is none. The request to the server simply returns a picture. By setting the MIME type on the response, the browser knows to read the bitstream for the image and render it as a JPG.

Thus, within a page, you could point an <img> tag at the page to get it to render these graphics. Here's an example:

```
<!DOCTYPE html PUBLIC "-//W3C//DTD XHTML 1.0 Transitional//EN"
"http://www.w3.org/TR/xhtml1/DTD/xhtml1-transitional.dtd">
<html xmlns="http://www.w3.org/1999/xhtml" >
<head>
    <title>Untitled Page</title>
</head>
<body>
    <img alt="No Image" src="GetPicture.aspx?picID=100" />
    <img alt="No Image" src="GetPicture.aspx?picID=102" />
    <img alt="No Image" src="GetPicture.aspx?picID=103" />

</body>
</html>
```

The <img> tags don't point to a JPG or another image, just to this service. So, when you render the page in the browser, the call is made to the service for each <img> tag, and the results are rendered by the browser. You can see this in Figure 11-7.

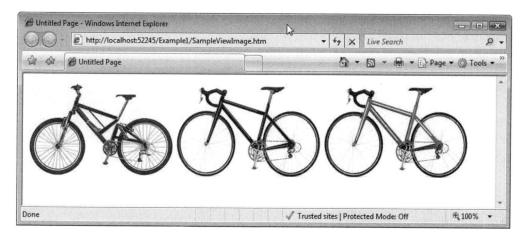

Figure 11-7. *Viewing several pictures from the server with <img> tags*

Writing the Forward-Caching Ajax Client

The principle behind the forward-caching Ajax client is very straightforward. You keep track of the ID of the current image and provide buttons that allow you to add and remove 1 from this ID. You then construct a URL to the image server, passing it the new ID and getting the response. Then you download the images that are 1 and 2 more than this value, as well as those that are 1 and 2 less than this value. When you call the URL and download the images, the browser will cache them.

For example, if the current image is 100, and you move forward to 101, the page will construct a URL call to the server asking for 101. If this has already been called, the results will be cached, and the image loaded from the cache. It will also construct calls to 102, 103, 100, and 99, and put the responses in the browser cache.

To do this, you need to use a slightly different technique from what you did in the simple example. You'll use two XMLHttpRequest objects: one with a callback that renders the image, and one that doesn't use a callback, but just gets the image and caches it.

Add a new HTML page to your application and call it AJAXPictureClient.htm. Change the body of the application to contain a <div> in which the image will be displayed, and two buttons—one for moving forward and one for moving backward. Here's the complete markup, including the JavaScript event-handler function calls that handle loading the page and clicking the buttons:

```
<body onload="initAJAX();">
    <div id="pic"><img src="GetPicture.aspx?picid=100" alt="not present" /></div>
    <input type="button" value="<<" id="btnPrev" onclick="DoPrev();" />
    <input type="button" value=">>" id="btnNext" onclick="DoNext();" />
</body>
```

Next, add a <script> tag to the head of your page, and add the following var declarations to it. They aren't part of a function within the <script> tag, so they are common to all functions.

```
var ajaxRequest
var cachedAjaxRequest
var currentPic = 100;
var theURL;
var theCachedURL;
```

As you step through the functions, you'll see the purpose of these. The first function that you'll need to implement is the initAJAX function called by the loading event of the page body. Here it is:

```
function initAJAX()
    {
        try
        {
            ajaxRequest = new XMLHttpRequest();
            cachedAjaxRequest = new XMLHttpRequest();
        }
        catch(error)
        {
            ajaxRequest = new ActiveXObject("Microsoft.XMLHTTP");
            cachedAjaxRequest = new ActiveXObject("Microsoft.XMLHTTP");
        }

        ShowPic(currentPic);
    }
```

This creates two XMLHttpRequest objects. The reason for using two of them is subtle. You may think that you can just use one instance, and only provide the callback function for calls to it where you want to display the image. Unfortunately, Ajax doesn't allow this. Once you set up a connection and specify the callback, the callback will be hit for all calls to that function.

This function also calls ShowPic, passing it the value of the current picture. You can see the ShowPic function here:

```
function ShowPic(thisPic)
    {
        theURL = "GetPicture.aspx?picid=" + thisPic;
        ajaxRequest.open("GET", theURL);
```

```
        ajaxRequest.onreadystatechange=DisplayPic;
        ajaxRequest.send();
    }
```

This is a simple Ajax function, constructing a URL to the GetPicture service using the value that was passed into it. It performs an HTTP-GET to that URL, and specifies DisplayPic as the callback function for state changes.

The DisplayPic function then checks for readyState being 4 (i.e., download complete), and loads the <div> with an <img> tag pointing to the same URL. As the image has already been downloaded, it will be instantly pulled from the cache. Note that the browser looks at the URI of a resource and determines if the current version is cached. If it is, it loads it from the cache; if it isn't, it downloads it.

```
function DisplayPic()
    {
        var divPic = document.getElementById("pic");
        if(ajaxRequest.readyState == 4)
        {
            divPic.innerHTML = "<img alt='not present' src='" + theURL + "' />";
        }
        GetPic(currentPic+1);
        GetPic(currentPic+2);
        GetPic(currentPic-1);
        GetPic(currentPic-2);

    }
```

In addition to this, it also calls the GetPic function, which kicks in the second Ajax function. This simply downloads (but doesn't display) the graphics. It calls this function four times, for currentPic+1, currentPic+2, currentPic-1, and currentPic-2. Many of these images will already be cached, so the call will be quick. This function could probably be a little smarter, but for the sake of simplicity, the brute-force method is used here.

The GetPic function is a standard Ajax call, but no callback is needed, as the image will not be rendered.

```
    function GetPic(thisPic)
    {

        theCachedURL = "GetPicture.aspx?picid=" + thisPic;
        cachedAjaxRequest.open("GET", theCachedURL);
        cachedAjaxRequest.send();
    }
```

Finally, you need to wire up the event handlers for the buttons, allowing navigation through the images. It's pretty straightforward—you simply increment or decrement the current picture ID and then call ShowPic with the new ID:

```
function DoPrev()
    {
        currentPic--;
        ShowPic(currentPic);
    }

    function DoNext()
    {
        currentPic++;
        ShowPic(currentPic);
    }
```

And that's it. You now have an Ajax page with forward (and backward) caching of images. You can streamline this page if you like—when you think about it, Ajax isn't necessary for the ShowPage call—you could simply construct an <img> tag from the current pic, but it is good to understand the technique, as you will use it in more complex apps.

You can see the application in action in Figures 11-8 and 11-9. The latter is the result of clicking the >> button shown in Figure 11-8. As you run the application, you'll see how quickly the pictures update and render.

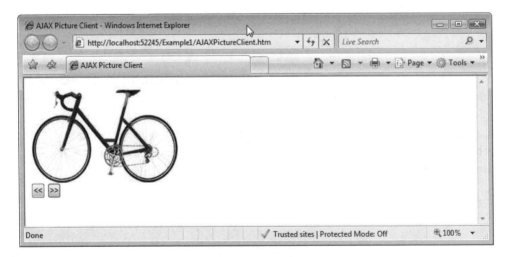

Figure 11-8. *Running the forward-caching Ajax application*

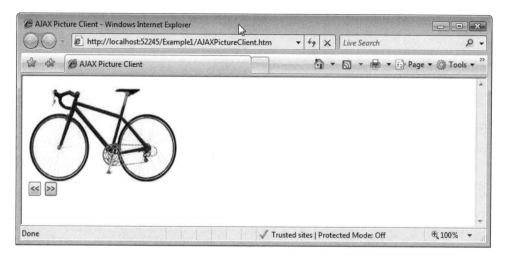

Figure 11-9. *Browsing to the next bicycle*

The entire code for the page is shown in Listing 11-4.

Listing 11-4. *Forward-Caching Client*

```
<!DOCTYPE html PUBLIC "-//W3C//DTD XHTML 1.0 Transitional//EN"
  "http://www.w3.org/TR/xhtml1/DTD/xhtml1-transitional.dtd">
<html xmlns="http://www.w3.org/1999/xhtml" >
<head>
    <title>AJAX Picture Client</title>
    <script type="text/javascript">
    var ajaxRequest
    var cachedAjaxRequest
    var currentPic = 100;
    var theURL;
    var theCachedURL;
    function initAJAX()
    {
        try
        {
            ajaxRequest = new XMLHttpRequest();
            cachedAjaxRequest = new XMLHttpRequest();
        }
        catch(error)
        {
            ajaxRequest = new ActiveXObject("Microsoft.XMLHTTP");
```

```
            cachedAjaxRequest = new ActiveXObject("Microsoft.XMLHTTP");
    }


    ShowPic(currentPic);
}

function GetPic(thisPic)
{

    theCachedURL = "GetPicture.aspx?picid=" + thisPic;
    cachedAjaxRequest.open("GET", theCachedURL);
    cachedAjaxRequest.send();
}

function ShowPic(thisPic)
{

    theURL = "GetPicture.aspx?picid=" + thisPic;

    ajaxRequest.open("GET", theURL);
    ajaxRequest.onreadystatechange=DisplayPic;
    ajaxRequest.send();



}

function DisplayPic()
{
    var divPic = document.getElementById("pic");
    if(ajaxRequest.readyState == 4)
    {
        divPic.innerHTML = "<img alt='not present' src='" + theURL + "' />";
    }
    GetPic(currentPic+1);
    GetPic(currentPic+2);
    GetPic(currentPic-1);
    GetPic(currentPic-2);


}

function DoPrev()
{
```

```
        currentPic--;
        ShowPic(currentPic);
    }

    function DoNext()
    {
        currentPic++;
        ShowPic(currentPic);
    }
    </script>
</head>
<body onload="initAJAX();">
    <div id="pic"><img src="GetPicture.aspx?picid=100" alt="not present" /></div>
    <input type="button" value="<<" id="btnPrev" onclick="DoPrev();" />
    <input type="button" value=">>" id="btnNext" onclick="DoNext();" />


</body>
</html>
```

This technique and methodology will prove very useful when you're building your applications. It also introduces a whole new way of thinking about the user experience. Forward caching changes the way in which many applications (e.g., maps) can be presented to the user. If you are building an application that could make the most of this, it's well worth thinking it through and building it into your site.

Summary

In this chapter, you took a look at Ajax, seeing some examples of applications where Ajax greatly improves the overall user experience, such as MSN MoneyCentral and Google Maps. You looked at the history of dynamic, partial page refresh technologies, leading up to the XMLHttpRequest object, for which the technique of Ajax was coined.

You looked into the architecture of Ajax and how you can use the XMLHttpRequest object in code, before delving into a couple of examples. The first example, though very simple, demonstrated straightaway that the instant-feedback nature of Ajax (as opposed to the traditional delayed-via-postback feedback of a web application) can improve your end users' experience.

You then looked into another major technique used by Ajax programmers: forward caching. This technique is used by applications such as mapping applications to allow users to get what seems to be instant access to data. Applications using this technique are smart enough to download and cache data that would likely be requested next. When the user actually requests it, the browser just pulls it out of the cache and displays it—far more quickly than if it were called from the server.

That wraps up this introduction to Ajax. In the next few chapters, you'll look into the toolkit from Microsoft that allows you to easily and rapidly develop Ajax applications using a server-side paradigm: the AJAX extensions for ASP.NET, formerly known as Atlas.

CHAPTER 12

■■■

AJAX Extensions for ASP.NET

The continued adoption of Ajax techniques to produce a better web user experience has brought about a new term: RIA (rich Internet application), to describe a postback-less environment containing pages that support partial updates and forward caching. As you saw in the previous chapter, this involved extensive JavaScript coding for even the simplest of applications. This has two major drawbacks. First, programming in JavaScript is not the most efficient of practices—it's a scripting language, and its support for development productivity (such as IntelliSense) and debugging is nowhere near as mature as it is for languages such as C# or Java. Second, as it is an interpreted language, it isn't designed for full-scale application development and will hit performance constraints.

Server applications are traditionally written in a language that runs on the server and emits HTML. These are compiled applications that are written in high-level languages, such as C# or Java, that are supported by a wide array of tools for debugging, management, profiling, and more.

As server-side applications emit HTML, it is a natural fit for them to emit JavaScript, too. As such, it is possible for a server-side development paradigm to give the developer the facilities to implement a client-side RIA. It then also becomes possible for this approach to give developers a controls/designer approach, allowing them to visually construct interfaces that support Ajax functionality, with the controls emitting the appropriate JavaScript to use the asynchronous XMLHttpRequest controls.

This is where the AJAX extensions for ASP.NET come into the picture. They enable the developer to quickly create web pages that include Ajax elements. As discussed in earlier chapters, ASP.NET brings a high level of productivity to web application development—and the same paradigm is now extended to allow Ajax/RIA development.

ASP.NET AJAX Overview

At the heart of Ajax is the XMLHttpRequest object. All Ajax applications ultimately use this object, but, as you develop applications on top of this technology, you'll soon see that there are a number of common, repeatable practices that you'll perform on it. For example, when requesting information from a page that you want to have updated asynchronously, you'll likely want to implement some form of progress update, or you'll have to carefully tweak exactly which parts of your page you'll want to have updated when you do a partial page refresh.

With these and many more potential scenarios in mind, ASP.NET AJAX has been designed to provide controls, script libraries, and technology support to make building RIA applications as easy for the developer as possible.

The functionality of ASP.NET AJAX has been broken down into two paradigms: *server*, containing the suite of ASP.NET controls to handle things such as partial refreshes, update progress, timers, and server-side integration with other applications across web services or other communications profiles; and *client*, which contains JavaScript classes to support value-added functionality, such as a browser-independent layer, extensions to support object orientation, and more.

You can see the basic ASP.NET AJAX server and client architectures in Figure 12-1.

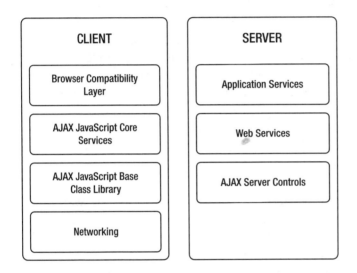

Figure 12-1. *ASP.NET AJAX client and server architectures*

The ASP.NET infrastructure provides many application services to server applications, including components that manage the UI and flow of an application (see Part 1 of this book for more details), handling serialization, validation, and extensibility, among other things. ASP.NET 2.0 also supports services such as database-backed user profiles and security and authentication methodologies. When using ASP.NET AJAX extensions, the whole ASP.NET framework is available for you to use, providing many value-added services, saving you time and effort in development.

ASP.NET also supports and provides web services that can be called from a client script that can work with the resources that ASP.NET provides. For example, you can use client scripts to help protect resources through forms authentication, or you can access user profiles, allowing user-specific settings to be stored on the server.

The major new additions to the server architecture are the ASP.NET AJAX server controls. There are a number of these, and they will be discussed in detail in Chapter 13. The major ones that you'll use in just about every application are the following:

ScriptManager: This component is used to manage the scripts that will be downloaded to the client. There are a number of client script libraries available to ASP.NET developers, and when a ScriptManager is used, only the relevant ones are downloaded to the client. You'll need to use a ScriptManager in just about every Ajax application.

UpdatePanel: This is used to visually design the part of the page that is used in a partial page update. Simply put, when you wrap an area of your page in an UpdatePanel, it will be automatically enabled for partial refreshes using Ajax.

UpdateProgress: This provides status information for the progress of the download occurring in the UpdatePanel.

Timer: The Timer performs postbacks at defined intervals. It can be used to trigger automatic updates (and therefore partial refreshes) to an area of the page that is wrapped with an UpdatePanel.

Despite being extensions to a server-side technology, the ASP.NET AJAX extensions also provide an abundance of client-side functionality, including the following:

Browser compatibility layer: If you look back to the Ajax examples in the previous chapter, you'll notice that at the Ajax declaration there are if...then scripts that handle instantiation of the XMLHttpRequest object on different browsers. The browser compatibility layer is designed to abstract this process—if you code to the AJAX extensions' JavaScript libraries, you do not need to worry about the underlying technologies that the browser supports.

Core Services: These provide extensions to JavaScript that allow you to create more robust applications, supporting classes, namespaces, event handling, inheritance, and more.

Base Class Library (BCL): The AJAX BCL includes components that are typically only available to developers of high-level languages, such as extended error handling.

Networking: This layer handles communication with server-side services and applications, allowing, for example, web services to be called directly from the browser.

You'll be looking into the client-side extensions of ASP.NET AJAX in Chapter 14.

Editions of ASP.NET AJAX

The web landscape is changing and evolving rapidly, and the tools needed to keep up also change and evolve. With this in mind, Microsoft has provided a number of optional add-ons to ASP.NET AJAX. These will change over time, but as of the 1.0 release, the options available to you are as follows:

ASP.NET AJAX Core: These extensions to ASP.NET include the server controls and client libraries discussed in this chapter and later in this book.

Control Toolkit: This provides a number of client-side controls that implement common functionality, such as calendars, tabs, watermarked text boxes, and more.

ASP.NET AJAX Futures: As the platform evolves, additional server and client controls and libraries are available on a Community Technical Preview (CTP) basis. These are kept separate from the core download.

AJAX Library: Should you not want to use ASP.NET on the front end, but make the most of the value-added functionality on the client side, the JavaScript libraries are made available for you to download and use in your applications.

For the rest of this chapter, you'll be looking at the core part of ASP.NET AJAX. In the next section, you'll look into downloading it and using it to create your first ASP.NET AJAX application.

Getting Started with ASP.NET AJAX

The ASP.NET AJAX Core library can be downloaded from the Microsoft AJAX site, at `http://asp.net/ajax/`. After downloading and running the installer, you'll see the Welcome screen (see Figure 12-2).

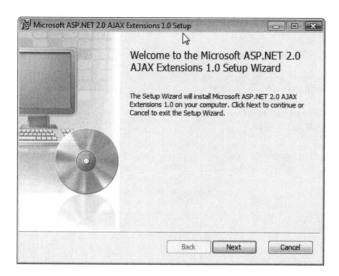

Figure 12-2. *Welcome screen for ASP.NET AJAX installation*

Clicking Next will begin the installation. You'll see the installation status screen (see Figure 12-3).

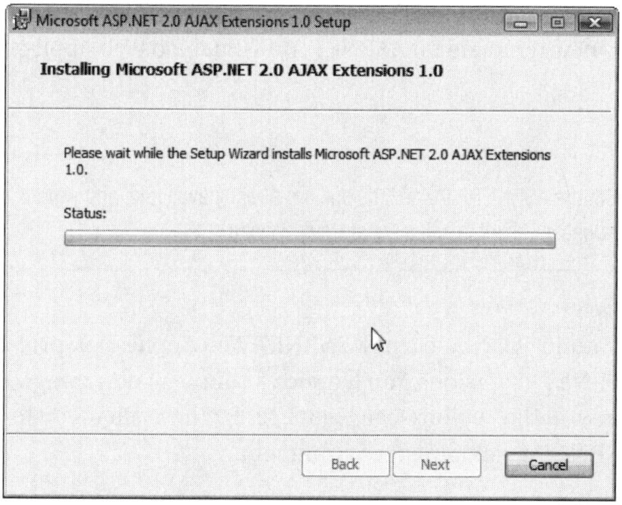

Figure 12-3. *Installation status screen*

The installation is pretty straightforward. Once it has installed successfully, you'll see a completion screen (see Figure 12-4).

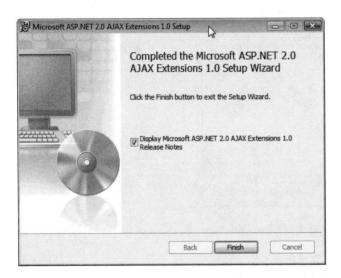

Figure 12-4. *Completing the installation*

Once this is done, you can launch Visual Studio 2005 and create a new project. In the New Project dialog box, you'll see a new template for ASP.NET AJAX-Enabled Web Application (see Figure 12-5).

■**Note** If you are using Visual Studio 2008, the ASP.NET AJAX extensions are already available, and you do not need to download them. However, the Control Toolkit is still a separate download.

Once you've done this, Visual Studio will create a new ASP.NET Web Application project that is configured to use the ASP.NET extensions. You'll notice a couple of new things. First are the AJAX Extensions controls in the Toolbox (see Figure 12-6). These allow you to provide Ajax functionality in an ASP.NET development environment.

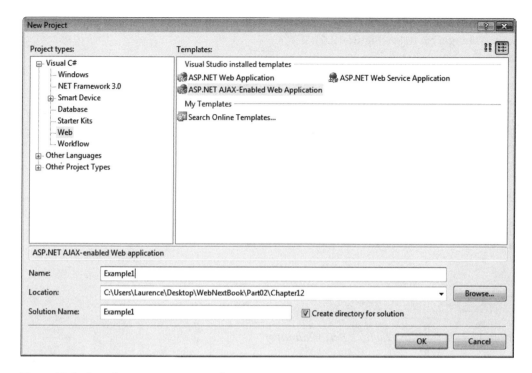

Figure 12-5. *Creating a new AJAX application*

Figure 12-6. *AJAX Extensions Server Controls Toolbox*

In addition, you'll see that the Default.aspx file created by the template will have a ScriptManager on it (see Figure 12-7).

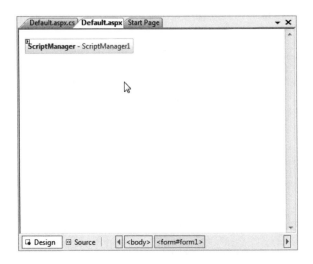

Figure 12-7. *Default.aspx with a ScriptManager*

Now take a look at the source code for the default page—you'll see the following, including the new `<asp:ScriptManager>` reference:

```
<%@ Page Language="C#" AutoEventWireup="true"
  CodeBehind="Default.aspx.cs" Inherits="Example1._Default" %>

<!DOCTYPE html PUBLIC "-//W3C//DTD XHTML 1.0 Transitional//EN"

  "http://www.w3.org/TR/xhtml1/DTD/xhtml1-transitional.dtd">

<html xmlns="http://www.w3.org/1999/xhtml" >
<head runat="server">
    <title>Untitled Page</title>
</head>
<body>
    <form id="form1" runat="server">
        <asp:ScriptManager ID="ScriptManager1" runat="server" />
    <div>

    </div>
    </form>
</body>
</html>
```

As you can see, this is a pretty straightforward ASP.NET page, with nothing new other than the fact that the ScriptManager control has been added. Now run the page and take a look at the source code that the browser sees. Here's an example:

```
<!DOCTYPE html PUBLIC "-//W3C//DTD XHTML 1.0 Transitional//EN"
  "http://www.w3.org/TR/xhtml1/DTD/xhtml1-transitional.dtd">


<html xmlns="http://www.w3.org/1999/xhtml" >
<head><title>
  Untitled Page
</title></head>
<body>
    <form name="form1" method="post" action="Default.aspx" id="form1">
<div>
<input type="hidden" name="__EVENTTARGET" id="__EVENTTARGET" value="" />
<input type="hidden" name="__EVENTARGUMENT" id="__EVENTARGUMENT" value="" />
<input type="hidden" name="__VIEWSTATE" id="__VIEWSTATE"

  value="/wEPDwUKLTYOMzg3MTYOM2Rk57fizSpOEsJIh1CKh3YgqVTdv1O=" />
</div>


<script type="text/javascript">
<!--
var theForm = document.forms['form1'];
if (!theForm) {
    theForm = document.form1;
}
function __doPostBack(eventTarget, eventArgument) {
    if (!theForm.onsubmit || (theForm.onsubmit() != false)) {
        theForm.__EVENTTARGET.value = eventTarget;
        theForm.__EVENTARGUMENT.value = eventArgument;
        theForm.submit();
    }
}
// -->
</script>


<script
 src="/WebResource.axd?d=
      yEDHQ59ZPl_l3mrZolNUQA2&amp;t=632968784944906146"
      type="text/javascript"></script>
```

```
<script src="/ScriptResource.axd?d=
    yfwYKTfiMeqOvuB4l8z1TrL35xfv6g8XP_WrOPfTwL66AB2oz
    8QRS5Lwfo666oDJgLW4Va2KNp_CEQC1pA2Sjb3Jm9uPm
    6XGO-wEIVg6lRA1&amp;t=633062590837065070"
    type="text/javascript"></script>

<script src="/ScriptResource.axd?d=
    yfwYKTfiMeqOvuB4l8z1TrL35xfv6g8XP_WrOPfTwL66AB2oz
    8QRS5Lwfo666oDJgLW4Va2KNp_CEQC1pA2SjaH2gXu3ERVLt
    TRI4HEwCJk1&amp;t=633062590837065070"
type="text/javascript"></script>

<script type="text/javascript">
//<![CDATA[
Sys.WebForms.PageRequestManager._initialize('ScriptManager1',
    document.getElementById('form1'));

Sys.WebForms.PageRequestManager.getInstance()._updateControls([], [], [], 90);
//]]>
</script>

    <div>

    </div>


<script type="text/javascript">
<!--
Sys.Application.initialize();
// -->
</script>
</form>
</body>
</html>
```

There's lots of new stuff here. You'll be seeing how this all hangs together as you work through this book, but for now consider the `<script>` blocks referencing `WebResource.axd` and `ScriptResource.axd`. These guys are downloading the various script libraries that the browser needs for this page. Part of this is to support the core extensions to JavaScript, adding object orientation so that calls like `Sys.Application.Initialize()` make sense.

Migrating ASP.NET to AJAX

One of the nicest things about ASP.NET AJAX is the fact that the UpdatePanel control can be used to add AJAX functionality to an existing ASP.NET application. This is simply achieved by wrapping the relevant controls with an UpdatePanel.

Consider the following example. Add a new web form to your application and call it AddWithUpdatePanel.aspx. On this form, add a couple of text boxes, a button, and a label, and call them txtA, txtB, btnAdd, and lblAns, respectively. The source of your page should look like this:

```
<%@ Page Language="C#" AutoEventWireup="true"
CodeBehind="AddWIthUpdatePanel.aspx.cs"
Inherits="Example2.AddWIthUpdatePanel" %>


<!DOCTYPE html PUBLIC "-//W3C//DTD XHTML 1.0 Transitional//EN"
  "http://www.w3.org/TR/xhtml1/DTD/xhtml1-transitional.dtd">


<html xmlns="http://www.w3.org/1999/xhtml" >
<head runat="server">
    <title>Untitled Page</title>
</head>
<body>
    <form id="form1" runat="server">
    <div>
        <asp:TextBox ID="txtA" runat="server"></asp:TextBox><br />
        <asp:TextBox ID="txtB" runat="server"></asp:TextBox><br />
        <br />
        <asp:Button ID="btnAdd" runat="server" OnClick="btnAdd_Click"
            Text="Add Em Up" /><br />
        <asp:Label ID="lblAns" runat="server"></asp:Label><br />
        <br />
         </div>
    </form>
</body>
</html>
```

Double-click the button to add an event handler, and add the following code to it:

```
protected void btnAdd_Click(object sender, EventArgs e)
{
    int a = Convert.ToInt16(txtA.Text);
    int b = Convert.ToInt16(txtB.Text);
```

```
        int c = a + b;
        lblAns.Text = c.ToString();
    }
```

Now when you run the application, you'll see something like Figure 12-8. When you type the numbers into the text fields, nothing happens until you click the button, which triggers a postback and a full refresh of the page. Depending on your system speed, you may or may not see a page blink, but you can notice the full page refresh by looking at the status bar.

You can convert this to an Ajax application without changing any code. To do this, drag and drop a ScriptManager control from the Toolbox onto the page. (Look back to Figure 12-6 to see the Toolbox.) After doing this, drop an UpdatePanel on the page, and then find the Panel control in the standard Toolbox and add a panel inside the UpdatePanel. The Panel resolves to a <div> at runtime, and can be resized within the Designer, causing the UpdatePanel to match it.

See Figure 12-8 for an example.

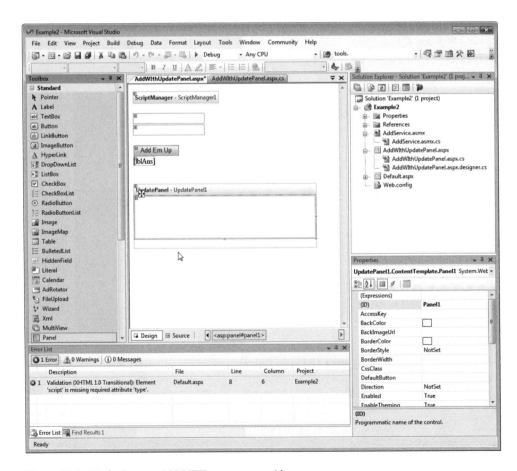

Figure 12-8. *Updating an ASP.NET page to use Ajax*

For the next step, you should drag and drop the text boxes, button, and label into the panel that you just added. Once you've done this, the source code of your page will look something like this:

```
<%@ Page Language="C#" AutoEventWireup="true"
CodeBehind="AddWIthUpdatePanel.aspx.cs"
Inherits="Example2.AddWIthUpdatePanel" %>

<!DOCTYPE html PUBLIC "-//W3C//DTD XHTML 1.0 Transitional//EN"

  "http://www.w3.org/TR/xhtml1/DTD/xhtml1-transitional.dtd">

<html xmlns="http://www.w3.org/1999/xhtml" >
<head runat="server">
    <title>Untitled Page</title>
</head>
<body>
    <form id="form1" runat="server">
    <div>
        <asp:ScriptManager ID="ScriptManager1" runat="server">
        </asp:ScriptManager>
        <br />
        <asp:UpdatePanel ID="UpdatePanel1" runat="server">
            <ContentTemplate>
                <asp:Panel ID="Panel1" runat="server" Height="88px" Width="388px">
        <asp:TextBox ID="txtA" runat="server"></asp:TextBox><br />
        <asp:TextBox ID="txtB" runat="server"></asp:TextBox><br />
        <asp:Button ID="btnAdd" runat="server" OnClick="btnAdd_Click"
            Text="Add Em Up" /><br />
        <asp:Label ID="lblAns" runat="server"></asp:Label></asp:Panel>
            </ContentTemplate>
        </asp:UpdatePanel>
    </div>
    </form>
</body>
</html>
```

And that's all you'll need to do to get this application to become an Ajax one. Run the application, and you'll see that when you run it, it no longer performs a full page refresh; it just does a partial Ajax-style one. You can see this in Figure 12-9.

Figure 12-9. *ASP.NET application using Ajax*

Building a Simple Ajax Application with ASP.NET

Now, the example of adding two numbers is all very good, but how does ASP.NET AJAX stack up when writing a more typical ASP.NET page—for example, one that uses a DataGrid to bind to a back-end data source?

■**Note** If you are amending an existing ASP.NET application to use Ajax, you should remember that some changes to your Web.config file will need to be made to reference the AJAX libraries. A good shortcut is to create a new ASP.NET AJAX application and copy the information from its Web.config file.

Let's put this together now. First, create a new web form and add a SqlDataSource control to it. Open the SqlDataSource Tasks pane, as shown in Figure 12-10.

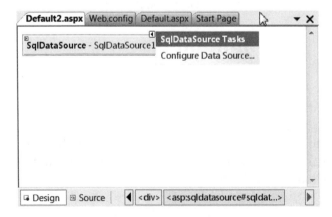

Figure 12-10. *Adding a SqlDataSource to an Ajax application*

Click the Configure Data Source link to go into the Configure Data Source wizard for the SqlDataSource. To see all the steps in this wizard, take a look back at Chapter 4, where the same connection is made. Otherwise, if you already have the AdventureWorks database set up with SQL Server, enter the configuration string on the first step on the wizard. See Figure 12-11 for details. Here's an example connection string:

```
Data Source=.\SQLEXPRESS;Initial Catalog=AdventureWorks;Integrated Security=True
```

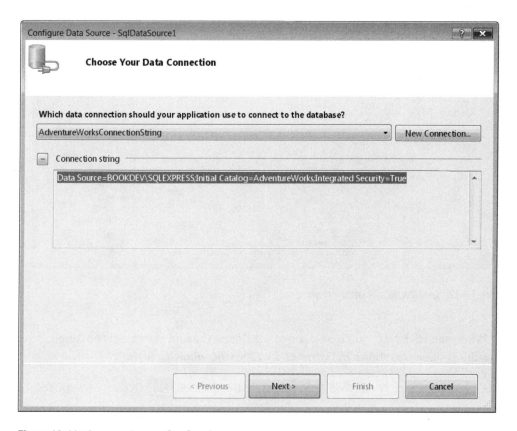

Figure 12-11. *Connecting to the database*

When you click Next, you'll be given the option to either use a custom SQL statement or specify columns from a table or view (see Figure 12-12). Select the former ("Specify a custom SQL statement or stored procedure").

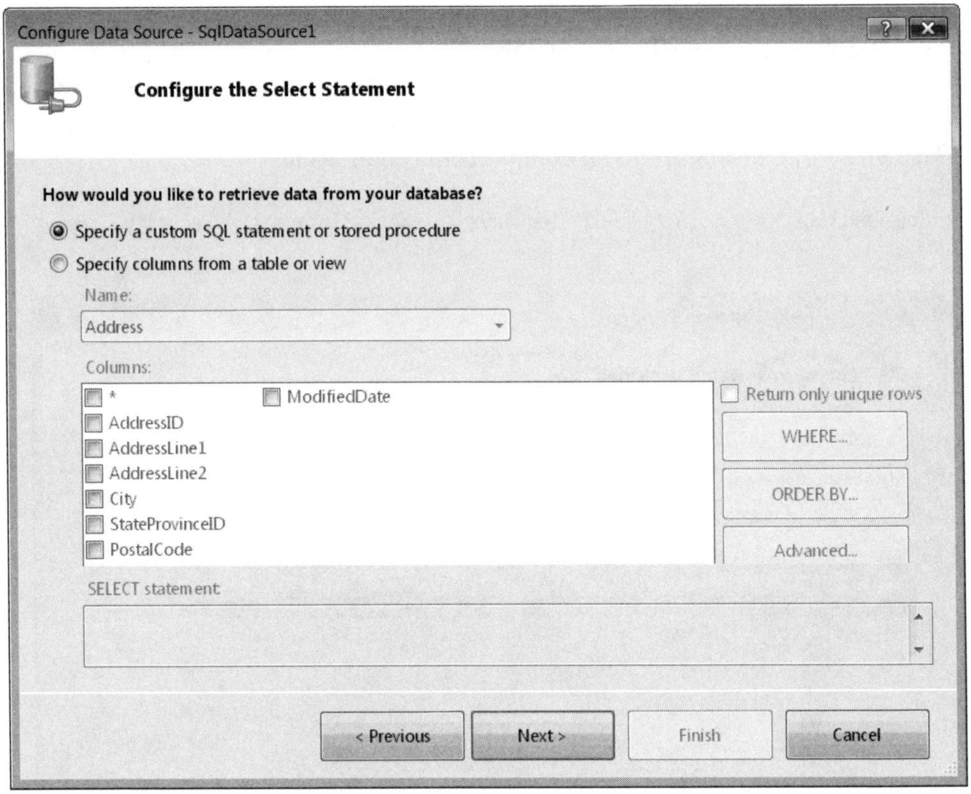

Figure 12-12. *Specifying the query type*

When you click Next, you'll be taken to the Define Custom Statements or Stored Procedures screen, as shown in Figure 12-13. Enter the following SQL:

```
SELECT AddressLine1, PostalCode FROM Person.Address WHERE (PostalCode = @PostalCode)
```

This selects the first line of the customer's address and their ZIP code when the ZIP code matches a parameterized value. You'll see how to set the default value in the next step.

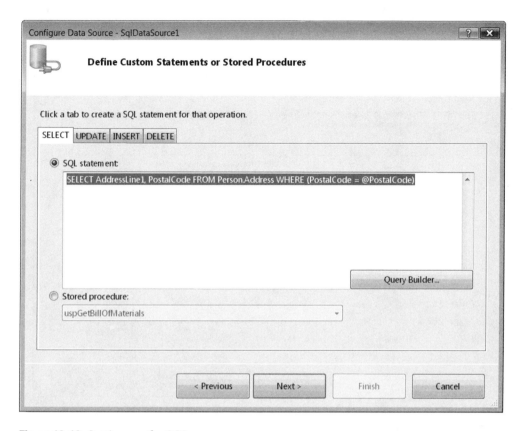

Figure 12-13. *Setting up the SQL query*

When you click Next, you'll be taken to the Define Parameters step (see Figure 12-14). Here you can set up default parameter values that will be used in your SQL query. Select QueryString as the parameter source, and the wizard will set up the code required to read the parameter from the URI that you use to call the service. Give the query string field a name (i.e., ZIP) and a default value. Now if you call your service using a URI like `http://server/pagename.aspx?ZIP=12345`, the `@PostalCode` parameter will be loaded with 12345 prior to calling the database.

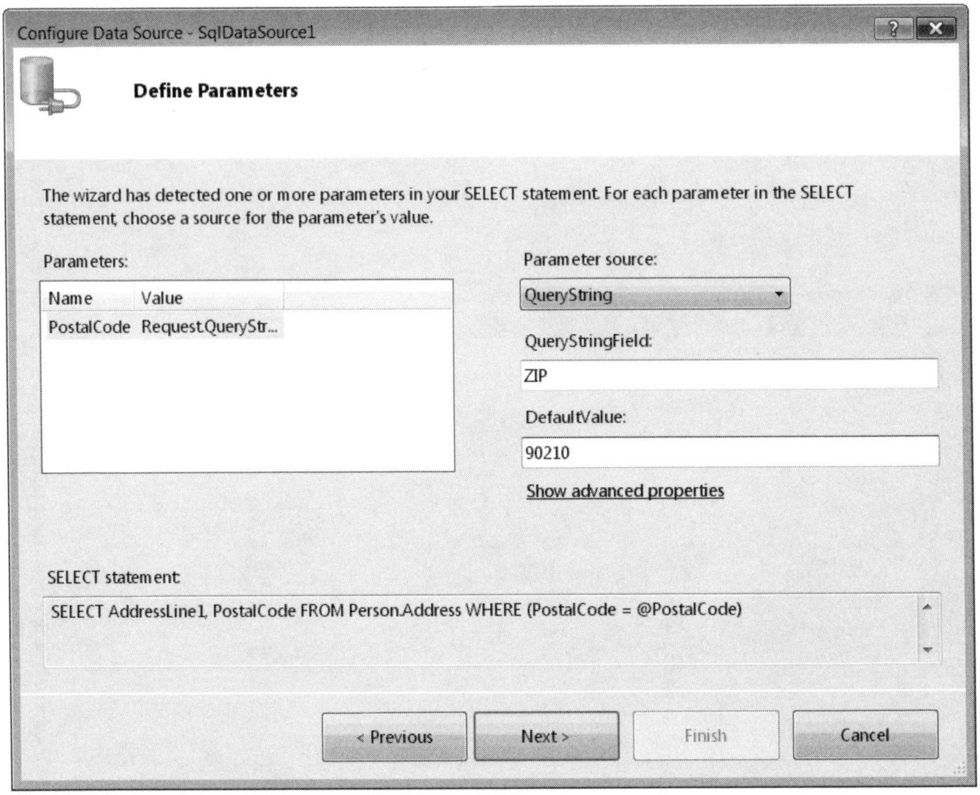

Figure 12-14. *Defining the parameters*

After this, you can finish out the wizard, and you'll have a configured data source.

The wizard has added some markup to your page to instruct the server at runtime to connect to the data and run the query, using the query string parameter that you defined. It should look something like this:

```
<asp:SqlDataSource ID="SqlDataSource1" runat="server"
ConnectionString=
   "<%$ ConnectionStrings:AdventureWorksConnectionString %>"
SelectCommand="SELECT AddressLine1, PostalCode FROM Person.Address
   WHERE (PostalCode = @PostalCode)">
      <SelectParameters>
         <asp:QueryStringParameter DefaultValue="90210"
            Name="PostalCode" QueryStringField="ZIP" />
      </SelectParameters>
</asp:SqlDataSource>
```

Now that you have your data connection, it's pretty easy to tie a DataGrid up to it to view the results of the query.

Drag and drop a GridView control onto the page, and open its Tasks pane (see Figure 12-15 for details).

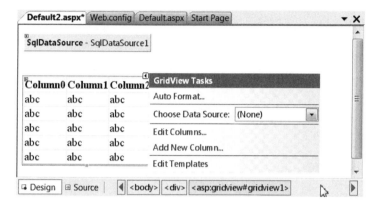

Figure 12-15. *Adding a GridView to your application*

Select SqlDataSource1 from the Choose Data Source drop-down, and you'll see the grid reconfigure itself to the fields that the data source exposes. Enable paging, sorting, and selection by selecting their check boxes in the Tasks pane, as shown in Figure 12-16.

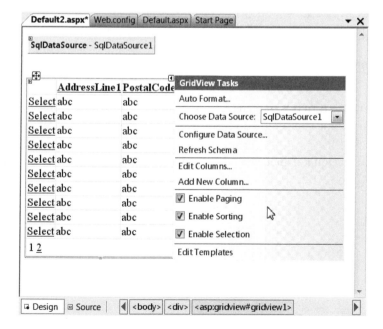

Figure 12-16. *Binding the grid to the data source*

Run the application. You'll see that you can select different pages on the grid, select items on the grid, and sort the items by clicking the column headers. However, every time you do this, you'll see a postback to the server and a page blink (see Figure 12-17). Notice the status bar progress at the bottom-left-hand side!

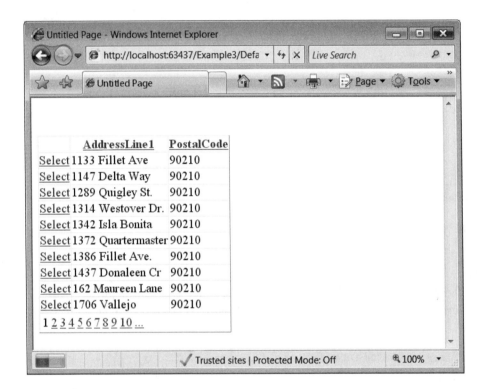

Figure 12-17. *Running the data-bound application*

Now let's see how easy it is to turn this into an Ajax application. As with everything else in ASP.NET AJAX, the first thing you should do is add a ScriptManager object to the design surface.

Once you have this, add an UpdatePanel. Drag the DataGrid onto the design surface for the UpdatePanel (see Figure 12-18).

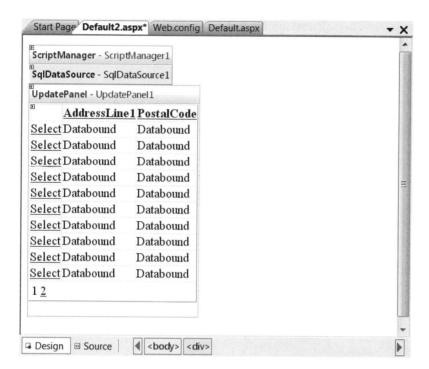

Figure 12-18. *Adding a ScriptManager and an UpdatePanel*

Now when you run your application, it will be an Ajax one, and you will not see the full page refresh when you perform an action on the DataGrid. For your reference, here is the full HTML markup for the page. Despite the pretty complex functionality, no C# or JavaScript coding was required.

```
<%@ Page Language="C#" AutoEventWireup="true"
  CodeFile="Default2.aspx.cs" Inherits="Default2" %>

<!DOCTYPE html PUBLIC "-//W3C//DTD XHTML 1.0 Transitional//EN"
  "http://www.w3.org/TR/xhtml1/DTD/xhtml1-transitional.dtd">

<html xmlns="http://www.w3.org/1999/xhtml" >
<head runat="server">
    <title>Untitled Page</title>
</head>
<body>
    <form id="form1" runat="server">
    <div>
        <asp:ScriptManager ID="ScriptManager1" runat="server">
        </asp:ScriptManager>
```

```
    <asp:SqlDataSource ID="SqlDataSource1" runat="server"
      ConnectionString="<%$ ConnectionStrings:AdventureWorksConnectionString %>"
      SelectCommand="SELECT AddressLine1, PostalCode FROM
        Person.Address WHERE (PostalCode = @PostalCode)">
        <SelectParameters>
            <asp:QueryStringParameter DefaultValue="90210"
                                      Name="PostalCode"
                                      QueryStringField="ZIP" />
        </SelectParameters>
    </asp:SqlDataSource>
    <asp:UpdatePanel ID="UpdatePanel1" runat="server">
        <ContentTemplate>
            <asp:GridView ID="GridView1"
                          runat="server"
                          AllowPaging="True"
                          AllowSorting="True"
                          AutoGenerateColumns="False"
                          DataSourceID="SqlDataSource1">
            <Columns>
                <asp:CommandField ShowSelectButton="True" />
                <asp:BoundField DataField="AddressLine1"
                                HeaderText="AddressLine1"
                                SortExpression="AddressLine1" />
                <asp:BoundField DataField="PostalCode"
                                HeaderText="PostalCode"
                                SortExpression="PostalCode" />
            </Columns>
            </asp:GridView>
        </ContentTemplate>
    </asp:UpdatePanel>

    </div>
    </form>
</body>
</html>
```

Using Ajax with Web Services

Some other useful technologies that come with the ASP.NET AJAX extensions are the ability to develop a web service that provides a JavaScript proxy, and client-side libraries that allow you to reference and use this proxy directly from the browser. This is very useful for developing mashup-style applications, where an interim server is not necessary to consume the web service and provide the data in HTML format, as is the typical design pattern when using web services. In this section, you'll build a web service, make it accessible to JavaScript, and build a simple client that accesses it.

For this example, you will build a web service that fronts the AdventureWorks database and uses its country code lookup table to allow you to convert a country code into a country name. For example, WS evaluates to Samoa and GL to Greenland. You can see this data in the Person.CountryRegion table.

If you haven't already set up an AdventureWorks database and connection to it in your application, it's a good idea to work through Chapters 4 and 5 and the samples earlier in this chapter before continuing. You can still use this sample, but if you have connectivity trouble (i.e., reading the connection string from Web.config), go through those earlier samples and you should be fine.

To get started, add a new ASMX web service to your solution and call it DataService. asmx. The full code for this service is listed following. This implements the simple web method GetCountryForRegion, taking in the region code and returning the country that matches it.

```
using System;
using System.Web;
using System.Collections;
using System.Web.Services;
using System.Web.Services.Protocols;
using System.Data;
using System.Data.SqlClient;
using System.Web.Configuration;


[WebService(Namespace = "http://tempuri.org/")]
[WebServiceBinding(ConformsTo = WsiProfiles.BasicProfile1_1)]
public class DataService : System.Web.Services.WebService {

    public DataService () {

        //Uncomment the following line if using designed components
        //InitializeComponent();
    }

    [WebMethod]
    public string GetCountryForRegion(string strRegion)
    {
        string strReturn = "";
```

```
       string connectionString = WebConfigurationManager.ConnectionStrings
            ["AdventureWorksConnectionString"].ConnectionString;
       SqlConnection sqlCon = new SqlConnection(connectionString);
       SqlCommand sqlComm = new SqlCommand();
       sqlComm.Connection = sqlCon;
       sqlComm.CommandType = CommandType.Text;
       sqlComm.CommandText =
          "SELECT * FROM Person.CountryRegion WHERE (CountryRegionCode = @strCRC)";
       sqlComm.Parameters.Add("@strCRC", strRegion);

       sqlCon.Open();
       SqlDataReader sRead = sqlComm.ExecuteReader();
       while (sRead.Read())
       {
           strReturn = sRead["Name"].ToString();
       }
       sqlCon.Close();
       return strReturn;


    }
}
```

For this web service to be consumed from JavaScript, it has to be a script service. This is a new attribute that has been added by the ASP.NET AJAX extensions.

To use scriptable services, you should first add a reference to them at the top of your service. It will look like this:

```
using System.Web.Script.Services;
```

Next, you'll attribute your service as a script service by putting the [ScriptService] attribute on the class declaration.

Your service is now ready to produce JavaScript proxies that can be consumed within the browser. You can test this by calling your service, and then appending /js to the URL. If your service is successfully set up, it will generate a .js file that the browser will download (see Figure 12-19).

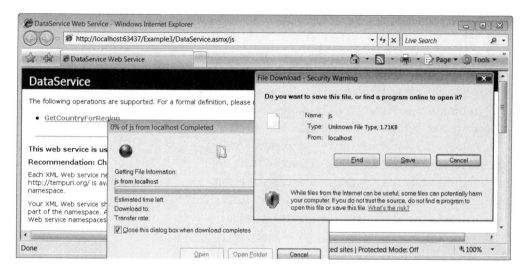

Figure 12-19. *Accessing the JavaScript proxy*

This proxy file will look something like this:

```
var DataService=function() {
DataService.initializeBase(this);
this._timeout = 0;
this._userContext = null;
this._succeeded = null;
this._failed = null;
}
DataService.prototype={
GetCountryForRegion:function(
    strRegion,succeededCallback, failedCallback, userContext)
    {

    return this._invoke(DataService.get_path(),
            'GetCountryForRegion',false,{strRegion:strRegion},
                succeededCallback,failedCallback,userContext); }}
DataService.registerClass('DataService',Sys.Net.WebServiceProxy);
DataService._staticInstance = new DataService();
DataService.set_path = function(value)
    { DataService._staticInstance._path = value; }
DataService.get_path = function()
    { return DataService._staticInstance._path; }
DataService.set_timeout = function(value)
    { DataService._staticInstance._timeout = value; }
```

```
DataService.get_timeout = function()
    { return DataService._staticInstance._timeout; }
DataService.set_defaultUserContext = function(value)
    { DataService._staticInstance._userContext = value; }
DataService.get_defaultUserContext = function()
    { return DataService._staticInstance._userContext; }
DataService.set_defaultSucceededCallback = function(value)
    { DataService._staticInstance._succeeded = value; }
DataService.get_defaultSucceededCallback = function()
    { return DataService._staticInstance._succeeded; }
DataService.set_defaultFailedCallback = function(value)
    { DataService._staticInstance._failed = value; }
DataService.get_defaultFailedCallback = function()
    { return DataService._staticInstance._failed; }
DataService.set_path("/Example3/DataService.asmx");
DataService.GetCountryForRegion=
    function(strRegion,onSuccess,onFailed,userContext)
        {DataService._staticInstance.GetCountryForRegion(strRegion,
            onSuccess,onFailed,userContext); }
```

This is pure JavaScript that has dependencies on the ASP.NET AJAX JavaScript libraries, so to use this service in a client, you'll have to make sure that the libraries are present. If you use ASP.NET to deliver the client page, then they are downloaded automatically when you use the <ScriptManager> component; otherwise you will have to deliver the libraries yourself through an HTML <script> reference. The libraries are freely downloadable from http://asp.net/ajax/.

The next step is to build a page that consumes this web service. To do this, add a new ASPX page to your solution, and call it CountryCode.aspx.

Add a ScriptManager component to CountryCode.aspx. Take a look at its Services property, and you'll see an ellipsis button that opens the ServiceReference Collection Editor. Use this to add a service reference to the DataService that you just set up (see Figure 12-20).

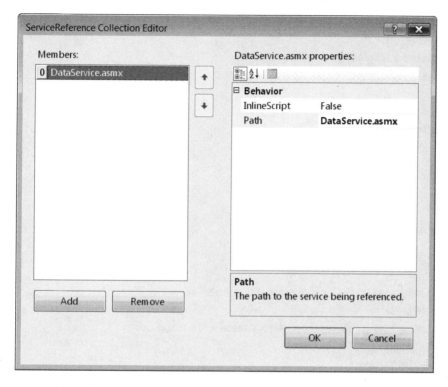

Figure 12-20. *Adding a service reference*

This will generate markup that looks like this:

```
<asp:ScriptManager ID="ScriptManager1" runat="server">
        <Services>
            <asp:ServiceReference Path="DataService.asmx" />
        </Services>
</asp:ScriptManager>
```

Next, add some HTML markup for an input text box and an input button. Double-click the button, and a JavaScript event handler will be created. Finally, add a <div> to your page and call it CC.

Your page markup will look like this:

```
<%@ Page Language="C#" AutoEventWireup="true"
    CodeFile="CountryCode.aspx.cs" Inherits="CountryCode" %>

<!DOCTYPE html PUBLIC "-//W3C//DTD XHTML 1.0 Transitional//EN"

    "http://www.w3.org/TR/xhtml1/DTD/xhtml1-transitional.dtd">
```

```html
<html xmlns="http://www.w3.org/1999/xhtml" >
<head runat="server">
    <title>Untitled Page</title>
<script language="javascript" type="text/javascript">
// <!CDATA[

function btnLookup_onclick() {
}

// ]]>
</script>
</head>
<body>
    <form id="form1" runat="server">
    <div>
        <asp:ScriptManager ID="ScriptManager1" runat="server">
            <Services>
                <asp:ServiceReference Path="DataService.asmx" />
            </Services>
        </asp:ScriptManager>
        <br />
        Enter Country Code
        <input id="txtCC" type="text" /><br />
        <br />
        <input id="btnLookup" type="button"
               value="Look Up" onclick="return btnLookup_onclick()" /><br />
        <br />
        <div id="CC"></div>

    </div>
    </form>
</body>
</html>
```

The next step is to add the JavaScript code that calls the web service when you click the button. The ScriptManager service reference handles the downloading of the proxy, so you'll have a class called DataService available to you. So, to call the GetCountryForRegion method using JavaScript, you just call it, specifying the parameter to pass and the call-backs for successful completion and timeout. Your call (with a hard-coded parameter) should look like this:

```
DataService.GetCountryForRegion(strCC, onReturn, onTimeOut);
```

Thus, to use the text box value to call the web service, you would use the button click event handler that was created earlier:

```
function btnLookup_onclick() {
    var strCC = document.all("txtCC").value;;
    DataService.GetCountryForRegion(strCC, onReturn, onTimeOut);
}
```

In JavaScript, you use `document.all` to look up an HTML control, pass it the ID of the control, and query its properties. So, the first line in this JavaScript takes the value of the text box and loads it into the `strCC` var.

Now all that remains is to implement the `onReturn` and `onTimeOut` functions. These are standard JavaScript functions that take a `result` parameter. You can see them here:

```
function onReturn(result)
{
    CC.innerHTML = result;
}

function onTimeOut(result)
{
    alert("You hit a timeout!");
}
```

The result that a successful call to the web service returns is a string, so you can set the `innerHTML` of the `<div>` to this result and it will appear on the page. And that's it—you now have a pure thin-client web application that directly consumes a web service via JavaScript-based proxies!

You can see this application in action in Figure 12-21.

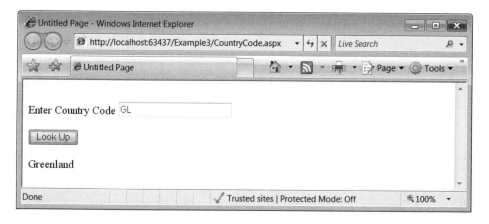

Figure 12-21. *Running the JavaScript service client*

Summary

In this chapter, you were introduced to the ASP.NET extensions that allow you to build AJAX applications easily using your familiar tools and skills. These extensions make Ajax applications a lot easier to write, as in many cases they emit the requisite Ajax code on your behalf, without you needing to explicitly code against the XMLHttpRequest API. You took a look at some examples of building new Ajax applications using Visual Studio, as well as how straightforward it is to amend *existing* ASP.NET applications for a better user experience using these tools. Finally, you looked at one of the more useful facets of ASP.NET AJAX—the facility to build a web service that exposes a JavaScript proxy, and how to consume this proxy, allowing web services to be called directly from the browser!

CHAPTER 13

■■■

Ajax Scripts and Services

As you saw in Chapter 12, ASP.NET AJAX has both server and client components. You saw how you use the ScriptManager to create a service reference so that a web service can be accessed directly from JavaScript.

In this chapter, you will look at some of the server controls and their supporting classes in some more detail. In particular, you will look at the ScriptManager control and how it can be used to link your server and client applications neatly. It enables ASP.NET AJAX applications to work within the browser, along with its partner control, the Script-ManagerProxy. You'll see how to deliver custom scripts to the browser, how to manage partial page rendering, and how to access web services directly from script.

You'll build on this to look at how Ajax applications can access ASP.NET services such as memberships and profiles, building out a role-based secured site in ASP.NET and then seeing how this can be accessed from JavaScript as well as ASP.NET.

The ScriptManager Class

The `ScriptManager` class is designed to manage the ASP.NET AJAX script libraries, all the script files that you use within your application, and proxy class generation for web services. In addition, it supports the UpdatePanel, UpdateProgress, and Timer controls to perform their partial page refreshing and timing functions. These controls will not work unless a ScriptManager is present. Finally, it offers the JavaScript classes that are necessary to access authentication and profiling services.

Partial Page Rendering

As you saw in the previous chapter, by storing page content and controls within Update-Panels, partial page updates become possible. This is managed by the ScriptManager component, which delivers scripts that interact with the page life cycle (you can see this in more depth in Chapter 3). The ScriptManager has an `EnablePartialRendering` property that allows you to override this. By default, it is set to `true`, meaning that partial rendering is automatically enabled, and all UpdatePanel controls will refresh upon postback (but not the whole page). Should you set it to `false`, then full page refreshes will occur on postbacks, unless you write JavaScript code that uses the `XMLHttpRequest` class to perform asynchronous postbacks and then manually update the page. Typically for Ajax pages, you will always set this to `true`. If your page is going to be relatively static (i.e., no post-backs to the server), and you want to use a ScriptManager to deliver JavaScript, then you can set it to `false` to reduce overhead.

Handling Errors in Partial Page Updates

In case you hit an error in the process of a partial page update, the ScriptManager has a property called `AllowCustomErrorsRedirect` (defaulting to `true`), which determines that the custom errors section of the `Web.config` file should be used when an error occurs—namely that you can redirect the user to a friendly landing page instead of crashing them out of your app.

Alternatively, you can catch and handle the `AsyncPostBackError` event, and/or set the `AsyncPostBackErrorMessage` property to manage errors. To do this, you define the `AsyncPostBackError` callback by setting the `OnAsyncPostBackError` attribute on the Script-Manager control. Here's an example:

```
<asp:ScriptManager ID="ScriptManager1" runat="server"
    OnAsyncPostBackError="ScriptManager1_AsyncPostBackError">
</asp:ScriptManager>
```

Then, in your server code, you can implement a function that handles this error. In this case, it takes the exception message and loads it into the `AsyncPostBackErrorMessage` property, which is accessible from client-side script via the PageRequestManager (you'll see more of this in the next chapter).

```
protected void ScriptManager1_AsyncPostBackError(object sender,
        AsyncPostBackErrorEventArgs e)
{
    ScriptManager1.AsyncPostBackErrorMessage = e.Exception.Message;
}
```

For example, if you add an `EndRequestHandler` callback to the PageRequestManager, like this:

```
Sys.WebForms.PageRequestManager.getInstance().add_endRequest(EndRequestHandler);
```

you can then access the `AsyncPostBackErrorMessage` from your JavaScript code as part of the args sent back to the `EndRequestHandler`:

```
function EndRequestHandler(sender, args)
{
    var errorMessage = args.get_error().message;
    alert(errorMessage);
}
```

Managing Custom Scripts

The typical way to add new scripts to a page is to use the <script> tag within HTML.
However, if your script library is using Ajax features, this is not always reliable. First, if the
browser accesses this script prior to reading the Ajax script libraries, it will hit parsing
errors. Second, if the script is accessing some of the security features of the Ajax library
(such as accessing profile information), it will fail. To get around these drawbacks in your
custom script, you can use the ScriptManager to deliver it for you.

Suppose, for example, you have a script like this, which uses the object-oriented
extensions of JavaScript that ASP.NET AJAX offers:

```
Type.registerNamespace("WebNext");

WebNext.House = function(streetName, townName, zipCode) {
    this._streetName = streetName;
    this._townName = townName;
    this._zipCode = zipCode;
}

WebNext.House.prototype = {

    getStreetName: function() {
        return this._streetName;
    },

    getTownName: function() {
        return this._townName;
    },

    getAddress: function() {
        return this._streetName + ' ' + this._townName + ' ' + this._zipCode;
    },

    dispose: function() {
        alert('removed ' + this.getAddress());
```

```
    }
}
WebNext.House.registerClass('WebNext.House', null, Sys.IDisposable);
if (typeof(Sys) !== 'undefined') Sys.Application.notifyScriptLoaded();
```

You can then ensure that it is correctly and cleanly delivered to the browser by declaring it as a script that the ScriptManager component will manage for you. Here's the markup to achieve this:

```
<asp:ScriptManager ID="ScriptManager1" runat="server">
    <Scripts>
        <asp:ScriptReference Path="House.js" />
    </Scripts>
</asp:ScriptManager>
```

Using Web Services from Script

A very powerful facet of the ScriptManager is that it allows you to declare references to web services. If these services are attributed as scriptable, and thus generate a JavaScript proxy, the ScriptManager can then initialize everything that is needed for a client to communicate directly with the service.

For example, consider the following simple web service. Note that it has been attributed as a [ScriptService]. In order to do this, you'll need to add a using reference to the System.Web.Script.Services namespace.

```
<%@ WebService Language="C#" Class="SimpleService" %>

using System;
using System.Web;
using System.Web.Services;
using System.Web.Services.Protocols;
using System.Web.Script.Services;


[WebService(Namespace = "http://tempuri.org/")]
[WebServiceBinding(ConformsTo = WsiProfiles.BasicProfile1_1)]
[ScriptService]
public class SimpleService  : System.Web.Services.WebService {

    [WebMethod]
    public int AddEm(int x, int y) {
```

```
        return x+y;
    }

}
```

The ScriptManager has a `Services` collection of `ServiceReference` objects that are used for this task. Each service is defined using a `ServiceReference` like this:

```
<asp:ScriptManager ID="ScriptManager1" runat="server">
    <Services>
        <asp:ServiceReference Path="SimpleService.ASMX"/>
    </Services>
</asp:ScriptManager>
```

The `ServiceReference` supports an `InLineScript` property that allows you to define whether the JavaScript proxy is stored inline in the page that contains the service reference, or whether it's downloaded as an external script. In some cases, security firewalls can prevent the external script from downloading, so the inline script will work nicely.

You can now access the web methods of the service directly from JavaScript. Here's an example of a page that references the simple service and accesses the `AddEm` method of the SimpleService that you just defined.

```
<%@ Page Language="C#" AutoEventWireup="true" CodeFile="ServiceReference.aspx.cs"
Inherits="ServiceReference" %>

<!DOCTYPE html PUBLIC "-//W3C//DTD XHTML 1.0 Transitional//EN"
  "http://www.w3.org/TR/xhtml1/DTD/xhtml1-transitional.dtd">

<html xmlns="http://www.w3.org/1999/xhtml" >
<head runat="server">
    <title>Untitled Page</title>
<script language="javascript" type="text/javascript">
// <![CDATA[

function Button1_onclick() {
    SimpleService.AddEm(3,4,onResult,onTimeOut);
}
function onResult(result)
{
    alert(result);
}
function onTimeOut(result)
{
```

```
        alert(timeout);
}


// ]]>
</script>
</head>
<body>
    <form id="form1" runat="server">
    <div>
        <asp:ScriptManager ID="ScriptManager1" runat="server">
            <Services>
                <asp:ServiceReference Path="SimpleService.ASMX"
                        InlineScript="True"/>
            </Services>
        </asp:ScriptManager>
        <input id="Button1" type="button" value="button"
                onclick="return Button1_onclick()" /></div>
    </form>
</body>
</html>
```

The key part of this to understand is the fact that the JavaScript proxy has been generated by the service. This creates a SimpleService class that is accessible via JavaScript.

With code like this, you call the service, passing the parameters (it takes two integers) and the name of the callback function for a successful result and the callback function for a timeout failure:

```
SimpleService.AddEm(3,4,onResult,onTimeOut);
```

Then, all you have to do is implement the callback function to inform the page (or user) of the results of the service call. This is where the number returned from the service is displayed in an alert dialog:

```
function onResult(result)
{
    alert(result);
}
```

Using Application Services from Script

In addition to accessing web services, ASP.NET AJAX gives you the facility to call ASP.NET 2.0 forms authentication and profile services directly from JavaScript. This allows you to continue presenting these services to your users without requiring non-Ajax full page refreshes. Using them is very straightforward, and the ScriptManager control is used to manage the generation and downloading of the correct proxies.

In this section, you'll first see how to add forms-based authentication to your ASP.NET AJAX site, and then you'll go into accessing the profile services.

Using Forms-Based Authentication in ASP.NET

Configuring forms-based authentication to use ASP.NET membership services is very straightforward, and very well handled for you by the framework. In this section, you'll go through, step by step, how to create a simple site that uses membership, authentication, and roles, and how ASP.NET and Visual Studio 2005 enable this for you. You'll then take what you've learned in this section to the next, where you will access the membership and profile data directly from JavaScript using your Ajax code.

Step 1: Creating a New Web Site Application

To get started, create a new ASP.NET AJAX–enabled web site in Visual Studio 2005. Use the HTTP location so that the site runs on IIS instead of the Cassini server. Call the site FormsSecured. Your dialog should look something like that in Figure 13-1.

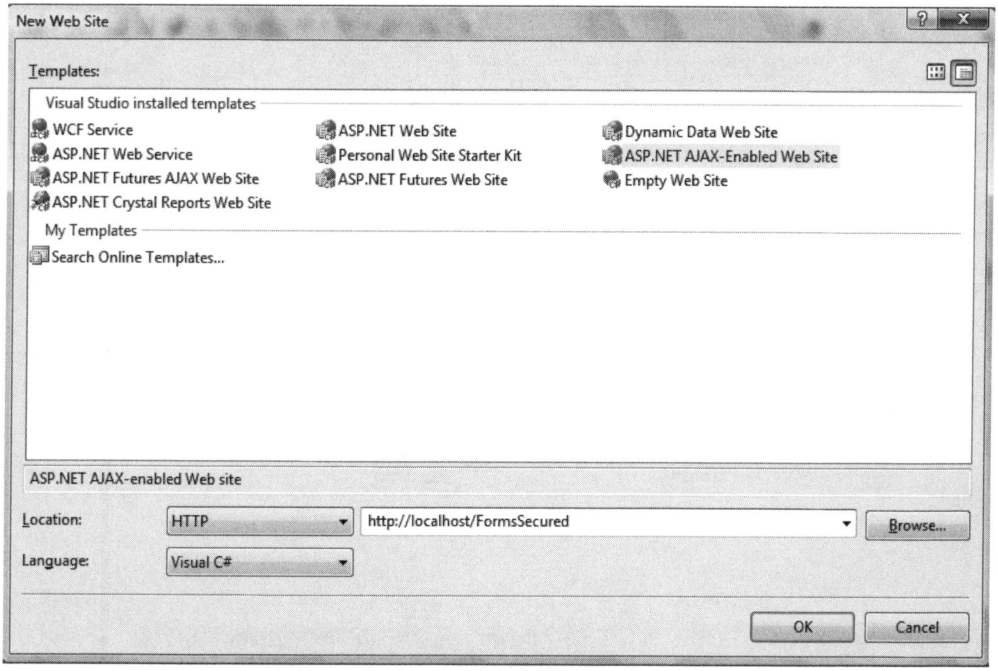

Figure 13-1. *Creating a new web site in Visual Studio 2005*

Once your site is created, use the Solution Explorer to create two new folders. Call one AdminFolder and the other UserFolder. Later, you will put content into these folders, which are accessed by Administrator and User profiles, respectively. You can see this in Figure 13-2.

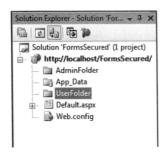

Figure 13-2. *Creating folders for the different roles*

Create some simple content in each folder. An ASPX file in each containing text to indicate which folder they are in should suffice.

Next, go to the Web Site menu in Visual Studio and select ASP.NET Configuration. The ASP.NET configuration utility will load in the browser (see Figure 13-3).

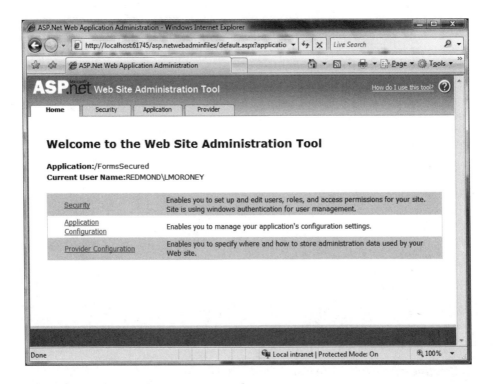

Figure 13-3. *Web Site Administration Tool*

This tool allows you to configure security, membership, and profiles, as well as specific settings for the application and different data providers for these services.

This application is using the security settings, so select the Security link and you'll be taken to the security administration screen (see Figure 13-4).

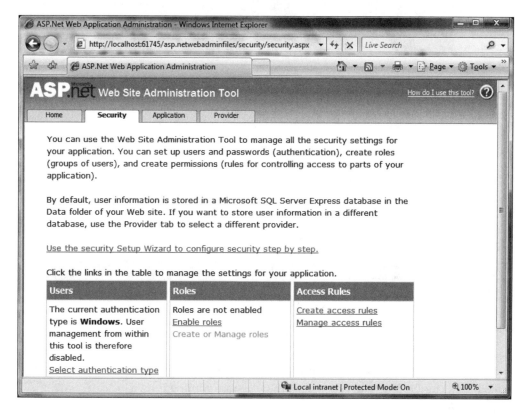

Figure 13-4. *Configuring security with the Web Site Administration Tool*

This allows you to configure users for your application, the roles that the users fit in, and access rules for those roles. Authentication is designed to use the Windows authentication type for local or intranet applications (this is the default) and the forms authentication type for external users. So, before you continue, you'll need to reconfigure this site for forms authentication. To do this, choose "Select authentication type" from the Users pane. After this, you should see something like Figure 13-5.

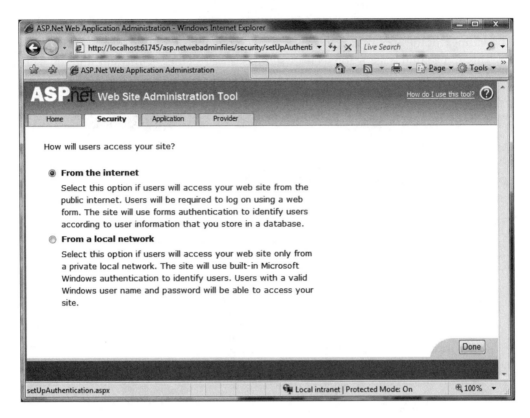

Figure 13-5. *Configuring the authentication type*

To use forms authentication, you specify that your users are from the Internet, and to use Windows authentication, you specify that they are coming from a local network. In this case, choose "From the internet."

Once you've done this, click the Back button to return to the security administration screen, and you'll be able to add new users from the Users pane. The Users pane is simple to fill out—you just need to specify the username, password, e-mail address, security question, and security answer. You could add a form like this to your own application quite easily, but for now, you will add a couple of sample users.

Add two new users, called Administrator and TestUser, respectively. Figure 13-6 shows an example of entering the Administrator user.

Now that you have a couple of users in the system (Administrator and TestUser), the next thing to do is set up a couple of roles. Typically, you will have at least two roles—one for administrative users, and one for everyone else. In many cases, you may have other levels of role, but the same principles apply—you create a role, assign users to a role, and configure access to a resource by role (but you can override this for specific users).

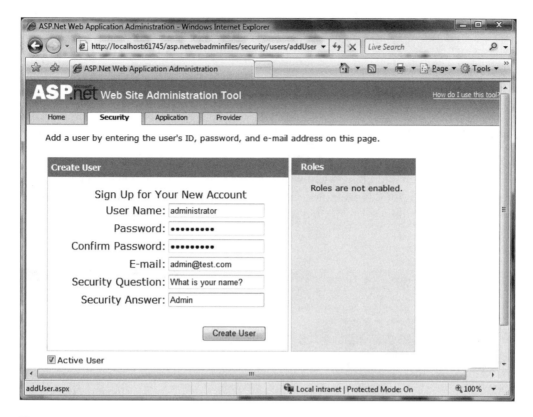

Figure 13-6. *Creating a new user*

Back on the Security tab, you'll see the Roles pane. In its default state, roles are not enabled (see Figure 13-7).

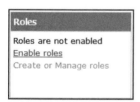

Figure 13-7. *The Roles pane*

Click the "Enable roles" link, and the pane will change to indicate that roles are enabled (see Figure 13-8). Once roles are enabled, you can disable them if you choose by clicking "Disable roles."

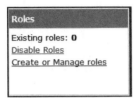

Figure 13-8. *Enabling roles*

Once they are enabled, you can now create new roles. As mentioned earlier, you will create two new roles for this example—one for administrators and one for users. Creating a role is as easy as typing in the desired name for the role and clicking Add Role (see Figure 13-9).

Figure 13-9. *Creating a new role*

When you are done, you'll see the full set of roles listed on your screen (see Figure 13-10).

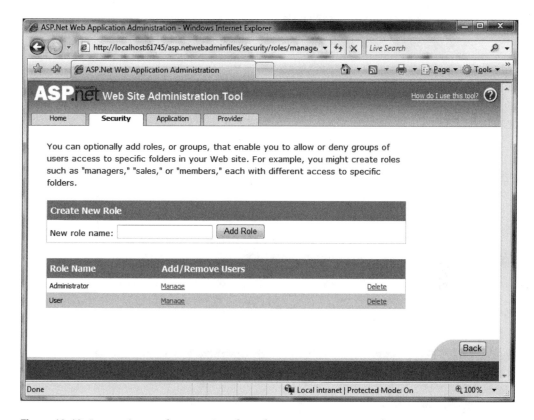

Figure 13-10. *Inspecting and managing the roles*

Now that your roles are set up, you can use them to create Access Rules for the content of your site. By default, every user (whether named or not) has access to everything. For example, if you want to give access to the root web to everyone, whether they are signed in or not, you don't need to do anything. If you want to give only regular users access to the UserFolder directory, you specify that all users are denied access first, and then specify that people in the User role are allowed. Similarly, for the administrative content (in the AdminFolder directory), you would first deny access to everyone, and then allow access only to those in the Administrator role (see Figures 13-11 and 13-12).

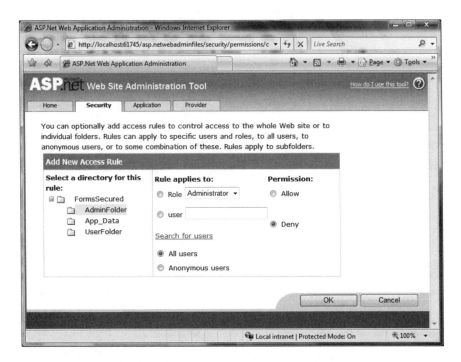

Figure 13-11. *Denying access to the AdminFolder directory*

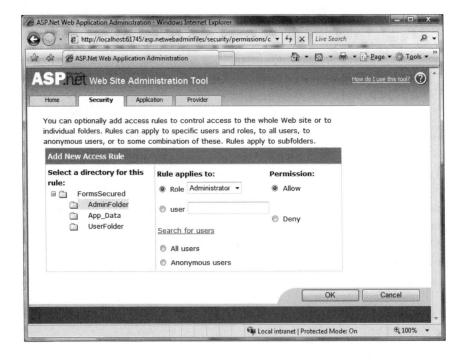

Figure 13-12. *Providing access to the Administrator role*

Finally, you can inspect or change your access rules from the Manage Access Rules screen (accessible from the Security tab) to see what your settings are. Figure 13-13 shows what the access rules for the UserFolder directory are. As you can see, anonymous users are not allowed, but regular users and administrators are. In a similar manner, anonymous users and regular users are not allowed to access the AdminFolder directory, but administrators are.

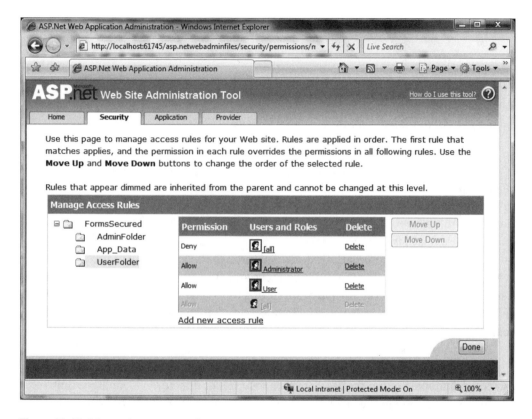

Figure 13-13. *Managing access rules*

Now that the site is configured, you can use ASP.NET server controls to provide login functionality.

Step 2: Creating the Sign-In Functionality

ASP.NET provides a number of server controls that make providing and managing forms-based authentication very easy. The first of these is the LoginStatus control, which provides the current status of the user. Drag an instance of this onto the Default.aspx page in the root folder of your web site. By default, this will create a Login link, which users will use to access your sign-in screen (see Figure 13-14).

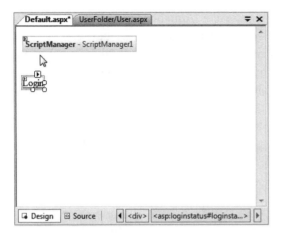

Figure 13-14. *Adding a login status to your home page*

This is then linked to a login page. So, create a new Login.aspx page in the root direc-tory of your web site and add a Login control to it. Note that the membership APIs are configured to work with a page of this name, so you do not need to configure the Login-Status control that you just created. If you want a login page with a different name, you can configure this in the Web.config file.

Login validation is automatically provided through the ValidationSummary control in ASP.NET. You'll find this in the Validation section of the Toolbox, and you can configure it simply by dropping it onto the page and setting its ValidationGroup property to the ID of the control that you want to validate. In this case, your Login control is likely called Login1, so simply use this.

You can see this in Figure 13-15.

You can now test the functionality of your site. Execute the site and try to access the protected content in either the UserFolder or AdminFolder directories—you'll see that ASP.NET redirects you to the login page. Similar behavior occurs if you try to access the AdminFolder folder and are not logged in as an administrative user.

This shows how straightforward it is to set up forms-based authentication for your ASP.NET web site. Now, with the ASP.NET AJAX extensions, you'll look at how you can access this information from JavaScript running in your browser.

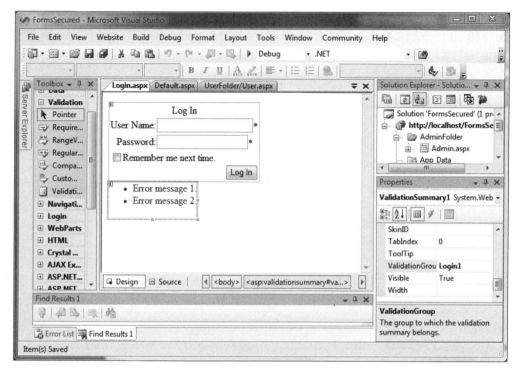

Figure 13-15. *Using login validation*

Adding Forms-Based Authentication to an Ajax Site

Before you can get started with building a forms-based authentication application, you will have to configure your server to use the built-in authentication service. This service is part of the Windows services on your server machine that manage the different methods of authentication. You can configure your site to use it by adding the following to your Web.config file:

```
<system.web.extensions>
  <scripting>
    <webServices>
      <authenticationService enabled="true"></authenticationService>
    </webServices>
  </scripting>
</system.web.extensions>
```

Accessing the authentication details is very straightforward within JavaScript. You can implement some simple HTML input controls to provide a user ID and password input box and a button.

```
<input type="text" id="username" /><br />
<input type="password" id="password" />
        <br />
<input type="button" id="btnSubmit"
        onclick="doLogin()" value="Login" />
```

Now, within JavaScript, you can implement the doLogin function, which uses the authentication service like this:

```
function doLogin()
{
   username = $get("username");
    password = $get("password");
Sys.Services.AuthenticationService.set_defaultLoginCompletedCallback(LoginComplete);
Sys.Services.AuthenticationService.login(username.value,
        password.value, false,null,null,null,null,"Logged in from my AJAX page");
}

function LoginComplete(validCredentials, userContext, methodName)
{
    alert(validCredentials);
    alert(userContext);
    alert(methodName);
}
```

Here you get the username and password, and then specify the callback function to be OnLoginCompleted.

Next, you call the login method of the authentication service. This takes a number of parameters:

Username: Text of username for sign-in

Password: Text of password for sign-in

IsPersistent: Persists the authentication ticket across browser sessions; defaults to false

RedirectUrl: URL to redirect to upon successful authentication; defaults to null, denoting that there will be no redirect

CustomInfo: Reserved for future use; defaults to null

LoginCompletedCallback: Name of function to call upon successful completion

FailedCallback: Name of function to call upon failed completion

UserContext: String containing user info to pass to the callback functions

The callback function takes three parameters:

validCredentials: true for successful login, false for bad credentials

userContext: Context data that was passed to the service in its UserContext property

methodName: Name of the method that triggered the callback (usually Sys.Services.AuthenticationService.login)

Using Profile Data

In a similar manner to adding user credentials and role membership, you can add free-form profile data to your web site using ASP.NET, and you can access this profile data directly from your JavaScript applications using Ajax.

The data itself gets stored on a user-by-user basis in the same database as the login and password information that you set up earlier.

Profiles are enabled using your Web.config file:

```
<system.web.extensions>
  <scripting>
    <webServices>
      <authenticationService enabled="true"></authenticationService>
      <profileService enabled="true"
          readAccessProperties="Property1, Property2"
          writeAccessProperties="Property1, Property2">
      </profileService>
    </webServices>
  </scripting>
</system.web.extensions>
```

The <profileService> node, as well as having an enabled attribute, also specifies the properties that may be read (in the readAccessProperties attribute) and those that may be written (in the writeAccessProperties attribute). These properties are specified in the <profile> node of Web.config.

You specify properties by using their name, type, and optional default value. So, for example, to add a couple of properties of type System.String, you could have a setting like this:

```
<profile enabled="true">
    <properties>
      <add name="Property1" type="System.String" defaultValue="P1"/>
      <add name="Property2" type="System.String" defaultValue="P2"/>
    </properties>
  </profile>
```

When using ASP.NET AJAX, you now have access to the Sys.Services.ProfileService service from JavaScript. In the next sections, you'll see how to use this to access your custom properties.

Accessing and Saving Properties in the Profile

The Profile service offers a load method that you use to read in the properties from the property store. This is usually called as part of the Login callback, which makes sense—you want to authenticate the user, and then use their validated credentials to load their profile data.

This takes a number of properties:

propertyNames: String array containing the names of profile properties to load

loadCompletedCallback: Callback function to call upon profile loading

failedCallback: Callback function to call upon failure of profile loading

userContext: String information to pass to the callback functions

For example, a simple call to load will look like this:

```
Sys.Services.ProfileService.load(null, OnProfileLoadComplete, null, null);
```

This sets up a simple load of the properties, specifying that the function OnProfileLoadComplete will be called when the properties are loaded.

The values of the properties are accessed via the Sys.Services.ProfileService. properties collection. So, if your properties are named Property1 and Property2, as used earlier, you can then use code like this to load their values into a couple of text boxes:

```
document.form1.txtP1.value = Sys.Services.ProfileService.properties.Property1;
document.form1.txtP2.value = Sys.Services.ProfileService.properties.Property2;
```

If you specified that the properties could be writable, then you could save the properties using the save method that is exposed by the Profile service. In a similar manner to the load method you saw earlier, it takes four properties:

propertyNames: String array containing the names of profile properties to save; can be null.

saveCompletedCallback: Callback function to call upon profile saving

failedCallback: Callback function to call upon failure of profile saving

userContext: String information to pass to the callback functions

Thus, you can specify how to save out your profile information using the following code:

```
Sys.Services.ProfileService.properties.Property1 = document.form1.txtP1.value;
Sys.Services.ProfileService.properties.Property2 = document.form1.txtP2.value;
Sys.Services.ProfileService.save(null, OnProfileSaveCompleted, null, null);
```

Summary

In this chapter, you looked at how the AJAX extensions for ASP.NET handle scripts and services. You looked at the ScriptManager component in some detail, looking at how to handle partial page updates and errors in partial page updates, before moving on to managing custom JavaScript libraries using the ScriptManager control. You then went into some detail on accessing the web services using the ScriptManager and how Ajax uses JavaScript Object Notation (JSON) to provide script-based proxies to web services. Finally, you looked at ASP.NET authentication, membership, and profiling, and how the AJAX extensions provide services that allow the JavaScript developer to access their information. In the next chapter, you'll see how the AJAX extensions beef up the JavaScript developer's toolbox through object-oriented extensions and more.

CHAPTER 14

■■■

JavaScript Programming with ASP.NET AJAX

ASP.NET AJAX offers many extensions to JavaScript, providing object-oriented features such as namespaces, inheritance, interfaces, enumerations, and more. These functionalities assist you in developing applications by providing more robust and structured language features, making it easier to maintain and add new features to your applications.

In this chapter, you'll look at these extensions to JavaScript, starting with the object-oriented extensions, and then moving into some of the data type extensions, including arrays, Booleans, and dates.

Object-Oriented Extensions to JavaScript

JavaScript, as its name suggests, is a scripting language, and thus hasn't been designed for higher-order functionality. As Ajax gains traction, requirements for applications are becoming more and more sophisticated, and the language in which they are being built needs to evolve in response.

Thus, ASP.NET AJAX has brought about object-oriented extensions to JavaScript to make the programmer's life a little easier. Please note that these aren't changes to the JavaScript interpreter—they are libraries built into JavaScript itself—so no changes to the browser are needed to make them work. In this section, you'll look through some of the object-oriented features, including classes, namespaces, inheritance, interfaces, enumerations, and reflection.

Using Classes in JavaScript

A class is how you define an object, where an object is an instance of a class. For example, a car may be a class, but a specific car such as Bob's 1995 Honda is an object that is derived from that class, because his Honda is, in fact, a car.

You use a class to define what the properties, methods, and events of an object will be. So, keeping the car example, a property is something that defines an attribute of the car, such as its color, a method is something that you can perform on the car, such as driving it, and an event is something the car informs you of and that you can respond to, such as the little red light that comes on when you are nearly out of gas.

In ASP.NET AJAX, properties are either set using dot notation or accessors. The rule of thumb is that you can use dot syntax when the property is a primitive type (such as a string), as follows:

```
MyCar.Color="Black";
```

Accordingly, you use the accessor syntax when the property is a complex object. The accessor syntax uses get_ and set_ methods to get and set the value of the property. For example, if your color settings are an object, then you will use the following:

```
MyCar.set_Color(ColorObject);
```

Methods are functions that you can call on an object, and that don't necessarily need a return parameter. For example, if you want to start the ignition on your car, you would do it using a method like this:

```
MyCar.startEngine();
```

Events are actions that take place on your object that raise a notification. In JavaScript, you specify the handler for the event by appending add to the event, specifying the handler name. For example, if you want to handle an event for the fuel running low in your car, you would write code like this:

```
MyCar.fuelLow.add(FuelLowHandler);
```

And you would then implement the specified function like this:

```
Function FuelLowHander(sender,args)
{
  ...
}
```

Using Namespaces in JavaScript

Namespaces are a methodology that you can use to group similar classes together to make for easier management. For example, if you are building a library of classes for common objects, such as car, boat, house, person, fruit, and dog, then it is a good idea to group these into different namespaces, for manageability and extensibility. For example, you could have a Vehicles namespace that car and boat live in. Then, if you were to create an airplane class, it would live in the same namespace. Also, consider the scenario where you have many classes, and a programmer wants to implement some functionality. If your classes are subdivided into namespaces, then the amount of searching that your user needs to do to find the class definition is a lot less.

The ASP.NET AJAX extensions provide methods that you can use when you define your class to register a namespace and add a class to the namespace.

When you are implementing a class and you want to add it to a namespace, you register it using registerNamespace, like this:

```
Type.registerNamespace("Boats");
```

And you add a class to the namespace using registerClass, like this:

```
Boats.PedalBoat.registerClass('Boats.PedalBoat');
```

Creating and Using a Simple JavaScript Class

In this example, you will look at creating a simple JavaScript class that represents a boat. The syntax may look a little strange at first, but you'll quickly get used to it—however, in order to understand what is going on, it's a good idea to go through it step by step. So, here goes!

The first line in your class should be where you register the namespace for the class. In this case, we are creating a Boat class, which is going to be in the namespace Vehicles, so we register the Vehicles namespace like this:

```
Type.registerNamespace("Vehicles");
```

The next step is to define the class constructor. You can overload this in ASP.NET AJAX JavaScript, but for the sake of simplicity, we'll keep it with a single constructor. Here's an example:

```
Vehicles.Boat = function(boatType, boatSize, boatName)
{
    this._boatType = boatType;
    this._boatSize = boatSize;
    this._boatName = boatName;
}
```

This defines that the Vehicles.Boat class is going to be constructed using three vars, called boatType, boatSize, and boatName.

The next step is to define the class itself, prototyping the properties, methods, and events that the class will support. In this case, we're just using properties and defining accessor functions, but later in this chapter you'll see how to register methods and events, too.

Please note the syntax that is being used here. You specify the prototypes as a comma-separated list of JavaScript functions. The functionality is defined inline in the declaration. So, to define methods that allow the values to be retrieved, you use the following syntax:

```
functionName : function() {...}, functionName : function() {...} etc.
```

You'll typically line break these for readability, but do remember that it is supposed to be comma-separated, and it is easy to leave out the commas when you break them.

Here's the example that defines the accessors to the boat functions, and a dispose that will fire when the object is destroyed.

```
Vehicles.Boat.prototype =
{
    getBoatType: function()
    {
        return(this._boatType);
    },
    getBoatSize: function()
    {
        return(this._boatSize);
    },
    getBoatName: function()
    {
        return(this._boatName);
    },
    getBoatDetails: function()
    {
        var strDetails = this._boatName + " is a "
                        + this._boatType + " boat that is size: "
                        + this._boatSize;
        return(strDetails);
    },
    dispose: function()
    {
        alert("destroying " + this.getBoatName());
    }
}
```

Finally, you register the class in the namespace:

```
Vehicles.Boat.registerClass('Vehicles.Boat');
```

You can see the full listing for this class, saved as Boat.js, in Listing 14-1.

Listing 14-1. *Defining a Boat Class*

```
// JScript File

Type.registerNamespace("Vehicles");

Vehicles.Boat = function(boatType, boatSize, boatName)
{
    this._boatType = boatType;
    this._boatSize = boatSize;
    this._boatName = boatName;
}

Vehicles.Boat.prototype =
{
    getBoatType: function()
    {
        return(this._boatType);
    },
    getBoatSize: function()
    {
        return(this._boatSize);
    },
    getBoatName: function()
    {
        return(this._boatName);
    },
    getBoatDetails: function()
    {
        var strDetails = this._boatName + " is a "
                        + this._boatType + " boat that is size: "
                        + this._boatSize;
        return(strDetails);
    },
    dispose: function()
    {
        alert("destroying " + this.getBoatName());
    }
}
Vehicles.Boat.registerClass('Vehicles.Boat');
```

To use this class in a page, create a new ASPX page containing a ScriptManager component. This ensures that the ASP.NET AJAX libraries are downloaded to the client at runtime, and thus the underpinnings for much of the object-oriented functionality in your class are available. However, you have to be careful about how you declare your class to the page. You can do it within a `<script>` tag that references the saved `Boat.js`, but you will end up with some problems if the browser tries to parse your class definition before it parses the supporting classes. In this case, it will not recognize the `Type` class in the very first line, and you'll get an error.

A better approach is to register your class with the ScriptManager, and have it manage downloading your script to the client.

When you place a ScriptManager on your page, you can select it in Visual Studio and inspect its `Scripts` collection using the Property Editor. This will call up the ScriptReference Collection Editor. On here, you can click Add to add a new `Scripts` reference and specify the path of the new reference to the script that you want to download—in this case, `Boat.js` (see Figure 14-1).

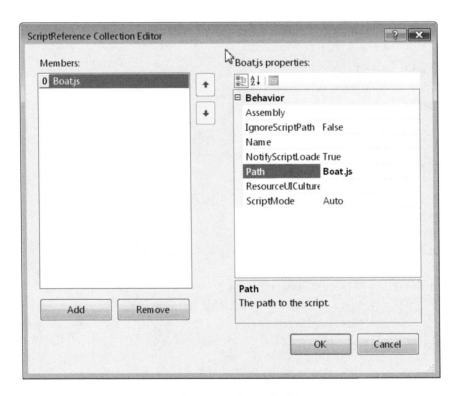

Figure 14-1. *Adding a script reference to the ScriptManager*

This will create a declaration on your page that looks like this:

```
<asp:ScriptManager ID="ScriptManager1" runat="server">
        <Scripts>
            <asp:ScriptReference Path="Boat.js" />
        </Scripts>
</asp:ScriptManager>
```

Now you can be sure that the JavaScript framework dependencies will be downloaded and parsed prior to your custom class, so you'll be in good shape.

To test the Boat class, you can now add an HTML button to the web form, and double-click it to have the IDE create an event handler. You can then create an object from the Boat class and use it with code like this:

```
function Button1_onclick() {
    var MyBoat = new Vehicles.Boat('Pedal','5','Stella');
    alert(MyBoat.getBoatDetails());
}
```

Listing 14-2 contains the code for the entire ASPX page.

Listing 14-2. *Using Custom JavaScript Class*

```
<%@ Page Language="C#" AutoEventWireup="true"
  CodeFile="Default2.aspx.cs" Inherits="Default2" %>

<!DOCTYPE html PUBLIC "-//W3C//DTD XHTML 1.0 Transitional//EN"
  "http://www.w3.org/TR/xhtml1/DTD/xhtml1-transitional.dtd">

<html xmlns="http://www.w3.org/1999/xhtml" >
<head runat="server">
    <title>Untitled Page</title>
<script language="javascript" type="text/javascript">
// <![CDATA[

function Button1_onclick() {
    var MyBoat = new Vehicles.Boat('Pedal','5','Stella');
    alert(MyBoat.getBoatDetails());
}

// ]]>
</script>
</head>
<body>
    <form id="form1" runat="server">
```

```
<div>
    <asp:ScriptManager ID="ScriptManager1" runat="server">
        <Scripts>
            <asp:ScriptReference Path="Boat.js" />
        </Scripts>
    </asp:ScriptManager>

</div>
    <input id="Button1" type="button" value="button"
           onclick="return Button1_onclick()" />
</form>
</body>
</html>
```

Now you can run the page and click the button to create a Boat instance, and the alert will return the value generated by getBoatDetails (see Figure 14-2).

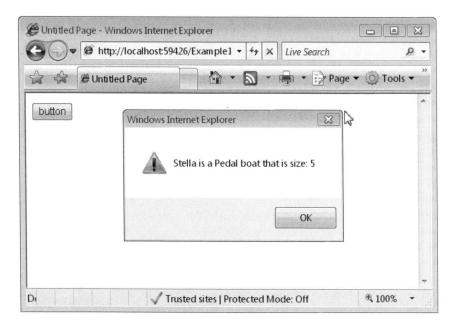

Figure 14-2. *Using the JavaScript class on a page*

Using Inheritance in JavaScript

The object-oriented concept of *inheritance* allows a class to derive from another class, saving you from defining common tasks multiple times. For example, earlier we defined a Vehicles namespace that contained a type of vehicle called a boat. Now, there are many types of boat, such as a speedboat, a yacht, a cruise liner, and so on. These all have something in common—that which makes them a boat—and something distinct, be it a motor, a sail, or a movie theater. Thus, the concept of inheritance means we can define a Boat class that contains the commonality and derive a SpeedBoat, Yacht, or CruiseShip class from this using inheritance.

Listing 14-3 demonstrates this, extending the Boat class that you defined earlier, and adding an outboard engine plus methods to activate it, giving us a speedboat.

Listing 14-3. *Using an Inherited Class*

```
Vehicles.SpeedBoat = function(boatSize, boatType, boatName, engineType)
{
    Vehicles.SpeedBoat.initializeBase(this,[boatSize, boatType, boatName]);
    this._engineType = engineType;
    this._currentSpeed = 0;
}
Vehicles.SpeedBoat.prototype = {
    getEngineType: function(){
        return this._engineType;
      },
    setEngineType: function(){
        this._engineType = engineType;
      } ,
    checkEngine: function(){
        if (this._currentSpeed>0)
            return ("Engine is running at speed" + this._currentSpeed);
        else
            return "Engine is off";
    },
    startEngine: function(){
        if(this._currentSpeed == 0)
            this._currentSpeed = 1;
        else
            return "Engine is already running";
    },
    openThrottle: function(){
        if (this._currentSpeed<10)
            this._currentSpeed++;
    },
    closeThrottle: function(){
        if (this._currentSpeed>0)
            this._currentSpeed--;
```

```
    }


}
Vehicles.SpeedBoat.registerClass('Vehicles.SpeedBoat', Vehicles.Boat);
```

Here, the first thing we do is declare the SpeedBoat class in the Vehicles namespace. It takes the same base types as Boat, but adds an engine type. Within this function, you pass the initial values to the base class with the initializeBase command, meaning that you don't have to handle boatSize, boatType, and boatName with getters and setters—they're already done in the base class.

Engine type and current speed are properties unique to the speedboat, so these have local member variables declared for them.

```
Vehicles.SpeedBoat = function(boatSize, boatType, boatName, engineType)
{
    Vehicles.SpeedBoat.initializeBase(this,[boatSize, boatType, boatName]);
    this._engineType = engineType;
    this._currentSpeed = 0;
}
```

Now that you have the class declared, you need to create the prototype, which contains the functions that are used as getters, setters, and object methods. The engine type requires a getter and a setter, so these are set up here:

```
getEngineType: function(){
        return this._engineType;
    },
    setEngineType: function(){
        this._engineType = engineType;
    },
```

You'll also need to provide methods for controlling the engine, to see if it is on or off, to start it, and to open and close the throttle. These are basic JavaScript functions, as shown here:

```
checkEngine: function(){
        if (this._currentSpeed>0)
            return ("Engine is running at speed" + this._currentSpeed);
        else
            return "Engine is off";
    },
    startEngine: function(){
        if(this._currentSpeed == 0)
            this._currentSpeed = 1;
```

```
        else
            return "Engine is already running";
    },
    openThrottle: function(){
        if (this._currentSpeed<10)
            this._currentSpeed++;
    },
    closeThrottle: function(){
        if (this._currentSpeed>0)
            this._currentSpeed--;
    }
}
```

The last step is to register the class in the namespace, declaring the class that it inherits from is Vehicles.Boat:

```
Vehicles.SpeedBoat.registerClass('Vehicles.SpeedBoat', Vehicles.Boat);
```

Now you can declare SpeedBoat objects in your code, accessing their methods or the base methods of the Boat class. For example, the getBoatDetails method is available on the base class, so the SpeedBoat can access it like this:

```
var MySpeedBoat = new Vehicles.SpeedBoat('Intimidator', '10', 'Arnie', '100cc');
    alert(MySpeedBoat.getBoatDetails());
```

Inheritance like this has limitations—the only methods that your class can use are those in the class that it inherits from (and the class that its parent class inherits from, and so on). In cases where you might want to implement common methods across different classes, you cannot do it with inheritance. For example, the speedboat implements throttle opening and closing, and you may want to implement these for a motorcycle also. You can't derive a motorcycle from a boat, so you'd end up having to implement them twice, and can end up with differences as a result, making for an untidy API (i.e., Motorcycle could have ThrottleOpen while SpeedBoat has openThrottle), which isn't desirable. The concept of *interfaces* is defined to help avoid this. You'll see how this works in JavaScript in the next section.

Using Interfaces in JavaScript

An interface can be used to specify a function prototype that crosses different class types, and is not dependent on an inheritance tree.

You can define functions that need to be in common across such classes—those that inherit from different base classes—by building them as an interface and having the class implement that interface.

Going back to our boat sample, we can now build an interface for all powered vehicles, which could be implemented by a motorcycle or an aircraft. If SpeedBoat implements this interface, then the prototypes for the engine functions are available to it.

First of all, you declare an interface as a prototyped set of JavaScript functions that you then register as interfaces using the registerInterface command. Here's an example:

```
Vehicles.IPowered = function() {}
Vehicles.IPowered.Prototype = {
    checkFuel: function(){}
}
Vehicles.IPowered.registerInterface('Vehicles.IPowered');
```

This creates and registers an interface called Vehicles.IPowered. So, if you want to make SpeedBoat implement this interface, you use the registerClass call. Earlier, when you registered the SpeedBoat class, you did it like this:

```
Vehicles.SpeedBoat.registerClass('Vehicles.SpeedBoat', Vehicles.Boat);
```

To change this to implement the interface, you use the interface name as the third parameter, like this:

```
Vehicles.SpeedBoat.registerClass('Vehicles.SpeedBoat', Vehicles.Boat,
Vehicles.IPowered);
```

Now if you want to use the function, you must implement an override within the SpeedBoat class, or just use the base declaration from the interface. Here's an example of overriding:

```
Vehicles.SpeedBoat.prototype = {
    checkFuel: function(){
        return "Yes, I use and need fuel, because I implement IPowered";
    }, ...
}
```

As you can imagine, your code can get pretty complex if you are defining large hierarchies of classes and using interfaces and inheritance to have coherent functionality across the set. In many cases, you would need to have an object check to see if it implements a certain interface or inherits from a certain class before invoking a method, in case it isn't implemented and you get an error. This is where *reflection*, the process of examining the structure of a component at runtime, comes in handy.

Reflection in JavaScript

This is the ability to examine the structure of your program at runtime, enabling you to get information about an object, including where it inherits from, which interface it implements, and what class it is an instance of.

Determining Inheritance

You can determine whether an item inherits from a particular class by calling the inheritsFrom method on it. This method is implemented in the base Type class, and as such it is available to all your JavaScript classes.

Consider the earlier scenario where we had two types of boat: a generic Boat class and a specific SpeedBoat class that inherits from it. We can now inspect the classes to see if they inherit from a particular class. If you query whether Vehicles.Boat inherits from Vehicles.Boat (itself), you'll get a false value returned, but if you query whether Vehicles.SpeedBoat inherits from Vehicles.Boat, you'll get true returned.

Here's the code:

```
Vehicles.Boat.inheritsFrom(Vehicles.Boat);
Vehicles.SpeedBoat.inheritsFrom(Vehicles.Boat);
```

Determining Instance Type

You can determine whether an object is an instance of a particular class by calling the isInstanceType function on the class definition and passing it the object in question. It will also match against classes that the class in question is derived from. This probably sounds confusing, and is best demonstrated by example.

If MyBoat is an object of type Vehicles.Boat and MySpeedBoat is an object of type Vehicles.SpeedBoat, declared in JavaScript like this

```
var MyBoat = new Vehicles.Boat('Pedal','5','Stella');
var MySpeedBoat = new Vehicles.SpeedBoat('Intimidator', '10', 'Arnie', '100cc');
```

then the following three alert boxes will return false, true, and true, respectively:

```
alert(Vehicles.SpeedBoat.isInstanceOfType(MyBoat));
alert(Vehicles.SpeedBoat.isInstanceOfType(MySpeedBoat));
alert(Vehicles.Boat.isInstanceOfType(MySpeedBoat));
```

The syntax is a little strange, as the method is on the class type, not the specific object. So, if you want to check if MyBoat is a speedboat, you would use Vehicles.SpeedBoat.isInstanceOfType(MyBoat). Obviously, MyBoat isn't a speedboat, it is just a boat, so this returns false.

Similarly, if I check whether MySpeedBoat is a SpeedBoat, I will get true, as this is indeed true.

Where it gets neat and interesting is in the fact that SpeedBoat derives from Boat, so if I check whether MySpeedBoat is a Boat, using this syntax, Vehicles.Boat. isInstanceOfType(MySpeedBoat), then I will also get true returned, as a MySpeedBoat is a Boat as well as a SpeedBoat.

Determining Interfaces

Finally, you will also want to check if a class implements an interface by calling the implementsInterface method on it. Note that you do the check on the class, not on instances of the class, so you cannot say MyBoat.implementsInterface(*whatever*). Instead you check it against the class, like this:

```
alert(Vehicles.Boat.implementsInterface(Vehicles.IPowered));
alert(Vehicles.SpeedBoat.implementsInterface(Vehicles.IPowered));
```

The first of these alert boxes will return false, because the Vehicles.Boat class doesn't implement the Vehicles.IPowered interface. But as the SpeedBoat does implement the interface, the second will return true.

Array Type Extensions to JavaScript

The Array object adds extensions to the base array handling functionality available to JavaScript. It achieves this through an abstract Array class that provides these methods, taking in a standard JavaScript array as one of its parameters.

Adding Items to an Array

To add an item to an array, you can use the Array.add command, passing in the array and the item. For example, you can create a JavaScript array called a like this:

```
var a = ['Item 1', 'Item 2', 'Item 3', 'Item 4'];
```

You can then add a new item to the array in Ajax JavaScript like this:

```
Array.add(a, 'Item 5');
```

Adding a Range of Items to an Array

To add a range of items to an array, you define the range as a JavaScript array, and then use the addRange method on Array to add the two of them together. Here's an example:

```
var a = ['Item 1', 'Item 2', 'Item 3', 'Item 4'];
var b = ['Item 4', 'Item 5'];
```

You can then add the arrays together with the following:

```
Array.addRange(a,b);
```

Clearing an Array

You can easily clear an existing array by passing it into Array.clear. The resulting array will be completely empty, so its length will be 0.

```
var a = ['Item 1', 'Item 2', 'Item 3', 'Item 4'];
Array.clear(a);
```

Cloning an Array

The Array.clone function creates a *shallow* copy of an array. This is a new array that contains all the elements of the original array. If the original array contains references, then the references in the new array will point to the same objects, but will not make copies of those objects.

```
var a = ['Item 1', 'Item 2', 'Item 3', 'Item 4'];
var b = Array.clone(a);
```

Checking Array Contents

You can check to see if a specific value or object is contained in an array by using the Array.contains function. It returns true if it finds a match; otherwise it returns false.

```
var a = ['Item 1', 'Item 2', 'Item 3', 'Item 4'];
var b = Array.contains(a,"Item 2");
// returns 'true'
Var c = Array.contains(a,"Green");
// returns 'false'
```

Dequeuing an Array

You can remove the first item from an array (a process called *dequeuing*) by using the Array.dequeue command and passing it the array in question. This is useful if you want to implement a first-in, first-out list using a JavaScript array, with the add method adding to the tail of the list, and the dequeue method removing from the head of the list.

```
var a = ['Item 1', 'Item 2', 'Item 3', 'Item 4'];
var b = Array.dequeue(a);
// b will now contain 'Item 2', 'Item 3', 'Item 4'
```

Looping Through an Array

You can call a function for each element in an Array object, looping through the contents of the array with the Array.forEach function. This takes three parameters:

Array: The Array object to enumerate.

Method: The function to call.

Context: A free-format string containing data that you can pass to the function. The function will get the context using this.

```
var result = '';
var a = ['Item 1', 'Item 2', 'Item 3', 'Item 4'];
Array.forEach(a, buildString, ":");
Function buildString(element, index, array)
{
   result+= element + this + index + ",";
}
// will output 'Item 1:0, Item2:1, Item3:2, Item4:3'
```

Finding a Specific Element in an Array

If you want to find the location of a specific item in an array, you can use the indexOf function to find it. It takes three parameters:

Array: The array to search.

Item: The item that you are looking for.

startIndex: This optional parameter specifies the index of the starting item for the search. So, if you want to start at the third item, use 2 here.

```
var a = ['Item 1', 'Item 2', 'Item 3', 'Item 4'];
    var b = Array.indexOf(a,'Item 2')
// returns '1'
```

Inserting an Item into an Array

Earlier, you saw the add command, which adds an item at the end of the array. If you want to add an item at a specific location within the array, you can use the insert function. It takes three parameters:

Array: The array that you are inserting the item into

Index: The location where you want to insert it (zero-based)

Item: The item to insert

```
var a = ['Item 1', 'Item 2', 'Item 3', 'Item 4'];
Array.insert(a,1,'Item 1a');
// Results: 'Item 1', 'Item 1a', 'Item 2', 'Item 3', 'Item 4'
```

Removing an Item from an Array

There are two methods for removing items from an array. The remove method takes an item as a parameter and removes the first instance of that item from the array, returning true when successful and false otherwise.

```
var a = ['Item 1', 'Item 2', 'Item 3', 'Item 4'];
Array.remove(a,'Item 2');
// will remove 'Item 2' from the array
```

The removeAt function removes the item at the specified index from the array.

```
var a = ['Item 1', 'Item 2', 'Item 3', 'Item 4'];
Array.removeAt(a,1);
// will also remove 'Item 2' from the array
```

Boolean Type Extensions

The Boolean language extensions provide for Booleans in JavaScript in a manner that may be more familiar to .NET programmers. In addition to the traditional Boolean enumerations of true and false, it provides a shortcut to instantiating a Boolean value through the parse function.

So, in JavaScript, you can now create Boolean objects in the following manner:

```
Var a = new Boolean(true);
Var b = new Boolean(false);
If (a==true)
  // Do Something
Var c = Boolean.parse("true");
If (c == true)
  // Do Something else
```

Date Type Extensions

ASP.NET AJAX provides a number of extensions to the Date object in JavaScript through its Date class. This gives extensions around locale specifics and easier instantiation of dates from strings.

Formatting a Date

The format function on the Date class provides a way to format a Date value into a set output format. It uses the standard DateTime format strings. For example, if you have a Date function and you want to render it using the default shortDatePattern type, you would simply say

```
var a = myDate.format("d");
```

where d is the standard format specified for shortDatePattern.

Formatting a Date Using Locale

If you want to format a date according to the current locale on the machine, you must first set the EnableScriptGlobalization property on the ScriptManager control to true. You will also need to ensure that the culture attribute of the web site is set to auto using Web.config.

Now if you use `localeFormat` and pass it a format string, the output will be formatted according to the current locale. For example, `d` gives MM/DD/YYYY in the United States and DD/MM/YYYY in the United Kingdom.

```
var a = myDate.localeFormat("d");
```

Parsing a Value into a Date

The `parseLocale` function allows you to create a locale-specific string by specifying the format. It takes two parameters: the date value and the format that you want the date to be formatted in.

```
var a = Date.parseLocale('2007-12-1', 'yyyy-mm-dd');
```

Error Type Extensions

These provide extensions to the JavaScript `Error` objects that provide exception details and different application compilation modes. The extension contains a number of error types that you can raise:

`Error.argument`: This lets you create an `Error` object that represents an exception in the arguments that you received in a function.

`Error.argumentNum`: This allows you to create an `Error` object that represents a null exception.

`Error.argumentOutOfRange`: This allows you to create an `Error` object that represents that an argument was out of the desired range.

`Error.argumentType`: This allows you to create an error that represents a type exception error.

`Error.argumentUndefined`: This allows you to create an error that represents that an argument is undefined.

`Error.create`: This allows you to create a free-format error with specifiable error text.

`Error.invalidOperation`: This allows you to create an error that declares that an `invalidOperation` was hit.

`Error.notImplemented`: This allows you to create an error that declares that the desired piece of functionality has not been implemented.

`Error.parameterCount`: This allows you to create an error that defines that the parameter set passed to the function is incorrect.

Number Type Extensions

These extend the base JavaScript `Number` object with some new static and instance methods.

Formatting a Number

You can format a number using the `format` function. This uses a culture-independent value, based on the en-US culture. For example, if you want to format a number as a currency (c format), you can use the following:

```
var a = 20;
var v = a.format("c");
```

To use the current culture to format the number, you can use the `localeFormat` function. This formats the number based on the current system locale. To understand how to configure this, you should check out the ASP.NET documentation on globalization and localization. The script to format the number according to the current culture is identical:

```
var a = 20;
var v = a.localeFormat("c");
```

Parsing a Number

You can create a new number var by parsing a string value. This is a static function and can be called without creating an instance of the object:

```
var n = Number.parseInvariant("23.2");
```

Additionally, you can parse a localized string to get a number using the `parseLocale` function, like this:

```
var n = Number.parseLocale("23,2");
```

String Extensions

String handling is always important, and the ASP.NET AJAX extensions provide a set of functions that make commonly used functions easier to implement.

String Matching

ASP.NET AJAX provides functions that allow you to check if the start or end of a string matches a specific value. These return a Boolean indicating whether there is a match. Here's an example:

```
var str = "This is a string";
var a = str.startsWith('this');
//returns 'false' because it is case insensitive
var a = str.endsWith('string');
//returns 'true'
```

String Trimming

String trimming involves removing whitespace from the start and end of the string. The ASP.NET AJAX extensions offer three methods:

Trim: Removes whitespace from the start and end of a string

TrimStart: Removes whitespace from the start of a string

TrimEnd: Removes whitespace from the end of a string

Summary

This chapter detailed the extensions to JavaScript that are provided by the ASP.NET AJAX extensions. You first looked at the programmer productivity enhancements brought about by the object-oriented extensions to JavaScript that provide for the ability to create classes. On top of this, the standard object-oriented methodologies of namespaces, inheritance, interfaces, and reflection were discussed.

Additionally in this chapter, you looked into what is available to programmers using arrays, Boolean values, dates, errors, numbers, and strings in ASP.NET AJAX.

With these tools on your belt, and with the server controls and services from previous chapters, you are now armed to go out and start building real-world applications using ASP.NET AJAX!

■ ■ ■

Enhancing the Web Experience with Silverlight

Users are increasingly demanding richer and easier-to-use experiences on the Web. Consider the design of a web site 15 years ago when we first started using the Internet. At the time, web sites were simply considered documents that were hosted on a server and could be linked with each other. Over time, the document paradigm moved away in favor of the application paradigm. And then applications themselves became increasingly more sophisticated in nature. Consider, for example, mapping applications. Internet-based maps of yesteryear would provide you with a pretty small map of the desired location. This map would have control buttons to allow you to pan and zoom around the map. Clicking these buttons would cause a page refresh (and thus, a delay), after which you would receive a new small map. Ultimately, the experience was inferior to picking up and using a paper map. Then, using Ajax, mapping applications improved to the extent that they gave a better user experience than paper maps, and now have become an indispensable tool to everyone who uses the Internet.

However, the basic technology hasn't really changed all that much since the days when web sites were simply hyperlinked documents. Thus, creating an application that has a high-quality and engaging UI requires a lot of engineering—which can be an expensive undertaking at best. Pushing the limits of what can be done with HTML and its associated scripting languages is no mean feat, and can lead to incompatibilities between different browsers.

Consider Ajax for example. Almost every Ajax application requires code a little like this:

```
function createRequestObject() {
    var ajax_object;
    var browser = navigator.appName;
    if(browser == 'Microsoft Internet Explorer'){
        ajax_object = new ActiveXObject("Microsoft.XMLHTTP");
    }else{
        ajax_object = new XMLHttpRequest();
```

```
    }
    return ro;
}
```

And this only differentiates between Internet Explorer and Firefox. If you are not writing an Ajax application, but one that uses a non-ubiquitous technology such as CSS or DHTML, you are left querying the user agent and trusting that the server returns an honest answer. The user agent string is simply a text field that contains what the server believes the browser that is communicating with it is. It is relatively easy to overwrite, and thus, a browser from a mobile device (which doesn't support CSS) could be spoofed into thinking that it is Internet Explorer, and incompatible data would be delivered to it.

It's pretty clear that HTML and scripting, while incredibly useful, are reaching the end of their serviceable lives with the growing expectations of users for richer and more dynamic applications. With that in mind, platform vendors have offered a number of technologies that enhance what HTML can do, with examples being things like Java applets, ActiveX controls, and Flash movies.

A new technology in 2007—and one that has a number of unique and distinct value propositions that make it a compelling one—is Microsoft Silverlight.

Introducing Silverlight

In Chapter 8, you looked at Windows Presentation Foundation (WPF) and a new technology that it provides called Extensible Application Markup Language (XAML). This language allows a UI and all its interactions to be defined with simple XML markup tags. This empowers a separation of design and development, so that the designer can become an integral part of the development process.

In the past, a designer would make a mock-up, or "comp," of the desired vision for the web site or application. This might be a set of wireframe drawings, pictures, simple animations, or scribbles on a piece of paper. The developer would have to take these visions and implement them, constrained by what the technology would permit. The result was often disappointing for both parties.

With XAML, the designer can use tools (such as the Microsoft Expression suite) to design the graphics, interactions, animations, and media that they desire to have in the site, and the developer can simply take this XAML and "activate" it by writing the code behind it that allows it to be used as an application.

Thus, the designer and the developer are working from a common set of artifacts, allowing next-generation designer-centric experiences to not just be possible, but to be relatively easy to implement.

Silverlight is a plug-in for the browser that renders XAML and exposes a programming model in JavaScript. Thus, web developers have a new suite of tools and technologies in XAML that will allow them to take their sites to the next level of richness, but they still have a familiar and flexible programming model in JavaScript that will allow them to continue to use their existing skills.

Silverlight Feature Highlights

While the high-level description of Silverlight as a browser plug-in that renders XAML and exposes a JavaScript programming model holds true, it leads to a number of questions around features and implications of building an application that uses such a plug-in.

In order to answer these questions, consider some of the highlights of this plug-in:

- It is a cross-browser, cross-platform technology. The Silverlight plug-in is supported consistently on Windows with the Internet Explorer and Mozilla Firefox browsers, and on Mac OS X with the Apple Safari and Mozilla Firefox browsers. In addition to this, an open source version of Silverlight called Moonlight, sponsored by Novell as part of their Mono initiative, will support various Linux distros and browsers.

- The experience of rendering XAML and the programming model is consistent across all browsers and operating systems.

- The download is intended to be completely self-contained, small, and easy to install. For example, all audio/video codecs needed to view supported content are part of the download. Thus, you will not need Windows Media Player on Mac OS X to view WMV video with Silverlight.

- The graphics are vector based, meaning that they are small to download and can be changed without loss of fidelity.

- It is fully compatible with web technologies such as JavaScript and Ajax, allowing standard techniques and skills to be used to build Silverlight applications.

- The XAML DOM is fully open to the programmer so that UI elements can easily be added or removed from it while it is running.

- It has no server-side dependencies, so Silverlight applications can be delivered equally well from ASP.NET, J2EE, PHP, and other server technologies.

Current and Future Versions of Silverlight

As has been discussed thus far, Silverlight is a browser plug-in that renders XAML and exposes a JavaScript programming model in version 1.0. However, early access versions of Silverlight 2.0 are available (they are called 1.1 in the downloads, but Microsoft plans to update them to a 2.0 early beta in spring 2008), and these enhance the programming model with a new, mini version of the .NET CLR, allowing applications to be built and coded using C# or other .NET languages. Silverlight 2.0 also includes these enhancements:

- The ability to run programs written with multiple programming languages has been added. In addition to JavaScript, the new mini CLR allows C# and Visual Basic to be used in building applications.

- The inclusion of a high-performance runtime has been included. Having your application logic compiled into .NET code can lead to drastic improvements in performance. For example, Microsoft has built a sample chess algorithm that does a look-ahead for chess moves, constrained to 1 second. You can play this game on www.silverlight.net. You will be able to see that the performance of the C# version (measured in the number of moves it can evaluate in 1 second) is generally 1,000 to 1,500 times faster than the JavaScript version. While this isn't a conclusive benchmark, it is certainly indicative of the improvements in performance.

- Extensibility to XAML has been added in version 1.1. Now you can create your own XAML controls to improve the overall experience.

- New XAML UI controls for application development have been added.

- Networking via the System.NET libraries has been added. Thus, Silverlight applications will be able to directly consume network resources in the services tier of a multitier application.

- Data enhancements such as LINQ are available.

- Cross-platform debugging is available, so an application running on Mac OS X will be debuggable from Visual Studio running on a Windows PC.

While these features are very compelling, at the time of writing this book, they are in a very early stage, and this book will focus only on Silverlight 1.0.

The Anatomy of a Silverlight Application

As Silverlight is a browser plug-in, using it could be as simple as using an `<object>` tag in HTML that refers to the plug-in, and defining a set of `<param>` tags to configure it.

So, you could easily add a Silverlight plug-in to your page like this:

```
<object type="application/x-silverlight">
<param name="source"  value="#xamlContent">
</object>
```

However, if you do this, you will be making life unnecessarily difficult for yourself, as you will have to manage the location of the XAML, manage the downloading and licensing of the component, and so on.

Instead, the Silverlight SDK provides tools that make the process a lot easier, and that provide a de facto standard methodology of using Silverlight on your site.

In the rest of this section, you'll look at all the pieces that you would use to build any Silverlight application, from a simple Hello World application to a full-featured web experience.

Using Silverlight.js

Microsoft provides the file `Silverlight.js` as part of the Silverlight SDK. This file contains everything that you need to instantiate and use the Silverlight plug-in on your page. It manages what to do with different browser versions, and provides a download location and terms-of-service and license information to the end user, making the download process safe, secure, and easy.

As Silverlight is a browser plug-in, it is hosted in an HTML page, and your page should have a script reference to this JavaScript file. This will look something like this:

```
<script type="text/javascript" src="Silverlight.js"></script>
```

The Silverlight SDK can be downloaded from the Microsoft Silverlight site, at `http://silverlight.net/GetStarted/`.

You'll see in a moment how this JavaScript library is used to create a Silverlight application—but first, let's look at the XAML that it will render.

Using XAML

You saw XAML earlier in this book as a markup language for WPF. Silverlight uses a subset of this language.

This sample contains a XAML Canvas, the basic drawing block and container in Silverlight, which in turn contains a TextBlock, which is used for rendering text. This text is a simple "Hello World!" message.

```
<Canvas
    xmlns="http://schemas.microsoft.com/client/2007"
    xmlns:x="http://schemas.microsoft.com/winfx/2006/xaml"
    Width="640" Height="480"
```

```
      Background="White"
      x:Name="Page">
      <TextBlock Width="195" Height="42" Canvas.Left="28" Canvas.Top="35"
            Text="Hello World!" TextWrapping="Wrap" x:Name="txt"/>
  </Canvas>
```

As you can see, this is straightforward XML, with the standard parent/child format. The `<TextBlock>` element is a child of the `<Canvas>` element, and thus it is contained by it.

This XAML would typically be saved as a file called `Page.xaml` or something similar. The rest of this example assumes that it is called `Page.xaml`.

Creating an Instance of the Silverlight Plug-In

The `Silverlight.js` library contains the `createObject` and `createObjectEx` functions, which are used to generate the correct `<Object>` or `<Embed>` tag to create the Silverlight component for the current browser. These functions perform identical tasks, the difference between them being that `createObjectEx` uses the JSON notation for bundling parameters as a matter of convenience.

It is good programming practice to separate this call from the page hosting it so that the details of the parameters used for the Silverlight component are externalized. So, for example, the HTML markup for the page would look something like this:

```
<body>
<div id="SilverlightControlHost" class="silverlightHost">
    <script type="text/javascript">
      createSilverlight();
    </script>
</div>
</body>
```

The `createSilverlight` function would be hosted in an external JavaScript file that is referenced by the HTML. This function would then call `createObject` or `createObjectEx` like this:

```
function createSilverlight()
{
  Silverlight.createObjectEx({
    source: "Page.xaml",
    parentElement: document.getElementById("SilverlightControlHost"),
    id: "SilverlightControl",
    properties: {
      width: "100%",
      height: "100%",
```

```
        version: "1.0"
    },
    events: {
        onLoad: handleLoad
    }
  });
}
```

There are a number of parameters being used in this case. They are discussed here:

- The source XAML is hosted in a file on this web site called Page.xaml.

- The Silverlight control is hosted in an HTML <div> called SilverlightControlHost (see the earlier HTML markup for this).

- The Silverlight control will have the ID SilverlightControl.

- It will fill its <div> horizontally and vertically (100 percent width and height).

- It is based on version 1.0 of Silverlight.

- A JavaScript function called handleLoad will execute when the Silverlight component is rendered by the browser.

Writing Application Logic

As shown in the previous section, a JavaScript function called handleLoad was defined as the event-handler logic to run in response to the Silverlight component being loaded and rendered by the browser.

Most Silverlight event handlers take two arguments, sender and args, which define a reference to the component on which the event was raised, and any associated arguments, respectively. One exception to this is the event that fires when Silverlight loads. This takes three arguments: control, userContext, and rootElement, which contain a reference to the Silverlight control, the user context of that control (a free-format string that can be assigned as part of the createObject or createObjectEx function, allowing the developer to differentiate multiple Silverlight controls on one page), and a reference to the root Canvas of the control, respectively.

Here's an example of JavaScript code that responds to the application loading, and that creates a new event handler on the TextBlock. This event responds to clicks on the TextBlock:

```
var SilverlightControl;
var theTextBlock;
```

```
function handleLoad(control, userContext, rootElement)
{
    SilverlightControl = control;
    theTextBlock = SilverlightControl.content.findName("txt");
    theTextBlock.addEventListener("MouseLeftButtonDown", "txtClicked");
}
function txtClicked(sender, args)
{
    theTextBlock.Text = "Hello to you too!";
}
```

Now what will happen is that when the Silverlight control is rendered, the code finds the TextBlock element and creates a new event listener that responds to a mouse click by calling the JavaScript function txtClicked.

This function will then change the contents of the TextBlock to "Hello to you too!" the end result being that the text will be changed as soon as the user clicks on it.

Putting It All Together in HTML

As you've seen already, HTML is at the heart of the Silverlight experience. Silverlight is a plug-in for the browser, after all. You've seen a number of pieces of this HTML already, but for reference, the complete HTML is here.

This contains the JavaScript references to the Silverlight.js, CreateSilverlight.js, and Code.js files, which are the Silverlight SDK script, the script containing the createSilverlight function, and the script containing the event-handler code, respectively.

It also sets up a <style> tag to define the dimensions of the <div> that contains the Silverlight control, and the <div> itself, which is populated by the results of the call to createSilverlight.

```
<html xmlns="http://www.w3.org/1999/xhtml">
<head>
    <title>FirstSilverlight</title>

    <script type="text/javascript" src="Silverlight.js"></script>

    <script type="text/javascript" src="CreateSilverlight.js"> </script>
    <script type="text/javascript" src="code.js"> </script>
    <style type="text/css">
        .silverlightHost {
            height: 480px;
            width: 640px;
```

```
            }
        </style>
    </head>

    <body>
        <div id="SilverlightControlHost" class="silverlightHost">
            <script type="text/javascript">
                createSilverlight();

</script>
        </div>
    </body>
</html>
```

Figure 15-1 shows how this looks in the browser when it is first run.

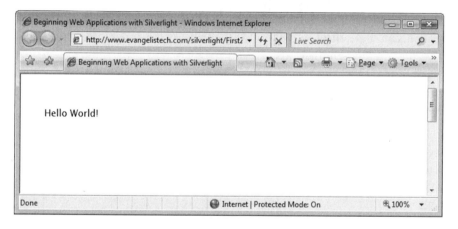

Figure 15-1. *Running your first Silverlight application*

When the user clicks on the TextBlock, the JavaScript event handler for it fires and changes the text. You can see the result in Figure 15-2.

In this section, you've seen the anatomy of a Silverlight application. You've seen how to create an instance of the Silverlight control using the standard library, and how to load XAML into it, rendering it and programming it using JavaScript.

In the next section, you'll look into the Silverlight control itself and its API in some more detail.

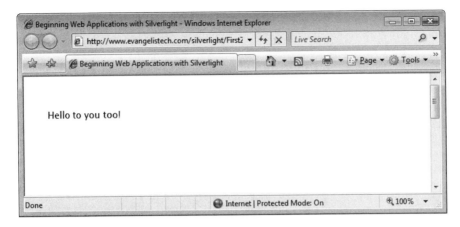

Figure 15-2. *The result of running the event handler*

Programming with the Silverlight Control

The Silverlight plug-in is a control, and like any other control it is programmed against using its properties, methods, and events.

The Silverlight Control Properties

The properties of the control determine its appearance, layout, and behavior. Earlier, you saw how they could be set as part of the createObject or createObjectEx method. In this section, you will look at each of the Silverlight control properties, and how you can use them to configure your Silverlight experience.

The Source Property

The Source property is probably the most commonly used one. Without it, Silverlight won't do much, because the Source property determines the XAML to load into the control for rendering. There are a number of ways that this property can be used:

Static file reference: When the XAML content is stored in a static file on the server (i.e., Page.xaml), setting this property to the URI of this file will download the file and render it.

Dynamic URL reference: As XAML is just XML, it can be generated by a server-side application running ASP.NET, J2EE, PHP, CGI, or anything else. If this is the case, you can set the Source reference to the URI of the server application, passing whatever parameters are needed.

Embedded XAML reference: XAML can also be embedded within a `<script>` tag within your HTML. Should you use this approach, you will need to name the tag, and then set the `Source` property of the Silverlight control to this value, prefixed with #.

Using Embedded XAML

Here's an example of a `<script>` tag that contains XAML:

```
<script type="text/xaml" id="xamlContent">
<?xml version="1.0"?>
<Canvas xmlns="http://schemas.microsoft.com/client/2007"
        Background="Wheat">
  <TextBlock Canvas.Left="20" FontSize="24">Hello World</TextBlock>
</Canvas>
</script>
```

As you can see, this script block has been called `xamlContent`. Thus, when initializing the Silverlight control, you would set its source to `#xamlContent`, like this:

```
function createSilverlight()
{
  Silverlight.createObjectEx({
  source: "#xamlContent",
  parentElement: document.getElementById("SilverlightControlHost"),
  id: "SilverlightControl",
  properties: {
      width: "100%",
      height: "100%",
      version: "1.0"
  },
  events: {
    onLoad: handleLoad
  }
});
}
```

The parentElement Property

This is the name of the `<div>` element that contains the Silverlight component within the HTML. In order for your Silverlight application to work correctly, this property must be set, and it must be set to the correct value.

The id Property

This is the required ID for the Silverlight control. If you want to reference the control from JavaScript in order to manipulate it or its DOM, it needs to be identifiable, and as such, the control needs an ID.

The width Property

This sets the width of the control in percent or pixels. This will be limited by the size of the <div> containing the control.

The height Property

This sets the height of the control in percent or pixels. This will be limited by the size of the <div> containing the control.

The background Property

This sets the background color for the control. This uses a XAML SolidColorBrush control to determine the color, which can be a named color (e.g., Blue) or an ARGB value for 8 bits each of alpha, red, green, and blue (e.g., #00FF00BB).

The framerate Property

This sets the maximum frame rate to allow for animation. It defaults to 24 frames per second. This is particularly useful for applications that use a lot of animation. Should you want to smooth out the animation, you can adjust the frame rate for the optimal effect.

The isWindowless Property

By default, the Silverlight plug-in runs inline in the page, meaning that HTML content flows around the plug-in. In many scenarios, you may want to write HTML content on top of the Silverlight content, perhaps to have an HTML form on top of your page, or to render a GIF or other graphics from a server that you don't want to inject into your XAML.

This is possible using the isWindowless property. When set to true, HTML content can be written on top of the Silverlight content. The default is false.

For example, here is the createSilverlight function amended to show isWindowless being set:

```
function createSilverlight()
{
  Silverlight.createObjectEx({
```

```
    source: "#xamlContent",
    parentElement: document.getElementById("SilverlightControlHost"),
    id: "SilverlightControl",
    properties: {
      width: "100%",
      height: "100%",
      isWindowless: "true",
      version: "1.0"
    },
    events: {
      onLoad: handleLoad
    }
  });
}
```

When using this property, if you write HTML in the same area of the screen as the Silverlight content, the HTML will be written over it. Here's an example:

```
<div id="SilverlightControlHost" class="silverlightHost">
  <script type="text/javascript">
    createSilverlight();
  </script>
  <div style="position: absolute; z-index: 1; left: 24px; top: 47px"
   id="layer1">
    <table style="width: 100%" cellspacing="1">
      <tr>
        <td style="width: 108px" class="style2">Name</td>
        <td><input name="Text1" type="text" style="width: 482px"></td>
      </tr>
    </table>
  </div>
</div>
```

As the HTML is within a <div> that is styled as position:absolute, it can be positioned anywhere on the page, including the same location as the Silverlight control. If the Silverlight control has isWindowless=true, then you will see it; otherwise, it will be hidden behind the Silverlight control.

The inplaceInstallPrompt Property

Silverlight has two modes of installation. These are set using the inplaceInstallPrompt property. This property defaults to false.

When this property is set to false and Silverlight is not installed on the client machine, a Silverlight medallion will appear on the page. When the user clicks the medallion to install Silverlight, they will be directed to the Silverlight install page hosted on the Microsoft web site. This will allow them to read the license agreement for using Silverlight, and download and install the control. Once done, they can return to the original page and view the Silverlight content.

When this property is set to `true`, a slightly different Silverlight medallion is presented. This medallion contains links to the license agreement, and clicking it implies acceptance. In this situation, the user isn't taken away from the site; instead, the download of the Silverlight plug-in will start automatically, and the user can install it in place. Once done, they can access the Silverlight application straightaway.

The FullScreen Property

Silverlight can run in full screen mode, where Silverlight content is drawn on top of all other windows. This is typically used for video playback, where the user wants to fill their monitor with the desired video. To do this, simply set the `FullScreen` property of the control to `true`. To change it back, set it to `false`.

The actualWidth Property

When the `width` property is set to a percentage value, the width of the Silverlight control changes based on the user's interaction with the browser. As a result, the value of the actual width of the control can be read using the `actualWidth` property. In addition, if this value changes, the `onResize` event will fire.

The actualHeight Property

When the `height` property is set to a percentage value, the height of the Silverlight control may change based on the user's interaction with the browser. As a result, the value of the actual height of the control can be read using the `actualHeight` property. In addition, if this value changes, the `onResize` event will fire.

The initParams Property

This is a string that you can use to set additional parameters on the control. These are completely free format, so you can do whatever you like with them. A typical scenario for this would be where you generate the Silverlight content from a server-side control, and you want to maintain the state of the parameters for it on the client side.

Here's an example of a `createSilverlight` function with the parameters set simply as `value1`, `value2`, `value3`. In this case, you would write code to read these parameters and respond to them as you see fit.

```
function createSilverlight()
{
    Sys.Silverlight.createObject(
        "Scene.xaml",
        document.getElementById("SilverlightControlHost"),
        "mySilverlightControl",
        {
            width:'300',
            height:'300',
            inplaceInstallPrompt:false,
            background:'white',
            isWindowless:'false',
            framerate:'24',
            version:'1.0'
        },
        {
            onError:null,
            onLoad:handleLoad
        },
        "value1, value2, value3", // Parameter List
        null);
}
```

The userContext Property

This is similar to the `initParams` property in that it is a free-format string that can contain any information you like. One difference is that its value is passed to the load handler, should you define one to respond to the application loading (see the `onLoad` event handler in the next section for details).

Thus, if you have multiple instances of the Silverlight control on the page, but want to write just one event handler to handle each of them loading, you can do so, and you can differentiate the controls based on their `userContext` property.

The IsLoaded Property

This property is read-only, and is set by the control based on the status of loading it. Once the control is loaded, it will be set to `true`; otherwise, it will be `false`.

The enableFrameRateCounter Property

A useful little tool to help you in debugging and testing your Silverlight applications is the frame rate counter, which displays the current render rate. It defaults to `false`, but you can turn it on by setting this property to `true`.

The EnableHtmlAccess Property

When set to `true`, this will allow the XAML content to be fully accessible from the browser DOM. It defaults to `true`.

The enableRedrawRegions Property

This is another useful debugging and optimization tool. When set to `true`, it shows the areas of the plug-in that are being redrawn with each frame.

The Silverlight Control Events

Silverlight offers a number of events that you can use to manage application events such as loading, unloading, and full screen changes.

The onLoad Event

This specifies the name of the JavaScript event handler that implements the code to execute upon the Silverlight control loading and running properly.

This event handler takes three arguments, `control`, `userContext`, and `rootElement`, which contain a reference to the Silverlight control, the user context of that control, and a reference to the root Canvas of the control, respectively. Here's an example:

```
function handleLoad(control, userContext, rootElement)
{
    alert("I loaded successfully!");
}
```

The `userContext` will receive whatever was set in the `userContext` property of the control.

The onError Event

This specifies the name of the JavaScript event handler that implements the code to execute whenever Silverlight encounters an error.

The event handler will contain the current XAML element in its `sender` argument, and an `errorArgs` object containing details of the error.

The `errorArgs` argument contains three properties: `errorType`, `errorMessage`, and `errorCode`.

For example, you could create an event handler for errors that provides details for runtime or XAML parsing errors like this:

```
function OnErrorEventHandler(sender, errorArgs)
{
    var errorMsg = "Error: \n\n";

    // Error information common to all errors.
    errorMsg += "Error Type:    " + errorArgs.errorType + "\n";
    errorMsg += "Error Message: " + errorArgs.errorMessage + "\n";
    errorMsg += "Error Code:    " + errorArgs.errorCode + "\n";

    switch(errorArgs.errorType)
    {
        case "RuntimeError":
            if (errorArgs.lineNumber != 0)
            {
                errorMsg += "Line: " + errorArgs.lineNumber + "\n";
                errorMsg += "Position: " +  errorArgs.charPosition + "\n";
            }
            errorMsg += "MethodName: " + errorArgs.methodName + "\n";
            break;
        case "ParserError":
            errorMsg += "Xaml File:     " + errorArgs.xamlFile     + "\n";
            errorMsg += "Xml Element:   " + errorArgs.xmlElement    + "\n";
            errorMsg += "Xml Attribute: " + errorArgs.xmlAttribute  + "\n";
            errorMsg += "Line:          " + errorArgs.lineNumber    + "\n";
            errorMsg += "Position:      " + errorArgs.charPosition   + "\n";
            break;
        default:
            break;
    }
    alert(errorMsg);
}
```

The onFullScreenChange Event

Silverlight allows you to go into full screen mode by setting the FullScreen property. This event will fire when that happens, allowing you to execute some code in response to the user changing to and from full screen mode.

The onResize Event

This event will fire when the actualWidth or actualHeight property of the Silverlight control changes. This is particularly useful if you want your control to dynamically resize itself based on the size of the browser window.

The Silverlight Control Methods

As with any object, the Silverlight control exposes a number of methods that allow you to manipulate it.

The createFromXaml Method

This extremely useful method allows you to add new XAML to the current render tree of the control. It takes two parameters: the first is a string containing the XAML that you want to use, and the second is a namescope, which if used will create unique names for the tags in this string so that they do not conflict with existing element names within the XAML tree.

When using this method, please note that you can only add new XAML elements that have a single root node—so if you have a number of elements to add, please make sure that they are all contained within a single container <Canvas>.

Additionally, createFromXaml does not immediately add the new XAML to the render tree. What it does is create a node within the render tree and return a reference to that node. You can then place this node in the correct position of the XAML render tree to add the new content to your Silverlight application.

Here's an example:

```
function handleLoad(control, userContext, rootElement)
{
  var xamlFragment =  '<TextBlock Canvas.Top="60" Text="Using CreateFromXAML" />';
  textBlock = control.content.createFromXaml(xamlFragment);
  rootElement.children.add(textBlock);
 }
```

As you can see, the xamlFragment is a string containing a new piece of XAML. This is created and a reference to it returned to the textBlock var. This reference is then added to the tree by adding it to the children of the root element.

The findName Method

XAML nodes may be named using their x:Name attribute. Should you want to manipulate the content of the XAML node (to, for example, change the contents of a TextBlock), you do so by using the findName method to get a reference to that node, and then editing the reference.

This was shown in our first example, in the event handler for clicking the TextBlock. Here's the code again:

```
var SilverlightControl;
var theTextBlock;
function handleLoad(control, userContext, rootElement)
{
    SilverlightControl = control;
    theTextBlock = SilverlightControl.content.findName("txt");
    theTextBlock.addEventListener("MouseLeftButtonDown", "txtClicked");
}
function txtClicked(sender, args)
{
    theTextBlock.Text = "Hello to you too!";
}
```

As you can see in the handleLoad function, the findName method was called to get a reference to the TextBlock (called txt). This reference was then manipulated by adding an event handler to it.

The createObject Method

This method allows you to create a new object for a specific purpose. In version 1.0 of Silverlight, only one object is supported: the Downloader object. The Downloader object allows you to download additional elements using asynchronous downloading functionality. It is very similar in scope to Ajax. It supports a number of properties, methods, and events that allow you to handle the download.

Using the Downloader Object

The Silverlight control provides a Downloader object (created using the createObject method) that allows you to get additional application assets in an asynchronous manner.

It supports the following properties:

DownloadProgress: This provides a value (between 0 and 1) representing the percentage progress of the download session.

Status: This gets the HTTP status code for the current download session status. It is a standard HTTP status code, containing, for example, 200 for a successful download, and 404 when the resource cannot be found.

StatusText: This gets the HTTP status text associated with the status code. For example, when the status is 200, the status text is "OK."

URI: This contains the URI of the object that you want to download.

In addition to this, you can call some methods on the Downloader object:

abort: This cancels the current download and resets all properties to their default state.

getResponseText: This returns a string representation of the downloaded data.

open: This initializes the download session, taking an HTTP verb as defined by the W3C. Silverlight 1.0 only supports the GET verb.

send: This executes the download request.

Finally, the Downloader object supports two events:

completed: This will fire once the download is complete.

downloadProgressChanged: This will fire while the content is downloading. It fires every time the progress changes by 5 percent or more, and when it reaches 100 percent.

To use the Downloader object, you must first create an instance of it. In JavaScript, this is very straightforward. Here's an example:

```
var downloader = control.createObject("downloader");
```

Then you need to initialize the download session by using the open method to set the URI of the resource to download, and the send method to start it downloading.

```
downloader.open("GET","movie.wmv",true);
downloader.send();
```

If you want to monitor the download progress and completion status, you can wire up the appropriate event handlers. Here's an example:

```
downloader.addEventListener("downloadProgressChanged", "handleDLProgress");
downloader.addEventListener("completed", "handleDLComplete");
```

Now you can implement these handlers:

```
function handleDLProgress(sender, args)
{
        var ctrl = sender.getHost();
        var t1 = ctrl.content.findName("txt1");
        var v = sender.downloadProgress * 100;
        t1.Text = v + "%";

}
function handleDLComplete(sender, args)
{
        alert("Download complete");
}
```

Summary

In this chapter, you took a look at Silverlight and how Silverlight applications are constructed. You worked your way through the anatomy of a typical Silverlight application before embarking on a tour of the Silverlight control and its various properties, methods, and events.

In the next chapter, you will look at XAML, and take a tour of the XAML controls that are supported by Silverlight. You'll also look into their JavaScript API, rounding out the programming aspects of working in Silverlight. This will hopefully serve as a launch board for you to go out and get more involved with the technology!

CHAPTER 16

■■■

Programming Silverlight with XAML and JavaScript

In Chapter 15, you took a look at Silverlight and the anatomy of a Silverlight application. In addition, you looked at the programming API for the Silverlight control itself. To wrap up the introduction of Silverlight, what is missing is a tour of the Silverlight XAML, including what it offers to you from the point of view of the attribute set that it gives you and the event handlers that you can declare and handle.

This chapter will do exactly that, starting with a tour of the XAML layout and visual elements, and then going into the controls that are available and their programming APIs.

When dealing with Silverlight XAML, the XML elements generally fall into these six categories:

- Layout elements, which are used to control your UI

- Brushes, which are used to paint your items

- Visual elements, which provide common functionality across different UI elements

- Shapes, which are used to draw your UI elements

- Controls for complex UI functionality

- Storyboards and their configurations for animation

Layout in XAML

The <Canvas> element in Silverlight XAML is the workhorse for application layout. The Canvas is a drawing surface on which you place other canvas elements. You place its location using its Canvas.Left and Canvas.Top properties. These properties specify the location of any XAML object relative to its container.

In addition, you can set the Z-order of the Canvas using the `Canvas.ZIndex` attribute. Z-order determines which item is drawn on top of another if multiple items are overlapping on the screen. Silverlight reads a XAML file from the top down, so that items that appear later in the document will be drawn on top of items that appear earlier.

Here is an example of a XAML document containing two Canvases. Each Canvas contains a rectangle.

```
<Canvas
  xmlns="http://schemas.microsoft.com/client/2007"
  xmlns:x="http://schemas.microsoft.com/winfx/2006/xaml"
  Width="640" Height="480"
  Background="White"
  x:Name="Page"
  >
  <Canvas Width="214" Height="145" Canvas.Top="59" Canvas.Left="8">
    <Rectangle Width="191" Height="104"
               Fill="White" Stroke="Black" Canvas.Top="19"/>
  </Canvas>
  <Canvas Width="254" Height="162" Canvas.Left="69" Canvas.Top="129">
    <Rectangle Width="211" Height="154"
               Fill="Black" Stroke="Black"/>
  </Canvas>
</Canvas>
```

There are a number of things going on in this listing, which, once you understand them, will help you to understand how to lay elements out in Silverlight XAML.

First, notice that each of the rectangles is contained within a Canvas. The first, or white, rectangle (the one with the `Fill="White"` attribute set) has its `Canvas.Top` property set to 19. This means that it will be drawn 19 pixels down from its container. Its container Canvas has a `Canvas.Top` of 59 and a `Canvas.Left` of 8. This Canvas is contained by the root Canvas—thus, the white rectangle will be drawn 78 pixels down from the top of the screen and 8 pixels from the left. Similarly, the black rectangle's position is determined by its `Canvas.Top` and `Canvas.Left` properties relative to its container Canvas.

Next, you will notice that the dimensions of the rectangles are set so that they are actually overlapping and occupying some of the same screen real estate. As mentioned earlier, Silverlight will draw later elements on top of earlier ones, so the black rectangle should be drawn on top of the white one.

Figure 16-1 shows how this will appear when it is rendered.

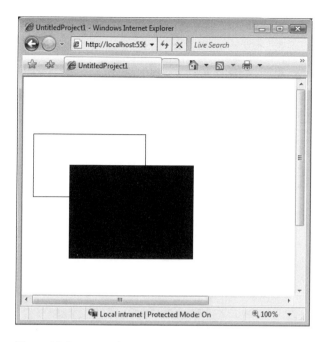

Figure 16-1. *Using the Canvas control to lay out content*

The Z-order behavior can be overridden using the ZIndex attribute of an element. In this case, you can set the ZIndex of either the rectangle or its containing Canvas. Higher numbered ZIndex values are drawn on top of lower numbered ones, so this XAML will cause the white rectangle to be drawn on top of the black one.

Here's the XAML code:

```
<Canvas
    xmlns="http://schemas.microsoft.com/client/2007"
    xmlns:x="http://schemas.microsoft.com/winfx/2006/xaml"
    Width="640" Height="480"
    Background="White"
    x:Name="Page">
        <Canvas Canvas.ZIndex="1" Width="214" Height="145"
            Canvas.Top="59" Canvas.Left="8">
          <Rectangle Width="191" Height="104" Fill="White"
                Stroke="Black" Canvas.Top="19"/>
        </Canvas>
        <Canvas Canvas.ZIndex="0" Width="254" Height="162"
            Canvas.Left="69" Canvas.Top="129">
          <Rectangle Width="211" Height="154" Fill="Black" Stroke="Black"/>
        </Canvas>
</Canvas>
```

You can see how this is rendered in Figure 16-2.

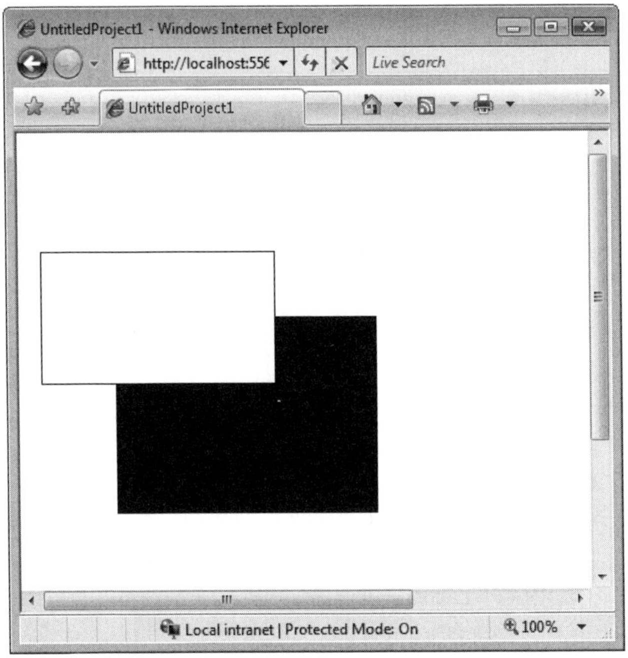

Figure 16-2. *Using ZIndex to fine-tune your UI*

Also note that a Canvas may contain another Canvas, and that each Canvas can contain multiple controls, giving you complete creative control over how your UI is laid out.

Using Brushes in XAML

XAML uses *brushes* to define how shapes will be drawn and filled. The earlier example showed rectangles that were filled with white and black and outlined in black. These were simple examples of using brushes to set the *fill* (how a shape is painted) and the *stroke* (how a shape is outlined). In this case, you filled the rectangles with a solid color, but there are other options. These are as follows:

SolidColorBrush: This paints with a solid color.

LinearGradientBrush: This paints with a linear gradient defined in two-dimensional space.

RadialGradientBrush: This paints with a circular (radial) gradient.

ImageBrush: This paints using a picture as the brush.

VideoBrush: This paints using a video as the brush.

These will be discussed in the next few sections.

The SolidColorBrush

The SolidColorBrush is used to paint with a solid color. This color can be a named value, such as Red or Black, or a hexadecimal value that describes the color intensity in alpha (transparency), red, green, and blue 8-bit values.

So, for example, to paint with the color black, you can use either the value Black or #00000000.

The LinearGradientBrush

This paints with a linear gradient defined in two-dimensional space. A gradient is what you get when you fade from one color to another. So, to define a gradient, you need at least two colors and a direction. When you use more than two colors, you will also need to define stops, which indicate at which point you should change to that color.

Colors are defined using either names or hexadecimal values in exactly the same manner as the SolidColorBrush.

The direction is defined using a normalized rectangle. This is a virtual rectangle that is 1 unit wide by 1 unit high. Thus, the top left-hand corner of this rectangle is at (0,0) and the bottom right-hand corner is at (1,1). This defines the direction of the gradient as being from the upper left to the lower right. Should you want to change this direction, you simply do it by specifying the coordinates of the start point and endpoint of your gradient direction using the coordinates of this virtual rectangle. These are set using the StartPoint and EndPoint properties of the brush itself.

Here's an example of a rectangle filled in using a LinearGradientBrush, and set to have a start point of (0,0.5) (i.e., halfway down the left side of the rectangle) and an endpoint of (1,0.5) (i.e., halfway down the right side of the rectangle), thus giving the gradient left-to-right horizontal movement.

```
<Canvas
  xmlns="http://schemas.microsoft.com/client/2007"
  xmlns:x="http://schemas.microsoft.com/winfx/2006/xaml"
  Width="640" Height="480"
  Background="White"
  x:Name="Page"
>
  <Rectangle Width="211" Height="176"
```

```
           Stroke="#FF000000" Canvas.Left="8" Canvas.Top="64">
    <Rectangle.Fill>
      <LinearGradientBrush EndPoint="1,0.5" StartPoint="0,0.5">
        <GradientStop Color="#FF000000" Offset="0"/>
        <GradientStop Color="#FFFFFFFF" Offset="1"/>
      </LinearGradientBrush>
    </Rectangle.Fill>
  </Rectangle>
</Canvas>
```

When you are using more than two colors, you need to define gradient stops to con-figure how they will behave in the gradient. This is because when you have two colors, it's pretty obvious that they will be at the start and end of the gradient. When you add a third, where should it go? It wouldn't be flexible if it were always in the middle of the gradient, so the concept of a gradient stop allows you to define its position.

A gradient stop is defined in one-dimensional space, with 0 denoting the beginning of the gradient and 1 denoting its end. So, if the stop is halfway in between, it would be at position 0.5; if it is three-quarters of the way along, it would be at 0.75; and so forth.

Here's an example of the same rectangle filled with several colors in a linear gradient. Note how the stops determine how the colors fade between the colors of the rainbow.

```
<Canvas
  xmlns="http://schemas.microsoft.com/client/2007"
  xmlns:x="http://schemas.microsoft.com/winfx/2006/xaml"
  Width="640" Height="480"
  Background="White"
  x:Name="Page">
  <Rectangle Width="211" Height="176" Stroke="#FF000000"
        Canvas.Left="8" Canvas.Top="64">
    <Rectangle.Fill>
      <LinearGradientBrush EndPoint="0,0" StartPoint="1,0.5">
        <GradientStop Color="Red" Offset="0"/>
        <GradientStop Color="Orange" Offset="0.17"/>
        <GradientStop Color="Yellow" Offset="0.34"/>
        <GradientStop Color="Green" Offset="0.51"/>
        <GradientStop Color="Blue" Offset="0.68"/>
        <GradientStop Color="Indigo" Offset="0.85"/>
        <GradientStop Color="Violet" Offset="1"/>
      </LinearGradientBrush>
    </Rectangle.Fill>
  </Rectangle>
</Canvas>
```

The RadialGradientBrush

This is similar to the LinearGradientBrush in that is paints a space using a gradient, but it does it in a circular manner, with 0 marking the center of the circle and 1 being its radius. Thus, if you have two colors defined, it will look a lot like the effect of a spotlight of the first color being shown on a wall of the second color, whereby the center of the circle will be the color of the light, the outer edge of the circle will be the color of the wall, and a gradient between the two will fill the space.

When using the RadialGradientBrush, you don't need to specify a start point or endpoint, as the gradient direction will always be from the center of the circle to its outside edge.

Gradient stops are used in the same manner as the LinearGradientBrush, with the Offset indicating the unit distance from the center.

Here's an example of a RadialGradientBrush using the same rainbow colors as the previous rectangle:

```
<Canvas
  xmlns="http://schemas.microsoft.com/client/2007"
  xmlns:x="http://schemas.microsoft.com/winfx/2006/xaml"
  Width="640" Height="480"
  Background="White"
  x:Name="Page">
  <Rectangle Width="211" Height="176"
      Stroke="#FF000000" Canvas.Left="8" Canvas.Top="64">
    <Rectangle.Fill>
      <RadialGradientBrush>
        <GradientStop Color="Red" Offset="0"/>
        <GradientStop Color="Orange" Offset="0.17"/>
        <GradientStop Color="Yellow" Offset="0.34"/>
        <GradientStop Color="Green" Offset="0.51"/>
        <GradientStop Color="Blue" Offset="0.68"/>
        <GradientStop Color="Indigo" Offset="0.85"/>
        <GradientStop Color="Violet" Offset="1"/>
      </RadialGradientBrush>
    </Rectangle.Fill>
  </Rectangle>
</Canvas>
```

The RadialGradientBrush gives you some extra control over how the gradient is painted. The GradientOrigin allows you to set the point at which the gradient emanates. It doesn't have to be the center of the circle, so setting it to a different value will "stretch" the gradient from the center of the circle to the specified point. You set it using a normalized (x,y) value, where (0.5,0.5) is the center of the circle, (1,1) is the lower right-hand side of the rectangle bounding the circle, and (0,0) is the upper left-hand side of the rectangle bounding the circle.

Here's an example of the GradientOrigin being set to (0.2,0.2):

```
<Rectangle Width="200" Height="128" Canvas.Left="8" Canvas.Top="8">
   <Rectangle.Fill>
      <RadialGradientBrush GradientOrigin="0.2, 0.2">
         <GradientStop Color="#FF000000" Offset="0"/>
         <GradientStop Color="#FFFFFFFF" Offset="1"/>
      </RadialGradientBrush>
   </Rectangle.Fill>
</Rectangle>
```

The SpreadMethod allows you to determine how the gradient repeats. It can be set to one of three values: Pad is the default, and it means that the gradient fades evenly between colors, and that the bounding rectangle is filled with the last color on the gradient; Reflect means that once the gradient is filled, it is reversed to fill in the remainder; and Repeat means that once the gradient is filled, it is repeated. These are particularly useful when used in combination with the RadiusX and RadiusY properties.

Here's an example of a RadialGradientBrush using the Reflect value in the SpreadMethod:

```
<Rectangle Width="200" Height="128" Canvas.Left="8" Canvas.Top="8">
   <Rectangle.Fill>
      <RadialGradientBrush SpreadMethod="Reflect">
         <GradientStop Color="white" Offset="0"/>
         <GradientStop Color="gray" Offset="0.5"/>
         <GradientStop Color="black" Offset="1"/>
      </RadialGradientBrush>
   </Rectangle.Fill>
</Rectangle>
```

RadiusX and RadiusY are used to set the desired radius of the gradient. The default value of this is 0.5, so specifying a value less than this will mean that multiple gradients will be used in the fill. This is probably best shown by example:

```
<Rectangle Width="200" Height="128" Canvas.Left="8" Canvas.Top="8">
   <Rectangle.Fill>
      <RadialGradientBrush RadiusX="0.1" RadiusY="0.1" SpreadMethod="Reflect">
         <GradientStop Color="#FF000000" Offset="0"/>
         <GradientStop Color="#FFFFFFFF" Offset="1"/>
      </RadialGradientBrush>
   </Rectangle.Fill>
</Rectangle>
```

You can see the result of this in Figure 16-3. As the radius is set to 0.1 on both x and y, five circles are used to paint the gradient; and as the SpreadMethod is set to Reflect, the gradient goes from black to white, and then white to black, and then black to white, and so on.

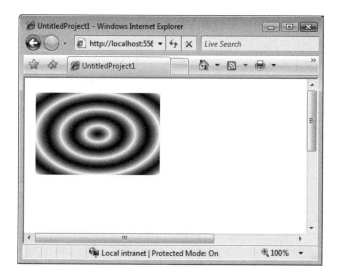

Figure 16-3. *Using the RadiusX, RadiusY, and SpreadMethod attributes*

The ImageBrush

In addition to filling a space with colors or gradients, you can also fill one with pictures using the ImageBrush. It offers a number of attributes that can be used to set the behavior, in particular how you control the image's aspect ratio and tiling behavior.

Here's an example of XAML to define filling a rectangle with an image using the ImageBrush:

```
<Rectangle Width="200" Height="128">
   <Rectangle.Fill>
      <ImageBrush ImageSource="apress.jpg" />
   </Rectangle.Fill>
</Rectangle>
```

You determine how the image is stretched using the Stretch attribute. This can take several different stretch modes:

None: Renders the image without changing it in any way.

Uniform: Scales the image to fit the dimensions of the fill area without changing the aspect ratio.

UniformToFill: Scales the image completely to fill the desired area, preserving its aspect ratio and clipping it if necessary.

Fill: Scales the image to fill the desired area using independent scaling on the x- and y-axes. This will distort the image to completely fill the available space.

To complement stretching the image, you can also set the image alignment using the AlignmentX and AlignmentY attributes. When the image doesn't fill the paint area, it can then be aligned as you desire by setting these properties. As you would expect, the values for AlignmentX are Left, Right, and Center, and the values for AlignmentY are Top, Bottom, and Center.

Here's an example of XAML that fills four rectangles with the same image, but sets each of them to a value from the different stretch modes, setting their alignments to the bottom right-hand corner.

```xml
<Rectangle Width="200" Height="200" Stroke="Black" Canvas.Left="23" Canvas.Top="17">
  <Rectangle.Fill>
    <ImageBrush ImageSource="apress.jpg" Stretch="None"
        AlignmentX="Right" AlignmentY="Bottom" />
  </Rectangle.Fill>
</Rectangle>
<Rectangle Width="200" Height="200" Stroke="Black"
      Canvas.Left="292" Canvas.Top="17">
  <Rectangle.Fill>
    <ImageBrush ImageSource="apress.jpg" Stretch="Fill"
        AlignmentX="Right" AlignmentY="Bottom" />
  </Rectangle.Fill>
</Rectangle>
<Rectangle Width="200" Height="200" Stroke="Black"
      Canvas.Top="245" Canvas.Left="23">
  <Rectangle.Fill>
    <ImageBrush ImageSource="apress.jpg" Stretch="Uniform"
        AlignmentX="Right" AlignmentY="Bottom" />
  </Rectangle.Fill>
</Rectangle>
<Rectangle Width="200" Height="200" Stroke="Black"
      Canvas.Left="292" Canvas.Top="245">
  <Rectangle.Fill>
    <ImageBrush ImageSource="apress.jpg" Stretch="UniformToFill"
        AlignmentX="Right" AlignmentY="Bottom" />
  </Rectangle.Fill>
</Rectangle>
```

You can see the results of this in Figure 16-4.

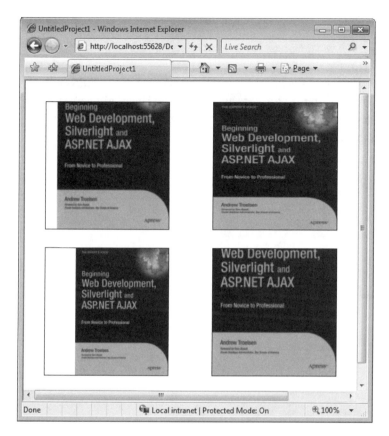

Figure 16-4. *The different stretch modes for the ImageBrush*

The VideoBrush

One of the more powerful features of Silverlight is its ability to paint a surface with video. This is achieved using the VideoBrush. You will use the VideoBrush in conjunction with the MediaElement control (which you will see later in this chapter).

To use the VideoBrush, you add a MediaElement to your canvas, name it, and set it to be invisible and not accessible to the mouse. Then you simply set it to be the source for the VideoBrush.

Here's an example:

```
<MediaElement x:Name="vid" Source="thebutterflyandthebear.wmv"
    Opacity="0" IsHitTestVisible="False" />
<TextBlock FontFamily="Verdana" FontSize="80"
    FontWeight="Bold" TextWrapping="Wrap"
```

```
      Text="Video">
  <TextBlock.Foreground>
    <VideoBrush SourceName="vid"/>
  </TextBlock.Foreground>
</TextBlock>
```

Here, the MediaElement loads a video called thebutterflyandthebear.wmv (this is a sample that can be downloaded from the QuickStarts page on the Silverlight web site, at http://silverlight.net/quickstarts/), and uses it to paint the text within a TextBlock.

You can see how this appears in Figure 16-5.

Figure 16-5. *Using the VideoBrush to paint text*

Using Strokes with Brushes

Each of the examples that you've seen in this section showed how an object could be filled using a brush. In addition to filling an item with a brush, you can also set its stroke to be painted with a specified brush. For example, if you are drawing a rectangle, you can fill it with one color and paint its outline with another.

Here's a simple piece of XAML that draws a white table with a black outline (stroke):

```
<Rectangle Stroke="Black" Fill="White" Canvas.Left="40" Canvas.Top="40"
    Width="100" Height="200" />
```

In this case, the stroke is a SolidColorBrush that is black. You could just as easily have painted it with a LinearGradientBrush instead, with XAML like this:

```
<Rectangle Fill="White" Canvas.Left="40" Canvas.Top="40" Width="100" Height="200">
<Rectangle.Stroke>
    <LinearGradientBrush >
        <GradientStop Color="Black" Offset="0"/>
        <GradientStop Color="White" Offset="0.5"/>
        <GradientStop Color="Black" Offset="1"/>
    </LinearGradientBrush>
  </Rectangle.Stroke>
</Rectangle>
```

When using strokes, you have a number of other properties that you can use to fine-tune their appearance.

The width of your stroke is set using the width property. When painting a stroke with something like a gradient brush, it is hard to see the gradient if your stroke is only 1 pixel wide, so it's very straightforward to change the width and have the brush show up a lot better.

The way the stroke is drawn is configured using the StrokeDashArray, StrokeDashCap, and StrokeDashOffset properties. The StrokeDashArray specifies how you would like the line broken into dashes by configuring it using an array of double values. This is a comma-separated list of values in which you set a value for the stroke length, followed by a value for the space length, and then repeat as necessary. For example, if you want your dash to be 3 units long, followed by a space 1 unit long, followed by a dash 2 units long, followed by a space 1 unit long, you would use a dash array that contains "3,1,2,1."

If you use this method and you have a large width on your lines, you'll see that your lines are in fact rectangles with sharp corners. You can change this using the StrokeDashCap property, which allows you to set your dashes to have the following end caps:

Flat: The default value, where the line ends flat, giving squared-off corners

Round: Specifies that the end cap is a semicircle with the same diameter as the line thickness

Triangle: Specifies an isosceles triangle end cap, where the base length equals the thickness of the stroke

If you are drawing a shape that has sharp turns on it, such as the corners of a rectangle, you may notice that the dashes do not join up cleanly in many cases due to their dash array not lining up with the specified widths of the shape. To control this a little better, you can specify how strokes will join up with each other when they go through a turn. This is set using the StrokeLineJoin property. You can set this to have the following join types:

Bevel: This shaves the edges off the join, thus smoothing it.

Miter: This keeps the default edging.

Round: This rounds off the edges of the join.

Using Visual Elements in XAML

Earlier, you saw several of the common visual elements that are used in XAML, including Canvas.Top and Canvas.Left. There are a number of other properties that many XAML elements have in common. In this section, you'll take a look at these, and from there you'll be able to understand the subsequent sections a little better!

Dimension and Position Properties

You'll typically use the Height and Width properties to set the dimensions of an item. These take a double value—so, for example, to create a 50×100 rectangle, you define its XAML as follows:

```
<Rectangle Fill="Black" Width="50" Height="100" />
```

The properties for setting the location of an item are Canvas.Top and Canvas.Left. These have a special syntax, called *attached properties*, as they are ultimately related to the parent element. So, to set the same rectangle to appear 50 pixels from the left and 50 pixels down from the top of its container, you would use this XAML:

```
<Rectangle Fill="Black" Width="50" Height="100" Canvas.Top="50" Canvas.Left="50" />
```

Opacity

Most shapes allow their alpha channels to be set. This can be done with the alpha channel on a shape's fill brush (with the exception of the VideoBrush). In addition, most elements allow you to use the Opacity property, which is a normalized double with 0 representing invisible, 1 representing visible, and everything in between representing a degree of opacity relative to the specified value.

Cursor Behavior

To provide good feedback to your users, it is often necessary to change the mouse cursor to indicate the type of action that is appropriate. XAML elements expose a Cursor property that allows you to set the following values:

Arrow: Displays the typical arrow cursor.

Default: No cursor preference set. This uses this element's parent cursor specifications.

Hand: Displays a pointing hand cursor, typically used for a hyperlink.

IBeam: Displays an I-beam, or text cursor. This is typically used to show an area where text entry or selection is used.

None: No cursor is used.

Wait: Shows an hourglass, indicating a busy state.

Using Shapes in XAML

Many of the XAML elements used to make up your UI are XAML shapes that are composited into more complex shapes. The shapes that are supported by Silverlight are as follows:

Ellipse: Draws a closed, curved shape. A circle is an ellipse with the same horizontal and vertical dimensions.

Rectangle: Draws a closed, straight-edged shape. A square is a rectangle with the same horizontal and vertical dimensions.

Line: Draws a line between the specified endpoints.

Path: Draws a series of connected lines and curves.

Polygon: Draws a closed shape made up of a connected series of straight lines.

Polyline: Draws a connected series of straight lines.

The Ellipse

The Ellipse is used to draw a closed, curved shape. Its Height property contains its vertical height (i.e., double its vertical radius), and its Width property contains its horizontal width (i.e., double its horizontal radius).

Here's an example of an Ellipse that is twice as wide as it is high, giving an egg-shaped element.

```
<Ellipse Fill="Red" Height="100" Width="200"/>
```

The Rectangle

This shape is used to draw a closed, straight-edged shape. As with the Ellipse, you control its dimensions with its Height and Width properties. For example, you can create a square with XAML like this:

```
<Rectangle Fill="Red" Height="100" Width="100"/>
```

You can round off the corners of a rectangle with the RadiusX and RadiusY properties. These take a double value specifying the radius of the circle that is used to round the corner. For example, to change the preceding rectangle to have rounded corners that are inscribed by a 10 pixel circle, you would use this XAML:

```
<Rectangle Fill="Red" Height="100" Width="100" RadiusX="10" RadiusY="10"/>
```

The Line

Lines are drawn in XAML using the Line object. You specify the starting point of the line using its X1 and Y1 properties, and its endpoint using its X2 and Y2 properties. Note that these are not absolute coordinates, but relative to the container of the line. For example, if you have the line within a Canvas that has a top of 50 and a left of 50, and X1 and Y1 are both set to 50, then the line will start drawing from (100,100).

The line itself can also have its Canvas.Top and Canvas.Left properties set to change its overall drawing position. Here's an example:

```
<Line Canvas.Top="50" Canvas.Left="50"
      X1="40" Y1="40" X2="100" Y2="100" Stroke="Black" />
```

The Path

The Path draws a series of connected lines and curves that are defined using a geometry. Silverlight uses the following geometries:

EllipseGeometry: Defines the path element as a simple ellipse.

LineGeometry: Defines the path element as a line.

RectangleGeometry: Defines the path element as a rectangle.

PathGeometry: Defines the path element using a complex set of different shapes, including arcs, Bézier curves, lines, poly Bézier curves, polyquadratic Bézier curves, and quadratic Bézier curves. When using a PathGeometry, you collect segments into a PathFigure, and one or more of these make up the PathGeometry. This goes beyond the scope of this book, but check out the MSDN documentation for more details.

In addition to using geometries, the Path object can be specified using a string that contains what is called the *path language*. This uses a simple syntax of space-separated values. These values contain a command letter, followed by a space, followed by a comma-separated set of numbers, which are the parameters for the specified command. Here's an example:

```
<Path Stroke="Black" Data="M 10,10 L 150,100" />
```

In this example, the M command (for *move*) moves the drawing head to position (10,10), and the L command (for *draw line*) draws a line to position (150,150).

The full set of path language commands are as follows:

M: Moves the draw heads to the point specified by two double values

L: Draws a line to the point specified by two double values

H: Draws a horizontal line to the point specified by a double value for its endpoint on x

V: Draws a vertical line to the point specified by a double value for its endpoint on y

C: Draws a cubic Bézier curve between the current point and the endpoint specified by six double values, which specify the x and y points of the two control points of the curve and the endpoint for the curve

Q: Draws a quadratic Bézier curve between the current point and the endpoint, specified by four double values, with the first two being the x and y of the curve's control point and the latter two being the x and y of the endpoint

S: Very similar to the Q command in that it takes four parameters, but draws the curve slightly differently, as the current coordinates are also used as a control point

A: Draws an elliptical arc between the current point and the endpoint

Z: Ends the current path and closes it by drawing a line between the current point and the overall starting point of this path

XAML Controls

In addition to the shapes, brushes, and visual elements mentioned previously, Silverlight has a number of XAML controls. These include the following:

- Image

- Glyphs

- TextBlock

- MediaElement

The Image Control

This control is used to draw a graphic. You use its Source property to set the URI of the image to draw. Silverlight supports Windows bitmap (.bmp), JPEG (.jpg), and PNG (.png) image formats.

Here's an example:

```
<Image Width="200" Height="200" Source="apress.jpg" />
```

You can also control the image using the same properties as you used for the Image-Brush earlier in this chapter—namely the Stretch, AlignmentX, and AlignmentY properties.

The Glyphs Control

This is used to render fixed text according to a defined font, using either the Unicode text directly or the offset of the character within the font. You use the character offset when there is no fixed keystroke associated with a character, such as with many of the graphical characters found in fonts such as Wingdings.

You specify the font using the FontURI property, setting it to the relative path of the font file. You can then specify the characters using either Indices as a comma-separated list of font offsets or UnicodeString as a string containing the desired characters.

The font size is controlled using the FontRenderingEmSize property, and the StyleSimulations property can be set to the following values to render the font in that style: BoldSimulation, ItalicSimulation, BoldItalicSimulation, and None.

Here's an example of using the Glyphs control to render Webdings characters using their font offset:

```
<Glyphs Canvas.Top="0" FontUri="webdings.ttf" Indices="201;188;196"
    Fill="Black" FontRenderingEmSize="48"/>
```

The TextBlock Control

This is a very lightweight control designed to display single or multiline text. The TextBlock control supports a limited set of web-safe fonts that work on multiple operating systems and do not require you to set or provide the font. These are the following:

- Arial

- Arial Black

- Comic Sans MS

- Courier New

- Georgia

- Lucida Grande/Lucida Sans Unicode

- Times New Roman

- Trebuchet MS

- Verdana

Additionally, you can download a font using the Downloader control, and then use the SetFontSource method of the TextBlock to assign the font to the text used in the TextBlock.

You can control how the text is rendered using the FontSize, FontStyle, and FontWeight properties. In the case of the latter, the possible values are Thin, ExtraLight, Light, Normal, Medium, SemiBold, Bold, ExtraBold, Black, and ExtraBlack.

You can add decorations to the TextBlock using the TextDecorations property. At present, it just supports Underline and None as values.

You can wrap text using the TextWrapping property. This can contain the values NoWrap (the text is clipped by the width of the TextBlock) or Wrap, where the text flows onto a new line when it goes beyond the available width. Note that when text wraps like this, the width of the text box may be reported inaccurately. Make sure that if you need to read the width, you check on the actualWidth and actualHeight properties for a correct read.

Here's an example of a TextBlock that uses TextWrapping and the Courier New font family:

```
<TextBlock Width="157" Height="101" Canvas.Left="47" Canvas.Top="72" Text="The Quick
  brown fox jumped over the lazy dog" TextWrapping="Wrap" FontFamily="Courier New"/>
```

Transformations

XAML allows you to define a transformation that affects how the element will be rendered on the screen. In computer graphics, items are managed using a mathematical construct called a *matrix*. Through use of matrix-based mathematics, coordinates can be easily manipulated, and thus transformations of objects are achievable. Silverlight gives you the facility to define your own matrices, which can be used to define the transformation for one or more objects, or to use one of a number of fixed transforms. The transforms available to you are as follows:

RotateTransform: Rotates the item through the specified angle

ScaleTransform: Changes the size of the object on the x-axis, the y-axis, or both axes

TranslateTransform: Moves the object to a new position

SkewTransform: Skews the object by the specified angle in a particular direction

MatrixTransform: Applies your custom transform

Transformations may be combined within a TransformGroup. In this scenario, Silverlight calculates a single matrix based on the defined transformations and applies this matrix as a single compound transform.

Storyboards and Animation

Animation in Silverlight is achieved by changing a property over a set amount of time using a timeline. Animations are contained within a storyboard, and come in a number of flavors:

DoubleAnimation and DoubleAnimationUsingKeyFrames: Used to change a double-based property, such as Canvas.Left or Opacity

PointAnimation and PointAnimationUsingKeyFrames: Used to change a point value over time

ColorAnimation and ColorAnimationUsingKeyFrames: Used to change a color value over time

You may have noticed that there are two types for each value: one standard animation and one that uses keyframes.

Programming with JavaScript

In the previous sections, you took a quick tour of the various controls that you can use in Silverlight XAML and looked at how to use their properties to set them. Typically, a designer will use a tool like Microsoft Expression Blend to put together the UI design, expressed as XAML, and may do some fine-tweaking by editing the XAML code.

In order to get the UI to do something meaningful, the programmer gets involved to activate the design. Here's where the JavaScript programming model comes in. You took a first look at this in Chapter 15 when you saw how scripting was used to instantiate and manipulate the control. In this chapter, you'll take a look at how you can manipulate your XAML UI. It's a very high-level overview, so for more details, take a look at a book such as *Introducing Silverlight 1.0* (Microsoft Press, 2007).

Editing Properties

In a programming sense, XAML tags should be treated as objects, with their attributes directly analogous to properties. Thus, when programming, you can just say `<OBJECT>.`
`<PROPERTY>=<VALUE>`. One exception to this is when you are addressing attached properties that already have a dot syntax, such as `Canvas.Left`. In this case, you will use `setValue` and `getValue` to write and read properties, respectively.

In JavaScript, your object will be a `var`, so you will need to set a `var` value to the object that you want to manipulate. You do this using the `findName` method of the Silverlight control to seek through its XAML content to get a handle on the object that you want. You can then access its programming model. To do this, the object must be named, and in XAML, you name an object using its `x:Name` attribute.

That's a lot of theory, which upon first reading might be a little confusing, but with a little practice, you'll see that it is straightforward.

Here's an example of a XAML document containing a TextBlock called `txt`:

```
<Canvas
    xmlns="http://schemas.microsoft.com/client/2007"
    xmlns:x="http://schemas.microsoft.com/winfx/2006/xaml"
    Width="640" Height="480"
    Background="White"
    x:Name="Page">
    <TextBlock Width="197" Height="59" Text="This is the first text"
        TextWrapping="Wrap" Canvas.Left="96" Canvas.Top="35" x:Name="txt"/>
</Canvas>
```

In JavaScript, you will need a reference to the Silverlight control. One way of getting this is by capturing the `Load` event of the control, which raises references to the control as well as its current context. See Chapter 15 for more details on this.

Once you have this reference, you can seek the item by using `findName` on the control's content.

```
function handleLoad(control, context, sender)
{
  var txtBlock=control.content.findName("txt");
  txtBlock.Text = "This is the new Text";


}
```

In this case, the txtBlock var is set to a reference to the TextBlock called txt. Now that you have this, you can just change its Text property using the standard dot syntax.

In addition to the dot syntax, you can use the setValue and getValue methods on the object. When using attached properties, you have to use this methodology. Here's an example:

```
txtBlock.setValue("Canvas.Top",200);
```

Using Common Methods

There are a number of methods that all XAML elements have in common. We'll first summarize them, and then look into the more important methods that exist on specific controls.

The AddEventListener and RemoveEventListener Methods

One of the nice things about Silverlight is how it separates the design and developer artifacts to allow them to work together more efficiently. You can specify an event handler for an item by using a XAML attribute to define the name of the function that will have the code to run in response to the event. For example, you can use the syntax MouseLeftButton = "handleClick" to declare that you want to use the JavaScript function handleClick when this element is clicked. The drawback with this is that it involves a developer editing the XAML from the designer directly, thus breaking the separation.

Silverlight allows you to avoid this by using AddEventListener to declare the handler at runtime. You'll typically do this as part of Silverlight loading. Your handler function will take two parameters: sender, which contains a reference to the control that the event was raised on; and args, which contains any arguments associated with the event. Here's an example:

```
function handleLoad(control, context, sender)
{
    var txtBlock=control.content.findName("txt");
    txtBlock.addEventListener("mouseLeftButtonDown", handleTxtClick);

}
function handleTxtClick(sender,args)
{
    alert("You clicked the Text Block");
}
```

You remove the event listener using the RemoveEventListener method on the control. You specify the event name and the handler token in the same way as you did when adding the event listener. Here's an example:

```
txtBlock.removeEventListener("mouseLeftButtonDown", handleTxtClick);
```

The CaptureMouse and ReleaseMouseCapture Methods

The CaptureMouse method allows the object to receive mouse events even when the mouse isn't within its borders. This is typically used for dragging events, so that once you start dragging an object, you don't have to be within its bounds to continue dragging it. This is released using the ReleaseMouseCapture method.

Here's an example where they are being used in conjunction with a handler for the MouseMove event, which will be discussed later in this chapter:

```
var isMouseCaptured;
function handleLoad(control, context, sender)
{
    var txtBlock=control.content.findName("txt");
    txtBlock.addEventListener("MouseLeftButtonDown","mouseDown");
    txtBlock.addEventListener("MouseLeftButtonUp","mouseUp");
    txtBlock.addEventListener("MouseMove","mouseMove");
    isMouseCaptured = false;
}
function mouseDown(sender,mouseEventArgs)
{
    sender.captureMouse();
    isMouseCaptured = true;
}
function mouseUp(sender, mouseEventArgs)
{
    sender.releaseMouse();
    isMouseCaptured = false;
}
function mouseMove(sender, mouseEventArgs)
{
    if(isMouseCaptured)
    {
        sender.setValue("Canvas.Top", mouseEventArgs.getPosition(null).x);
        sender.setValue("Canvas.Left", mouseEventArgs.getPosition(null).y);
    }
}
```

The GetHost Method

This method allows you to get a handle on the Silverlight control, and is useful if you don't want to keep a global reference to it. Here's an example:

```
function someEvent(sender,args)
{
    var slControl = sender.getHost();
}
```

The GetParent Method

Similar to GetHost, this returns a reference to the parent element of a particular XAML element. This is particularly useful if you want to walk up the XAML tree. Here's an example:

```
var txtBlock = control.content.findName("txt");
var txtBlocksParent = txtBlock.getParent();
```

Using MediaElement Methods

In addition to the common methods, the MediaElement also exposes the methods described in the following subsections.

The Play Method

This will start playback of the current media if it is not currently active or resume playback if it is in a paused state. Here's an example:

```
var med = sender.content.findName("mplayer");
med.Play();
```

The Pause Method

This will pause an active playback. Some types of media may not be paused (i.e., streaming media), and in this case the pause command will be ignored. You can check to see if the media can be paused by using the CanPause property. Here's an example:

```
var med = sender.content.findName("mplayer");
if(med.CanPause)
    med.Pause();
else
    // do nothing
```

The Stop Method

This will stop the current media playback, regardless of whether it is currently playing or paused. Here's an example:

```
var med = sender.content.findName("mplayer");
med.Stop();
```

Handling Events

In this section, we'll first look at the common events that are available to all XAML elements in Silverlight, and then toward the end of the section, we'll look into those that work specifically with the MediaElement.

Managing Focus with the GotFocus and LostFocus Events

The only object that can receive Focus events in Silverlight 1.0 is the root Canvas. When it receives focus, the GotFocus event will fire. When it loses it, the LostFocus event will fire. You can use this to determine when the user has selected the Silverlight content within the browser.

Capturing Keyboard Input with the keyDown and keyUp Events

As only the root Canvas can receive focus, only the root canvas will receive these events.

The keyDown event will fire when a key is pressed and the Silverlight control has focus. It raises two arguments: sender and keyEventArgs. The first parameter will always contain a reference to the Canvas. The second will contain the necessary metadata to extract the key information. It exposes the following properties:

keyEventArgs.key: This is an integer that represents the key that was pressed. It is not operating system–specific. This uses a portable key code that is not operating system–specific. The full key set is available in the SDK documentation.

keyEventArgs.platformKeyCode: This is an operating system-specific integer that represents the key that was pressed.

keyEventArgs.shift: This is a Boolean that determines the state of the Shift key when the key was pressed.

keyEventArgs.ctrl: This is a Boolean that determines the state of the Ctrl key when the key was pressed.

The keyUp event will fire when the key has been released. It exposes the same parameters as the keyDown event, and can be handled in the same manner. When processing input, it is often better to capture it on keyUp instead of keyDown—that way, you can more accurately assess the state of the Shift and Ctrl keys. For example, when the user types Shift+S for an uppercase *S*, you'll get two keyDown events: one for the initial Shift, and then one for the *S*. However, for keyUp, you'll only get an event for Shift+S.

Handling the Loading of Controls with the Loaded Event

Every XAML element exposes a Loaded event, which can be captured to do some processing once the element is loaded. In most examples, you'll see a Loaded event being captured on the control itself, but if you want finer-grained processing, you can do it for each element. This is very useful when you want to add event listeners at runtime. If you have a lot of controls that you want to set up event listeners for, and you do them all in the control's Load event, you'll end up with a lot of code in there that is difficult to maintain.

Note that if you specify the Load event for an element and that element's child, the child event will fire first, followed by the parent.

Handling Mouse Events

Controls can be interacted with using the mouse, and several events are provided that allow you to control their behavior in different circumstances. Each of these events provide a reference to the control as their first argument, and a MouseEventArgs object as their second argument.

The MouseEventArgs object exposes a getPosition method that returns an object containing x and y properties that are used to get the coordinates of the mouse on the screen. In addition, it exposes a shift property that is used to determine whether the Shift key was pressed, and a ctrl property that is used to determine if the Ctrl key was pressed.

The events that can be captured are as follows:

MouseEnter: This fires when the mouse enters the bounds of this control.

MouseLeave: This fires when the mouse leaves the bounds of this control.

MouseLeftButtonDown: This fires when the left mouse button is held down over the control.

MouseLeftButtonUp: This fires when the left mouse button is released over the control after being held down over the control.

MouseMove: This fires when the mouse is moved within the bounds of the control.

MediaElement Events

The MediaElement provides events that give you fine-grained control over writing media-oriented applications in Silverlight. It exposes the following events:

`BufferingProgressChanged`: This event will fire when video is being buffered into the MediaElement. When playing back a streaming media source, a certain amount is buffered (depending on bandwidth) so that the overall playback is as smooth as possible. The event will fire when the buffer amount has changed by 5 percent or more, and when the buffer is full.

`CurrentStateChanged`: This will fire when the state of the MediaElement has changed. The state may be read using the `CurrentState` property. The possible states are Buffering, Closed, Error, Opening, Paused, Playing, and Stopped.

`DownloadProgressChanged`: If you are playing back a media file that isn't being streamed, the media element will download it to your browser cache before playing it back. As it downloads, this event will fire every time the amount downloaded has increased by 5 percent, and when the download completes.

`MarkerReached`: Markers can be encoded into video streams, and when Silverlight encounters one of these markers, the `MarkerReached` event will fire. It includes a `markerEventArgs` argument that contains a `Text` property containing metadata about the marker.

`MediaEnded`: This event will fire when the MediaElement is no longer playing back media.

`MediaFailed`: This event will fire when the MediaElement has a problem accessing or playing back the requested media.

`MediaOpened`: This event will fire once the media has been successfully accessed. At this point, the `NaturalDuration`, `NaturalVideoHeight`, and `NaturalVideoWidth` properties will be available.

Putting It All Together: Creating a Casual Game in Silverlight

In Chapter 15, you took a look at how to use Silverlight on your web page, and in this chapter, you've taken a look at the XAML and JavaScript used to build Silverlight applications. Now it's time to roll up your sleeves and put it all together with an example.

Figure 16-6 shows the example—a simple yet addictive memory game where you have to repeat a sequence of colors. Each time you succeed, the sequence will repeat with one new color added. See how high you can go before you forget the sequence. My record is 17!

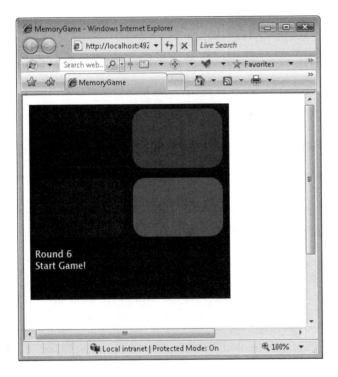

Figure 16-6. *Silverlight memory game*

Designing the Game XAML

The first step in building a game like this is to create the XAML. This can be built using the Expression Blend tool (www.microsoft.com/expression).

When using Blend, first create a new project, using File ➤ New Project (see Figure 16-7).

You'll see an option to create a Silverlight 1.0 site, which creates a file system web site (not an IIS one) containing everything you need to get up and running with Silverlight. The .NET Orcas option is for the Silverlight 1.1./2.0 preview only.

Once you've done this, you'll have a project containing a XAML page (Page.xaml) and its associated code-behind (Page.xaml.js), which can be used for the design and the implementation, respectively.

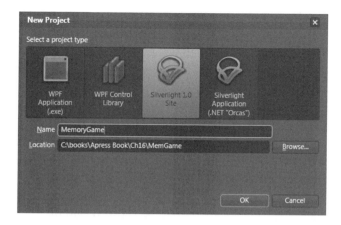

Figure 16-7. *Creating a project in Expression Blend*

You can see Expression Blend, with the Project and Design windows open, in Figure 16-8.

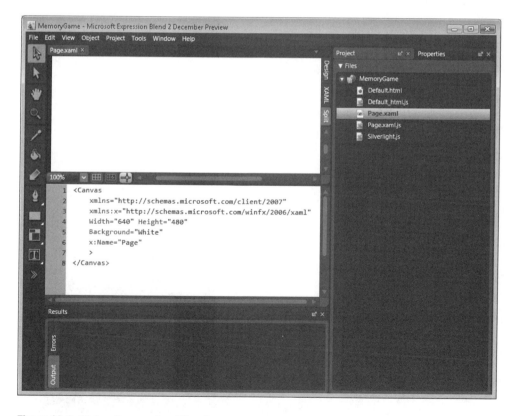

Figure 16-8. *Using Expression Blend*

You can edit your XAML with the Visual Designer, with the Property Editor, or in code view. For example, you can see that the background of the main Canvas is white, so you can edit this by selecting the Properties view and editing the background property to a different color, or by simply going into the code view and typing a new color (e.g., Black) into the contents of the Background attribute.

Next, you can draw each of the color cells that are used by the animation game. These are drawn as rectangles with rounded corners.

On the toolbar at the left of the screen, you can see the Rectangle tool. Select this and drag out a rectangle. You should see a white rectangle on the screen. You can round off its corners using the RadiusX and RadiusY properties. Set these to 20 to get nice rounded corners. Now fill in the rectangle with a color.

What I did for the game was default the colors to a "dim" mode. Then, to light them up, I raised the intensity by using an animation. You'll see the animation shortly, but first I'll show you how to set the color. Silverlight uses 8-bit values for each of the red, green, and blue channels. Under this, pure blue would involve setting 0 for red, 0 for green, and 255 for blue. My "dimmed" blue would have half of this value—so 0 for red, 0 for green, and 127 for blue.

Figure 16-9 shows the rectangle being colored in this way.

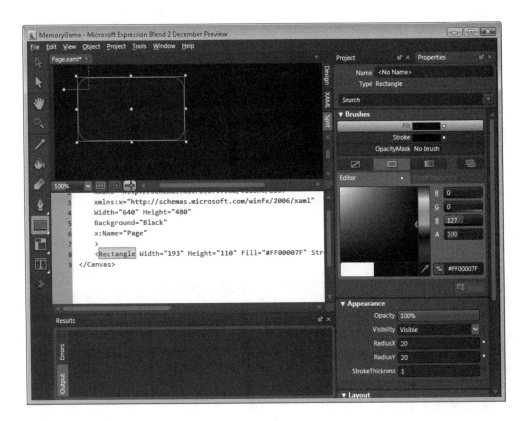

Figure 16-9. *Filling in the rectangle*

While you are in the Property Editor, it's good to give your rectangle a name. You'll see the default <No Name> at the top of the window. Change this to something like rBlue.

Next, you can generate an animation to change the value of this color over time. From the Window menu, select Animation Workspace to open up the animation designer. Make sure that the Objects and Timeline pane is visible (it may be collapsed and shown vertically—if so, click the down arrow on it to open it up). Your screen should look something like Figure 16-10 when you are ready.

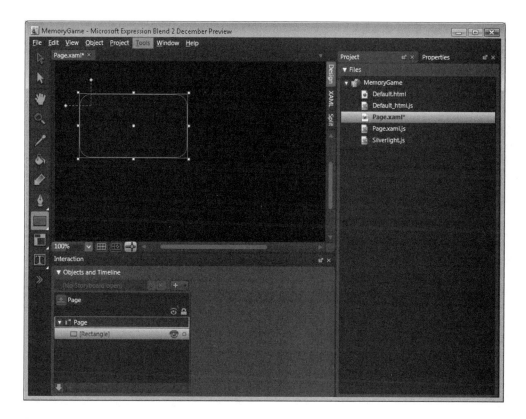

Figure 16-10. *Using the animation workspace*

You'll see on the Objects and Timeline pane that there is no storyboard presently open. Add a new storyboard to define the animation that brightens the blue rectangle by clicking the + to the right of this message. This will show the Create Storyboard dialog, which allows you to create a storyboard. Make sure that the Create as a Resource option is checked, otherwise the animation will be defined as one that runs when the XAML is first loaded (see Figure 16-11).

Figure 16-11. *Creating a new storyboard*

Now that you've done this, the timeline editor will appear. This is a very simple tool that allows you to generate animations quickly and easily (see Figure 16-12).

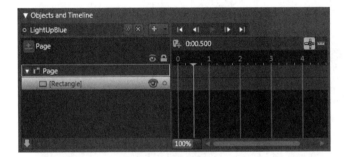

Figure 16-12. *Using the timeline editor*

Drag the yellow time indicator to the 0:00.500 mark (half of a second) and add a keyframe at this point. To add a keyframe, you use the tool with the green + on it, located immediately above the timeline window. You can see it just to the left of the 0:00.500 label in Figure 16-12. A blob will appear on the timeline, indicating that there is a key frame there.

Now, with the timeline still on 0:00.500, use the Property Editor to change the color of the rectangle to full blue (0 red, 0 green, 255 blue).

Then return to the timeline editor, drag the yellow bar to the 1 second mark, add a new key frame, and go back to the Property Editor to change the color back to 0 red, 0 green, 127 blue.

You've now defined an animation that will change the intensity of the blue from 127 to 255 over 0.5 seconds, before returning back to 127 over the next 0.5 seconds.

Repeat this process for three other rectangles—one red, one green, and one yellow. For yellow, use equal values of red and green (e.g., dimmed is 127 red, 127 green, 0 blue).

Once you've created them all, defined their animations, and added a couple of TextBlocks that will be used for starting the game and showing your current round, you should have XAML that looks like Listing 16-1.

Listing 16-1. *XAML Source for the Memory Game*

```
<Canvas
  xmlns="http://schemas.microsoft.com/client/2007"
  xmlns:x="http://schemas.microsoft.com/winfx/2006/xaml"
  Width="324" Height="304"
  Background="Black"
  x:Name="Page"
>
<Canvas.Resources>
  <Storyboard x:Name="LightUpBlue">
    <ColorAnimationUsingKeyFrames BeginTime="00:00:00"
        Storyboard.TargetName="rBlue"
        Storyboard.TargetProperty="(Shape.Fill).(SolidColorBrush.Color)">
          <SplineColorKeyFrame KeyTime="00:00:00.5" Value="#FF0000FF"/>
          <SplineColorKeyFrame KeyTime="00:00:01" Value="#FF000080"/>
        </ColorAnimationUsingKeyFrames>
    </Storyboard>
    <Storyboard x:Name="LightUpGreen">
      <ColorAnimationUsingKeyFrames BeginTime="00:00:00"
        Storyboard.TargetName="rGreen"
        Storyboard.TargetProperty="(Shape.Fill).(SolidColorBrush.Color)">
          <SplineColorKeyFrame KeyTime="00:00:00.5" Value="#FF00FF00"/>
          <SplineColorKeyFrame KeyTime="00:00:01" Value="#FF008000"/>
        </ColorAnimationUsingKeyFrames>
    </Storyboard>
    <Storyboard x:Name="LightUpRed">
      <ColorAnimationUsingKeyFrames BeginTime="00:00:00"
          Storyboard.TargetName="rRed"
          Storyboard.TargetProperty="(Shape.Fill).(SolidColorBrush.Color)">
          <SplineColorKeyFrame KeyTime="00:00:00.5" Value="#FFFF0000"/>
          <SplineColorKeyFrame KeyTime="00:00:01" Value="#FF800000"/>
        </ColorAnimationUsingKeyFrames>
    </Storyboard>
    <Storyboard x:Name="LightUpYellow">
      <ColorAnimationUsingKeyFrames BeginTime="00:00:00"
        Storyboard.TargetName="rYellow"
        Storyboard.TargetProperty="(Shape.Fill).(SolidColorBrush.Color)">
          <SplineColorKeyFrame KeyTime="00:00:00.5" Value="#FFFFFF00"/>
          <SplineColorKeyFrame KeyTime="00:00:01" Value="#FF808000"/>
        </ColorAnimationUsingKeyFrames>
    </Storyboard>
```

```
    </Canvas.Resources>
    <Rectangle Width="145" Height="92" Fill="#FF000080"
        Canvas.Left="8" Canvas.Top="8" RadiusX="20"
        RadiusY="20" x:Name="rBlue"/>
     <Rectangle Width="145" Height="92" Fill="#FF008000"
        RadiusX="20" RadiusY="20" Canvas.Left="168"
        Canvas.Top="8" x:Name="rGreen"/>
    <Rectangle Width="145" Height="92" Fill="#FF800000"
         RadiusX="20" RadiusY="20" Canvas.Left="8"
         Canvas.Top="115" x:Name="rRed" />
    <Rectangle Width="145" Height="92" Fill="#FF808000"
         RadiusX="20" RadiusY="20" Canvas.Left="168"
         Canvas.Top="115" x:Name="rYellow"/>
    <TextBlock Width="187" Height="27" Canvas.Left="8" Canvas.Top="222"
        Text="" TextWrapping="Wrap"
        Foreground="#FFFFFFFF" x:Name="txtRound"/>
    <TextBlock Width="187" Height="27" Canvas.Left="8" Canvas.Top="240"
        Text="Start Game!" TextWrapping="Wrap"
         Foreground="#FFFFFFFF" x:Name="txtStart"/>
</Canvas>
```

Now that the design is done, it's time to start looking at the code.

Implementing the Code

You can load the project into Visual Studio for editing. To do this, you use File ➤ Open
Web Site, and find the site on your hard drive in the location that you created it using
Expression Blend.

The Page.xaml.js file should be used to create the code for the application. You don't
have to use it, but it's good practice to put code associated with a XAML file in its code-
behind. JavaScript programming can be done using delegate-based functions, as you can
see in the basic code provided by the Expression Blend template, or "normal" functions,
which is my preference.

So, before continuing, take a look at the Default.html.js file, and you'll see code like
this to define the event handler that responds to the onLoad event for the Canvas:

```
onLoad: Silverlight.createDelegate(scene, scene.handleLoad),
```

Change this to use the standard declaration, as you'll see later that the code itself will
be written using a standard function syntax.

```
onLoad: handleLoad,
```

Now it's time to implement the logic for the game itself. Listing 16-2 shows the full code for Page.xaml.js.

Listing 16-2. *JavaScript Source for the Memory Game*

```javascript
var theMoves = new Array();
var currentMove = -1;
var currentFrame = -1;
var currentUserMove = -1;
var currentUserCol = -1;
var slControl;
var inAnim=false;
var inMovesPlayBack=false;
var inGame = false;

function handleLoad(control, userContext, rootElement)
{
    slControl = control;
    setUpEventHandlers();
}

function gameOver()
{
    alert("Game Over: You scored: " + currentMove);
    slControl.content.findName("txtRound").Text = "";
    currentMove = -1;
    currentFrame = -1;
    currentUserMove = -1;
    currentUserCol = -1;
    inGame = false;

}
function handleStart()
{
    if(inGame)
    {
        // Do Nothing
    }
    else
    {
        gameloop();
    }
```

```javascript
}
function gameloop()
{
    addToMoves();
    playMoves();
    getUserMoves();
}


function getUserMoves()
{
    currentUserMove =-1;

    // Do nothing else, just wait for user mouse events
}
function handleMouseDown(sender, eventArgs)
{
    // The following line of code shows how to find an
    // element by name and call a method on it.
    if(inAnim || inMovesPlayBack)
    {
        // Do Nothing
    }
    else
    {
        currentUserMove++;
        switch(sender.name)
        {
        case "rBlue":
            inAnim = true;
            currentUserCol=0;
            slControl.content.findName("LightUpBlue").Begin();
            break;
        case "rGreen":
            inAnim = true;
            currentUserCol=1;
            slControl.content.findName("LightUpGreen").Begin();
            break;
        case "rYellow":
            inAnim = true;
            currentUserCol=3;
            slControl.content.findName("LightUpYellow").Begin();
            break;
```

```
        case "rRed":
            inAnim = true;
            currentUserCol=2;
            slControl.content.findName("LightUpRed").Begin();
            break;
    }
  }
}

// Sample event handler

function addToMoves()
{
    currentMove++;
    theMoves[currentMove] = Math.floor(Math.random()*4);
    slControl.content.findName("txtRound").Text = "Round " + (currentMove+1);
}

function playMoves()
{
    currentFrame=-1;
    inMovesPlayBack = true;
    doNextFrame();
}

function doNextFrame()
{
    currentFrame++;
    if(currentFrame<=currentMove)
    {
      switch(theMoves[currentFrame])
      {
        case 0:
            slControl.content.findName("LightUpBlue").Begin();
            break;
        case 1:
            slControl.content.findName("LightUpGreen").Begin();
            break;
        case 2:
            slControl.content.findName("LightUpRed").Begin();
            break;
        case 3:
```

```
            slControl.content.findName("LightUpYellow").Begin();
            break;
        }
    }
    else
    {
        inMovesPlayBack = false
    }

}

function handleAnimComplete()
{

    if(inMovesPlayBack)
    {
        doNextFrame();
    }
    else
    {
        if(currentUserCol == theMoves[currentUserMove])
        {
            // We can keep going
            if(currentUserMove>=currentMove)
            {
                gameloop();
            }
        }
        else
        {
            // We hit an error -- game OVER
            gameOver();
        }
    }
    inAnim=false;

}

function setUpEventHandlers()
{
  slControl.content.findName("rBlue").addEventListener("MouseLeftButtonDown",
      handleMouseDown);
```

```
slControl.content.findName("rGreen").addEventListener("MouseLeftButtonDown",
    handleMouseDown);
slControl.content.findName("rYellow").addEventListener("MouseLeftButtonDown",
    handleMouseDown);
slControl.content.findName("rRed").addEventListener("MouseLeftButtonDown",
    handleMouseDown);
slControl.content.findName("LightUpBlue").addEventListener("Completed",
    handleAnimComplete);
slControl.content.findName("LightUpGreen").addEventListener("Completed",
    handleAnimComplete);
slControl.content.findName("LightUpYellow").addEventListener("Completed",
    handleAnimComplete);
slControl.content.findName("LightUpRed").addEventListener("Completed",
    handleAnimComplete);
slControl.content.findName("txtStart").addEventListener("MouseLeftButtonDown",
    handleStart);
}
```

The operation of the game is very simple. For each round, the computer adds a new random move to the current stack of moves (implemented using a JavaScript array), and plays them back. Once they are all played back, it is now the user's turn. If the user can select them in the same order that the computer played them back, then they progress to the next round, where the process is repeated, but with one new move added to the stack.

In Silverlight, the core of this is managed using events. At the end of the JavaScript, you can see the setUpEventHandlers function, where events are wired up to the various controls. The important events are handleMouseDown, which manages the user clicking the rectangle, and handleAnimComplete, which handles what to do once an animation has completed.

So, when the computer is playing back the moves, the process is to do the following:

- Get the next move (doNextFrame function)

- Figure out which piece it belongs to

- Play the animation for that piece by finding the storyboard and calling its Begin method

Then, when the animation is complete, it goes back to the beginning and gets the next move again. It has to be done this way, otherwise the animations would not play in sequence.

When the computer is playing back the moves, the user clicks should be ignored. This is managed using the inMovesPlayback Boolean, which is set to true at the beginning of the cycle, and set to `false` once all the animations have played back. You'll see in the `handleMouseDown` event handler that if this is set to `true`, then no action will be taken.

Additionally, as the animation is timeline-based, it would be possible for the user to click many times and cause many animations to play back concurrently. For this game, it has to be in a sequence, so once an animation begins, the `inAnim` Boolean is set to `true`—so when Silverlight catches a mouse click, the event handler also checks this. If it is `true`, the handler will ignore the mouse event.

The moves themselves are kept in an array, so when the user is clicking the sequence, their current move is checked against what it should be. If it is correct, then the user can continue. If not, then we enter the game over state, where the score is reported and all variables reset.

And that's it. From first principles, this game was written in a little under two hours. It shows how powerful the Silverlight framework is, and when combined with the flexibility of JavaScript, it shows how your existing skills can be reused to build rich interactive applications.

Summary

In this chapter, you continued your look at Silverlight and at what is possible in programming Silverlight 1.0 applications using JavaScript. You took a tour of XAML, looking at the available controls and elements, before going into what they expose to the JavaScript programmer. Then you put it all together with a simple game example. This was hopefully enough to whet your appetite for the possibilities that are opened by the Silverlight platform. As this book goes to press, Silverlight version 2.0 will be entering beta, and while it adds the power of the .NET Framework for programmability purposes, the basic architecture of an application will remain the same, and the skills you earn from building 1.0-based applications will transfer right across, so why wait?

Index

▪Symbols

@ character, 90

<%@ %>, denoting ASP.NET directive, 28, 109

▪A

A path language command, 391

ABC (Address, Binding, and Contract), 161

access rules, 321

accessor syntax, for properties, 332

action attribute, 39, 40

ActiveX controls, 255

activities, 209–228

  available out of the box, 223

  Code, 214, 221, 228

  Compensate, 223

  ConditionedActivityGroup, 223

  Delay, 223

  EventDriven, 223

  FaultHandler, 223

  IfElse activity, 219

  InvokeWebService, 223

  Parallel, 223

  Replicator, 224

  Sequence, 224

  Terminate, 224

  Throw, 224

  WebServiceInput, 224

  WebServiceOutput, 227

  While, 224

actualHeight property, 366, 393

actualWidth property, 366, 393

add command, for arrays, 344

AddEm() method, 313

AddEventListener() method, 396

addRange command, for arrays, 345

address service, 168–176

  client for, 172–176

  creating, 112–120, 168–172

Address, Binding, and Contract (ABC), 161

AdminFolder directory, 321, 324

ADO.NET, 69–103

  building data-driven applications with, 82–91

  commands for, 86–91

  data binding and, 91–102

  reading data and, 88

AdventureWorks (sample) database, installing, 79

Ajax, 23, 253–278, 353. *See also* ASP.NET AJAX

  forward caching and, 265–277

  history of, 253–257

  migrating ASP.NET to, 289–292, 298

  server/client architectures and, 280

  web services and, 300–307

AJAX Extensions for ASP.NET. *See* ASP.NET AJAX

Ajax scripts. *See* ScriptManager control

AlignmentX property

  Image Control and, 392

  ImageBrush and, 384

AlignmentY property

  Image Control and, 392

  ImageBrush and, 384

AllowCustomErrorsRedirect property, 310

animations, 203, 394, 405

App.config file, address service client and, 173

application layer, 3

application performance, 8

application pooling, 139

application references, 27

application services, 314–327

415

applications. *See also* Ajax; ASP.NET;
    Silverlight; sample applications
  adding Ajax functionality to, 289–292,
    298
  Blend, 196–203
  compiled, 279
  connected, 155
  creating, 9, 131, 284
  data-driven, 69, 82–91
  maps and, 255, 265
  parameters, adding to, 218–223
  rich Internet, 279
  start options for, 25
  stateful, 39
  stateless, 38
  testing/debugging, Cassini web server
    for, 173
  tightly coupled/loosely coupled, 105
  Windows client applications and, 37
  workflow, 211, 224–230
App_Code folder, 20
App_Data folder, 17
architecture, ASP.NET and, 32
ARPANET, 3
Array class, 344
array type ASP.NET AJAX extensions to
    JavaScript, 344–347
Array.add() method, 344
Array.addRange() method, 345
Array.clear() method, 345
Array.clone() method, 345
Array.contents() method, 345
Array.dequeue() method, 346
Array.forEach() method, 346
Array.indexOf() method, 346
Array.insert() method, 347
Array.remove() method, 347
.asmx file extension, 108
ASMX Web Services, 156
ASP, 7, 9
ASP.NET, 9–36, 280
  applications, creating, 9
  architecture of, 32
  folders, creating, 20

  forms, creating, 41–46
  history of, 7
  side-by-side execution and, 138
  theme capabilities and, 21
  web forms and, 37–67
  web services and, 105–127
ASP.NET AJAX, 23, 279–308
  extensions/add-ons for, 282
  JavaScript programming and, 331–351
  migrating ASP.NET applications to,
    289–292, 298
  scripts and, 309–329
  server controls and, 281
  server/client architectures and, 280
ASP.NET AJAX Core library, 282–288
ASP.NET HTML controls, 41, 46
ASP.NET Literal control, 46
ASP.NET server controls, 12, 39, 59
.aspx file extension, 17
assemblies, adding references for, 21
Asynchronous JavaScript and XML.
    See Ajax
AsyncPostBackError event, 310
AsyncPostBackErrorMessage property, 310
atomic transactions, 160
attached properties, 388
authentication
  configuring, 318
  forms-based, 315–327
authentication mode, for SQL Server, 76
automatic postbacks, 52, 58
AutoPostback property, 53, 55, 58

■ B

background property, 364, 404
BCL (Base Class Library), Ajax and, 281
.bmp files, Silverlight and, 392
Boat (sample) class, 333–340
Boolean ASP.NET AJAX extensions to
    JavaScript, 348
branching, 209
browsers, 37
  browser compatibility layer, Ajax and,
    281

default, 26
XMLHttpRequest and, 256
brushes, Silverlight and, 378–388
BufferingProgressChanged event, 401
business transactions, 160

▬C

C path language command, 391
caching, Ajax and, 265–277
CAG (ConditionedActivityGroup) activity, 223
CanPause property, 398
Canvas, 357, 375, 388
CAPICOM.dll, 240
CaptureMouse() method, 397
cards, 233
adding to CardSpace wallet, 235
managed, 233
using on the Internet, 237
CardSpace, 233–251
CardSpace wallet and, 235
certificates and, 241
preparing development environment
for, 240–244
Cassini (Visual Studio 2005 Web Server), 9, 173
certificates, CardSpace and, 241
CGI applications, 6
classes, in JavaScript, 331–344
inheritance and, 338–341
namespaces and, 332
cleanup, 59
clear command, for arrays, 345
client-side functionality, 41
client tier, 148
clients, for address service, 172–176
clone command, for arrays, 345
Close() method, 86
code
managed cross-platform, 6
reuse of, 160
Code activity, 214, 221, 228
code conditions, 220
code initialization, 57

code reuse, 160
code-behind pages, 17, 108
ColorAnimation/ColorAnimationUsing-
KeyFrames, 394
Command class, 70
commands, in ADO.NET, 86–91
CommandText property, 86
CommandType property, 86
Compensate activity, 223
compiled applications, 279
composability, 158
ConditionedActivityGroup (CAG) activity, 223
configuring
App.config file and, 173
authentication, 318
connections, 140–145
databases, 139
physical path, 132
security, 317
SQL Server, 140
SQL Server 2005 Express, 72
Web.config file and. See Web.config file
web sites, via IIS Manager, 129
connected applications, 155
Connection class, 70, 82
connection leaks, preventing, 86
connection strings, 82, 93
connections, 82
choosing, 92
configuring, 140–145
testing, 84
<connectionStrings> section, 83
console (sample) application, 211–223
contents command, for arrays, 345
contracts, WCF services and, 161–176
controls, 12, 39, 59
ActiveX, 255
creating at runtime, 64
layout, 188–196
XAML, 391
cookies, 55
Copy Web Site tool, for web site
deployment, 146

copying web sites, 25
Core SQL Server Express, 72
country code converter (sample)
        application, 301–307
createFromXaml() method, 370
createObject() method, 358, 362, 371
createObjectEx() method, 358, 362
createSilverlight() method, 358, 360
    initParams property and, 366
    isWindowless property and, 364
creating
    address service client, 172–176
    address service, 168–172
    applications, 9, 131, 196–203, 284
    ASP.NET folders, 20
    controls, at runtime, 64
    data-driven applications, 82–91
    folders, 20
    roles, 320
    web references, 23
    web service clients, 120
    web services, 108
    web sites, via IIS Manager, 131
    workflows, 211–223
credentials. *See* CardSpace
cross-platform interoperability, 158
ctrl property, 400
.cs file extension, 17
CurrentState property, 401
CurrentStateChanged event, 401
Cursor property, Silverlight and, 388
custom scripts, 311

■D

DARPA, 3
data adapters, 117
data binding, 59, 91–102
    DataList control and, 99–102
    GridView control and, 96–99
    SQLDataSource control and, 92–95
    web services and, 122
data connections. *See* connections
data link layer, 4

data providers, 70
data stores, 70
data-driven applications, 69, 82–91
DataAdapter class, 70
database files, attaching to
        AdventureWorks database, 80
database login, configuring, 142
databases, configuring, 139
DataContractAttribute, 165
DataGrids, 292
DataList control, 99–102
DataReader class, 70
DataSet class, 70
DataSets
    adding to web services, 113
    address service and, 168
    using in web methods, 117
DataSource control, 91
Date class, 348
date type ASP.NET AJAX extensions to
        JavaScript, 348
debugging applications, Cassini web
        server for, 173
default browser, 26
Default.aspx file, 17, 40
Default.aspx.cs file, 44
Delay activity, 223
deploying
    client tier, 148
    service tier, 146
    web sites, 129–151
dequeue command, for arrays, 346
Design view, 28
digital identity. *See* CardSpace
Dispose() method, 86
doLogin() method, 326
doNextFrame() method, 413
dot notation syntax, for properties, 332,
        395
DoubleAnimation/DoubleAnimation-
        UsingKeyFrames, 394
Downloader object, 371

DownloadProgressChanged event, 401
downloads
　AdventureWorks database, 79
　ASP.NET AJAX Core library, 282
　ASP.NET AJAX JavaScript libraries, 304
　Silverlight SDK, 357
　SQL Server Express, 71
　SQL Server Express with Advanced
　　Services, 72
　Windows Workflow Foundation, 211

E

Ellipse shape, Silverlight and, 389
Empty Workflow Project, 212
EnableFrameRateCounter property, 368
EnableHtmlAccess property, 368
EnablePartialRendering property, 309
EnableRedrawRegions property, 368
EnableScriptGlobalization property, 348
EnableViewState property, 56
encapsulation, 160
EndPoint property, LinearGradientBrush
　　and, 379
Enterprise Services, 156
error type ASP.NET AJAX extensions to
　　JavaScript, 349
errors, 18
　handling in partial page updates, 310
　onError event (Silverlight) and, 368
EventDriven activity, 223
events, 52, 58
　JavaScript classes and, 332
　XAML elements and, 399
ExecuteCode property, 214, 221
ExecuteNonQuery() method, 87
ExecuteReader() method, 87
ExecuteScalar() method, 87
ExecuteXmlReader() method, 87
Expression Blend (Microsoft), 182–207,
　　394, 402
Extensible Application Markup Language.
　　See XAML

Extensible Markup Language. *See entries
　　at* XML
Extensions for ASP.NET. *See* ASP.NET AJAX

F

FaultHandler activity, 223
feedback, server control for, 46
Fill() method, 117
fill, Silverlight and, 378
finally block, 86
findName() method, 371, 395
flow between server and users, 53
folders, creating, 20
FontRenderingEmSize property, 392
FontSize property, 393
FontStyle property, 393
FontURI property, 392
FontWeight property, 393
forEach command, for arrays, 346
form tag, 39, 40
format() method, 348, 350
forms authentication services, 315–327
forward caching, Ajax and, 265–277, 279
forward-caching client, Ajax and, 271
framerate property, 364
FTP protocol, 5
FullScreen property, 366

G

Garrett, Jesse James, 253
geometries, Silverlight and, 390
GetAddress() method, 122
GetData() method, 117
GetHost() method, 398
GetParent() method, 398
getPosition() method, 400
getValue() method, 396
get_ method, accessor syntax and, 332
Glyphs control, 392
Google Maps, Ajax and, 255
GotFocus event, 399
GradientOrigin property, 382
grid layout control, 188–193
GridView control, 96–99, 126, 297

■H

H path language command, 391
handleAnimComplete event, 413
handleInput() method, 262
handleLoad() method, 359, 371, 395
handleMouseDown event, 413
head tag, 62
Height property, XAML and, 364, 388
"Hello World!" message, Silverlight and,
    357
hosts file, CardSpace and, 243
HTML, 5, 7
    image servers and, 270
    Silverlight and, 354–368
HTML controls, 12, 39
HTML forms, 39–46
HTMLHead, 62
HTTP, web services and, 106
HTTP-GET verb, 39
HTTP-POST verb, 39
HTTP request, 39, 66
        HTTP response, 66
HttpRequest class, 44
HttpResponse class, 46
HTTPS, CardSpace and, 241
hypertext, 5

■I

id attribute, 46, 49
id property, 364
IDE (integrated development
        environment), 12, 113, 120
Identity Metasystem, 233
identity selectors, 233
IfElse activity, 219
IFrame, 254
IIS (Internet Information Services),
        129–138
    CardSpace and, 240, 244
    version 7.0 of, 130
IIS Manager, 129, 134–138
Image control, 392
image servers, 266–271

ImageBrush, Silverlight and, 379, 383
<img> tag, 270
implementsInterface() method, 344
inAnim boolean, 414
indexOf command, for arrays, 346
Indigo. See WCF
InfoCard. See CardSpace
inheritance, in JavaScript, 338, 343
inheritsFrom() method, 343
initAJAX() method, 261, 272
initParams property, 366
InLineScript property, 313
inMovesPlayback boolean, 413
inplaceInstallPrompt property, 365
InputActivityName property, 227
insert command, for arrays, 347
install-certificates.vbs script, 241
integrated development environment
        (IDE), 12, 113, 120
integrated security, 141
integration, 155, 158
interfaces, in JavaScript, 341, 344
InterfaceType property, 225
Internet, history of, 3
Internet Information Services. See IIS
interoperability, 155, 158
InvokeWebService activity, 223
IsActivating property, 225
isInstanceType() method, 343
IsLoaded property, 367
IsPostBack property, 58
isWindowless property, 364
items, adding to projects, 19

■J

Java, 7
JavaScript
    for ASP.NET AJAX, 331–351
    Silverlight programming and, 354–373,
        394–414
JavaScript proxies, 312
.jpeg files, Silverlight and, 392
JSP, 7

K

keyUp/keyDown events, 399

L

L path language command, 391
layout controls, 188–196
layout, Silverlight and, 375
LinearGradientBrush, Silverlight and, 378, 379
lines, Silverlight and, 390
Literal control, 46
Load event, 400
load() method, 328
Loaded event, 400
localeFormat() method, 349, 350
location, for web applications, 11
Login control, 324
login functionality, 323
login() method, 326
LoginStatus control, 323
loosely coupled applications, 105
LostFocus event, 399

M

M path language command, 391
managed cards, 233
managed cross-platform code, 6
manual deployment, 138–151
mapping applications, 255, 265
MarkerReached event, 401
matrix-based mathematics, 393
MatrixTransform transform, 394
.mdf file extension, 80
MediaElement class, 385
    events and, 401
    methods and, 398
MediaEnded event, 401
MediaFailed event, 401
MediaOpened event, 401
membership services, 315–327
memory game (sample) application, 401–414
messaging, 156, 159
method attribute, 39, 40

methods, 332, 396
Microsoft
    AJAX Extensions for ASP.NET. *See* ASP.NET AJAX
    Expression Blend, 182–207, 394, 402
    Silverlight, 353–373
Microsoft Message Queuing (MSMQ), 156
Microsoft Remote Scripting, 255
Mixed Mode authentication, for SQL Server, 76
mouse
    CaptureMouse/ReleaseMouseCapture methods and, 397
    mouse events and, 400
MouseEventArgs class, 400
MouseMove event, 397
MSMQ (Microsoft Message Queuing), 156

N

name property, 43
name/value pairs, 83
namespaces, in JavaScript, 332
naming conventions, for HTML forms, 43
NaturalDuration property, 401
NaturalVideoHeight/NaturalVideoWidth properties, 401
.NET Framework 3.0
    WCF (Windows Communication Foundation), 155–176
    WPF (Windows Presentation Foundation), 177–208
network layer, 4
number multiplier (sample) application, 257–265
number type ASP.NET AJAX extensions to JavaScript, 350

O

OASIS (Organization for the Advancement of Structured Information Standards), 159
<object> tag, 356
Object Linking and Embedding for Databases (OLEDB) provider, 71

object orientation, 160

object-oriented ASP.NET AJAX extensions to JavaScript, 331–344

ObjectDataSource control, 91, 122

ODBC (Open Database Connectivity) provider, 71

Offset property, RadialGradientBrush and, 381

OLEDB (Object Linking and Embedding for Databases) provider, 71

onError event, 368

onFullScreenChange event, 370

onLoad event, 368

OnLoginCompleted() method, 326

OnProfileLoadComplete() method, 328

onreadystatechange property, 256, 262

onResize event, 370

Opacity property, Silverlight and, 388

Open Database Connectivity (ODBC) provider, 71

open() method, 256, 262

OperationContractAttribute, 164, 168

Oracle provider, 71

O'Reilly, Tim, 255

Organization for the Advancement of Structured Information Standards (OASIS), 159

OSI seven-layer model, 3

■P

Page class, 66

page initialization, 57

page processing, 37

page state management, 33

Page.Controls collection, 61

Page.Init event, 57

Page.Request property, 44

PageRequestManager, 310

pages, controls on, 59

Page_Load() method, 44, 50, 57

Page_PreRender event, 59

paging data, GridView control and, 98

Panel control, 290

Parallel activity, 223

parameters, in ADO.NET commands, 90

parentElement property, 363

parseInvariant() method, 350

parseLocale() method, 349, 350

partial refreshes, 254

partial updates, 279, 309

path language, 391

Path, Silverlight and, 390

Pause() method, 398

performance, 8

PHP, 7

physical layer, 5

physical path, configuring, 132

Play() method, 398

.png files, Silverlight and, 392

PointAnimation/PointAnimationUsing-KeyFrames, 394

polymorphism, 160

postal code finder (sample) application, 87–102

postbacks, 38, 44
    automatic, 52, 58
    partial page rendering and, 309

PreRender event, 59

presentation layer, 4

printf statements, 7

processing flow, 53

product photos (sample) browser, 266–277

productivity, WCF and, 156

profile services, 314

profiles, 110, 327

projects
    solutions and, 17
    start options for, 25

properties, 331
    attached properties and, 388
    XAML elements and, 395

property pages, 26

proxies, 24, 312

push/pull models, 40

Q

Q path language command, 391

R

RadialGradientBrush, Silverlight and, 378,
    381
RadiusX property
    RadialGradientBrush and, 382
    Rectangle shape and, 404
RadiusY property
    RadialGradientBrush and, 382
    Rectangle shape and, 404
Read() method, 88
readers, 88
readyState property, 257, 263, 273
Rectangle shape, Silverlight and, 390, 404
references, 21, 27
reflection, in JavaScript, 343
registerClass() method, 333, 342
registerInterface() method, 342
registerNamespace() method, 333
ReleaseMouseCapture() method, 397
reliability, 155, 160
    message delivery and, 156–159
    WCF and, 168
Remote Scripting (Microsoft), 255
Remoting, 156
remove command, for arrays, 347
RemoveEventListener() method, 396
Replicator activity, 224
Request object, 66
Request.Form array, 44, 50
resources for further reading
    ASP.NET theme capabilities, 21
    CardSpace, 251
    IIS, 151
    Silverlight, 395
    WCF, 171
    WF, 231
    WPF, 208
Response object, 66
responseText property, 263
reuse of code, 160

RIAs (rich Internet applications), 279
roles, 318
RotateTransform transform, 394
Ruby, 7
rule conditions, 220
runat=server attribute, 40, 46, 49

S

S path language command, 391
sa login, 76
SAAS (Software as a Service), 160
sample applications
    country code converter, 301–307
    memory game, 401–414
    number multiplier, 257–265
    product photos browser, 266–277
    stock quote, 9, 24, 30
    temperature converter, 224–230
    workflow console, 211–223
    ZIP/postal code finder, 88
save() method, 329
scalability, 69
ScaleTransform transform, 394
<script> tag, 272, 288, 311
    Boat (sample) class and, 336
    containing XAML, 363
ScriptManager control, 281, 286–288,
    309–329
    adding to pages, 290, 298, 304
    application services and, 314–327
    web services and, 312
ScriptReference, 336
ScriptResource.axd, 288
scripts. See ScriptManager control
security, 155, 160
    address service and, 168
    configuring, 317
    SQL Server, configuring for, 141
    WS-Security and, 159
SelectedIndexChanged events, 59, 64
selection, GridView control and, 99
self-describing systems, 161
send() method, 256, 262
Sequence activity, 224

Sequential Workflow Console Application, 212

Sequential Workflow Library, 212, 224

sequential workflows, 209

server controls
ASP.NET AJAX and, 281
data binding and, 91–102

server-side functionality, 41

server-side Java, 7

servers, 38

service harness, 165

service orientation
building WCF services and, 161–176
rules/tenets of, 161

Service-Oriented Architecture (SOA), 107, 160

service tier, 146

ServiceContractAttribute, 164, 168

ServiceReference class, 313

services, 309–329

servlets, 7

session layer, 4

session state, 55

sessions, 39

SetFontSource() method, 393

setUpEventHandlers() method, 413

setValue() method, 396

set_ method, accessor syntax and, 332

shapes, Silverlight and, 389

shift property, 400

side-by-side execution, 138

sign-in functionality, 323

Silverlight, 353–373
animations and, 394, 405
brushes and, 378–388
JavaScript programming and, 354–373, 394–414
layout and, 375
shapes and, 389
transformations and, 393
visual elements and, 388
XAML controls and, 391
XAML programming and, 354, 375–394, 401–414

Silverlight control, 362–373
events and, 368
methods for, 370
properties for, 362–368

Silverlight SDK, 357

Simple Object Access Protocol. *See* SOAP

SkewTransform transform, 394

.skin files, 21

SOA (Service-Oriented Architecture), 107, 160

SOAP (Simple Object Access Protocol)
web services and, 106
WS-* standards and, 159

Software as a Service (SAAS), 160

SolidColorBrush, Silverlight and, 379

Solution Explorer, 17–27

solutions, 17

sorting data, GridView control and, 99

Source property
Image control and, 392
Silverlight control and, 362

Source view, 28

SpeedBoat (sample) class, 338–342

SpreadMethod property, 382

SQL injection attacks, 58

SQL queries, 86, 268, 295
address service and, 114
specifying, 93

SQL Server
configuring, 140
database access and, 86

SQL Server 2005 Express, 71–82
authentication mode for, 76
downloading, 71
installing/configuring, 72

SQL Server 2005 Express with Advanced Services, 72

SQL Server Configuration Manager, 140

SQL Server Express Edition Toolkit, 72

SQL Server Express with Advanced Services, 72

SQL Server Management Studio Express tool, 72, 78

SqlCommand class, 86

SqlConnection class, 86
SqlDataReaders, 88
SQLDataSource control, 92–95
StartPoint property, 379
state, 38, 70
State Machine Workflow Console
    Application, 212
State Machine Workflow Library, 212
state workflows, 210
stateful web applications, 39
stateless web applications, 38
stock quote (sample) web application, 9,
    24, 30
Stop() method, 399
storyboards, 394, 405
Stretch property
    Image Control and, 392
    ImageBrush and, 383
string ASP.NET AJAX extensions to
    JavaScript, 351
string matching, 351
string trimming, 351
StrokeDashArray property, 387
StrokeDashCap property, 387
StrokeDashOffset property, 387
StrokeLineJoin property, 387
strokes, Silverlight and, 378, 386
<style> tag, 360
StyleSimulations property, 392
.svc file extension, 162
svcutil.exe tool
    for address service clients, 172
    for WCF services, 167

T
tabs, 13
TCP/IP protocol, 3, 140
templates, for workflows, 211
Terminate activity, 224
testing
    applications, Cassini web server for, 173
    connections, 84

Text property, 396
TextBlock control, 386, 392
    memory game (sample) application
        and, 406
    txt (sample) XAML document and, 395
TextChanged events, 53, 259
TextDecorations property, 393
TextWrapping property, 393
themes, folder for, 21
Throw activity, 224
tightly coupled applications, 105
timeline animations, 203, 394, 405
Timer control, 281, 309
Token class, 250
Toolbox, 12
tools. *See* utilities
transactability, 155, 160, 168
transactions, WS-Transactions and, 160
transformations, 393
TransformGroups, 394
TranslateTransform transform, 394
transport layer, 4
try . . . catch block, 86
txtClicked() method, 360
Type class, inheritsFrom() method and,
    343

U
UpdatePanel control, 281, 289, 298, 309
UpdateProgress control, 281, 309
URLs, 6, 134–138
userContext property, 367
UserFolder directory, 321, 324
users, web application building and, 37
using reference, 312
using statement, 86
utilities
    Copy Web Site tool, 146
    SQL Server Express Edition Toolkit, 72
    SQL Server Management Studio Express
        tool, 72, 78
    svcutil.exe, 167, 172

■V

V path language command, 391
validation, 58
ValidationSummary control, 324
value property, 43
.vb file extension, 17
Vehicles (sample) namespace, 333
VideoBrush, Silverlight and, 379, 385
view state, 38, 46, 55, 69
virtual directories, 129
Virtual Directory wizard, 131
Visible property, 96
visual elements, Silverlight and, 388
Visual Studio, 9–31
    Blend artifacts, using with, 206
    workflows and, 211–223
Visual Studio 2005 Web Server (Cassini),
    9, 173
VWDE (Visual Web Developer Express),
    9, 41

■W

WCF (Windows Communication
    Foundation), 155–176
    building services and, 161–176
    interoperability and, 158
    productivity and, 156
    service orientation and, 160
Web 2.0, 255
web browsers. *See* browsers
web development
    basics of with ASP.NET, 9–36
    future technologies and, 160
    history of technologies and, 3–8
web forms, 17, 37–67
    processing, 56–59
    types of, 39–56
web methods, address service and, 117
web references, 23, 27, 120
web servers, XMLHttpRequest and, 256
web services, 8, 105–127
    Ajax and, 300–307
    clients for, 120
    creating, 10, 108

    data binding and, 122
    running, 110
    scripts and, 312
    technologies and, 156
    web references for, 23, 27, 120
    workflow applications and, 224–230
Web Services Description Language
    (WSDL), 23, 106, 108
Web Services standards (WS-* standards),
    158, 233
Web Site Administration Tool, 35
web sites
    CardSpace and, 240–251
    copying to new location, 25
    creating, 10, 129, 315–323
    deploying, 129–151
    workflow applications and, 224–230
Web.config file, 34, 166
    address service and, 169
    address service client and, 173
    ASP.NET AJAX and, 292
    connection strings stored in, 83
WebMethod attribute, 110
WebResource.axd, 288
webs, installing, 244
WebService directive, 109
WebServiceBinding attribute, 110
WebServiceInput activity, 224
WebServiceOutput activity, 227
WF runtime engine, 211
WF. *See* Windows Workflow Foundation
WHERE clause, 94
While activity, 224
Width property, XAML and, 364, 388
Windows authentication, 76, 318
Windows Bitmaps, Silverlight and, 392
Windows CardSpace. *See* CardSpace
Windows client applications, vs. web
    applications, 37
Windows Communication Foundation.
    See WCF
Windows Presentation Foundation.
    See WPF

Windows Workflow Foundation (WF),
        209–231
    creating applications and, 211–223
    downloading, 211
Workflow Activity Library, 212
workflow applications, 211, 224–230
workflow console (sample) application,
        211–223
workflows, 209–231
    creating, 211–223
    sequential, 209
    state, 210
World Wide Web, history of, 3
WPF (Windows Presentation Foundation),
        177–208
    building applications and, 196–207
    Expression Blend and, 182–196
    XAML and, 177–181
WS-* standards (Web Services standards),
        158, 233
WS-AtomicTransaction, 160
WS-BusinessActivity, 160
WS-Coordination, 160
WS-I, 110
WS-ReliableMessaging, 159
WS-Security, 159
WS-Transactions, 160
WSDL (Web Services Description
        Language), 23, 106, 108
WSE, 156

X

XAML (Extensible Application Markup
        Language), 177–181
    App.xaml/Window1.xaml files and, 182
    Blend application building and,
        196–203
    createFromXaml() method and, 370
    embedded within an HTML <script>
        tag, 363

events and, 399
findName() method and, 371
methods and, 396
properties, editing, 395
Silverlight programming and, 354,
        375–394, 401–414
Source property and, 362
XAML Canvas, 357, 375, 388
XAML controls, 391
XML (Extensible Markup Language), 105
    ADO.NET and, 70
    web services and, 106
XMLDataSource control, 91
XMLHttpRequest, 255, 310
    ASP.NET AJAX and, 279
    callback and, 263
    caution with, 256
    communicating with web servers and,
        256
    forward-caching client and, 271
XMLWriter, 170
XSLT, 105

Z

Z path language command, 391
Z-order, for Canvases, 376
ZIP code finder (sample) application,
        87–102

You Need the Companion eBook

Your purchase of this book entitles you to buy the companion PDF-version eBook for only $10. Take the weightless companion with you anywhere.

We believe this Apress title will prove so indispensable that you'll want to carry it with you everywhere, which is why we are offering the companion eBook (in PDF format) for $10 to customers who purchase this book now. Convenient and fully searchable, the PDF version of any content-rich, page-heavy Apress book makes a valuable addition to your programming library. You can easily find and copy code—or perform examples by quickly toggling between instructions and the application. Even simultaneously tackling a donut, diet soda, and complex code becomes simplified with hands-free eBooks!

Once you purchase your book, getting the $10 companion eBook is simple:

❶ Visit **www.apress.com/promo/tendollars/**.

❷ Complete a basic registration form to receive a randomly generated question about this title.

❸ Answer the question correctly in 60 seconds, and you will receive a promotional code to redeem for the $10.00 eBook.

THE EXPERT'S VOICE™

2855 TELEGRAPH AVENUE | SUITE 600 | BERKELEY, CA 94705

Offer valid through 8/08.